Da Capo
BEST
MUSIC
WRITING
2004

Da Capo
BEST
MUSIC
WRITING
2004

The Year's Finest Writing on Rock,
Hip-Hop, Jazz, Pop, Country, & More

Mickey Hart
GUEST EDITOR

Paul Bresnick
SERIES EDITOR

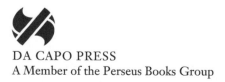

DA CAPO PRESS
A Member of the Perseus Books Group

Set in 10- point Janson Text by the Perseus Books Group

Cataloging-in-Publication data for this book is available from the Library of Congress

First Da Capo Press edition 2004
ISBN 0-306-81380-7

Published by Da Capo Press
A Member of the Perseus Books Group
http://www.dacapopress.com

Da Capo Press books are available at special discounts for bulk purchases in the U.S. by corporations, institutions, and other organizations. For more information, please contact the Special Markets Department at the Perseus Books Group, 11 Cambridge Center, Cambridge, MA 02142, or call (800) 255–1514 or (617) 252–5298, or e-mail special.markets@perseusbooks.com.

2 3 4 5 6 7 8 9—06 05 04

CONTENTS

Introduction

For the Love of Music

It seemed easy enough. Read one hundred articles on music, pick the best thirty or so, then write a foreword to a book containing the articles. I begin to read and am amazed at the quality and scope of these marvelous words. Doubts race through my mind. Where do I begin? What to cut? I'm doomed. This has turned into one of the hardest editing tasks I have ever attempted.

First, my apologies to those who did not make the cut. It is not because of content; it has only to do with limitations placed on the length of this book. All one hundred articles deserve to be included. They speak of the struggles, the hardships, the ups and downs, the love and the magic music evokes. Describing invisible feelings is hard enough, but doing so in a way that grabs readers by the throat and shakes them is another thing entirely. That is what the writers whose tales you will read in this book have accomplished.

Music, of course, is the one element that ties these diverse pieces together. The articles consider the eternal questions: why does music inspire and entrance both listener and performer? Why, in essence, can't we live without music? If we wonder why we are compelled to make the vibratory world our home, we must first try to understand the basis of this desire.

So then, why music?

There is no shortage of information, quotes, stories, and anecdotes about music. Through the ages there has always been music, and it is simple fact that no culture has or can exist without it. When asked to write the foreword for this compendium, I thought long and hard on what there is to say about the totality of these articles.

The one thought that kept coming to mind was that whereas every person loves some kind of music, the real question is why. I see this as the skeleton key that unlocks the mystery of our love affair with the world of vibrations around and inside of us.

Music is part love potion, part healer-communicator, and part soundtrack of our lives. Describing music is like trying to draw a picture of spirit: everyone has a different image in mind, and no two renderings are alike.

Music rises from the subconscious to reveal itself in countless forms. It can be described in many ways, but in the end it is one of the most important languages we use to explain the range of emotions we experience in life. Listening, composing, and playing music transform spirit into something concrete, show us that we are not alone, and connect us to the world around us. As I write this, we are a world in conflict, a world on fire, a world at war. In the articles contained herein, the authors speak of music as an antidote for hate. Musicians and their audience find their answers in sound.

The magic of music is what is interesting to me: victory over divisiveness, making sense out of nonsense, chasing an invisible creation with all of your might. The muse can be strong and relentless, and there is no mercy for the weak or timid. The struggle to turn the spirit that is deep within you into form is the goal. Of course, that goal is expressed in a variety of ways: something beautiful to one person may sound like absolute garbage to someone else. If you consider the diversity of styles that are described in these articles, from Johnny Cash to 50 Cent, Stevie Wonder to Eminem, it is clear that today's music reflects the wide range of sensibilities that exist in our society.

A song has the ability to bring forth the sense of place from where the music came. An enormous body of diasporic music has landed on our shores and reappeared, like ritual, in the identities of Bobby Bare, Mel Tillis, Lauryn Hill, the Beatles, the Beach Boys, and innumerable artists most of us will never hear. Music has sprung from social movements, wars, economic hardships, discrimination, political causes, and religious fervor. Not a day goes by without a new song being born.

I got a call from Pete Seeger the other night. He raved about the "power of music" and how "music could save the world." At 85, he knows very well the power of music to unite, to make whole, to heal, and to uplift. He has seen music work magic in political rallies and in circles of children and with the handicapped, the destitute, the powerful, the rich, and the poor. People, he says, "are beginning to play musical instruments again, realizing their power, not just listening, but making music of their own." This folk singer has seen it all and has devoted his life to the innate power of music. He is possessed by the notion of music as emancipator-savior of the species. I listen and learn from this master musical activist.

However, when a style of music does not serve a purpose within a community, it may cease to be. Likewise, when a community dies, certain music within it dies as well. Some styles and instruments are reborn from the old; others just disappear. In fact, throughout history we have made and remade instruments to produce the sounds we want to hear. There are saxophones, a world of percussion instruments, turntables, electric guitars, and a panoply of digital contraptions squealing to be heard above the din. Some sounds are pleasant, others strange and weird. The point is that music is right up there with sex and food. Music is not a luxury; it is a necessity of life.

There is a need on this blue-green spinning rock to organize, hybridize, immortalize, and create new and exciting musical sounds, and we tend to write about these goings-on. All kinds of combinations, fusions, and reinventions abound. From fantasy to reality, the musical imagination is limitless.

Music makes us feel good and brings us real joy. Joy is distinct from fun. Fun is ephemeral. Joy is something deeper, like family. You don't just have fun watching your family, you experience joy. Making or listening to music will open you up. Music is freedom and life. It is medicine for the soul. Go try some and see!

The work you are about to read will speak volumes. I hope you enjoy these marvelous stories as much as I have.

Mickey Hart

April 15, 2004
Sebastopol, California

DAN BAUM

Jake Leg

How the Blues Diagnosed a Medical Mystery

Dr. John Morgan, a professor at the City University of New York Medical School, likes to call himself a pharmaco-ethnomusicologist. His first love is early-American vernacular music, and his apartment, on the Upper West Side, is stacked with ancient records. Some years back, Morgan was listening to the Allen Brothers' "Jake Walk Blues," released in 1930. In a kazoo-backed Tennessee twang, the brothers sang, "I can't eat, I can't talk, drinking mean jake, Lord, I can't walk."

The lyrics pinballed through Morgan's memory and lit up twice. First was a lecture he'd heard in medical school, in 1961: a professor had mentioned a strange paralysis called "jake walk" that he had observed during his residency in Cincinnati in the thirties. Next was a face from Morgan's childhood in Ohio, that of a legless beggar called Nigger John. Nigger John had had the "jake leg," Morgan recalled his mother telling him. She had said it in a way that discouraged further inquiry.

Stout and bearded, Morgan, who is sixty-three, delicately set the arm of a turntable on a thick, spinning record, and after a moment's hiss we heard what sounded like pure despair. "Ishmon Bracey, one of the Mississippi greats," Morgan whispered. From seven decades back, Bracey wailed, "Jake leg, jake leg, what in the world you trying to do? Seems like everybody in the city's messed up on account of drinking you."

Morgan has collected a number of songs about the jake leg or the jake walk. "From them we learn that some new kind of paralysis appeared in 1930," he said. "No songs mention it before then." He began bending back blunt fingers. "The paralysis was brought on by drinking something called 'jake.' It afflicted enough souls to instigate an entire subset of folk music. Blacks and whites were affected. It rendered men impotent. And it was no longer inspiring musicians by 1934, which meant it was a cataclysmic but discrete event." He sat back and spread his hands. "Behold the study, through folk music, of a substance-induced epidemic," he said. "Pharmaco-ethnomusicology."

Morgan has been researching the jake leg on and off for twenty-seven years. He has put together a CD collection of seventeen tunes mentioning it, including one by Gene Autry, and he has written half a dozen medical-journal articles on the subject. In the nineteen-seventies, he interviewed a number of the epidemic's surviving victims and collected his data, a teeming bazaar of anecdote and chemistry, in a huge manuscript that has been gathering dust for years. He also has a filthy carton full of clippings. With a little prodding, he agreed to turn all the material over to me. "I'm not giving up on the story myself," he said. "I just don't mind someone else telling it, too."

As far as we know, the outbreak was first detected in Oklahoma City, by Ephraim Goldfain, a thirty-four-year-old physician who had emigrated from Romania as a child and had put himself through medical school by operating a streetcar. He was bookishly handsome, with swept-back red hair, a cleft chin, and round horn-rimmed glasses. With a few partners, he ran a thirty-five-bed clinic called the Reconstruction Hospital. On February 27, 1930, a man whose name is lost to history staggered in off the street. The patient's feet dangled like a marionette's, so that walking involved swinging them forward and slapping them onto the floor. He told Goldfain that he had strained himself lifting an automobile, and a couple of days later his calves had begun to tingle. Then his legs went useless below the knee. He wasn't in any pain, he said, but he could barely get around.

Sudden paralysis in those days usually meant polio, but to Goldfain, who recounted the patient's history in a medical journal, this didn't look like polio. He didn't pay much attention to the story about lifting the car. Goldfain thought the man's symptoms suggested lead poisoning. He ordered blood and spinal-fluid tests. They came back negative.

Later that day, another man appeared, exhibiting the same bizarre palsy. And then another. By the end of the day, Goldfain's clinic had admitted five patients with the distinctive paralysis. One of them, a podiatrist, claimed he had caught the illness from his own patients, and handed Goldfain a list of the ones who had gone foot-floppy in the past few days. The list had sixty-five names.

Oklahoma in 1930 was a hard-luck place. Thanks to price-killing oversupplies of wheat and cotton, its people had gotten a head start on the Depression. The same day that Goldfain saw his five patients, the American Hospital Association criticized Oklahoma City's medical preparedness, noting that it had fewer hospital beds per capita than any other city of its size. Now it was struggling with what looked like a full-blown epidemic.

In one frenetic day, Goldfain visited thirty men on the podiatrist's list, and in the succeeding weeks followed up with other visits. The men's feet dangled, their legs hung dead below the knee. Some could get around on crutches, some couldn't make their legs move at all, some could use neither their legs nor their hands. Goldfain knew at once that this was no contagion. No children were sick, and hardly any women. The men Goldfain saw all lived in a seedy part of town known for bootlegging. They struck him as being ashamed of their illness. He had only to look at them, and the grimy scratch houses they lived in, to know they were stewbums, boozegobs, hooch histers, drunks.

Within a few days, in various locales in the East, the South, and the Midwest, men began folding up. Some found that they couldn't climb out of bed in the morning. Those who could still walk all had the same rubber-legged gait; one doctor in a Rhode Island hospital flooded with victims said that the men walked as if they were passing through "a field of wet grass." In Providence, a seventy-year-old hobo was stricken at 11 A.M. at the corner of Friendship and Plain Streets; he sat down and couldn't get up. The numbers were frightening: fifty-five cases in Worcester, Massachusetts. Five hundred practically overnight in Wichita. Six hundred and ninety in Topeka.

A thousand in Mississippi. The mystery plague smote Johnson City, Tennessee, particularly hard. "A great many of the victims for the first three or four weeks were ashamed to come on the streets, but they finally came out," a Johnson City victim wrote in a letter to the Surgeon General's office. "You can go on the streets of Johnson City now, and in the run of a day, you can count three or four hundred people in the same condition that I am in."

In New England, as in the South, the typical victim was an alcoholic man living alone in a cheap rented room, unemployed or holding a menial job. Many were veterans of the Great War. A pair of Cincinnati doctors examined a hundred and seventeen victims and found their median age to be forty-seven; almost all of them were earning less than forty dollars a week. "A fair proportion led lonesome lives," the doctors wrote. "Indeed, it would be difficult to imagine anyone having less contact with the people about them than some of these patients."

The economics of Prohibition, then in its eleventh year, painted a bull's-eye on the urban and small-town poor. City swells could buy bonded liquor from Canada; backwoods hillbillies often had access to stills. Low-income townsfolk drank what they could get—rubbing alcohol, hair oil, Sterno, doctored antifreeze. What many of them preferred, though, was jake.

Jake was Jamaica ginger extract, one of the hundreds of dubious but harmless patent medicines that Americans had been relying on for a century. A pale-orange concoction packaged in a two-ounce glass bottle, it was supposed to treat catarrh, flatulence, and "late menstruation." Because it was as much as eighty-five-percent alcohol, it packed the kick of four jiggers of Scotch. And it was legal. Patent medicines had been providing an end run around temperance laws since Maine became the first state to go dry, in 1851. A bottle costing thirty-five cents was available in many pharmacies, groceries, and even dime stores. Preachers and schoolmarms could slip the flat, clear-glass bottle into a pocket for a discreet nip at home. Common rummies, though, often took a bottle into the store's back room, which many jake sellers kept as low-rent speakeasies. There they could mix the jake with Coca-Cola and have their own furtive little party.

The Pure Food and Drug Act of 1906 had purified neither. It required only honest labeling. If a patent medicine contained alcohol, morphine, opium, cocaine, heroin, alpha or beta eucaine, chloroform, cannabis indica, chloral hydrate, or acetanilide, the label had to say so. Furthermore, if the medicine was listed in a compendium of drug standards such as the United States Pharmacopeia (U.S.P.), the medicine had to meet those standards and the bottle could carry the U.S.P. label. Jake, as a "fluid extract," fell under the U.S.P. requirement of four-per-cent solids (in this case, ginger) in a solution of alcohol and water. In 1919, the Volstead Act turned every state dry, but it banned only beverage liquor; jake and other alcoholic medicines remained legal. When the mysterious outbreak of paralysis occurred, eleven years later, there was no reason initially to suspect jake had any role.

The first person to record a connection between jake and the paralysis may have been Ishmon Bracey, the black blues singer who cut "Jake Liquor Blues" in Grafton, Wisconsin, in March of 1930, only weeks after Goldfain saw his first case. Bracey was one of half a dozen Mississippi bluesmen—Son House, Willie Brown, and Charley Patton among them—whom Paramount Records had invited to Grafton that spring to make "race" records. (This was only ten years after the first black blues hit was recorded—Mamie Smith's "Crazy Blues," on Okeh Records—and Paramount had heard from furniture-store owners, who sold record-players, that they could move more stock if there were more black blues records available.) In addition to Bracey, Tommy Johnson, who had made a name for himself in 1928 by recording "Canned Heat Blues," about drinking Sterno, cut his "Alcohol and Jake Blues" at Grafton. He was, according to his biographer, David Evans, a hopeless alcoholic who in a drunken stupor became convinced that he had signed away his rights ever to record music again. Johnson's brother recalled for Evans, "See, when Tom get broke, he would sell anything to get a drink of whisky or a drink of alcorub or anything that'd bring on drunk. He'd take this old black Three-in-One shoe polish and strain it through a powder muff. It would be just as clear as water." Though he lived and performed for another twenty-six years, after the Grafton session Johnson never recorded another song. Daddy

Stovepipe, a singer who liked to perform in formal attire, and his wife, Mississippi Sarah, also apparently recorded a jake-leg song, though John Morgan has never found it.

Morgan believes that no other incident has inspired as much popular music as the jake-walk epidemic. Generally, one song comes out of a disaster, maybe two. "There is nothing to equal the jake walk," he told me. As a pharmaco-ethnomusicologist, Morgan pays particular attention to the portrayal of intoxicants. "Alcohol songs, like heroin songs, tend to be negative and warning, and the jake songs fit that pattern. Marijuana songs are almost always funny."

Newspaper writers came up with nicknames for the ailment: jake leg, jake walk, jakeitus, jakeralysis, gingerfoot. "The worst has happened," a one-paragraph story in the Topeka *Daily Capitol* said. "Emporia, the Athens of Kansas, has 'jake leg.'" In the country as a whole, as many as a hundred thousand people were affected, many ending up in the poorhouses, county farms, veterans' homes, and pogeys that constituted the social safety net in those days.

Right behind the stories of outbreaks came reports of miracle cures: "galvanic current," sodium thiosulfate (a cure for "heavy-metal" poisoning), and baths in cider vinegar. An Oklahoma City man said he recovered from the jake leg by being "bumped around on a long trip by automobile." An Alabama jake-legger told his doctor that corn whiskey was the "specific treatment" for his condition. A Texas woman told a judge that her doctor had recommended beer. Dr. Robert Kidd, of Columbus, Ohio, treated a hundred and twenty-five jake-leg cases by removing forty cc.'s of spinal fluid from each patient and replacing it with a product called Lille's horse serum. Aside from "terrific anaphylactic reaction," rise in temperature, severe headache, backache, nausea, and vomiting that required Adrenalin and morphine to combat, everything went swimmingly. O. B. Van Fossen, a chemist at the Golden Rule oil refinery, in Wichita, looked out his window one day to see a dozen jake-leg victims bathing in the slush ponds of warm petroleum refuse and mud. The lime and sulfur of the slurry, they'd been told, might do them good.

Some victims, for whatever reason, did recover varying degrees of mobility; for others, the paralysis was permanent. John Morgan tracked down some severe jake-leg victims in 1977. By then, the muscle floppiness they'd experienced in the nineteen-thirties had evolved into a spastic rigidity, but they were still crippled. Autopsies of jake-leggers who died from other causes showed damage to the central nervous system, including the spinal cord's anterior horn cells—the same that go bad in cases of polio and amyotrophic lateral sclerosis (A.L.S., or Lou Gehrig's disease). But the spinal column's pyramidal tract cells also suffered from the jake, which gradually led to spasms and rigidity. Higher brain functions weren't affected, a team of University of Oklahoma researchers concluded, although their methodology raises questions. They dosed a chicken with enough jake to make its legs go limp and noted, "The expression in the eyes seemed to indicate that the mind was not impaired."

Once jake was established as the vector, there was no escaping the awkward truth that the victims had brought the affliction upon themselves. "God is hanging out a red flag as a danger sign to those who violate His law," thundered a Johnson City Baptist minister. Shame was an additional burden on the sufferers; the jake leg's distinctive limp betrayed everybody. Fear of disgrace made it hard for doctors to get a patient history. A paralyzed operator of a Georgia mill, for example, vigorously denied drinking jake until his doctor tricked him by offering a prescription that he said might help but could kill any patient who'd been drinking ginger extract. The patient declined the prescription.

Not all victims were poor or alcoholic. In the nineteen-seventies, Morgan interviewed "James Thomas," a highly respected white retiree who had served on the boards of several Tennessee banks. When he was seventeen, Thomas and his brother and some friends had bought some jake in Johnson City at a roadside store run by a man named Will Kite and his daughter. Two weeks later, Thomas, who drove a truck for an oil company, noticed that something was wrong. He suddenly found it hard to depress the brake and clutch pedals. He began working indoors, but noticed that his hands were weak as well; soon he couldn't walk. "After months in bed," Morgan recalled, "he was able to struggle to his feet and walk with crutches, and began working on his parents' farm. He would hold tightly to the plow handles and drag his feet behind the horse, who initially supplied most of the locomotive power. His hands returned to normal, a process that took years, and he became a retail grocer. He never walked without crutches again."

According to another Johnson City resident, the Kites denied that their Jamaica ginger extract had caused the illness. "They pointed out that the bottles were all labelled 'United States Pharmacopeia 70% alco,'" Morgan explained. "Because it was labelled so and carried a governmental certificate, it couldn't be the cause of the illness, they argued. They backed up their beliefs by openly consuming the jake in the store. The Kites continued to operate the store for a time. This was accomplished with difficulty, because they both had to crawl on hands and knees from the back rooms of the store to the counter to wait on customers."

None of the contemporary news or medical accounts mentioned what appears to have been the disease's most embarrassing consequence. "It's the doggonest disease ever heard of since I been born," Bracey sang. "You get numb in front of your body, you can't carry any lovin' on." In the jake songs, "limber leg" or "limber trouble" seems to have been the bluesmen's code for impotence. "Mama cried out and said, 'Oh Lord, there's nothin' in the world poor daddy can do, 'cause he done drank so much jake, oh Lord, that he got the limber leg, too,'" moaned Willie Lofton. Bracey was the most explicit: "Aunt Jane, she came runnin' and screamin', tellin' everybody in the neighborhood, 'That man of mine got the limber trouble, and his lovin' can't do me any good.'"

Every song by a black singer mentions the limber leg. "If it hadn't made men impotent, there might not have been any music at all," Morgan said. In 1976, he tracked down a sixty-nine-year-old jake-leg victim named Gwin Davis. When the epidemic began, Davis had been a mill-worker living in a boarding house in Elizabethton, Tennessee. He'd bought his jake at a roadside stand that also sold ice cream, sandwiches, and moonshine. He and all but one of the eight or nine other young men at the boarding house went limp at the same time. Initially, they made a game of it. "We thought it was fun, in a way. Slap our feet and fall down, this and that," Davis said. "We didn't know we was going to get to where we couldn't walk at all. Yeah, finally got to where we couldn't walk at all." When Morgan asked him if he'd ever thought of marrying, Davis looked at his feet and wept.

It is impossible to determine how many black people suffered from the jake leg; they weren't welcome at many hospitals, where they might have been counted. Only whites gathered statistics on the epidemic, and, again, the research methods were often questionable. The researchers at the University of Oklahoma asserted that they had not found "a single case of a Negro being affected" in their region, but they seem to have doubted their own observations. (Oklahoma was ten per cent black.) To see if African-Americans enjoyed a natural immunity to the jake leg, the researchers devised yet another experiment with the chickens, this time dosing black and white chickens with known paralytic ginger extract. Secure in the belief that black feathers in chickens were the genetic equivalent of African heritage in humans, they watched the black and white chickens fall ill indiscriminately and concluded that "color plays no part." An Ohio doctor noted that ten per cent of the cases he saw were Negroes, and felt compelled to report that, among the remainder, seventy-five per cent were "brunettes." The songs of Ishmon Bracey, Willie Lofton, and Tommy Johnson remain the best confirmation that the jake leg hit black communities hard.

The jake-leg epidemic broke out during the last golden moments of the Republican Elysium, before the full effect of the crash set in, when the country was feverishly denying how poor it was getting. Government was small, regulations were skimpy, enforcement was an afterthought, and mass product-liability suits were yet to be pioneered. The federal budget was less than four billion dollars, and the biggest items were defense spending and veterans' benefits. Drug standards were policed, to the limited extent allowed, by the Agriculture Department's tiny Bureau of Chemistry, which in 1927 changed its name to the Food, Drug, and Insecticide Administration. Its annual budget was little more than a million dollars, a pittance even then. The very idea that the federal government should play a role in fighting the jake leg was controversial.

In any case, the government had no Centers for Disease Control from which to dispatch regiments of epidemiologists. As jake leg whipped across the land, plenty of theories circulated: that a batch of jake had been contaminated with lead, arsenic, nicotine, creosote, or carbolic acid; that an unscrupulous bootlegger had used toxic wood alcohol or petroleum alcohol instead of grain alcohol; that the jake-leggers suffered from "lathyrism, which results from the eating of certain species of beans"; that gatherers of wild ginger on the island of "Santo Domingo" in "Central America" had accidentally harvested a poisonous root called "derringue." One old jake victim in Elizabethton, Tennessee, told Morgan that, because the biggest local employer at the time of the outbreak was a German-owned rayon factory, a lot of people thought that the Germans were poisoning the jake to soften up America for another war.

The only public-health watchdog was the federal Hygienic Laboratory, a miserably underfunded outgrowth of the Ellis Island clinic, which had been established in 1887 to screen immigrants. It was in the process of changing its name to the grander National Institute of Health, but it had a budget of less than a million dollars, and a staff of only twelve doctors. One of them was a bespectacled forty-two-year-old Russian immigrant named Maurice Isadore Smith, who, like Ephraim Goldfain, had come to the United States as a child and worked his way through medical school to become a pharmacologist. In early 1930, he decided that he needed to get his hands on a sample of poisoned jake.

It wasn't easy. As word of the epidemic spread, storekeepers, fearful of being prosecuted, removed jake from their shelves. Consumers smashed their bottles to keep family members from getting poisoned. More than once, Smith's investigators had to recover bottles from cesspools and outhouse pits. They found their first sample in Findlay, Ohio, and rushed it back to Washington, where testing on animals revealed something odd. Though poisoned jake killed rabbits and paralyzed calves, it was relatively harmless to monkeys and dogs, animals commonly used to test for toxicity in humans.

Looming in the background of Smith's investigation was the Treasury Department's Bureau of Prohibition, which had jurisdiction over any incident involving alcohol and a budget roughly nine times that of either the F.D.I.A. or the N.I.H. It also had badges and tommy guns. Some health officials held the dry agents in contempt as power-hungry, moralistic cops. "It will do us no good to be identified with the Prohibition Unit," one F.D.I.A. official wrote his boss, reasoning that it would "hinder our work in the future if manufacturers think we are snoopers for the Prohibition outfit." But the Prohibition Bureau had the resources and labs for analyzing alcohol. Its chemists quickly identified a surprising chemical in the suspect jake: tri-ortho-cresyl phosphate, or TOCP, a plasticizer formulated to keep synthetic materials from becoming brittle. Two companies made it: Eastman Kodak and the Celluloid Corporation of Newark, New Jersey, which used it for lacquers, resins, and rubber compounds. TOCP was not considered toxic.

Why would anyone add plasticizer to jake? The most persuasive theory was put forward by several investigators and chemists. From the start of Prohibition, the Treasury Department had sought to tackle the problem of people getting too much pleasure from patent-medicine tippling by ordering that the solids in fluid extracts be doubled. In the case of jake, this transformed a tasty pale-orange liqueur into a black syrup so bitter it could be endured only if heavily diluted.

To enforce compliance, government agents sometimes pulled jake off shelves, boiled off the alcohol, and weighed the solids. Agents didn't thoroughly test the solids, though, and this provided an opportunity for the clever chemists of a multimillion-dollar industry devoted to subverting Prohibition. Bootleggers were already stripping methyl alcohol out of denatured "industrial" alcohol to make it drinkable and distilling potable hooch from aftershaves and perfumes. What they needed was a way to boost the solids in jake enough to satisfy the T-men without spoiling the taste.

They tried molasses and various herbs, but what worked best, at least until 1930, was castor oil. It had a higher boiling point than alcohol and so stayed behind, to be weighed with the ginger, when the alcohol was gone. Its drawback was its tendency to rise to the top of a bottle, tipping off the buyer that something other than ginger and alcohol lurked inside. The plasticizer TOCP solved that.

After testing Smith's samples, Prohibition Bureau chemists described TOCP in a letter to the Food, Drug, and Insecticide Administration as "a tasteless, odorless substance, viscous in character, soluble in alcohol, insoluble in water" which "behaves very much like oleoresin of ginger." It was cheap, perhaps even cheaper than castor oil, and certainly cheaper than ginger. And the textbooks said it was safe. As Smith had seen, even if the bootleggers had scrupulously tried TOCP on dogs and monkeys—the most expensive and human-like of test animals—it would have seemed harmless. "Only a chemist of some ability could have thought of [using

TOCP]," Smith wrote in the October, 1930, issue of the journal *Public Health Reports*. "And had there been anything known about the pharmacologic action of this substance and the possible dire consequences, it is probable that it would never have been used and the disaster would never had happened."

Some newspaper editorials blamed the epidemic on Prohibition's arcane rules—a view that was expressed more eloquently when the Mississippi Sheiks, a black string band, recorded "Jake Leg Blues," in June of 1930. "You thought the lively man would die when you made the country dry, when you made it so that he could not get not another drop of rye," the Sheiks sang. "Well, I know that you will feel bad when you see what he has had . . . He's got those jake limber-leg blues."

The poisoned jake samples eventually led investigators to Harry Gross and Max Reisman, two Boston brothers-in-law who had undertaken various shady ventures together during the nineteen-twenties. They traded a big country house back and forth, and Reisman ran it briefly as a resort called Breezy Meadows. They dabbled in penny-ante food jobbing, handling canned goods, jams, and extracts. But they never used the same business name for very long, and constantly rearranged ownership of their enterprises in a complicated shell game, no doubt to conceal their dealings at the fringes of the illegal-liquor business. Gross wangled a valuable Prohibition Bureau permit in 1921 to handle various types of alcohol, but the Bureau revoked it two years later. Reisman was indicted at one point for shipping five gallons of pear extract to an Indian reservation, in violation of a federal law banning alcohol on reservations. By 1926, the Prohibition Bureau had the brothers-in-law pegged as likely bootleggers. A surveillance memo from the jake investigation describes "several well-dressed men of the bootlegger type . . . loafing about" their office, and one can almost see the fedoras and spats.

In 1927, police found a still on the grounds of the country house. Somehow, though, no one was arrested. In 1928, Gross and Reisman rented the third and fourth floors of a building at 65 Fulton Street in Boston, renamed themselves Hub Productions, installed Goldie Sprinsky, a sister-in-law, as their secretary, and threw themselves into full-time production of Jamaica ginger extract. They shipped the jake around the country in big barrels, which they filled at night and labelled "liquid medicine in bulk." The brothers-in-law apparently cut corners from the start; now and then, customers would complain that the jake they received from Hub didn't conform to U.S.P. standards, and Gross would type firm, businesslike answers defending the product.

Like a lot of good bootleggers, Gross and Reisman were shade-tree chemists, and in the summer of 1929 they decided to supplement the castor oil in their jake with something cheaper and better. They ordered barrels of dibutyl phthalate, a plasticizer like TOCP, and three solvents: fusel oil, butyl Carbitol, and Cellosolve. All were clear, oily liquids with high boiling points. But the brothers-in-law wisely rejected all three; they're lethal. Instead, they asked one of their chemical suppliers, Martin Swanson, for some ethylene glycol, another odorless, oily chemical that was common in antifreeze and nontoxic to most people. Alas, the ethylene glycol boiled off too quickly. A few days later, Gross called Swanson and asked him to find something less volatile. Swanson was puzzled; volatility was not an issue when ethylene glycol was used as intended. Swanson sent Gross some diethylene glycol, which is similar but has a higher boiling point. That didn't please Gross, either. "Well, I don't know what on earth you are doing with this stuff and how you are handling it," Swanson told Gross. Apparently, Gross was mimicking the boiling trial that federal agents would use if they tested his jake, and was finding that diethylene glycol evaporated with the alcohol instead of staying behind with the ginger. That was lucky for jake hounds everywhere: it was as deadly as the other chemicals. Swanson told Gross that the only thing he had that was less volatile was Lindol, the Celluloid Corporation's trade name for tri-ortho-cresyl phosphate.

Gross and Reisman twice asked Swanson if Lindol was toxic, and asked him to write Celluloid to make sure. On January 18, 1930, Swanson received confirmation from Celluloid that Lindol was harmless, and he told Gross. Hub bought a hundred and thirty-five gallons of it, enough to adulterate six hundred and forty thousand bottles of jake. Gross would load each shipment into the elevator, take it alone to the fourth floor, and send down the empty barrels.

Somebody working for Gross and Reisman may have had second thoughts. On March 1st, a man identifying himself as an employee

of the Dolan Drug Company, which was a shell operated by Gross
and Reisman, called the warehouse that was storing the jake and
said, "Those sixteen drums of ginger which you have stored in my
name are poison. I don't want them." If an employee was having
pangs of conscience, Gross and Reisman were not. On March 15th
and 19th—more than a week after the first stories about the jake
epidemic hit the papers and two weeks after the call from the Dolan
Drug Company—Gross and Reisman shipped two last barrels of
jake. The F.D.I.A. and Prohibition cops found plenty of distributors
who could finger Hub as the source of their bad jake. In December,
Gross and Reisman were indicted by a federal grand jury.

Because Gross and Reisman had paralyzed tens of thousands of
people, everybody involved in the prosecution wanted to hit them
with Prohibition charges, which carried jail time, instead of merely
the administrative fines that would likely be levied by the F.D.I.A.
But patent medicines came under the jurisdiction of the Prohibition
Bureau only if they were used as "beverages" rather than as medicine, a legal distinction almost impossible to prove, especially since
jake labels often carried a warning: "This preparation must not be
used for beverage purposes under penalty of law." Gross and Reisman eventually pleaded guilty to violating the Prohibition laws as
well as the Pure Food and Drug Act. The hitch was that they
insisted they were only middlemen. If the judge went easy on them
and put them on probation, they would turn over the much more
important criminal. The judge complied.

In reality, Gross and Reisman were the ones who not only had
made the jake but had ignored early news reports indicating that
their product was responsible for the outbreak of paralysis. They
also neglected to mention, during plea bargaining, the two barrels
shipped in March. When those showed up in Los Angeles the following year and paralyzed another two hundred people, the judge
revoked Gross's probation. In April, 1932, he began serving a two-
year prison sentence. Reisman never did time.

A few people tried to sue the distributors who sold them the bad
jake, but nobody went after the one entity with deep pockets: the
Celluloid Corporation. In May of 1931, some Oklahomans orga-

nized the United Victims of Jamaica Ginger Paralysis, which claimed to speak for thirty-five thousand stricken people across the country. Unfortunately, the Federal Rules of Civil Procedure, which effectively enabled class-action lawsuits, were seven years in the future, and product-liability law was in its infancy. "To have brought such suits would have been almost unthinkable," according to Andrew Popper, a torts professor at the Washington College of Law at American University. "They'd have thrown you in bad-lawyer jail." All the victims could do, really, was petition the government officials for relief. There wasn't much hope. When United Victims first formed, Oklahoma's governor, William (Alfalfa Bill) Murray, declared, "There are three kinds of people I haven't much use for. One is the man with 'jakeitis,' another is the investor on the stock exchange, and the other I won't mention." The victims persisted anyway. "I have a wife and two children dependent on me, and we have been kicked and cuffed about without any home just very little to eat ever since I got crippled," a thirty-year-old man named Joe Gordon wrote to his senator in a spidery hand from Hot Springs, Arkansas, in 1933. "And I'll tell the world Life looks almost hopeless for me and my little family, and God knows we have struggled so hard to Live since this awful injustice." Congress was lobbied for years, but it never passed a bill for victims' relief.

"The jake-leg story is almost completely about class," John Morgan says. "If someone had poisoned the Canadian source of bonded Scotch, something would have been done. But these men were mostly migrants. They came to the city, leaving their women, to get work. They were seen as poor, sloppy drunks." And so the jake-leg tragedy dropped down the national amnesia hole. With its unwelcome implications about Prohibition and poverty, and its falling thirty years before the era of class-action lawsuits, the epidemic would have probably remained forgotten but for the efforts of the Allen Brothers, Ishmon Bracey, Tommy Johnson, the Mississippi Sheiks, Willie Lofton, and Daddy Stovepipe and Mississippi Sarah.

Even Ephraim Goldfain, the first doctor to treat the illness, took little apparent pride in his role. He went on to make a name for himself locally, pioneering the use of gold in arthritis therapy. He was also celebrated in Oklahoma for rheumatism serum he mixed himself, handblowing the glass vials that held the doses and fashioning, instead of the usual teardrop top, whimsical animal-head stoppers. With his granddaughter Suellen in the passenger seat, he would drive among the tiny farm communities surrounding Oklahoma City, injecting his patients. He died in 1983. Suellen Singer still enjoys telling family stories about him, but she says she knows nothing about the jake leg. He never mentioned it.

ELIZABETH MÉNDEZ BERRY

The Last Hustle

You can now walk a mile in Jay-Z's shoes. As of April 2003, two different S. Carter by Reebok models went on sale for $99.99. So not only can you drink the Armadale vodka he hawks at the club he owns and dress your entire family in outfits from his Rocawear clothing line, you can buy footwear with his signature on the back. But after listening to Jay-Z's most revealing record ever, *The Black Album*, you still won't understand how it feels to inhabit his pristine 10-and-a-halfs.

Jay-Z wears each pair a maximum of twice. "I've noticed that when people have had money for a long time, they never talk about it, they don't show it," he told me during an interview at Baseline Studios in New York—wearing jeans, a jacket, and S. Carters, of course. "But I'm that same kid from that neighborhood with that insecurity, who feels like if I get the car I'll feel better about myself because it's been too long feeling bad about myself. Lyor Cohen wears New Balances 80 times. If I wear Reeboks two times, I gotta get rid of 'em." He paused and smiled. "I'll get there one day." After saying "If I wear," Jay-Z began an almost imperceptible "N" sound, but stopped himself before completing the word "Nikes," replacing that financially inconvenient stutter with "Reeboks." Jay-Z has the first sneaker deal for a non-sports star to protect.

He's also got a reputation to look after. Jay-Z is a confidence artist, and he's gotten rich by not making it personal—teaching the swagger but seldom betraying the emotional limp that caused it. Now, after nine studio albums and undisclosed millions in revenue, Jay-Z says he's retiring from rap. He claims that he's no longer inspired by the hip-hop world, but the content of *The Black Album* and his contemplative conversational tone suggest that he isn't just bored by what other people are doing—he's bored by the alter ego he's outgrown. The risk-averse rapper calculates, however, that it's the smooth criminal the public has fallen for—the reason he can sell athletic footwear without a jump shot—and he's not about to jeopardize his financial future. Instead, he's doing his best to preserve the myth for posterity.

On a Metro North train the day after *The Black Album* is released, a young woman carrying a Rocawear bag listens to the album on her headphones. She's mouthing the lyrics already. Jay-Z's recording persona is so compelling because though he's still a caricature—certain features are disproportionately emphasized—he's an elegantly rendered one. Says Kanye West, the producer responsible for some of Jay's most sinuous beats, "Jay-Z can't be a loser. He can't say anything that could come off as uncool. And if he does he has to figure out the coolest way to say it." Somehow, in spite of the disposables he's picked up along the way—shiny shirts, Shaquille O'Neal collaborations, rotating cast of Roc-A-Fella sidekicks, endless product placements—Jay-Z's Teflon nonchalance seems timeless.

"Coming up, I experienced the worst pain a person can experience, period," Jay-Z said. "Your pop is your superman, and when that's taken away from you, you never want to put yourself in that position again." He explained the birth of his cool candidly. "I always grew up [thinking], if you say you don't care about it, then no one can hurt you. People called me jazzy, I was a cool guy for my age, but that's where it stemmed from."

Jay-Z patented his chilly brand of calm on his classic debut, 1996's *Reasonable Doubt*, which is still his favorite. "It was my first album, so I didn't have a target audience," he said. "I didn't know anything about making music. That was the best album for me because I was just doing what came naturally." *Reasonable Doubt* is honest not in the sense of soul-baring but in the sense of unselfconscious. "I was just trying to tell a story and keep it in rhyme form so that my friends would be like, 'Wooo,'" he said. Concealed within the album are a wealth of tricky lines you brush past at first. On the hustler reality check "D'Evils," he raps, "You know the demon said it's best to die/And even if Jehovah Witness, bet he'll never testify." "I call that the Easter egg hunt," Jay-Z told me. "With every album I try to do that, but I think that was the one that had the most Easter eggs."

Since *Reasonable Doubt*, writing has become an exercise in restraint for Jay-Z. He admits as much on *The Black Album*'s "Moment of Clarity," where he rhymes, "I've dumbed down for my audience and doubled my dollars/They criticize me for it yet they all yell holler." Jay-Z explained: "Now I know how to make a song so I know when to turn it on and turn it off. I know when to take my foot off the pedal, when I'm gonna lose everyone." By his next album, *In My Lifetime, Vol. 1*, he was playing the market—Jay-Z worked with Puff Daddy and commissioned dubious Hype Williams videos. At the beginning of the record comes a stage whisper that sets the tone: "Man look at these suckers/I ain't no rapper, I'm a hustler."

Jay-Z's friend Notorious B.I.G.—who was able to balance his street persona with pop success, and whose posthumous *Life After Death* earned 10 platinum plaques—provided the template, not to mention the producer. Jay uses *Vol. 1* to play homage to B.I.G. while claiming his recently deceased friend's King of New York crown. Jay-Z may also have been inspired by the third member of the holy trinity of rap he anoints on the razor-sharp *Vol. 1* track "Where I'm From": Nas. Nas's debut, 1994's *Illmatic*, was a cognoscenti record that sold gold. Right after *Reasonable Doubt* came out in June of 1996, Nas released *It Was Written*, which made concessions to commercial radio, notably via the single "Street Dreams." *It Was Written* was certified double platinum in two months, just as *Reasonable Doubt* was certified gold. Since then, none of Jay-Z's albums has sold less than platinum. But though he'd prioritized his cash flow, Jay-Z didn't put all his Easter eggs in that basket. Throughout his career, he has often enlivened the radio with cunningly addictive tracks like 2000's "I Just Wanna Love U." And even when his music is mediocre, there's a line or two hidden in there for the close listeners—and maybe for him too. One gets the sense that he's trying to keep himself amused.

In 1998, shortly after the release of the mega-selling *Vol. 2 . . . Hard Knock Life*, Jay wanted to make an album for his original audience. "I'll never forget that day," said DJ Premier, who has collaborated with Jay-Z since he was down with Big Daddy Kane. "The phone rang, and it was Jay—at that time we had each other's numbers," recalled Premier. "He said, 'I want to do this thing called the *Black Album*. I want to take a good two or three weeks and just lock in with you, you do nothing but this album. I want you to produce the entire thing. I'm not gonna do no singles. I'm not gonna do nothing, just throw it out.' I was down, and then there was talk of a *Black Album* in the street, but it never happened."

Five years later, Jay-Z has released a very different *Black Album*— one that doesn't include any production from Primo—but he still feels constrained by fame. "We as artists are faced with keeping it real and going back to the 'hood and making the hardcore record, so we don't get criticized like 'Aw, he fell off,'" he said. "Whenever a person tries to go and do different things, they condemn it as a sell-out attempt. Myself included, we can't be afraid to grow. What's the point if we can't talk about the things we've seen?" Andre 3000's album is one of his favorites right now: "'Y'all don't hear me, y'all just wanna dance.' I can relate to that. He wants to be totally honest, he wants to tell the truth, but 'Y'all just wanna dance.' I know what he feeling right there."

That frustration shows on *The Black Album*. Though Jay-Z never steps out of character—he does the dancefloor ditty, the narco-nostalgia, the ego trip—he no longer seems entirely comfortable playing his role. When during a listening session, he played the track "99 Problems" for a group of journalists, he took great pains to explain that the word *bitch* as used in the song doesn't refer to a woman, and therefore isn't misogynistic. Either he thought we were a very gullible bunch or he felt conflicted about his use of the term, embarrassed even. I doubt he offered any such disclaimer when he played "Can I Get a . . ." back in 1998. Later on, when I asked him about the fluffy phoned-in Neptunes single "Change Clothes," he said, "It's not degrading at all," as if that justified its existence.

Having come clean about his crowd-pleasing career path on the new album, Jay-Z claimed in person that he was trying to recapture the uncompromising rhyme style of *Reasonable Doubt*. "I stopped dumbing down more than ever," he said. Maybe, but Jay-Z has sold his character so well that he seems afraid to swap it for a newer model. Said Kanye West, "I think Jay probably does want to rap about more honest stuff, but that's not what he came into the game to rap about." He fulfills his audience's expectations for quick-fix singles like "Change Clothes." And he still plays the intelligent gangster who, like the Eskimos, has a hundred words for snow— when he said, "I'm running on fumes" during the brief Q&A after the listening session, he could have been referring to the long dissipated crack smoke that he still conjures in rhyme. According to Kanye West, "Jay wanted to take it back to before he was in the industry, to the drug game, to make it like how *Reasonable Doubt* was." But back then, Jay-Z's life and his recording persona coincided; he had barely retired from street life. That's no longer true, which may be why, though he offers the finessed violence of old on "Threat," Jay-Z adds an unmistakable wink to the track. He doesn't carry a gun anymore.

Instead of illuminating the person he is now—a grown man who golfs—Jay applies his newfound insights to his past, delving into his motivations for hustling. "At least let me tell you why I'm this way," he says on the first track, "December 4th," and proceeds to use the album to explain, justify, and even apologize for his past. On "Allure," he raps, "I put my feet in the footprints left to me, without saying a word/the ghetto's got a mental telepathy/man, my brother hustled so naturally up next is me." Of course, this introspection isn't simply a function of his artistic integrity. Jay-Z is adding nuance to his personal mythology to make his legacy more compelling. Nowhere is this more evident than in his mother's guest spot on "December 4th," in which she describes the auspicious debut of her 10-pound, eight-ounce son Shawn: "[He] didn't give me any pain when I gave birth to him, and that's how I knew that he was a special child."

In his own words, Jay-Z is irreplaceable. So whether you buy the brown-on-beige S. Carters or the *Black Album* special edition color scheme, Jay-Z reminds you on "Justify My Thug" that you can't really wear his shoes. "Try to put your dogs in it/Ten-and-a-halfs, for a minute-and-a-half/Bet that stops all the grinning and the laughs." But though he's concerned with protecting his mystique,

Jay-Z seems to genuinely crave inspiration. When I met with him, I gave him a copy of a critical—and I do mean critical—essay on *Reasonable Doubt, Vol. 3: Life and Times of S. Carter,* and *The Blueprint* that I contributed to the book *Classic Material.* The following day, he called to tell me that it provoked him to write a new second verse for "Public Service Announcement." He said that what he appreciated most about the piece was its honesty, and invited me to come to Baseline and hear the cut.

After a long scheduling delay, I finally returned to the studio, as E!, Extra, CNN, and New York 1's celebrity chaser George Whipple waited for on-camera interviews. I ran into Jay-Z and he said he thought he'd be able to play it for me. An hour later, however, he got pulled into a two-hour meeting with Reebok, and that was that. When I heard it a few days later in the comfort of my own home, I was struck by part of the new verse: "Hope you don't think users are the only abusers niggas getting high within the game/If you do then how would you explain I'm 10 years removed still the vibe is in my veins/I've got a hustler's spirit, nigga period."

Those lines clarify a lot. In hip-hop, a culture that confuses cleverness with wisdom, Jay-Z is certainly one of the best. But he's a hustler first, an artist second. Producer Kanye West is also a rapper, with his solo debut due early next year. In an interview I did with him in August for *Vibe,* he told me, "My claim to fame is to be honest." So towards the end of our recent conversation, I asked West what would happen if Jay-Z talked about all the things he's seen, not just the safe, dangerous stuff—if he started making music from the pit of his stomach. He paused, and then said: "Can you imagine that? I wouldn't have a chance."

ANDREW BONAZELLI

Five Nights, Five Karaoke Bars

Don't Let the Sun Go Down on Me

Two maxims warm my heart whenever I'm fraught with doubt about my lot in life: "Those who can, do; those who can't, write reviews" and "No statue has been put up to a critic." Naturally, I mean "warm my heart" in the drop-the-blow-dryer-into-the-bathtub sense.

Sauntering onstage and unleashing some pretentious, indecipherable, extended metaphor about my ex in a sexy, detached Marlboro rasp? I'm pretty sure the four horsemen of the hipster apocalypse—Old, Fat, Wrinkled, and Ugly—will throw me a good old-fashioned boot party before my first paying gig.

The only surrogate is karaoke. I spent five consecutive nights in five different karaoke venues last week and heard an MC summarize the experience as "your chance to be a rock star . . . for three minutes at a time." Thanks, MC Plato, but I've developed my own enduring philosophies on hara-karaoke.

SUNDAY—TWILIGHT EXIT,
2020 E. Madison St., 206-324-7462

The moment my acquaintance Austin informed the semipro, no-fucking-around Twilight regulars that "this shong's goin' out to Jee-shus," it was clear that all were in for a transcendent version of Creed's "Higher." As I urged the masses to "take me to a place where blind men see," Austin harmonized with a just-right, five-minute-and-16-second "RAAWRRRRRRRRGHHHH!!!"

Our bro-down evidently had nothing on Avril Levigne's "Sk8er Boi," during which—despite the fact that my microphone was apparently never on—I was brutally dry-humped by an exuberant lady who screamed, "I fuckin' love this song!" mid-thrust. Trust me: My "moves" had nothing to do with this. The Twilight is the kind of place where Carrot Top comes off like Enrique Iglesias. Your pants may not survive.

MONDAY—BAR, 1525 E. Olive Way,
206-322-1788

I arrived alone to find seven jocks playing billiards; I left vibing an undiscovered gem that I shall reluctantly espouse. Bar's T-shaped stage, fog machine, off-Pine/Pike location, and nonexistent early crowd gave me the opportunity to growl, "I wanna fuck you like an animal," in all Reznorian glory to . . . the Ms. Pac-Man machine. Come early enough and you'll enjoy similar playlist autonomy.

Easy highlight: A guy in a Tool shirt performed, no shit, a Tool song. I complimented him earnestly in the bathroom, he asked if I was a cop, and we did something that may or may not have been illegal but ultimately put my body on lockdown until I finally breached . . .

TUESDAY—R PLACE, 619 E. Pine St., 206-322-8828

Walking home from my nightly booze 'n' bullshit rounds, I often gave up covetously at R Place. Every night seems to be an onslaught of No Doubt and gyrating silhouettes that—as a straight dude who hangs out with 85 percent straight dudes—I stupidly disregard.

I'd always assumed that Tuesday karaoke ignited such fervor, but the event was surprisingly subdued, awash in balladry and dedications. Thankfully, my cohorts, Heather June and Simon, applied electroshock. He literally shoved her off the stage during "Don't Let the Sun Go Down on Me," igniting an hour-long pissing match that culminated when I negotiated "Wild Wild West" (my Heather duet) to bump "P.I.M.P" (my Simon duet). Worse, Heather June's mike was inexplicably shut off during said Escape Club classic. Not the best day for a woman who regularly owns the Twilight dance party covering Lita Ford, but considering the depth of my pre-karaoke jitters—I was considering Elvising a bottle of valium—a home run for yours truly.

WEDNESDAY—SUNSET TAVERN, 5433 Ballard Ave. N.W., 206-784-4880

Rockaraoke: an entirely different beast. No TV screens. No vocal cues. Actual working musicians. Monster stage. Blinding lights. Only one sign-up per set. Everyone knows it's impossible to drink enough to make your first attempt remotely tuneful, and I was not in company that I wanted to make a spectacle of myself before. Perfect recipe for a fuckup.

So I fucked up. I selected "Enjoy the Silence" and froze. Not "choked" froze; just meowed monotonously, looked at the guitarist like a bunny for every cue, stormed to the john afterward, dry heaved, then slumped back to my table in ignominy.

Having suitably alienated everybody, I drove back to Bar, met my friends Arlie and Kelley, and, in familiar, nonthreatening confines, blasted through the Strokes, Green Day, 50 Cent, and Limp Bizkit with such depraved gusto that the MC yelped "Marshall (long story . . .), you're a karaoke whore!" If he only fucking knew.

THURSDAY—FENIX UNDERGROUND, 323 Second Ave. S., 206-467-1111

Dream finale. Rusty, yesterday's rockaraoke axman, recognized me right away, coddled my ego, insisted that we try "Silence" again instead of "Blue Monday," and voilà: I danced, I hit my spots, and he told everyone to "give this guy a big fucking hand" during the outro. For three minutes at a time, I was Cinderella. Maybe next week I can graduate to Ratt.

GEOFF BOUCHER

Beat at Their Own Game

Sometimes the past isn't hard to find. Leave Los Angeles, drive 125 miles into the oven heat of Palm Desert, down Sonny Bono Memorial Highway and across Frank Sinatra Drive, and the past might even greet you at his front door. "You found me," Hal Blaine says from behind huge sunglasses. "Come on in."

Inside, a few gold records adorn the wall, all hits by John Denver, all featuring Blaine on drums. What's missing from the walls of his modest home says far more about the backbeat of Blaine's life today. "I used to have, oh, 150 other ones, but I had to sell them all." Blaine kept time on some of the most memorable American recordings of the 1960s—"California Dreamin'," "Strangers in the Night," "Good Vibrations," "Mrs. Robinson," "Can't Help Falling in Love," "I Got You Babe" among them—but that was during what he calls "the absolute golden age of session musicians."

It was also, he adds, before "those machines" changed the making of music.

Blaine says the phone that never stopped ringing in the 1960s and early 1970s went silent in the following decade as the drum machine arrived and music trends veered away from him. A bitter divorce left him without his Rolls-Royce, yacht and the house above Mulholland. "I have to be honest with you. I'd be homeless today without my pension." Blaine was the king of Los Angeles session drummers, and today the weary, 74-year-old royal in the desert reflects his former kingdom. It would be hyperbole to say the session drummer is dead, but, like John Henry hammering away at that steel, you wonder what the long-term health is for a profession that tries to match swings with a machine.

"It's a tough time now, a real tough time, especially if you're one of those young people trying to get in," says Jim Keltner, the drummer who became a titan of the field in the 1970s, playing on major recordings by Bob Dylan, John Lennon and many others. Keltner remains a player in great demand, but now that makes him a rarity in his field. "There has been an erosion. Things aren't the way they were. But you really have to say that you could see it coming. It shouldn't have been a surprise to anyone."

The rudimentary drum machines of the 1970s were alarming to many of the old guard who predicted then that the robotic drumstick eventually would elbow out the human player. They were right. Entire pop albums are sometimes recorded today without a traditional drummer in the studio, and one of the premier genres of the age, hip-hop, is almost defined by the computer creation of beats by celebrity producers, not by a drummer.

Then there's the overall malaise in the session recording business. Laptops and modest home studios can be used to make professional-level albums now, and many of the lavish recording studios in Los Angeles and New York are wondering if in a few years they will have the allure of, say, an extremely well-appointed typewriter factory.

Album sales are down, record labels are shaky and cutting back, and film and television work—the lifeblood for players in Local 47 of the American Federation of Musicians—is often taken offshore for the discounted costs. It makes the local's president, Hal Espinosa, long for the days in the 1960s when he and other players scrambled across town to play session after session.

"There were 11 or 12 variety shows going on. I was doing Dean Martin's show, the Bob Hope specials, Carol Burnett's show. We were running from one studio to the next. Today you don't have that because of new technology. It's gone. It's not coming back." At least Espinosa was a trumpet man. "It's changed for all of us. But I imagine it's the worst for the drummers."

*   *   *

Some Learned to Adapt

Jimmy Bralower once believed drumming was a science only in the way boxing and whistling are sciences. "Look. Playing drums is holding two clubs in your hand. It doesn't get much more primitive than that, right?" Bralower is a New York record executive these days, a prominent vice president at Atlantic Records, but once he was a scrappy Long Island kid who dreamed of being a drummer. He bounced among bands in the 1970s, and by the 1980s he was working in the session rooms of SoHo with artists such as early hip-hop figure Kurtis Blow. It was cusp time—live R&B music and disco were giving way to the protean sound of hip-hop, and the beat of the new music was still being shaped.

"So one day someone brings in this box—it was a foot long and a foot wide and it had all these buttons on it. It was a Roland TR–808, a drum machine. They turned it on and, well, it was pretty daunting. There were beats and rhythms that were kind of impossible to play. This box could do stuff I couldn't do. It was a very threatening moment." Bralower came to embrace the new technology, at first out of career desperation, but then with the zeal of a painter finding whole new colors and canvas.

"Then I became the guy in New York who could program the drumming machines and I had reinvented myself," he said. He would work on some major albums, among them "So" by Peter Gabriel and "Back in the High Life" by Steve Winwood. Not all of his peers smiled on his success, and some producers, worried that the technology compromised their integrity, would ask the programmer if his name could be omitted from the credits. But the work kept coming.

The drummer was the most vulnerable of session players—a beat, a pulse, is the most mechanical of music, and therefore the easiest for a machine—but the synthesizer age has diminished the role of session players of all kinds as samples and swaths of sound made it easier to make music without musicians. The membership of Local 47 was once 16,000; now it's below 9,000. The refinements in technology continue too, so the declines continue. Just five years ago, more than 30,000 of the local's musicians were contracted for sound recordings. By last year, the number sagged to 23,500.

Advocates of the machines and software that create beats for so much of today's pop albums say they are cheaper, faster and easier than bringing in a human drummer. But veteran producer Rick Rubin (Beastie Boys, Red Hot Chili Peppers, Johnny Cash) says it goes beyond practicality. He says the rise of hip-hop in the 1980s created in pop an artist and audience taste for the relentless, inhumanly perfect beats of the machines instead of more expressive and organic rhythms of Blaine's era.

"If you buy an album by somebody like Britney Spears today, you won't find a drummer on it, and it's because the sound, the flavor, of the drum machine is what people want now," Rubin said.

He added that there is also a quality control issue: "Now anyone with a good idea for a beat can program that into the machine and hear it at its very best rendering. Now it's more about the idea than the skill. There are only a couple of handfuls of truly great drummers out there. But there are thousands and thousands of drum machines."

Rubin is in the studio now with rapper Jay-Z and, instead of a live drummer, the beats will be created by the vintage TR–808, the same analog drum that had alarmed Bralower and was used in the 1980s by artists such as Public Enemy and Afrika Bambaataa. The TR–808 can create a variety of sounds, from congas to cowbells. By working its buttons, you can create the rhythm patterns for entire songs. Specialized gear like the TR–808 isn't even needed now; the software age has made computer hard drives into the newest drum kits.

There may be unexpected downsides to the new downbeats. Bralower worries that the ability to shape entire albums with little or no collaboration is creating a generation of musical loners.

"The idea of having a roomful of people there when you presented your ideas, that's kind of gone away," he says. "You could never make an album by yourself before; you could never create without working with other musicians. . . . There's also this whole generation now very used to computer-correct rhythm. That breathing thing that is people playing music is not presented as much. Even rock bands run their music through computers to clean it up. You know, once upon a time, Hal Blaine would just count it off. He was the metronome. Then came the ignorant third party, the technology that doesn't know what's going on in the room."

*   *   *

A Hall of Famer

Ask people about session drummers and the name Hal Blaine always comes up. When the Rock and Roll Hall of Fame created the category of sidemen, Blaine was the first inductee. He played on 42 songs that hit No. 1 and more than 150 that cracked the Top 10. The Grammy Record of the Year is the most coveted trophy in music—Blaine played drums on seven of them. He became a band name, a must-have guy whether it was for a Frank Sinatra single, an Elvis Presley film or a Coca-Cola commercial. "If the music in the second half of the 20th century were the Empire State Building," Art Garfunkel once said, "Hal Blaine would be the ground floor."

Blaine first hit the recording session scene in Los Angeles in the late 1950s. He had by then served in Korea, and played drums in Chicago strip joints, Las Vegas comedy shows and San Bernardino R&B clubs. He hooked up with Phil Spector, the successful and eccentric producer, and a group of session players who became known as the Wrecking Crew. The L.A. scene's veteran players inspired the nickname. "They're wrecking the business," the muttering went when the new rock 'n' roll generation came in.

There was a measure of truth in the old-timers' appraisal. The concept of the self-contained rock or pop band that took hold in the wake of the Beatles and Rolling Stones began a gradual downsizing of the session players' role. Still, by the 1970s, rock had grown so large and lucrative that the top session players lived like the stars themselves.

Many of the premier session drummers of that era have moved on. Rick Marotta was known for his work with Steely Dan, Paul Simon, Carly Simon, Aretha Franklin, James Taylor and many others. "Back then, I couldn't take all the jobs that were offered," he said. "Now, if I was doing just that, I wouldn't be able to make a living."

Instead of rock albums, Marotta now works in sitcoms. He's the composer for "Everybody Loves Raymond" and other shows, writing the music needed for background environments and the show's breaks.

In his studio behind a dentist office in Hollywood, Marotta admits that the gig is not as completely satisfying as his session days, but he also feels fortunate to have the strong, steady work. As he flips on the electronic drum pads to give an example of the modern craft, he glumly confides that one of his well-known peers from the 1970s is now working at a car dealership. He also says a friend who sells, rents and tunes drums for pro players in Nashville is watching his business shrivel.

Marotta marvels at what his nest of computer equipment can do as he weaves music together for television shows, but he marvels even more that the gadgetry could replace artists. "I don't know how they got lost. I really don't. Machines are machines. There are things that I hear people did on records that machines can't do. There are things that drummers like Steve Gadd did, things that Jeff Porcaro did and Keltner did—machines cannot do those things."

Keltner may be his generation's equivalent of Blaine. After working in the early 1970s with Joe Cocker, he quickly reached the stratum of star session player. He would go on to sit with stars ranging from Pink Floyd to B.B. King, Jackson Browne to the Bee Gees, Elvis Costello to Willie Nelson, Barbra Streisand to Fiona Apple.

Keltner remembers a fellow drummer who told him in the 1970s that he was leaving the L.A. scene because the drum machines were gobbling up work. "I told him that instead of going back to Tulsa, he should get one of those machines," Keltner recalls. The technology of today does not alarm or offend Keltner but it occasionally disappoints him. He says he hears a steady stream of new albums that are so filtered and finessed that he can almost see the numbers inside the digital sound.

"You suddenly realize: These albums have real likable songs, they have likable performances from everybody, all the singing is good and very in tune, all the playing is good and the guitars are in tune," Keltner says. "But then you realize maybe that's what is wrong. That's why I don't like it. It's more like a mannequin. From a distance it looks like a really beautiful human being, but you get up close and it's not alive. It's standing there with painted-on features. That is the technology being abused."

The drummer is not dead in rock music, not by any means. In bands, drummers, be they Dave Grohl, Meg White, Larry Mullen Jr. or Lars Ulrich, have inspired a new generation to pick up sticks, and they will continue to do so. ?uestlove of the Roots has even brought a live player into the rap world. For session drummers, the new model may be Josh Freese, the gifted young player who also has ongoing and formal membership in three bands: Perfect Circle, the Vandals and Devo.

Blaine has no idea what the future will be for session drummers, but he expresses a solemn gratitude that he was at the right place and time. He moved into the Palm Desert home late last year and, for the first time in his adult life, there are no drums under his roof. His famous drum kits are now in museums or with collectors.

"I played the drums for years, and they played me," he says with a smile. "It's a different time now."

WILLIAM BOWERS

I Think I'm Going to Hell

A Descent into My Morning Jacket Fandom

An ominous ninety-nine-second rumble: Is that a looped growl? A funnel cloud in an echo chamber? Is somebody's work-truck under-water? What noisome thing is being wrought in the foul rag-and-bone shop of Kentucky? Keyboards and drums announce themselves teasingly, and build, mastered as if emerging from the disagreeable soundcloud. So beginneth my favorite album by my favorite rock band, My Morning Jacket's seventy-four-minute *At Dawn* (one hundred and eighteen if you count the bonus disc). The whole mess is organic and mechanized, tribal and industrial, ancient and futuristic, and when that rumble fades and frontman Jim James belts out the words "At daw-awwn," he sounds, well, predestined; his eruption is the messianic moment to which the intro's murk had been lumbering all along. Dawn is, of course, the prime context for a melodramatiza-tion of potentiality, and James nails it, providing his listeners with the same anything-can-happen tingle one gets from a vacation bender, a breakup, a layoff, or sometimes just from being on-line. The song is secular gospel, and in this initial exclamation, James is invoking the Big Bang.

He goes on to quote an enemy's perspective, proclaiming, "All your life is obsceee-eene!" As someone burdened with strange guilt about preposterous American comfort, and as a fan of original sin, and of Kafka's heightened sense of fraudulence, and of Goethe's awareness that each of us is capable of committing every possible horror (Philip Larkin had a point with that whole "man hands on misery to man" thing, huh?), I am inclined to agree with the accuser. Yessirree, all my life, obscene: check.

James sings the line with a singular strain that hints that he, too, is tempted by its teetotaling negation. But James is on a musical mission, and to him, the meaning of *obscene* probably goes to the word's roots, which would imply being "off stage," or out of sight, i.e. not in front of a microphone. Instead of surrendering to despair, though, James tells us how he handles the detractor: "That's when my knife rises/Their life ends/And my life starts again/Again . . . /Ageeeeaeeein." I don't think what he's describing has anything to do with the standard exaltations of rebirth. He's dealing with the will to power, with Cain, with rock 'n' roll.

It is—I can't believe I'm saying this, in a world full of mothers and children—the most inspiring song about murder I've ever heard. If it were playing, and you were my guest, I'd position you by the stereo and stop just short of *forcing* you to listen. If you resisted, and yammered, I'd ask you to leave the room. If you then made too much noise in the kitchen, I might escort you to the front stoop, and plant you in a rocking chair beside the bottle-packed recycling bin. Your civil rights, the mosquitoes, and that cat-pee-smelling chemical with which the neighborhood spray truck tries to combat the mosquitoes would keep you company while I finished listening to the song in the respectful silence it deserved. Our juxtaposition would befit *At Dawn*, an album as rich on a night when friends are coming over as it is the nights when one would give anything to have friends coming over.

The excuse for my ridiculous behavior splits sweetly into matters of nature and nurture. Heredity: I descend from song obsessors who either made people listen along or neglected them for their neglect. Habitat: I was subject to their obsessions, interpolated as pop hostage and exile, and now I pass the savings onto my guests.

God love him, Dad turned our "living room"—intriguing what this phrase implies about a house's other rooms—into his "music room." He removed the standard furniture and filled the space with stereo equipment and album stacks. My sister and I were pretty much banned from this chamber, even though it was the only route to our bedrooms. So on a daily basis we'd have to hotfoot incognito, best we could, through an audiophile's danger zone. Sometimes Dad spread albums on the floor in flowcharts representing an ideally sequenced listening session. These arrangements looked like vinyl hopscotch to a kid. Once my sister pounced on a Lionel Richie record and was dispatched to Mom for discipline. Dad didn't beat us; that would have interrupted his reverie.

Dad's father, though, was worse, and still is. He also did away with the concept of a family-gathering forum and converted his parlor to an all-stereo layout, but in a much larger and older house. With a beautiful smile, he'd turn up the amplifiers and engineer cracks along the wall that fissured to reach the cathedral ceiling.

On some of my visits to his house, he doesn't speak to me or anyone accompanying me; he just blasts his stereos, playing one song per album, for an hour or so. After each song with that certain *it*, he barks, "That's got it!" He'll move from Junior Wells into some Van Halen into some Johnny Cash into some Herbie Hancock, et al. Music keeps this eighty-year-old young: He drives a vintage Mustang with fifteen-inch "booming" speakers; he has subdued, and pistol-whipped, would-be burglars; one Christmas he gave me a mix tape consisting of selections by Paul Simon, Ween, and Bass Master Funk.

My older brother's music obsession was metal. Its clamor and celebration of communal deviance clashed with his quiet, insular nature, but he'd come out of his room to declare that Quiet Riot and Billy Squier and Judas Priest and Kiss and Twisted Sister were titans. He'd skulk around me, lupine, explaining what a virtue it was to play a tape until it wore out, until some part of it disintegrated. Then he'd skulk, lupine, into his (also off-limits) room, where, we later learned, he'd head-banged a hole into the wall behind his framed hologram poster of an eagle and wolf atop jagged rocks.

All of these men were Christians, and I accompanied them to sermons during which we were told that we should eschew faith in worldly possessions. One church even hosted—pregnant gulp—album bonfires. I would dream of Christ showing up at our house, his brilliant purity difficult to behold against our redneck-rococo décor; he would proceed to overturn the house's music collections the same way that, in TV movies and Easter skits, he trashed the moneychangers' tables in the temple. A friend's Presbyterian mother told me that in heaven we'd listen to a beautiful choir all the time, and I couldn't believe that we would have no say in selecting the eternal soundtrack. I guess I was like a tribesman confused by the shiny watches and jewelry of the missionaries; I couldn't grasp the salvation-message because I wanted to grasp the *stuff*. Who cared to matriculate to an afterlife without one's record collection?

Though the logistics of divorce conspired to separate me at an early age from my father, brother, and grandfather, I too became a packrat of sound, "joining" my clan of man-children, and, I soon learned, a pervasive larger fraternity of collectors. For gift-exchanging holidays, we don't ask for CDs or box sets. We ask for big, ornate, customized CD cabinets. My genus of collector is very different from the hoarder of 78s who covets each rarity as an individual artifact. Nor does our ilk have much in common with the high-minded curators certain that their classical repository will sustain post-apocalyptic humanity's faith in itself. The separatist sophisticateurs who hole up with their mineral water, their flyswatters, their crossbows, and their Sun Ra discographies find my kind blasphemously indiscreet—for we are abstract, fetishizing quantity and variety. Our stockpiles are manifestations of an ownership virus, and there is something latently colonial about how we conceive our collections as a vast domain. We forge and sever bonds via the burning of exceedingly cosmopolitan mix CDs that all but exclaim, "Look how indiscriminate my discriminating palate is!"

Many of us think we're better than those paraphernaliens who collect sports cars, Beanie Babies, *Star Wars* leavings, or those little porcelain boots, but we are wrong. Our fixed attachment to our stashes is obviously a type of compensation for some pointed lack. The dominant psychobabble on Grandpa is that because he had nothing during the Great Depression, he must define and protect himself by (or, burden himself with) surplus now. No matter what kind of sensitive aesthetes we obsessives think we are because we collect music (which, we'd argue with rectitude, is culturally superior to, say, collecting Nazi jewelry), we can be just as pathetically contentious and bullying as the next buff or self-elected aficionado. Our collections can be abysses: An hour can be spent packing seventeen hours' worth of music for a two-hour drive. My teeth can fall into disrepair, but my music shelves will be severely ordered and maintained.

With loving self-mockery John Cusack played one of us music-obsessives in the film of Nick Hornby's *High Fidelity*, a performance made more interesting by its being an extension of Cusack's role in *Say Anything*. In the climactic scene of that film Cusack woos the object of his affection by standing outside her window in dramatic rain, hoisting a boom box blaring Peter Gabriel's "In Your Eyes." (The universal "awwws" this scene triggered are why *Entertainment Weekly* named the film "the number one Modern Romance of all time.") The moment is a sign that something profoundly transgressive has happened; the romantic tradition of Romeos and Cyranos who spoke in self-composed verse beneath their sweethearts' windows has been supplanted by a Lloyd Dobler merely pressing the play button on a machine to unleash a supposedly passionate commodity he selected. In James Joyce's "The Dead," which is careful to include a reference to Romeo's "balcony scene," the doomed, weather-braving Michael Furey at least used his own voice to sing someone else's song to Gretta. Suddenly with Lloyd—a creation of lifetime music-geek Cameron Crowe—we are happy to let our albums communicate for us; the lazy courtier is a DJ who earns/expresses the same value as the song's performer. (Think of the scene in *24 Hour Party People* in which the Tony Wilson character points out that the club DJ receives the applause that bands used to get. Though some DJs actually do make art, in the majority of American clubs the DJ is praised merely for selecting the work of other people. This "privilege the messenger" ethic is unique to music; imagine a projectionist getting laid for his successful looping of a film. Such is the minor-league deification we obsessives seek to obtain as a perk.)

Enter My Morning Jacket, an amazingly multivalent five-piece originating and operating from Louisville, Lexington, and Shelbyville, Kentucky. To my veteran ears, the band was *everything*: The performances crystallized on their releases spanned disparate genres and synthesized the shopworn approaches of all the music I'd overheard growing up. But MMJ was still somehow strikingly original, as if Neil Young were dragging the Beach Boys across an abstract plane to have a cookout on a shipwreck. When considering their obvious influences and their disorienting freshness, I think of that complaint on a Forest Service comment card: "The places where trails do not exist are not well marked." And their Southern goulash covered a stately-to-shambolic spectrum that could please fans of Chet Atkins's protean virtuosity as well as fans of the Silver Jews' casually articulate slopcountry. My Morning Jacket's music cultivated in me an acute esteem. I became, for them, the music-obsessive equivalent of a junkie: a completist. The fool completist must have it all, and therefore spends a great amount of time and money hunting a band's every recorded and performed morsel, eventually spiraling off into a bootleg-archiving delirium. It's not pretty. Listservs, file-sharing sites, and eBay are our crackhouses, our venues-as-middlemen: I once sold a tour-only Songs:Ohia CD to another completist for $83 (who won the on-line auction against several similarly desperate obsessives), so that I could spend the money on an illegal compilation of rare My Morning Jacket material. My conundrums flounder outside the realm of good and evil: I've lain awake nights on tragically unchanged pillowcases, fretting over not being able to find a copy of the Louisville sampler on which MMJ covers "Take My Breath Away," Berlin's love theme from *Top Gun*. I had obviously sidestepped the designated saviors of my spiritual upbringing and (to bastardize William James) used music to fill the faith-hole. When pressed to explain my fanaticism for My Morning Jacket, or to argue the band's relevance, I pause: Like many a modern Southerner, I teem with fairly illogical aversions and often indefensible convictions. Just as my neighbor can't fathom anyone challenging his WHY AREN'T YOU SAVED? bumper sticker, I think: Who are these skeptics kidding? Is it not just plainly obvious that My Morning Jacket is the greatest band in the world?

No Guralnick-style approach will do: Though I want to ascribe a myth to the band ("While kayaking in Boulder, Colorado, James encountered Buddha. . . . "), they aren't dead. Sticking to band history seems ridiculous, since their legacy is just beginning; they're currently recording their major-label début, and besides, they're younger than I am, damn them. In his contribution to the anthology

Rock Over The Edge: Transformations in Popular Music Culture, R.J. Warren Zanes (himself an estimable star, as a member of the Del Fuegos) analyzes the subtexts of fandom, examining how fans fantasize about, and over-identify with, their mutual heroes—Zanes seeks to add to that list of responses the possibility of "queer desire." Despite being at ease with recognizing Jude Law's fineness, and despite having formed a few My Morning Jacket-inspired best-friend supergroups with names like Trust Bucket, Falcon Stirrup, Birthmark Jones, and Commemorative Stoneware that only lasted one drunken night, I can safely say that no part of my loyalty to Jim James's sublime quintet involves wanting to lick him, or be him, or master him, or be mastered by him. I just enjoy hearing him make good on his musical gifts.

Any trial requiring my testimony would be wise to have me swear with my hand on a copy of *At Dawn.* Such allegiance—slightly aggravated, of course—breeds cretinism, and I have often become one of the band's chauvinists, despite the world's not needing another asshole. I scorn acquaintances who resist my missionary dotage. Believing that My Morning Jacket should always headline, I hold grudges against the acts for whom I've seen them open. When folks attempt to lump MMJ in subgenres such as alt-country or indie-pop, I am quick to assert that Jim James regards his troupe as a rock band, plain and simple. Still MMJ typically plays to "indie" crowds, made up of people who attend club performances with a churchgoer's regularity and emphasis on dress, though these shows are more democratized than church: The indie-faithful occasionally flock to concerts in order to critique, or even mock, the pulpiteers.

When they aren't trying to fake an ever-changing vernacular, the hipsters' anything-goes, endocannibalistic conversations will begin with greetings along the lines of, "Hey, has your bumper sticker freed Tibet yet?" Aware of the pressures that lead them to disdain sincere enthusiasm, I can sympathize with their retreat into irony. Their heads are busy with cultural minutiae, the result of survey-style education and commercial grooming; they are trying to keep straight Malcolm McLaren from Marshall McLuhan, and to sort the Cavity Creeps from the Flavor Crystals. The multiplicity of delights competing for their attention can impoverish their sense of the especial. But as Mark Dery wrote, "Irony is a leaky prophylactic against consumerism, conformity, and other social diseases spread by advertising." Though My Morning Jacket can indulge in some healthy stage badinage, and though I've seen Jim James use bizarre accessories to distance himself from the audience (hiding his face behind a stuffed buffalo head, draping himself in a tie-dyed muumuu), the band champions earnestness, a trait that distinguishes them from Louisville's killjoy, "post-rock" scene. The band's emotivity can trigger a hipster's nag reflex, and when less-dedicated fans begin their jabs, we overzealous MMJ disciples wince with the agony that drove Kierkegaard to call the burden of enduring glib criticism "the long martyrdom of being trampled to death by geese." The band even volleys with audience members moved to indulge in Ironist's Tourette's, the strange, indie variation on heckling: an urge to shout random phrases during hushes. (Jim James once announced, "This next one's called 'Jesus and God,'" off our album *Desert Storm*," after a sozzled ticketholder yelled, between numbers, "Jesus and God!" and "Desert Storm!") Americans' freedom to carouse notwithstanding, the more garrulous the crowd gets, the more petulant we Nietzschean superfans get. When someone near me at a show called the band My Boring Racket, I was ready to throw down, but for the good sense of an accompanying female who pointed out the insufferable silliness of my would-be centurionship.

That said, My Morning Jacket concerts leave a majority of their attendees agog. The band grew out of Jim James's solo performances at sundry open-mics, and he has honed a still-malleable stage mystique. Stout and wide-eyed, he veers from coming across as a spacey barefoot farm-bred ragamuffin to a fully cognizant, self-consciously sexy bandleader extraordinaire to an intimidating, head-banging, Flying-V-pummeling Black Sabbath and Slayer devotee to an intimate, approachable, crooning, hippie reification of John the Baptist. Bassist Two-Tone Tommy, resembling a lankier and more worried Nirvana-era Dave Grohl, seems to take his flail-or-chill cues from James. Guitarist (and cousin to James) Johnny Quaid, prone to triumphantly playing his Gibson high above his head during intense passages, is a curious mix of Adonis and Gremlin, embodying the "ruggedly handsome" hero/villain of a thousand unfilmed screenplays. These three core members have been

together five years. Keyboardist Danny Cash, distant kin to The
Man In Black and a talented graphic designer whose look suggests a
mellow greaser, joined before the recording of *At Dawn*. The band's
third and seemingly permanent drummer, Patrick Hallahan, is
James's childhood best bud—he's a giant guy with a wavy mop that
suggests a grunge hybrid of a Louis XIV wig and the Cowardly
Lion's mane. In this epoch of casting-call "bands" with prefabri-
cated images, you'd be hard-pressed to summon a rollicking five-
some more hirsute and oleaginous than these mugs.

This assemblage of ponytails, wires, t-shirts, boots, and flip-flops
has ruined at least one version of my life. See, I was in love with that
aforementioned woman, the one who sparingly pointed out the
lameness of my fascist fandom, and we'd bonded over the course of
a half dozen My Morning Jacket concerts. She was the givingest and
most creative woman I'd ever known, and MMJ's handling of
romantic material can do wonders for a blossoming couplehood;
James allowed us to imagine that our union was some uncanny heterosexual masterpiece, the way he portrays love as the validating and
visceral miracle-burden that it can be when it, as the dialect-poet
David Lee wrote, "sparkles like a diamond in a goat's ast."
      MMJ songs were in the background during our abortive efforts
to get wine stains off the ceiling with OxiClean, and when she
passed out on the trampoline and I woke her by pelting her with
moldy scones, and when she expressed her reticence to skinnydip
while silkworms dangled from the tree behind her like tiny, larval
paratroopers. She even painted a sign for my album-crowded house
reading, HOME IS WHERE THE STUFF IS.
      Ah, those were the days; we seemed bound for glory: marriage,
death, some freckly kids left to handle our CD estate. But when we
started to suck, as complicated people often will, our reliance on
MMJ became a problem. James's nonchalantly gorgeous songs, once
so reinforcing, now conjured an affectionate atmosphere that we
failed to emulate. The songs were mafia thugs, putting pressure on
us to live up to their drama. Even "Lowdown" became a sore spot:
on the surface a bouncy, flippant ditty brimming with impossible
promises, but actually about wounded people vowing not to put
each other through any more crap. Its refrains of "you never gotta

fight with me" and "you only gotta dance with me" seemed like buoys we'd already drifted beyond. We'd go to parties and perform the combative vaudeville of an unspooling relationship. "Hi, yes, we're here together, but don't be bourgeois and presume we're in love." "Yes, in fact, we steadfastly refuse to love each other." And people would laugh at the meta-couple's antics, and wonder what was the secret of our salubrious, self-correcting rapport.

So we drove two hours south to see My Morning Jacket one last time. They were awesome. Awesome. But we didn't even stand together. And after the show, we reached out, separately, to the band, freighting strangers with our speeches about what they meant to us. When she and I found ourselves, rather incidentally, in proximity to each other again, she said, giddily, "He's my new boyfriend!" When I traced the beeline from her big brown eyes to discern the identity of the beau nouveau, I realized, to my horror, that she was looking at *all of them.*

Not necessarily a damning infraction, but we were eager to implode. Suffice to say, later that night this wonderful woman found reason to strand me in Orlando. She drove off just after whipping out her digital camera and taking a picture of me in the street, shooting her a gallant bird, capturing perfectly the climax of a pattern of abuse and dismissal that manifested only in gestures. She spent the night at a notorious gay bar/hotel with comforters assuring her that I was a good man, and I spent the night at a Greyhound station with a drunk explaining to me that manhole covers were "nature's pancakes." Before she moved away, we cleaned her apartment without speaking, all hard feelings. I don't recommend playing My Morning Jacket albums, which consist of fifty percent heartbreakers, in an empty house where you used to have fun and comfort. She's a union organizer in the Motor City now, getting buckets of dirty water thrown on her by frustrated factory workers and taking orders from a puckish Albanian. If some horrible Detroitian circumstance befell her, surely that would be My Morning Jacket's fault, and not mine, right?

My Morning Jacket is an ideal divergenic fix. Music's transportative power must explain why those men to whom I am bloodbound love it so; music provides escape, and hoarding it equips their rooms—

and lives—with multiple escape routes. The work of Jim James and his boys is admittedly better suited to accompany your slightly seedy, loafering lost twenties than it is your thirties' reductive Sisyphean quests for money, or orgasm, or that gross attention called respect.

With My Morning Jacket on my headphones, a bike constitutional can be epic (though technically against the law). Their music delivers me past the house where the black woman who told me she used to call whites "ofays" sits in her bra and jean shorts on the porch and it takes me past the office of the ophthalmologist who calls blacks "equatorials." It helps me pedal around the mother whose son carries her oxygen tank, the hose between them a kind of umbilical leash.

On a fitness kick, I listened to MMJ while I jogged around the upper level of a gym where a depressing basketball camp was being conducted, the unremarkable gloryhounds colliding with their own teammates in oversized logo-billboard outfits and shoes that resembled tanks. MMJ soothed me and some friends on a road trip when sleep deprivation and caffeine mania had us groupthinking that the deer on the shoulder were teasing us with suicidal lunges. *At Dawn* shepherded me through that dolorous day that my cactus died and it didn't symbolize anything.

Once, tipsy at a beach hotel, I dove into the pool with my headphones still on. And I hope to never grow so foggy that I forget the spring afternoon I spent playing MMJ and watching a Carolina wren build a nest in a guitar amp I'd used to prop open a kitchen window. Am I blathering yet? Forgive me, I've been recruited by a music that accentuates the purgative, that makes me sick for how radio was ruined, that situates itself at all the best crossroads—it's gothic but transparent, smart and sentimental, slippery but firm, demotic and difficult, weapon and tourniquet. . . .

Reverb is such an integral component of My Morning Jacket's galvanism that it could be regarded as the band's sixth member. The same way that black-and-white footage is used to communicate filmic pasts, reverb provides MMJ with an instantly fermented, nostalgic sound, that of an oldies station struck by magic lightning, hearkening to the cavernous levels used to inflate the minimal arrangements of so many legendary Sun sessions and so many doo-wop and r&b classics. (For a band often labeled as modern hillbilly psychedelia, MMJ's soulfulness runs deep. Anyone doubting Jim James's worship of various incarnations of Marvin Gaye need only consult "War Begun," "The Bear," or "Come Closer." See also "They Ran," which functions as a nitrous-oxidized homage to Berry Gordy, and the band's cover of nubian diva Erykah Badu's "Tyrone," which holds its own against Wilco's magnificent, Mayfield-lite "Jesus, Etc." as an artful slab of Caucasian soul.) The reverbiana of Joy Division and Galaxie 500—two rock touchstones for placing MMJ—was ascribed to those bands by their madmen producers Martin Hannett and Kramer, respectively, whereas My Morning Jacket inflicted reverb on themselves—possibly, initially, like so many do-it-yourselfers trying to maximize the scope of their four-track cranny, to make up for their low-budget recording apparatus (on Quaid's grandparents' farm). And then, possibly, because it suited them so well, like it did Roy Orbison, enshrining his bellows with a nebulous quality, an interiority—the resonance of the psyche's amphitheater.

Whether James is singing in his punk wail, soft "black," deep country, nimble swain, or spastic castrato mode, reverb is his substrate. *At Dawn*'s mixer is listed in the liner notes as Dave "Would you like a little music to go with your reverb?" Trumfio, no doubt based on a comment he made regarding how this band lets reverb affect their music the way certain narcotics transmogrify thought, or the sex drive. I have watched Jim James rattle soundmen during concert setups. "More reverb," he'll ask. "But that's already way too much." "Uhnh-uhnh. More." Minor adjustment. "More." Adjustment. "More," James will say until the monitors are threatening to succumb to a feedback skree. MMJ's tunes involve but also go beyond the exaggerated industrial-wasteland solitude of Joy Division and the plastic vastness of Galaxie 500; James can sound aquatic, or like he's broadcasting from some interplanetary outpost, a ranger station that the budgetary committee ceased to fund but forgot to shut down. (This cosmic tincture made MMJ's desolate cover of Elton John's "Rocket Man" a no-brainer.)

"Phone Went West," arguably the band's most instantly hummable, and thus crowd-pleasing, song is lacquered just to the point of amniotic stillness that the poet Joe Wenderoth conveyed when he called an empty fast-food restaurant "the false eternity of the womb." While the band delivers an otherworldly reggae-prom arrangement whose drums explode around the five-and-half-minute mark, James yowls and re-yowls a passive prophecy, "There will be a knock on your back door!" The listener infers that the knock won't be acknowledged. The song's refrain, "Tell me there's nobody else in the world," works both as a slogan for a poisonously exclusive relationship, and as a plea for confirmation of the speaker's grandiose loneliness, like Beckett's Krapp, who guesses from his living room filled with sound equipment that the "earth might be uninhabited." It's as if a biblical rapture transpired, and the speaker is relieved to be left behind.

As an ardent dabbler in mix-CD alchemy who strives to produce a rewarding mood arc with each compilation, I must say that the Bible's orthodox DJs did a mean job of sequencing that thing, especially with that four-book stretch during which the praise songs of Psalms lead into the advice columns of Proverbs following the rational doom-treatise of Ecclesiastes, ending with the erotica of Song of Solomon. My Morning Jacket wanders gracefully through the turf of Psalms, Proverbs, and Solomon, offering nuggets of appreciation for the gift of life, of can-do positivity, and of fleshly magnetism. James frequently cites his intuition that he is being guided by things beyond his understanding, by voices and spirits. Demos from *At Dawn* include "Lead Me Father," which could be sung at a Wesleyan picnic. The band is always thanking a "God," and like the Power Team, those weightlifting Christian motivational speakers, the band takes the stage with an athletic confidence, huddles, sometimes high-fives, and openly discusses what they see as their music's redemptive mission. I've never seen them drink. When James sings about stealing or cocaine, or kicking someone's head in, he does it with an innocence that takes me back to how pure even a toxic scrapyard seems after snowfall. MMJ's mysticism doesn't belie their capitalism, however; just like late-night televangelists, the band are mantrapreneurs, business-minded spiritualists who want their product to reach everyone. ("Old September Blues" is awkwardly beautiful; it's a cost-benefit-analysis as ballad, with James expressing his

gratitude for someone who was "always . . . an asset" and "never . . .
a drawback.") MMJ even participated in the commodification of the
holy days by making an "Xmas" record.

For all that gusto, their discography bogs down considerably, as
the Bible does, in the despairing acceptance of Ecclesiastes' existential morass. How can I not think of MMJ's reverb when I read, "Better is a handful of quietness than two hands full of toil and a striving
after wind"? The author, pen-named Qoheleth, or the Teacher, is
bummed, big-time, and thankfully my *New Oxford Annotated Bible*
does me the favor that my bubbly, biased *New Student Bible*
wouldn't; it admits that the book's God's-in-control, "it's all
good" moments were tacked on by a cautious editor. James's line,
"There will be bigotry and there will be open minds," from "I
Will Be There When You Die," parallels the passages in Ecclesiastes that inspired the Byrds' "Turn! Turn! Turn!" and T.S. Eliot's
"The Love Song of J. Alfred Prufrock."

The book's refutation of novelty complements MMJ's retrofitted
tones. "Take me out of this dead-end nightmare," the speaker of
MMJ's "Nashville To Kentucky" cries, as worn down as Qoheleth,
who doesn't sound very different from contemporary absurdists
frustrated with their estrangement from purpose and authority. All
is vain toil under the sun to Qoheleth, and we moderns have the
rank benefit of knowing that even the sun's only got about five billion years left.

Though on some tracks James vaunts a chipper faith in hard
work, he addresses the anhedonia brought on by torpor and the idea
that "trying gets nothing done," on "Death Is The Easy Way," voic-
ing concern for a person whom nothing "gets . . . high." Anyone
who flinches when the weather forecaster says "tomorrow will be
almost exactly like today" could commiserate with MMJ or
Qoheleth. When James sings of not letting your "silly dreams/Fall
in between/The crack of the bed and the wall," you know that to
have focused on that dead space, the speaker is hurting, or lying
awake nights. Qoheleth holds forth on the transience of youth, and
James sings of a lost urgency, "I needed it most/When I was eigh-
teen/But now that I'm older/I don't need many things." The song
goes on to bemoan a relationship that even the "heavens" can't help.
Things just are how they are, Qoheleth says, and they repeat, and

we don't know why, and he adds, "Who can straighten what God
has made crooked?" James prefers to let his own creations' crooked-
ness speak for itself, reluctant to explain where his songs come from,
or how one is supposed to regard the twenty-four-minute "Cobra,"
which shifts from a bizarre Prince-meets-the-Oak-Ridge-Boys
groove into the flophouse Hendrix, into ambient drone, into banjo
drone, finishing with a slurred "shout-out." I think James would like
the short section called "Hurrah!" from "The Dog Among The
Rills" by Winfield Townley Scott:

> *Madam, your little boy has*
> Bat ears;
> And, Madam, some of my poems are
> Cock-eyed;
> But we had 'em—
> *Didn't we!*

The band's two bleakest songs are the ones chosen to provide the
last words on each MMJ full-length, before chill-out instrumental
codas. "I Think I'm Going To Hell" closed *The Tennessee Fire*, and
it's, uh, self-explanatory. *At Dawn* wraps up with "Strangulation,"
perhaps an extension of "The Dark," on which James sang of "God's
fingers choking me." "Strangulation," though, looks outward, as
much of *At Dawn* does, at people who fell optionless and plundered.
The characters' nihilist wish is to not "feel a thing," and the song's
final fourth is a two-minute caterwaul, with James screaming as if
being forcibly escorted toward the vestibule beneath this world's
blinking exit sign. Chapter 9, Verse 4: "But he who is joined with all
the living has hope, for a living dog is better than a dead lion."

A church-faith, once indoctrinated, can be difficult to de-bug.
Even Ecclesiastes' doubting author says my writing and book-love
won't save me, that knowledge and sadness increase correlatively.
Plus: "Of making many books there is no end, and much study is a
weariness of the flesh." As for the obsessive music collecting, I can
sometimes hear, mentally, slightly reverbed, a visiting preacher from
one of the mountaintop camp meetings I attended as a lad telling
me that my CD racks are altars I've built to false gods. Pity me for
clinging to a child's literalism, but what would heaven even *be*?

Everybody sporting J. Crew, gathering berries and corn? I can't buy the capitalist streets-of-gold thing, and that version of eternal paradise in which we are supposed to become spirit-blobs may free us of our troubling bodies and thoughts, but it underscores the sci-fi nonsensicality of "perfection" and "total fulfillment." Hell is simply more understandable, more navigable, a concept. Even if you don't go for envisioning it as the Dantean torture-scape, or a Bruckheimer fireball, you could comprehend the tastefully simple all-darkness format. Then again, our nightmares seem more linear than our sweeter dreams. I pick on the religion I inherited, and quasi-shirked, but my faith in bands isn't any more rational. The rockist and the fundamentalist carry hot, hero-clogged heads. We don't outgrow our extremism because we're so invested in it, and, needing our lives to make sense to us, we construct self-fulfilling prophecies.

Jim James sings, "[I] try to walk this earth an honest man, but evil waves at me its ugly hand." He understands not only Ecclesiastes' moral that all is vanity, but also that, conversely, vanity is, sometimes, all. On the ponderous "Bermuda Highway," he makes the very anti-Christian confession, "I wonder why that meek guy got all the fame/Maybe I'm to blame/For his short, bitter, f—ed-up life." And no matter how a life is spent, dying is losing to Jim James, as was evident from the first MMJ show I saw without the woman I'd squandered. The concert was August 16, in Washington D.C., and James opened with a soul-charring solo cover of "Suspicious Minds," the King's chronicle of a smothering, paranoid relationship. James introduced the song with a warm smile, saying, "Twenty-five years ago tonight, Elvis Presley lost his way." Then came the reverb, and he began to sing: "We're caught in a trap. . . . "

At my day job, I have regular encounters with a kid whose sadistic, Cromwellian, fundamentalist parents lock him in his room at night to keep him from becoming "worldly." He is one of the most tormented and traumatized people I've ever met. I try to help him view his parents' treatment of him as abuse, and to set up an intervention, but he declines, having adjusted to the hopelessness of his plight. He is eighteen, but they've got him terrified of even the most mundane daily maneuvers. One day I invited him to grab some take-out with me, and My Morning Jacket's *At Dawn* was cued up on my car stereo, sounding majestic despite having to poot out of my ruined speakers. Neither of us made conversation; I wanted to hear some MMJ, and I thought he was nervous about not having permission from his censors to join me for a drive. We ate in the car with the music on, sucked Cokes as we watched lovers in the park across the street compose their own concordances. On our way back, he pointed to my CD player and said, "I'm not allowed to listen to music." I thought, *Who are his parents, the Taliban?* He continued, "But if I could listen to music, I would want to listen to this."

Keepin' It Unreal

$elling the Myth of Bla¢k Male Violen¢e, Long Past Its Expiration Date

> *Yeah, they want reality, but you will hear none/*
> *They'd rather exaggerate a little fiction.*
>
> —N.W.A, "EXPRESS YOURSELF"

The promotion of 50 Cent from bootleg king to god of the streets was PR genius. His handlers have played the angle magnificently. The attempts on his life come up repeatedly in interviews, and 50 is happy to provide embellishment. Even critics have bought into the mystique—review after review of 50's *Get Rich or Die Tryin'* cites his battle scars as evidence of his true-to-life depiction of the streets. On the cover of *Rolling Stone*, he posed with his back to the camera, exposing one of his wounds. Who knew nine bullet holes could be such a boon?

Now the banners are unfurling: "2003: the year hip-hop returned to the streets." You can thank 50 for that. *Get Rich* has been hyped as the most realistic representation of the ghetto since the heyday of Biggie. To its credit, the album turns down the bling factor considerably. 50 could care less about what whip you're pushing or the cut of your Armani. All that concerns him is your (preferably violent) downfall. Add in 50's work history in the narcotics trade and his random swipes at supposed wanksta Ja Rule and you have the makings of the most legitimate gangsta rapper since Jay-Z.

But not much more. At its core the hubbub around *Get Rich* and the return of gangsta rap is crack-era nostalgia taken to the extreme. Imagine—articulate young black men pining for the heyday of black-on-black crime. Like all nostalgia, neo-gangsta is stuck in history rather than rooted in current reality. The sobering fact is that the streets as 50 presents them, brimming with shoot-outs and crack fiends, do not exist. Of course, drugs are still a plague on America's house, and America's gun violence is a black mark on the developed world. But millennial black America is hardly the Wild West scene it was during gangsta rap's prime. Gangsta could once fairly claim to reflect a brutal present. Now it mythicizes a past that would fade away much faster without it.

In the late '80s, young black men—gangsta rap's creators, and its primary constituency—became their own worst enemies. Drug dealing was becoming a legitimate, if deadly, life option, and with it came an arms race that turned Anyghetto, U.S.A., into Saigon. The Harlem Renaissance drew its power from the optimism of the New Negro, the Black Arts movement pulled from Black Power, gangsta rap tapped the crack age. If Motown and Stax were the joyful noise of us unshackling ourselves into the dream ("Are you ready for a brand-new beat?"), gangsta rap was the sound of us crashing back into the desert of the real ("Life ain't nothin' but bitches and money").

The crash is complete, and in any black community you can find the rubble—uneducated, unemployable young black men. Their narrative no longer rings with the romance of a Nino Brown. Crack is played, and so, apparently, is fratricide—murder rates in the black community have been dropping since the mid '90s. The way of the gun still takes its toll, but Saigon has been pacified. Mundane afflictions like unpaid child support and industrial flight have once again come to the fore.

The streets that gangsta rappers claim as their source are no longer as angry as they are sad. For that reason alone, gangsta rap should be dead by now. But still it lingers, fueled by America's myth of the menacing black man. Gangsta rap today is about as reflective of reality as, well, a reality show. And yet still it lumbers across the landscape of pop, shouting "I'm Real."

*   *   *

Step away with your fistfight ways/
Muthafucka this ain't back in the days.
—THE NOTORIOUS B.I.G., "THINGS DONE CHANGED"

Some 17 years ago, I was ambling past a local 7-Eleven on my way home from school. There in front of the store where I frequently leafed through copies of *X-Men*, I met gangsta rap in its most tangible form. It was 1986—the year Schoolly D birthed the genre with his single "PSK (What Does It Mean?)"—and the old order of Afro-America was coming apart. Black fathers were going M.I.A., guns were flooding the streets, and crackheads were multiplying. I was young and too obsessed with *Transformers* and *Galaxy Rangers* to notice the walls caving in around me.

And then at that 7-Eleven I watched a kid unveil the biggest, blackest handgun I'd ever seen. He and his friends had been arguing with another clique when the one kid dropped the trump card. It was like something out of the dollar flicks, scored by my heart pounding like a timpani. No cars pulled into the parking lot. No one ducked or screamed. I did not move. With his point made, the kid returned his tool to his jacket and walked away laughing with his friends, taking my innocence with him.

Whatever I had left was beaten out of me during my first year of middle school. I got jumped so often that I spent that year searching for alternate paths home, some of them integrating bus routes even though I lived around the corner. A new road map might save me from a critical beatdown. But as the gangsta rap era geared up, the bumrush became the least of my worries.

These were the days when fashion became a health risk. Mothers started shunning Jordans, Lottos, and Diadoras, fearing their sons would come home in their socks, or not at all. Schools ran damage control, implementing uniforms and banning book bags for fear of what kids might be packing. And still the crazy reports kept filtering through—young boys attacking their mothers or smoking each other over an accidental footprint on someone's suede Pumas.

Then the entire dialogue changed. Nationalists declared black males an officially endangered species and screamed genocide orchestrated by the invisible white hand. I was 12 and understandably short on grand theories, save one—the world had gone crazy. One day I was living for *Jayce and the Wheeled Warriors*, the next my older brother was flashing me a hot .38.

The nationalists were right about one thing. It was a white hand fueling black America's dementia—the white hand of crack cocaine. "When crack arrived in the city it increased the level of gun violence. You had lots of young people with the money to buy guns and an arms race came with that," says Peter Reuter, professor of criminology at the University of Maryland and co-author of *Drug War Heresies*. "It was no longer shootings over territory, but over transactions. The amount of money you could steal from someone was a lot larger now, and the drugs themselves made people more violent."

Crack also had the good luck to arrive in cities just as the rust belts were completely eroding employment. Whereas once a man could support his family with a job at the plant, manufacturing was being phased out by automation and the factories' retreat from the cities. Add Reagan's and then Bush's neo-conservative attack on social programs, and you have the ingredients of an epidemic.

"This is the Reagan/Bush era, when you have massive social disinvestments in schools, and in urban areas altogether," says Robin Kelley, professor of history and Africana studies at NYU. "Reagan cut back significant amounts of social funding in urban areas and expanded the police force. Playgrounds, community centers were no longer getting funded and they were disappearing."

While experts opined on the damage wrought on urban communities, gangsta rap laid out the new reality for the young. "PSK" was the foreshadowing. But when KRS-One growled his murderous vocals over a pulsing bassline ("Knew a drug dealer by the name of Peter/Had to buck him down with my 9 millimeter") and then N.W.A's "Dopeman" hit with its high whistle and crashing drums, a new age in black urban America was ushered in.

Initially, gangsta rap's interpretation of the times was complex. Some acts reveled in the image of boys gone wild, while others deplored the effects of crack on their communities. Most early gangsta rappers, and some of the best (Scarface comes to mind) lived somewhere in between. What was made clear by all gangsta rappers, however, was that the life of crime was becoming a far more appealing career track than flipping burgers.

Harry Holzer, professor of public policy at Georgetown, was involved in a 10-year survey of attitudes among black males toward employment. In 1979, as the manufacturing decline set in, the researchers asked black men whether they had a better chance making a living illegally or legally. Sixty percent preferred to stay straight. When Holzer's team asked the same question again in 1989, the number fell to 40 percent. However hyperbolically, N.W.A's classic *Straight Outta Compton*, released the year before, reflected this trend.

"Think of a world where people make a choice between work in the legal sector and work in the illegal sector, and make it on monetary concerns and whatever risk they might encounter," says Holzer. "What happened was that the labor market for less educated African American men really disintegrated. The legal sector became less and less attractive, and then with the crack boom, the illegal sector became more attractive. Then there was the glamour. Early on you saw this wholesale shift."

The brilliance of gangsta rap was in how it embodied that shift. *Straight Outta Compton*'s frantic ambience and the sparseness of *Criminal Minded* translated the chaotic and impoverished conditions of black Americans into sound. And their lyrics outlined the changes that were enveloping the community.

The form was most moving when it eschewed shock tactics that haunted it from day one, in favor of bleak, candid shots. Ice Cube's "A Bird in the Hand" was a detailed account of why, for black men, the illegal sector so often trumped the legal one. His "Alive on Arrival," about bleeding to death in the emergency room, presaged the health-care debates of the '90s, while "My Summer Vacation" humorously examined the exportation of gang culture nationwide. Ditto for Biggie. At its best, his seething debut *Ready to Die* bleeds pathos and tragedy. "Things Done Changed" defined the schism between civil-rights-movement African Americans and their cracked-out progeny. Equally astute was Nas's *Illmatic*, which shunned all urges toward didacticism or shock, instead opting for a wide-angle view of the Queensbridge projects. "NY State of Mind," "Memory Lane," and "One Love" constitute a stark and striking black-and-white photo album of Nas's black America.

"Gangsta rap was a critique of ghetto life. So much of it was about turning the cameras on crime and violence and the police," says Kelley. "It wasn't meant to be any kind of uplift narrative. It was a form of reportage—turning the mirror back on the black community."

But as the '90s wore on, and MTV noticed the big dollars generated by gangsta rappers and their associates, the mirror began to crack. Ice Cube faded into Mack 10, Biggie was replaced by the LOX, and Nas gave way to Nastradamus. As the music became more popular, it became more of a cartoon—eventually, the only cartoon in town. Despite an occasional hit by the Roots or Talib Kweli, the popular face of rap has been defined by acts in the mold of Biggie or Tupac, but with less talent and almost no perspective.

Perhaps worse, the music has devolved into a misleading caricature of the world it claims as inspiration—the streets. Crack isn't nearly the force that it was in the late '80s and early '90s. "Very few people have started using crack in the last 15 years," says Reuter. "Now you have older, sadder crack buyers, less violent, unable to hold a job, and involved with a lot of property crime."

The consequences of crack's rampage still haunt the communities it once infested. But the epidemic is over. "Basically you can think of this like a regular epidemic," says Reuter. "At first people want to try it. Some go and use it regularly, and become negative role models. After two or three years it was clear that crack was a very nasty drug, and all you are left with are the people who first started using it."

The decline of crack has brought an attendant decline in the murder rate among the population at large, and African Americans in particular. In 1991, 50.4 African Americans per 100,000 were killed. By 2000, that number had halved itself. Actual murders committed by young black males dropped from 244.1 per 100,000 youths in 1993 to 67.3 in 1999.

*   *   *

The sunset looks beautiful over the projects/What a shame, it ain't
the same where we stand at/If you look close you can see the bricks
chipped off/Sometimes niggas miss when they lick off.
—MOBB DEEP, "STREETS RAISED ME"

None of this means urban black America is experiencing a renaissance. During the '90s the fortunes of almost every segment of society were buoyed by the surging economy. Welfare reform, a
frequent and sometimes deserving target of criticism from the left,
sent poor women back into the job market in droves. At the same
time, Clinton-era programs, such as the expansion of the earned
income tax credit, lightened the load of the country's working poor.
Only one group seemed to miss the gravy train—young black men,
gangsta rap's original constituency.

Over the past two decades, black America made impressive gains
in the job and education sector—or anyway, half of black America
did. In a study of young, "less educated" African Americans with
only a high school diploma, Holzer and his partner Paul Offner discovered that the employment rate for women rose from 37 percent
in 1989 to 52 percent in 2000. The rate actually fell for men, from
62 percent to 52 percent. According to Holzer, in the 16–24 age
range there is actually a higher percentage of black women
employed than black men—a stunning statistic, given that many
black women in this demographic are also unwed mothers.

Why hasn't gangsta rap morphed to address the new reality of
African American men? In short, because the narrative of today's
black man makes a lousy cowboy flick. A central element of gangsta
rap was the lionizing of drug dealers as cool, smooth black males
fighting their way out of the ghetto. Although the portrayal was
highly exaggerated, it definitely wasn't a complete fantasy—the
drug trade did produce a few legitimate entrepreneurs. But no
amount of hyperbole could salvage the current narrative of the black
male—that of the habitual loser.

Gangsta rappers and their advocates argue that they are simply
doing what other artists do in emphasizing certain elements of their
world. "It's drama, and in drama you take the mundane elements of
life and you infuse them at times with hyperbolic meaning," says
Todd Boyd, professor of critical studies at the University of South-

ern California. "When people look at *Scarface* they don't criticize the film because it overly dramatizes Tony Montana's cocaine use. In reality, if anyone snorted that much cocaine, they would be dead in five minutes, but nobody applies that same standard to hip-hop. That doesn't make it any less authentic. It's not reality, it's a representation of reality from one individual's perspective."

Increasingly, that perspective is skewed. It sounds more like mythology cobbled together from a few shreds of personal experience and a lot of Donald Goines, Biggie Smalls, and *GoodFellas.* For sure, the violence that rappers love to harp on still happens—the murder rate among black men remains several times higher than that of white men. But MCs conveniently ignore less glamorous forms of violence that exert as much, if not greater, influence on their lives.

A true narrative of "the streets" and the black men who inhabit them would depict a deadbeat ex-con, fleeing mounting child support, unable to find work, and disconnected from the lives of his kids. It would chronicle his gradual slide off the American radar even as his mother, daughter, and girlfriend (not wife) make inroads. It's a story that doesn't lend itself to romance. More importantly, it doesn't fit the image of black men in the American imagination.

White America has always had a perverse fascination with the idea of black males as violent and sexually insatiable animals. A prime source of racism's emotional energy was an obsession with protecting white women from black brutes. Since the days of *Birth of a Nation* up through *Native Son* and now with gangsta rap, whites have always been loyal patrons of such imagery, drawn to the visceral fear factor and antisocial fantasies generated by black men. Less appreciated is the extent to which African Americans have bought into this idea. At least since the era of blaxploitation, the African American male has taken pride in his depiction as the quintessential man in the black hat. It is a desperate gambit by a group deprived of real power—even on our worst days, we can still scare the shit out of white suburbanites.

"These are the corporate-made images," says Kelley. "It's not that the image is new, it's an image that always sold, this idea of a dominant black man—they are violent, they are out of control. But we've established that a lot of these narratives are just made up from Italian gangster movies."

The narrative of the post-crack era black male—poor, unemployable, and long resigned—is a direct challenge to that mythology. The inglorious plight of the black male is a disturbing reality that might make for compelling art. But for the record industry, that's a nonstarter.

Too bad. Because those few exceptions to this rule offer a glimmer of what post-gangsta hip-hop could look like. OutKast began as gangsta rap but evolved with the times and came up gold with—among other gems—"Ms. Jackson," which brilliantly evokes the complexities of black America's skyrocketing rate of out-of-wedlock births. Or think of Andre 3000's verse in the Grammy-winning "Whole World." Instead of clichéd crack dealers, Dre shouts out laid-off airport workers.

OutKast is a platinum act several times over, but rappers pledging loyalty to "the streets" have been uninclined to follow suit and observe the ghetto through an honest lens. What they do instead is live out an overblown stereotype. That such an image has little resemblance to reality is irrelevant. The image of black men that sells to the rest of America wasn't mapped out by Biggie Smalls, but Bigger Thomas.

MICHAEL CORCORAN

The Soul of
Blind Willie Johnson

When Jack White of the red-hot White Stripes announced, "It's good to be in Texas, the home of Blind Willie Johnson," at Austin venue Stubb's in June 2003, most in the sold out crowd likely had never heard of the long dead gospel blues singer/guitarist from Marlin, who pioneered a ferocity that still lives in modern rock. We have become used to being saluted as the home of T-Bone Walker, Stevie Ray Vaughan and others. But who is this Blind Willie Johnson?

The first songs he recorded, on a single day in 1927, are more familiar. "Nobody's Fault But Mine" was covered by Led Zeppelin, Eric Clapton did "Motherless Children," Bob Dylan turned Johnson's "Jesus Make Up My Dying Bed" into "In My Time of Dying" on his 1962 debut LP and "If I Had My Way I'd Tear the Building Down" has been appropriated by everyone from the Grateful Dead to the Staple Singers.

Johnson's haunting masterpiece "Dark Was the Night (Cold Was the Ground)" was chosen for an album placed aboard the Voyager 1 in 1977 on its journey to the ends of the universe. Foreseeing an extraterrestrial intercept, astronomer Carl Sagan and his staff put together "Sounds of Earth"—including ancient chants, the falling rain, a beating heart, Beethoven, Bach and Blind Willie.

Should aliens happen upon the spacecraft and, with the record player provided, listen to that eerie, moaning, steel-sliding memorial to the Crucifixion, they will know almost as much about the mysterious Blind Willie Johnson as we do.

Beyond five recording dates from 1927–1930 that yielded 30 tracks, the singer remains a biographical question mark. Only one picture of him, seated at a piano holding a guitar with a tin cup on its neck, has ever been found. A search on the Internet or a browse of libraries and bookstores reveals the slightest information on this musical pioneer, and almost all of it is wrong.

Months on the trail of Johnson turns up a living daughter and a death certificate—and little else. Finding witnesses who knew Johnson is about as easy as interviewing folks who lived through World War I. Many are dead or too old to remember.

Or, like Sam Faye Kelly, the only child of Blind Willie and his backup singer Willie B. Harris, they're too young to realize what was going on six, seven decades ago. "I remember him singing here in the kitchen and reciting from the Bible," said Kelly, 72. "But I was just a little girl when he went away."

And while the death certificate corrects some previously accepted misinformation (he was born in 1897 near Brenham, not 1902 in Marlin, and died in 1945, not 1949, in Beaumont), the document doesn't tell you how he lived from 1930, when his recording career ended, until his death. It doesn't tell you how many times he was married and how many kids he fathered. It doesn't verify the widespread legend that Willie was blinded when a stepmother threw lye in his face at age 7 to avenge a beating from his father. The certificate reports the cause of death as malarial fever, with syphilis as a contributing factor. But when it also lists blindness as a contributor, the coroner's thoroughness becomes suspect.

Unquestioned is the opinion that Johnson is one of the most influential guitarists in music history. "Anybody who's ever played the bottleneck guitar with some degree of accomplishment is quoting Blind Willie to this day," said Austin slide guitarist Steve James. An instinctive virtuoso, Johnson made his guitar moan, slur and sing, often finishing lyrics for him, and throughout the years, Clapton, Jimmy Page, Ry Cooder and many more have expressed a debt to the sightless visionary.

And yet, the 1993 double-disc "Complete Blind Willie Johnson" has sold only about 15,000 copies on Sony/Legacy. No doubt, more than half of those sales were to guitarists. 1930s Mississippi Delta blues man Robert Johnson grew into a full-blown rock icon in part because of the mysteries of his life and death, but Willie Johnson has not benefited from his enigmatic existence. Even though his guitar-playing inspired a host of Delta blues men, from Johnson and Son House to Muddy Waters, Blind Willie refused to sing the blues, that style of pre-war music preferred by collectors and historians. He sang only religious songs, which explains a big part of his relative obscurity. His gruff evangelical bellow and otherworldly guitar were designed to draw in milling mulling masses on street corners, not to charm casual roots rock fans decades later.

When word got out late last year through the community of music historians and record collectors that Blind Willie had a daughter, who was still living in Marlin, 28 miles southeast of Waco, there was a collective gasp of hope that new information would surface. Maybe there was a box with pictures, letters or gospel programs that would fill in the huge gaps. Maybe Willie B. Harris had told her daughter details about her father, like how he lost his sight and where he learned his songs.

The discovery of an heir also stirred the interest of musical estate managers, such as Steve LaVere of Mississippi's Delta Haze company, who visited Kelly in November. In his role managing the estate of Robert Johnson, LaVere has aggressively collected back royalties from Columbia Records and such performers as the Rolling Stones and Led Zeppelin.

"It's all about getting the pennies to roll in your direction—we're talking about eight cents a record (in songwriter royalties)," LaVere said. "Eventually, the pennies turn into dollars." LaVere estimates that in the 13 years since the release of the Robert Johnson boxed set on Columbia, Johnson's catalogue has earned well over $10 million, with LaVere taking a 50 percent commission.

But when LaVere left Marlin to return to his offices in Greenwood, Miss., he didn't have a signed contract that would give him the right to represent the estate of Blind Willie Johnson. "I was a little miffed," he said. "I thought we had laid out the groundwork on the phone and would be able to sign a deal, but some people just don't know what they have, what it's worth, and they'd rather do nothing than feel like they might get cheated."

Kelly said she just didn't want to rush into anything. "You know, old people don't like to sign stuff right away," she said as she maneuvered her wheelchair through the cramped quarters of 817 Hunter St., where Blind Willie lived with Kelly's mother in the early '30s. It's a four-room box with a sagging roof and walls warped by the heat.

Kelly said that she's never received a penny from her father's music.

But first she has to fly the flag, said lawyer William Krasilovsky, who wrote "This Business of Music," the industry bible. "You say, 'Here we are. We represent the heirs of Blind Willie Johnson.'" Until an estate is established, there's no place to send royalties.

But just how much money might she be due?

First off, forget about lucrative songwriting royalties. Almost all of Johnson's material was derived from such public domain sources as religious hymns and old "Negro spirituals."

But Krasilovsky said the Blind Willie estate could earn money by copyrighting his arrangements. "Does the work have distinctive fingerprints of originality that qualify for a new derivative copyright of public domain material?" he asked, reading from a copyright law book.

"Distinctive fingerprints" fits Blind Willie's truly original style like the steel cylinder he used to slide over his pinky. ASCAP and BMI, organizations that collect songwriting royalties for artists and publishers, pay about half as much for copyrighted arrangements as they do for original compositions.

Blind Willie Johnson's recordings were probably made under the "work for hire" agreement prevalent at the time, which means that Sony can claim ownership of the masters. But that's a contention that makes music historian Mack McCormick bristle. "The can't produce a contract, they can't produce the masters," he said. "They had to borrow 78s from collectors. Sony claims they own the music and they don't even have copies of the fuckin' records!"

California-based estate manager Nancy Meyer, whose Bates Meyer company represents the heirs of T-Bone Walker and many other vintage blues and jazz players, said if she were hired by Kelly, she'd form a publishing company and file copyrights for all Blind Willie's recordings. "Since the material was never copyrighted, the clock hasn't started," she said, referring to the amount of time that passes before the material is deemed "public domain" and therefore free for anyone to use. Copyrights are protected for a 28-year term from the date the copyright was originally secured, with a 28-year renewal period, followed by a 19-year term of renewal, for a total of 75 years.

"I guess I should hire someone to see about getting some money for the family," Kelly said. "I need to make a move here."

"Z'rontre!" Kelly called out to her great-grandson, her voice cutting through the loud cartoons watched in the living room by two kids lying on the floor. "Come here and get Mama that box of papers." A little boy bounded in from the bedroom and climbed up on a chair to reach a rectangular plastic box. "This boy's only three years old and he can do everything for me, even fetch me some water," said Kelly, who's stricken with arthritis and other ailments. "He's my legs."

She pulled out a few fragile documents, including a birth certificate which says that she was born June 23, 1931, to Willie Johnson, occupation listed as "musician," and a mother whose maiden name was Willie B. Hays.

Kelly said she remembers her father staying with her mother until she was about seven or eight years old. That would put him in Marlin until at least 1938. But two years after Kelly's birth, her mother had a daughter, Dorothy, with a man named Joe Henry, according to Kelly. Six years later came Earline, from another father. Kelly recalls that her parents had remained married even as Willie B. Harris was having kids with other men and Blind Willie was drifting from street corner to church to train station for months at a time.

"We was working people, see," said Kelly. "My mother understood that my father had to leave Marlin to make money. She worked seven days a week as a nurse. I'd say, 'Mama, please stay home today' and she'd say, 'But I gotta work' and I'd understand."

During the era in which Blind Willie recorded, artists didn't expect royalties. They took whatever the labels paid them, usually around $25 to $50 per record, and the music they recorded was considered work for hire. The labels claimed all rights. "They had just made a record," Columbia field recorder Frank Walker, who helmed Johnson's remarkably fruitful 1927 session, said in an interview in the '60s. "To them that was the next best thing to being president of the United States."

Johnson's first 78 rpm—"If I Had My Way" backed with "Mother's Children Have a Hard Time" (titled "Motherless Children" by Clapton)—sold a remarkable 15,000 copies, even more than Bessie Smith's recordings of the day. By 1930, however, the Depression dried up demand for gritty country blues/gospel, and Blind Willie's recording career was history. But as was his nature, Johnson kept on the move, playing "from Maine to the Mobile Bay," according to what his touring mate Blind Willie McTell told John Lomax in a 1940s interview.

"People recalled hearing him at times over KTEM in Temple and on a Sunday-morning church service broadcast by KPLC in Lake Charles," said McCormick. "He left memories in Corpus Christi during WWII when there was a fear about Nazi submarines prowling the Gulf of Mexico. Someone must have told him submarines often listened to radio stations to triangulate their position. He went on the air with new verses to one of his songs, probably 'God Moves on the Water' about the Titanic, offering grace to his audience, then followed with a dire warning to the crew of any listening U-boat with 'Can't Nobody Hide from God.'"

Blind Willie's music was revealed to a new generation of country blues enthusiasts (including Bob Dylan) with the 1952 release of the Harry Smith anthology "American Folk Music," which included Johnson's "John the Revelator." The "Blind Willie Johnson" album came out on Folkways in 1957, with a key detail wrong. Second wife Angeline Johnson, who was tracked down by music historian Samuel Charters in 1953, was credited with the backing vocals performed by his first wife, Willie B. Harris.

This error was uncorrected until the mid-'70s, when a Dallas music collector named Dan Williams drove down to Marlin to see if he could find anyone who knew Blind Willie. "I approached a group of elderly black people near the town square and one of them said he was related to Blind Willie's ex-wife, the one who sang on his records, and I thought I was going to meet Angeline Johnson," Williams recalls. "Nobody knew anything about a Willie B. Harris."

After hearing Harris sing along to the Blind Willie records and talk about details of the recording sessions that only those present would know, Williams ascertained that she was, indeed, the background singer.

"She talked about meeting Blind Willie McTell at the last session in Atlanta (April 20, 1930) and I did some research and found out that, sure enough, McTell recorded at the same studio the same day."

Charters made the correction, crediting Harris, in his notes to the 1993 boxed set, but repeated Angeline Johnson's contention that she married Blind Willie in Dallas in 1927. There is no record of such a marriage in Dallas County, or in the county clerks' offices of Falls, McLennan, Bell, Milam, Jefferson or Robertson counties. But then, neither is there evidence, besides Kelly's birth certificate listing her as legitimate, that Blind Willie and Willie B. were ever married.

Researching history about long dead blues men is fueled by random payoffs, much like slot machines and singles bars. You run your fingers down the pages of big, dusty books for hours and then you find a bit of information, a bit of new evidence, and it all becomes worth it.

But dozens of hours in search of details on the life of Blind Willie Johnson resulted in almost zero positive reinforcements. A five-hour drive to Beaumont yielded the slightest new info; a city directory shows that in 1944, a Rev. W.J. Johnson, undoubtedly Blind Willie, operated the House of Prayer at 1440 Forest St. That's the address listed on Blind Willie's death certificate as his last residence.

Besides the entry on the death certificate, there is no evidence that Blind Willie Johnson is buried in Beaumont's "colored" Blanchette Cemetery, a seemingly untended field littered with broken tombstones and overrun with weeds. If Johnson had a headstone, it's gone now. When the cemetery floods, a man who lives across the street said, sometimes wooden coffins can be seen floating away amongst the debris. There is no peaceful rest, no solitude for the ages, for the migrant musician.

His music, meanwhile, continues its journey to the galaxy's back yard.

Ry Cooder, who based his desolate soundtrack to "Paris, Texas" on "Dark Was the Night (Cold Was the Ground)," described it as "The most soulful, transcendent piece in all American music." On that Voyager 1 disc is hard evidence that we are a spiritual people, that we hurt and we heal, that we do indeed have souls that live long after we're buried.

MICHAEL ELDRIDGE

Remains of the Day-O

A Conversation with Harry Belafonte

Say the name Harry Belafonte at a dinner party, and some aging hipster will break into a plummy chorus of "Day-O." That Belafonte can still be thought of as a camp icon is more than a little unfortunate. If they dug a little deeper, the same people who write Harry Belafonte off as a silk-shirted purveyor of pseudo-Caribbean schlock might just as easily see him as one of the twentieth century's bona fide organic intellectuals. When you get right down to it, even "The Banana Boat Song"—commonly known as "Day-O"—dramatizes the drudgery of alienated labor in the colonial produce trade.

In some sense, though, Belafonte's rather one-dimensional reputation isn't surprising. Pop stars are doomed to be remembered as caricatures of themselves, and Belafonte helped invent the very notion of pop stardom. He was the first artist ever to sell a million albums in one year, and for the better part of two decades, Harry Belafonte was everywhere: his name sold out nightclubs and concert halls; his face emblazoned playbills and movie posters and magazine covers; his performances brought home a Tony, an Emmy, and Grammy after Grammy. Though he's spent much of the past thirty years working in the wings as a producer, when he takes center stage he can still pack them in. Then there are his progressive credentials: after *Brown v. Board of Education* in 1954, Belafonte refused to perform in southern states. A close friend and confidant of Martin Luther King, Jr., he worked as spokesman, strategist, benefactor, and fund-raiser for the civil rights movement. By the end of the fifties, he'd joined the struggle against South African apartheid; in this capacity, he would introduce exiled musicians like Miriam Makeba and Hugh Masekela to American audiences, cofound the Trans-Africa lobby with Randall Robinson, and arrange Nelson Mandela's celebratory visit to the U.S. in 1990. For the past fifteen years, Belafonte has also been a UNICEF Goodwill Ambassador, focusing his most recent efforts on the AIDS epidemic among South African children.

It's tempting to tally these accomplishments in two separate columns, as if the entertainer and the activist were parallel personae, or celebrity merely a convenient platform for social action. But Belafonte maintains that the two strands are tightly interwoven. His whole career, he says, has been an attempt to reconnect African Americans to their diasporic heritage, while insisting upon their central place in American culture. Henry Louis Gates, Jr., recalls the thrill of watching Belafonte's coolly provocative performance as guest host of the *Tonight Show* in 1968. At that tense moment in American history, says Gates, Belafonte seemed "the perfect hybrid of popular culture and political conscience."

Of course there are those who regard any such hybrid as a doomed compromise—at times, even Belafonte himself seems to hold this opinion. Still, Belafonte has succeeded in the rather paradoxical task of bringing "folk" to the masses. And *the folk* and *the masses* are not terms Belafonte throws around lightly: they're informed by the leftist ideologies he grew up with in the 1930s, and they're central to his old-school cultural politics, which sees art as a tool of enlightenment, music as an instrument for erasing racial prejudice and building race pride.

Belafonte was born in Harlem in 1927, but his mother, alarmed by the race riots of 1935, moved the family to her native Jamaica for a stretch of his childhood. (They returned to New York in 1939, when England went to war against Germany.) After dropping out of high school, Belafonte did a stint in the Navy, eventually joining the American Negro Theater (where he met Sidney Poitier) and enrolling in a master class in drama at the New School (where his classmates included Marlon Brando and Tony Curtis). Work for black actors was sparse, though, and in 1949 a friend who'd heard

him sing persuaded him to perform at a midtown nightclub's amateur night. Much to Belafonte's surprise, the dare led to a gig, then
good notices in *Down Beat* and *Variety*, which earned him further
bookings around the country. But the promising debut turned out
to be a false start: uninspired by his jazz-pop material and disen-
chanted with his prospects, Belafonte called it quits. He took a year
off, and when he emerged from the wilderness, he'd transformed
himself into a folk singer.

Belafonte may have decided that his chances were better against
Burl Ives and Josh White than Mel Tormé and Billy Eckstine, with
whom he'd been frequently compared. Just the same, it was a singu-
larly inauspicious moment for anyone, let alone a black man with
radical sympathies, to launch a career in folk. To begin with, late
1951 was roughly the midway point in the transition from swing to
rock, and while many musical styles were fighting for the swing
throne, folk no longer looked like a contender. The Weavers, who'd
had an enormous hit in 1950 with an anodyne cover of Lead Belly's
"Goodnight Irene," were now being hounded as communist subver-
sives, and all the African American folk singers from the forties were
implicitly tarred with the same brush—tainted, like the Weavers, by
their association with the left-wing People's Songs cooperative.
Indeed, McCarthy's witch-hunt was reaching its stormy peak, and
African Americans caught their share of bad weather. Josh White had
caved before the House Un-American Activities Committee, as had
Langston Hughes. Paul Robeson, an unrepentant fellow-traveler and
a particular idol of the young Belafonte, had been all but lynched at a
People's Songs–sponsored concert in Westchester County two years
earlier, and now his career was being systematically destroyed. Belafonte's other hero, W. E. B. Du Bois, had been arrested by the State
Department in 1950 on trumped-up charges of serving as a "foreign
agent." Under these circumstances, who could blame Belafonte for
dressing his folk music in satin shirts and tight trousers and all the
other accoutrements of show business?

At the same time, his slick presentation was a challenge to one of
the folk-purist articles of faith: it implicitly questioned the notion
that "the folk," particularly "the black folk," made no distinction
between their lives and their art—that their lives *were* their art.
Belafonte was a consummate performer, a professional, and he

never let you forget it. And while he was a passionate critic of capitalism, he realized that folk music could no longer afford to shun the fame and fortune bestowed by commercial success. The shrewdness of his gambit was borne out at the box office. Within months, he was playing extended engagements to sold-out rooms; record companies, Broadway producers, and movie studios all came calling.

As his career took wing, he also used his innocuous image to sneak some subversive ideas under the McCarthyist radar, camouflaging his internationalism with a cosmopolitan repertoire. At the same time, he was able to turn American nationalism to his advantage: in that hyperpatriotic era, Belafonte realized he could promote African American music by affirming that black folk cultures were not un-American but paradigmatically American—to be antiblack was, in some sense, to be anti-American. So in 1954, at the height of his early fame, he conceived of a project that would prove his point.

At first Belafonte envisioned it as a touring show representing the historical variety of black contributions to American oral and musical culture. Next, it was to form part of a series of television specials devoted to a broad survey of Americana. But eventually it took shape as a multivolume record album—a counterpart, perhaps, to Harry Smith's idiosyncratic *Anthology of American Folk Music*, which had appeared on Folkways Records in 1952. (In its earliest incarnation, Belafonte's album was to be titled *Anthology of Negro Folk Music*.) Following the phenomenal success of his *Calypso* album, Belafonte got the go-ahead from RCA, and after several more years of preparation (archival sources were largely nonexistent, so he set out to "reconstruct" the music in the studio), recording began in earnest in 1961. The project's scope kept growing, however: eventually it would aim to survey the musical culture of African Americans from the time of their arrival in America until the turn of the twentieth century. By the time it was finished another ten years had passed, and the cultural landscape had changes. A skittish *Reader's Digest* pulled out of a longstanding partnership to market and distribute the anthology (now named *New World A-Comin'*), and the project was shelved. It languished in the vaults for nearly thirty years, until Bertelsmann, RCA's new corporate parent, revived Buddha Records, an old bubblegum-pop label, for the express purpose of mining the RCA archives. When they stumbled upon Belafonte's anthology, Buddha executives were fairly seized with missionary zeal. They labored for almost three years, and although there was one final, horrible obstacle—the anthology was released on September 11, 2001—they eventually managed to bring Belafonte's gospel to the world.

Earnestly conceived by Belafonte and his collaborators, lovingly reassembled by Buddha's engineers and producers, and superbly packaged by International Paper, *The Long Road to Freedom: An Anthology of Black Music* received justifiably respectful notice from critics, who praised it in the reverent language reserved for outsized projects by living legends. (Grammy nominations were a foregone conclusion.) It features stunning performances by folksingers both amateur and professional—Erzaline Jenkins and Bessie Jones as well as Sonny Terry and Brownie McGhee—though soul singer Gloria Lynne and jazz crooner Joe Williams offer some epiphanies, as well. While Belafonte mainly takes a back seat, he saves two of the most sublime numbers, "Hark 'E Angel" and "Wonderful Councillor," for himself. It's a remarkably catholic compilation: *The Long Road to Freedom* includes eighteenth-century black Creole music and post–Civil War minstrel tunes alongside chestnuts like "Follow the Drinking Gourd" and "John Henry."

Yet like most sacred texts, *The Long Road to Freedom* is also a bit strange. Its governing aesthetic, for instance, is more Fisk Jubilee Singers than Georgia Sea Islands: musical director Leonard DePaur tends to recreate musical history as if he were staging a Broadway show. And then there is the musty odor of its antiquated mission. This anthology was addressed to a rather different cultural moment, of course, so we can't help but receive it as a kind of time capsule that tells as much about America (and about Harry Belafonte) between 1954 and 1971 as about black music before 1900. Belafonte has held on to a faith in the humanizing power of culture—particularly in its ability to foster sympathy and understanding across cultures—that might seem quaint if it weren't so fervent, and if the alternative weren't so bleak.

Now, Belafonte is hardly the first person to try to prove African Americans' humanity by demonstrating the greatness of their art. Nor is he the first to see them as the "potential salvation of commerce-ridden, soulless America" (as historian Steven Watson paraphrased the views of the 1920s), or to hear their music as the supreme embodiment of American culture. In other words, to note that this vision is dated is also to acknowledge that it has roots. For Belafonte, roots still matter, especially in a world that's grown dubious of them, and especially if what you're rooted in is a diaspora. And so the anthology, for all its anachronism, couldn't have appeared at a better time, for we now find ourselves at yet another of those moments when "roots culture" is on the rise. In 1959, writing with Nat Hentoff, Belafonte prophesied that "we may be close to a time when a repertory with roots will be much more common among popular singers than it is not . . . [when] the exasperation and frustration of the times in which we now live will eventually level off and people will have the time and the peace of mind to come back to songs, with roots in their culture, and to create new ones, however urbanized, of real meaning."

In retrospect, he was announcing the advent of the folk revival, which was right around the corner. But he might as well have been looking forward to the end of one century, and the beginning of the next. O brother, where art thou? Harry Belafonte's known the answer all along.

MICHAEL ELDRIDGE: Listening to the *Anthology*, I was struck by the variety of it—the sense that black life in America has taken on so many different forms. That's an idea that's been important in your career, too.

HARRY BELAFONTE: You know, I came out of the West Indian community in Harlem. I didn't move around in an environment of the intellectuals or academics. But when I was thrown into the war, into a segregated division of the navy, our all-black unit was quite diverse, quite eclectic. There were bourgeois blacks, rich blacks, educated blacks, ignorant blacks, poor blacks, light-colored blacks, dark-colored blacks, et cetera . . .

ME: Diaspora in the flesh.

HB: But *totally*. And I gravitated—perhaps out of instinct, perhaps out of conscious choice—toward those who were expressing some interesting point of view on what it meant to be black and in that war. I listened to men who knew A. Philip Randolph, who knew

Walter White, who were members of the NAACP. Our units were split up right after basic training; those who were the most educated, the most articulate, went on to become officers. I never finished high school, but my IQ score was so high that I fell in with a group of men who were high school graduates, even college graduates. We went to Hampton Institute to prepare for what they called the quartermaster corps—to take care of provisions and bookkeeping. But I didn't get to do that—I was too rebellious. Finally, they made me a munitions loader, which was one of the dirtiest and most dangerous jobs you could have in the armed forces on the domestic side.

ME: That was the fate of a lot of black men in the service during World War II, right?

HB: Yes. And the men who were stuck with munitions loading were very bitter, very angry. And in our bitterness and anger we went out and got drunk. We wanted to beat up everybody we met, including each other. But there were also those of us that decided to study, to learn, to find out how to organize. We were asking, What would we become when we got out of there? How could we help make things different? So I began to read the Du Bois pamphlets and things that these college men had given to me. Du Bois made no room for remedial students; you had to struggle to understand what he said. But I made that struggle.

ME: In the early 1950s, when your career was taking off, a lot of newspaper and magazine stories took great pains to highlight your personal connection to West Indian folk music: "These were the songs that Belafonte heard in his youth, and they stayed with him," and so on. But you made no secret of the fact that you'd actually come to folk music fairly late. In fact, your move from pop to folk, between 1950 and 1951, was largely the result of research in the Library of Congress. Throughout the 1950s, you even carried a tape recorder with you on tour, going out to gather material from chain gangs and sharecroppers. So how would you describe your connection to folk music? Is it a lived connection or a scholarly connection?

HB: I think there's another dimension to this question. I had been a very serious student of theater. So rather than define me as somebody who moved from pop music to folk music—although that is the truth—you might say that the real driving force was my deep involvement with the literature of the twentieth-century theater. Most of the theater before and during and shortly after World War II was driven by great social writers, great social thinkers: Clifford Odets, Arthur Miller, along with the books of Steinbeck and Hemingway and Faulkner and Baldwin. So although pop music satisfied a kind of a limited musical need, I was hunting for something that was closer to the literature and theater I had studied.

In the war, I had seen how propaganda was used in film and theater and songs and everything else—not only to inspire support for the war, but to explain the ideology of that war to the citizens. So when I came out of the service, I needed to extend that. I saw how much trouble this nation was in—what it was doing to Indians, to Hispanics, to women, and especially to black people. As an artist, how do you articulate this? I couldn't really do it in the theater; I'm not a playwright. But in folk music, I found an opportunity to speak to issues of great human and social concern, and to do it in ways that were quite artful. In that tradition, I found people who did it magnificently, and they influenced me: Paul Robeson, Lead Belly, Josh White, Mahalia Jackson.

ME: Can you connect the dots, then? How, exactly, can culture—whether it's pop culture or folk culture—lead to racial and social justice?

HB: Well, it depends on how you view what culture does. If you're talking about Hollywood, then it does very little—as a matter of fact it may divide people more than it brings them together.

But as a kid growing up in New York City, I came to know the Jew through the *culture* of the Jew: I saw Jewish comics; I heard Jewish singers; I listened to stories told by the interpreters of Shalom Aleichem. At the same time, I was listening to Irish bards and folksingers, and I was reading the plays of Sean O'Casey. This was the culture that captivated the mind of a young black kid, born in poverty in Harlem, growing up in the plantations of Jamaica.

All of that put me in touch with worlds that I did not know, made me see how relevant these people were to my world—and how relevant I was to theirs. I became an instrument through which all this expressed itself. I commanded millions of people who listened to my voice. And I think millions of people have acted on that, to some degree or another. I brought them to the civil rights movement, and the civil rights movement brought them somewhere else. So if you look at culture—not the narrow Hollywood definition, but in its broadest and subtlest and most communicative sense—then you can see that culture is hugely relevant. And we suffer deeply in this country, trying to bridge divides, because we have stifled culture.

ME: So in your experience, culture can bridge ethnic divides if you're open to its transformative power. But following that logic, racism would be rooted largely in a lack of compassion. That's an old-fashioned view of culture that's really quite hopeful—though perhaps not self-evidently true. How would you argue with the cynics?

HB: Well, in the early part of the twentieth century, culture was filled with the mission of telling the truth about the peoples of the world. The culture of Islam, the culture of the oppressed in Africa, the culture of the peasants in Latin America—they can still tell that kind of truth. But since culture has become the playground of commerce, and since commerce owns communication, it has determined the culture you get.

ME: When we think of folk artists, we usually think of people being born into a specific cultural circumstance and transmuting that culture into art. But with you, it was almost the other way around: you set out to find a cultural form that suited your artistic and political vision. What was that process like?

HB: In my youth, I listened to Lead Belly and Woody Guthrie and Big Bill Broonzy and others, and I was just stunned by the power and the beauty of it. And then, in the Library of Congress, I heard more songs, songs that helped me develop my own repertoire. The work I have done is quite eclectic, it sings the languages and themes of other cultures and other people. There's no single thread tying it all together except the human thread.

ME: And yet what your early admirers especially liked about you was that you didn't treat folk songs as solemn anthems or museum pieces; you brought out the drama in them, the theater.

HB: I brought out the *contemporary* in them.

ME: At that moment, the popular press was starting to dismiss folk singing with code words like "arty." *Variety* gratefully wrote that you'd taken folk singing out of Greenwich Village and made it attractive to middlebrows and sophisticates, as well as bohemians and radicals. Was that a conscious strategy?

HB: Absolutely.

ME: Would you say you set out to commercialize your material by giving it this showbiz aesthetic?

HB: Well, I guess the fact that it became commercial means that it was commercialized. I wanted to use some cunning and find a way to introduce an art form into an environment that was extremely limited—to be able to make a social and political statement to listeners without them suspecting it.

ME: By that point, of course, folk music was closely identified with the labor movement and the left.

HB: Yes, and it was the labor movement that created an environment where blacks were recognized for their contributions to American music. Prior to that, we lived in a very contained place: we were the blacks of the 1920s who did the Charleston; our purpose was to keep white folks happy and entertain them. The labor movement and the progressive environment of the 1930s—the WPA, the strikes and the bread riots, the antifascist movement in Spain—allowed black music and black art to be seen in its proper perspective.

This was right in the heyday of the folk song movement, Woody Guthrie and "This Land Is Your Land." It was remarkable. And that's what I grew up in. But after the war, when that period was over, America went on an imperialist march to dominate the world. If you were at all critical of America, you were branded a communist. There were very, very few black forces at work who stood up against that onslaught. Paul Robeson was one; W. E. B. Du Bois was another. And when he was arrested, I was down at Foley Square, a young kid with a picket sign saying, "Release Dr. Du Bois."

ME: Still, once your career took off, in spite of your rigorous research into folk musics and cultures, the public saw you mainly as a pop star. And in the mid–1950s, when you were at the heart of the calypso craze, the press promoted you as "King of Calypso." Although I know you resented that title . . .

HB: Let me hasten to add something that very few people have understood: I was never embarrassed that I lived in a place—the Caribbean—that gave rise to this cultural form. What I resisted and disliked intensely was the callous, indifferent, almost racist way in which marketing people defined me as the "King of Calypso," with very little reverence for the fact that there was a place called Trinidad, a tradition called Carnival, and a history of great poets coming together and writing these very witty songs. Consequently there was a sense in the Caribbean that I was somehow complicit in the pirating of a culture. So I resisted that title, because I had not earned it, and they had no right to give it to me.

ME: At the same time—in part because of this "King of Calypso" stuff—there was some criticism of the music you were making.

HB: You know, a lot of people said, "As a voice of the Caribbean, he doesn't sound very authentic." I understood what they meant. But why blame me for failing to be something that I never set out to be? When I took the music beyond its "authentic" boundaries, it spawned a whole new audience—an audience that had never existed before.

What bothered me most was the invocation of authenticity as the measure by which music is to be critiqued. If you're going to look at it from that perspective, the most authentic song is, "Ugh!" It was sung by men in loincloths, bashing each other with clubs. Everything since then is just a variation on "Ugh!" So what is "authentic" art?

What I said is, "Why should I be limited by how you think I should sound, when there's a whole public out here that says, 'We like what we hear'?" If you look at the *New York Times* and the *Herald-Tribune*, the drama critics who wrote about me when I did theater back in the early 1950s understood what I was doing. And they rewarded it. Most journalists are lazy; they are limited by their own experience. But you have to stay the course if you believe in what you do. And I'm still here today.

ME: I wonder if we could talk about your "coming out" as a politically committed artist. Nowadays, you're known as an outspoken commentator on everything from racial politics to U.S. foreign policy to the flaws of capitalism. But when you were starting out, you weren't doing overtly political stuff, you weren't leading audiences in rousing choruses of "Which Side Are You On" or "We Shall Overcome." Did you feel you had to put your radical sympathies under cover for the sake of your career?

HB: There's no question. There was a conscious awareness of how hostile the environment was, and how clever you'd have to be to outsmart the predator. So there was selection and choice. But there was never compromise in the content. The fact is that I didn't sing a lot of protest songs back then because most of that material had been written or covered by others, and because I saw another way to move my image and my cause through the ranks of the human family. The question was this: if you bring to the table prejudices that cause you to question my very humanity, how do I get you to see me as a man? Suppose I sing "Scarlet Ribbons" or "Try to Remember" or "Take My Mother Home" or "Danny Boy" or "Hava Nageela," and you're moved by the subject. You take a step back and look at the man singing it—the man you'd thought of as merely black, or Caribbean, or American, or political, or whatever. And you're forced to square those preconceptions against the fact that I've moved you. Have I not won you over in a more substantive way than if I'd just . . .

ME: Shouted a slogan.

HB: Right. So, yes, a lot of people say, "Oh, we accept him because he's so good-looking, so close to white; his features are so Eurocentric. That's the kind of Negro I'd like to have my son be friends with, that's the kind of Negro I'd like my daughter to date."

ME: You were kind of a "stealth" radical, then?

HB: Yeah, well, I feel it really is incumbent upon me to make you feel that I'm more like you than not—that my fears are exactly the same as yours, and my hopes should be the same as yours, too. Because I really want to take nothing from you—but I *would* like to lead you to another place, since you've taken so much from me.

ME: I'd like to ask you about the gestation of *The Long Road to Freedom*, about the cultural context that led you to believe that some-

thing like this was important—or even possible—when you conceived the project over forty years ago.

HB: Well, everything that I loved as a child was art that identified
itself with a social mission. There was Charlie Chaplin. In the
Depression, every poor person in the world delighted in his ability
to outsmart the rich, to outsmart oppression. It was there in all the
great writers of the time, but it was also there in the dance of
Katherine Dunham, and the painting of Diego Rivera and Charles
White, the music that was being sung and played at the Apollo
Theater.

ME: So how did you persuade the record company to underwrite a
project with a similar social mission?

HB: I had asked George Marek at RCA if he would be interested in
a series of works that would reflect the cultures of other places in
the world. I started with the Caribbean because I was more familiar
with that environment, and because when I looked at he music from
that community that was getting heard here in the United States, I
found it wholly unacceptable. It was a one-dimensional kind of
experience. Most of the calypsonians who enjoyed any popularity
here at all were liked for their sexual double-entendres, which
struck me as a kind of "antiblack" content. I saw us very differently,
and I'd grown up with very different songs. So I went to that source.
And in the beginning, there was a great resistance from within
RCA. But George Marek stayed with the project, and I was making
enough money for RCA that he could convince them to let me do it.
When the *Calypso* album finally came out, everybody was astonished
at how successful it was: it was the first album ever to sell a million
copies in a year. All of a sudden, the world was delighting in the
songs of this strange, exotic place called the Caribbean.

After that, Marek decided he would let me do another project,
and he gave me more freedom. And I immediately thought that I
must do a black anthology of American music, because no other culture had the same sense of diversity. So that's how I started thinking
about *The Long Road to Freedom*. When I found people like Leonard
DePaur, and I developed relationships with people like Sonny Terry
and Brownie McGhee, I saw the opportunity to do this in a way that
was a little different from the traditional methods of folk music. I

wanted to create a historical chronology that would touch the high points of our experience and let the world know that this was a mere thread in a vast blanket of music and culture—and with these people involved, I had the chance to bring in art and musical mastery and high fidelity.

ME: You began recording the project in 1961, and it took ten years to finish. So why has it taken so long for the anthology to appear? And why now? I know the official story: the set didn't appear in 1971, as originally planned, because the partnership between RCA and *Reader's Digest* dissolved. But do you think there were political factors, too? For example, were you more openly identified with leftist causes in 1971 than you had been in 1954?

HB: Absolutely.

ME: Still, it seems a bit odd. That same year, the other major record labels brought out multivolume sets devoted to the Woodstock festival and to the Concert for Bangladesh. So why couldn't RCA bring out a project you and they had worked on for ten years?

HB: Well, first of all, Woodstock was a white experience, and Bangladesh is a foreign country. It's easy for us to engage with problems that don't exist here. We can always have open discussions about Bangladesh, the same way we can have open discussions of human rights in China—just don't talk about what's happening here.

Also, George Marek died. He was an Austrian Jew, very much an intellectual, hugely sensitive to oppression. He loved culture, and he was very open toward all kinds of music. He was the man who signed Leontyne Price and me and Elvis Presley and Jefferson Airplane, all in the space of one decade. He made us feel as if the world could not exist without us. After he died, the new regime came in, the bottom-line boys from Harvard. At the same moment, the civil rights movement was at a crisis point and the antiwar movement was at its peak. Nobody wanted to be provoked on the subject of race.

ME: Things are different now, I suppose. I've read that some of BMG's current executives were genuinely excited to rediscover this material. Just the same, BMG isn't a charity organization. So I guess that's why I'm curious about the timing of this. Does the anthology seem "safer" now? Or more marketable, somehow? What's changed?

HB: What's changed is that America is no longer legally segregated. What's changed is that Colin Powell is secretary of state and Ken Chenault is CEO of American Express. What's changed is that we have the Congressional Black Caucus. We have Michael Jordan, and black music dominates the pop charts, and we have black people at every level of public and private life. Moreover, we have this thing called "world music," so that even as we contain Cuba with our blockades, one of the country's most popular albums is *Buena Vista Social Club.*

ME: And there's the so-called roots music revival, too. Ever since Smithsonian reissued Harry Smith's *Anthology of American Folk Music*—or maybe even earlier—record labels have been rummaging through their archives and coming up with new boxed sets of old music, much of it black music.

HB: I just think there's no more flour to be bleached. And when you've run out of bleach for the flour, you have to go back and deal with the flour itself. I mean, white society is dying from the cholesterol of its own design. Where are their books, where are their paintings, where are their philosophers, where are their poets, where are their singers? On the other hand, look at the developing world—its music, its art, its literature. White youth are sucking up everything out of the black ghetto—especially rap—because it's the most interesting place to be.

ME: Why is it always black culture that's called upon to fulfill this role?

HB: Because it is still the only culture—I mean, there are some exceptions—but in America it is still the only culture that's a protest culture. It's still the only culture in America that speaks out against inequity. And there's a genuineness in black culture that makes people feel that they're dealing with something far more authentic than what white culture produces on its own.

ME: Sure, but let's take just two examples from my generation, going back twenty-five years: punk and hip-hop both emerged as

underground movements that thought of themselves as being outside the mainstream, even antagonistic to it, and they both had a
pretty well-articulated political consciousness. And yet it didn't take
all that long for corporate rock and corporate rap to co-opt that
music and sell it right back to us. Nowadays, the cycle between
opposition and co-optation has grown exceedingly short. How do
you circumvent that?

HB: Well, I think it's already being circumvented. When you go
around the world, you see rap in Soweto, in Portuguese Africa, in
French Africa, in Cuba, in Nicaragua, in Brazil. And that global rap
culture has come back to New York. They had what they called a
"hip-hop globalization" conference here, and rappers from around
the world spoke about social content. Rap is reaching back to
reclaim what it was when Afrika Bambaataa and Melle Mel and
those guys were doing it out of the South Bronx. So I think that the
music is doing what you're talking about—it's reclaiming its truth,
its identity, its social and political mission—and white kids are very
much into it. It's a culture of protest, it's a culture of analysis, it's a
culture of difference, and it's got a great beat.

ME: You're talking about a commercial music returning to its origins as a true folk music. And I think that brings us back to your
early career, when you were a pop star whose only real rival in the
world of recorded music was Elvis Presley. Even if you weren't
singing protest songs, you went on record then with some fairly
strong opinions about the mediocrity of commercial culture and the
integrity of folk culture. Folk music, you said, was the spontaneous,
organic expression of a people's culture, and that was a type of
expression that has become increasingly scarce under capitalism, as
people consumed and produced music commercially rather than
communally. Do you still feel that way now, almost fifty years later?

HB: More than ever. And I don't shy away from the fact that my art
was influenced by Marxism—that was the code of the day. The
socialist ideal was what most culture in the world aspired to in the
middle of the twentieth century. All of the artists I mentioned as the
great voices of culture were socialist, or socialist-influenced.

ME: Nowadays, historians and cultural critics tend to be skeptical
about concepts like "the authentic expression of a people's culture,"

just as you're skeptical about the notion of a "pure" folk culture. Some of them have pointed out that many of our notions of "authenticity" and "tradition" and "the folk" were manufactured in order to serve an assortment of ideological ends. Yet there's still this idea that black culture is the embodiment of everything vital and natural and pretechnological—the antithesis of Euro-American modernism. The Barbadian poet Kamau Brathwaite made a similar point when he dismissed ethnomusicologists like Alan Lomax, Samuel Charters, and Moe Asch as purveyors of "fakeways" rather than "folkways." I'm up on my soapbox, I guess, but—

HB: Just don't push me off mine! [They laugh.]

ME: It's a deal. But does any of this temper your continued belief in folk music as the spontaneous expression of a people's culture?

HB: I think there are contradictions, but I don't know that the contradictions are total. If you take black music, if you take what has been traditionally described as the folk voice, what is unique about that voice is that there is a depth to its character. It takes time to develop. It's something that is handed back and forth by people who mold that expression to define their pain, their hopes, their aspirations, their dreams.

On the other hand, commercial art insists on mass production and disposability, so that nothing lingers too long—you always have to get people to buy the next thing. After a while, you have to eliminate that long process of development. You don't have the time, for example, to look for humanity in the midst of tragedy in order to evoke laughter. So you write something superficial and you trick the public into thinking it's funny by putting in a laugh track. All that's left is the packaging, because commercial art is not made through suffering and struggle and solidarity. And as a consequence, I think our culture is diminishing. Rather than looking for content to drive audiences, we have developed technology. Come and be razzle-dazzled by what mechanisms can do to your visual senses.

ME: But what's the alternative? I think the other thing that Brathwaite was getting at had to do with people like Lomax, tramping around the world in order to "archive" and "preserve" other people's cultures. A lot of people argue that the whole folkloric enterprise has certain colonialist undertones, inasmuch as it repeats the patterns of colonial rule: powerful people—usually powerful white people—marching off into various dark corners of the world and gathering up raw materials to take home and exploit for their own profit or enjoyment. For instance, Paul Simon was accused of neo-colonialism and cultural imperialism for his work with South African musicians on the *Graceland* album. Did you ever have to worry about that kind of criticism?

HB: Sure. But so what? You know, I encouraged Paul Simon to go to South Africa. I arranged some of the meetings, and when *Graceland* came out, I was delighted that millions of people who had never paid much attention to that culture were all of a sudden alive to it. Granted, I found the content a little . . . well, let me not criticize him. I thought there were a lot of things that could have been said, lyrically, which would have given us a greater sense of the environment from which those sounds came, and those things wouldn't necessarily have disturbed Paul Simon's style of writing.

ME: I guess you could argue that Simon was relatively upstanding about the whole affair: the concerts in support of the album seemed to be as much about Ladysmith Black Mambazo and Miriam Makeba as they were about Paul Simon, and he arranged for them to get major-label releases in the States.

HB: Well, there are those who will tell you that had not the response from the ANC been so swift and intense, the *Graceland* tour might have turned out a little differently. So he took Miriam Makeba and Ladysmith Black Mambazo and Hugh Masekela on tour with him, and that took some of the venom out of the ANC's sting. But incidentally, the ANC never critiqued the content of Simon's work, it critiqued the process. There was a certain arrogance in him saying, "I'm not political, I don't get into politics."

ME: He was involved in politics whether he wanted to be or not.

HB: Exactly. But still, Columbus came to this hemisphere, and despite all the villainy that he brought with him, that's a fact of life. With Lomax, and others who went around the world in that colonial fashion, there are aspects of villainy: Lomax was a racist, et cetera. And yet this work was done, and we have this collection, and I don't know who would have done it if he hadn't. Thomas Jefferson and all those other slaveholders wrote a proclamation that has done much to design where mankind has gone in its evolution. Is all of that villainous, or is all of it positive? I don't think we should reject the good because there was some bad, or ignore the bad because there was so much good. I think it's both, and I think what we should do is talk honorably about both.

ME: Still, the whole business makes you wonder about how Americans get interested in "foreign" music. Over the past hundred years or so, there's been a series of musical fads that seem to get so blurred in the popular imagination that they've become almost interchangeable. First there was rumba, then tango, then samba and calypso and mambo and cha-cha-cha and salsa and merengue—on and on it goes. Do you think Americans have a genuine desire to understand other cultures, or is it merely boredom with the perceived blandness of their own mainstream culture?

HB: I think it's all of that, not any one explanation. You know, when you ran off your litany of musical genres, almost everything you mentioned has its roots in Africa. Now, if you look at "world music," it often seems like a euphemism, a label for people who are still incapable, for racist reasons, of saying "this is African music" or "this is black music." So, "world music" becomes a safe zone in which dominant society can domesticate something that it cannot resist. How much easier is it to say "world music" than it is to say "the music of Africa" or "the music of a people who come from a slave diaspora"? If you can't understand the evolution of music in Cuba and how deeply rooted it is in slavery, then that's unfortunate, because you are still unable to understand that the thing you enjoy comes from struggle with oppression.

That's why I say in the anthology: look at the beauty of this music, listen to these voices, listen to what people are saying about their suffering over a couple of hundred years. And if you like what you hear, if you are moved by what you hear, doesn't that make you want to know more about how this music came to be?

ME: Why do you think we always seem to need some familiar, established figure to act as our interpreter? How come it takes Paul Simon to introduce us to South African music, or David Byrne to tutor us about Brazilian music? For that matter, why did we need Harry Belafonte to introduce us to calypso?

HB: Because our culture teaches us to be highly skeptical and suspicious of what we don't know. We wait for someone to tell us it's safe—that's what America's all about. Anything that is different is going to be held in abeyance until someone comes along and tells us it's acceptable.

ME: Part of your stated purpose for *The Long Road to Freedom* is to convey the complexity and sophistication of African American history and culture and the centrality of that experience to the American experience at large. Do you think that mission is still as relevant or as urgent now as it was in 1954, when you first conceived the project, or 1961, when you began recording it, or 1971, when it was finally finished? Since then, we've seen the establishment of African American Studies programs in dozens of American universities, and the inclusion of the history of culture of black Americans and other under-represented groups in other, more traditional disciplines; we've also seen the advent of Black History Month and the publication of several major anthologies of African American literature, and even the release of other historic collections of black music. Couldn't you argue that this part of the battle has already been won?

HB: I think we're still fighting the battle. I don't believe that the battle will have been won until the art of Africa and the culture of the African diaspora is fully embraced and understood. Even today, I think that black Americans are more Eurocentric in our values and our interests than we are Afrocentric. First I was colored, then I was Negro, then I was black, and now I'm African American—a whole lifetime spent in search of the right terminology. And yet, you ask most black Americans: Where's Mali? Who is the president of Kenya? Forget it! And what can they tell you about Caribbean culture, or about Brazil?

Now is this something to be ashamed of? Have we done something sinful? Absolutely not. This is a symptom of the devastation of our slave experience—we're the only slave group in the world that still lives inside the belly of the beast. Everybody else has extricated themselves: Brazilians, Cubans, Jamaicans, Africans. And they have created societies that do not aspire to values that were set by their former slave masters. Yet here in America, our tastes are very Eurocentric: when we leave the ghetto, the minute we get a buck, we're moving to where white people live, rather than focusing our attention on the rehabilitation of our own communities, rather than letting the power of our own culture and art come to life. So when Miriam Makeba or Youssou N'Dour or Salif Keita or Gilberto Gil or Milton Nascimento comes here, we have no frame of reference— our taste buds are not alive.

ME: You're saying that black Americans haven't succeeded in achieving some kind of "American" identity and also haven't succeeded in achieving any kind of diasporic consciousness.

HB: Yes—as a matter of fact, that's perfectly put. We sit, straddling—that's why we are so schizophrenic. It's a kind of split personality disorder.

ME: What about you? From your very first appearance as a folk singer, you adopted a deliberately cosmopolitan approach. And in your career as an activist you've been concerned with issues that span the breadth of the diaspora. Yet from the very first song you wrote and performed professionally—"Recognition"—all the way through to the release of *The Long Road to Freedom*, you've also identified yourself as an African American. Looking back, how would you characterize your relationship with African America?

HB: I would like to eliminate the "America" part and keep the "African" part. I'd say I identify with African culture and African diaspora culture, and African Americans are a part of it. Even on my earliest albums, you'll hear this: the spirituals I sang—"My Lord, What a Morning," "Take My Mother Home"—were sung in an African American voice, and yet it was clear that they were African-rooted.

ME: It sounds as if you'd like to be rid of the national component altogether.

HB: Had my mother not sent me to Jamaica for much of the first twelve years of my life, I would never have understood how international we are. Because when I was thrust back into Harlem, back into the black American rhythm of life, there was a constant sense that we were very much alike. And even within my own community—immigrant blacks living in black America—it was curious that we sought to see the differences in one another, when there was so much that bound us together. And then, of course, when you began to hear about people like Marcus Garvey and Haile Selassie, and you saw what happened to people like Robeson and Du Bois, there was no other way to see us except as part of a diaspora. And that, I thought, was where our strengths truly lay.

ME: Which makes the history of sometimes testy relations between American blacks and West Indian American blacks all the more unfortunate.

HB: Or the strained relations between American blacks and African blacks. When I go to Africa today—South Africa, or Nigeria, or wherever I go—I find huge resistance to the . . . I mean, there is some envy of our material goods and whatnot, but by and large, I find there's very little about black Americans that Africans want. In intellectual circles in South Africa, for example, there's vigorous criticism of black Americans, and a strong unwillingness to be like them.

ME: When you see rifts like this, even within the diaspora, is it realistic to think that music—even folk music—can repair the damage? It makes me wonder about something Charles Shaar Murray once said—about how whites in America like black music just fine, they don't like black *people*. White folks will gladly pay to hear you sing "Day-O," but that doesn't mean they want to live in the same neighborhood or send their kids to the same schools as you do. As someone whose audiences are, in fact, largely white—a fact you've noted quizzically, maybe even ruefully, now and then—is it hard for you to remain optimistic about the potential of music?

HB: I think that black culture commands a global audience because of the sheer power of it, the beauty of it—it is hard to dismiss. And because it brings so much delight, it can easily be embraced. The physical presence of black people, however, is something else: it reflects a history of oppression that white people don't want to deal with, not because they wouldn't like to see the oppression go away, but they don't want to pay the price for it to be gone. "Entertain me, don't agonize me": we play that role every day, and it's how we've achieved most of our economic success. We're paid most for what we do as entertainers, not for what we do as scientists or professionals or intellectuals or provocateurs. As black Americans in the midst of all this, we face a dilemma. First and foremost: What are we? If we are Americans, then what does the flag mean to us? And are we going to let this country be defined by the Bush ilk, or by the likes of Dr. King—whom we have allowed to become just a holiday rather than a living, breathing presence, a source of genuine inspiration? Why isn't Dr. King or Robeson or someone like that in our pantheon? We have no gods—except for white gods.

And I don't think these problems will just will themselves away. I sat the other night with Chris Tucker and some other people from the young black culture. These guys treat me with real reverence and respect. And I said, "You guys have really just dropped the ball here. You're all making $26 million a movie—which in itself is vulgar, no matter who you are. But how much do you need to insulate yourself from poverty before you can begin to think about where to put your energy and your celebrity and your voice to stimulate that which is the best in us?" They kind of look at you. They heard the question, but they don't have an answer. But I know a lot of them are grappling with it, because they say, "Can we meet with you again?"

ME: I suppose your own career is a model of how to combine entertainment and activism—not just fund-raisers, but real political work. Your work in South Africa, for example—how did that come about?

HB: I was one of the founders of Trans-Africa. We needed a lobbying force in this country to speak up about relationships with Africa and the African diaspora. We were dealing not only with South Africa but with the independence of Africa in general.

As for my work with the global antiapartheid movement, that arose because of my relationship with the ANC and Oliver Tambo. I chaired the committee that brought Nelson Mandela here, and I shaped his itinerary: what unions he met with, what churches he visited, what synagogues he went to, his congressional visit. But this wasn't a stand-alone project; it was a natural extension of where I came from: Dr. King, Robeson, Eleanor Roosevelt. I'm naming the

luminaries because they're the most easily identifiable. But most of
the people that I've worked with are people you never heard of,
people with no college education who made a critical difference.

Right now I'm working with gangs, the Bloods and the Crips, in
the American prison system. The system—the privatization of the
prisons, the disenfranchisement of ex-felons—is part of the same
instrument of oppression that existed when I was a boy. It's the same
banks, the same people, the same villainy.

ME: I also want to ask you about the World Conference against
Racism last summer in Durban, which you attended. What dominated the media reports here in the States was the U.S.'s decision
not to participate. But even some commentators on the left dismissed the conference as a colossal waste of time.

HB: Those critics on the left who dismissed that conference as irrelevant and said nothing good could come of it—I've long seen those
people as dilettantes who have no stomach for getting into the heart
of the struggle, who are too cowardly to surrender their image as
liberals or as positive thinkers, even though they have long since
given up their moral responsibility. In some ways, I find those people much more problematic than the people who are clearly evil. So
I don't even bother with them. I go where I have to go.

I would readily accept the view that America's absence from the
conference was a disgrace. But that's not the whole story. We need
to understand that this wasn't just some casual snub, instigated by a
disgruntled Mr. Colin Powell, acting as the house slave for George
Bush. It was calculated. It was just that they didn't want to discuss
the Israeli-Palestinian question, and it wasn't just that they didn't
want to discuss reparations. There is a whole list of issues that are
not to be discussed: sexism, the feminist movement, globalization,
the World Bank, the IMF. The people who control this country
don't want to be exposed to that kind of criticism.

What disturbs me is not so much that all this villainy exists—as a
matter of fact, not to expect it would be naïve. What bothers me is
the extent of our capitulation. I don't see any fight left in the black
caucus in the Congress, I don't see it among intellectuals and the
presidents of universities. I see no institution where our passion for
political articulation and political unity survives.

ME: Do you think that's because people have been worn down or disillusioned by the lack of progress over the years? Is it because black people in America are divided along class lines or ethnic lines? Or is it something else?

HB: I think it's all of the above; I don't think it's any one thing. But mostly it's that the enemy has successfully led the broad population—black, white, yellow, Native American, everyone—to embrace a value system that has crippled our capacity for social agitation and dissent. We're all trapped in the abyss of greed. Black people are going to have to understand that the issue here is more than race. We are the souls, we are the people that must save the soul of this nation. But like the rest of the country, we're caught up in the rush to the well of materialism. Therefore, we are willing to watch Rwanda, Congo, the upheaval of societies in the Caribbean, and even our sixty-nine churches burnt down, and the election stolen from our black voters in Florida—all without a whimper. It is tragic. And it's going to be very costly.

Dr. King said it clearly. The very last conversation we had, he said, "Harry, I think we're integrating into a burning house." I asked him, "Well, how do we fix that?" And he said, "We're going to have to become firemen."

BILL FRISKICS-WARREN

Johnny Cash, 1932–2003

The Man in Black—and Other Colors

I had the privilege of spending a couple of hours with Johnny Cash twice; on neither occasion was he dressed, head to toe, in his signature black. The first time, at the Cashes' sprawling home on Old Hickory Lake in Hendersonville, he had on jeans and an untucked blue Oxford cloth shirt with a button-down collar. The second, at the cottage that he and his wife June shared at the Carter Fold in the Clinch Mountains of southwestern Virginia, he wore black sweatpants and an embroidered white work shirt.

That second encounter was in September of last year, on the final day of summer. The leaves were starting to turn, but I was still hot and sticky, and storms were gathering to the west. I was on assignment and had driven from Nashville to interview Johnny at the Fold, the old homestead of the "first family of country music"—the place where A.P. Carter was born and where he and his ex-wife and singing partner Sara are buried. The Cashes were there, at the house that used to belong to June's parents, Mother Maybelle and Ezra Carter, to work on her latest album, an unvarnished musical memoir called "Wildwood Flower" that the Dualtone label released after her death this spring.

Johnny was propped up in a black leather recliner as I was shown into their modest, memento-lined living room, his feet elevated to prevent swelling due to water retention brought on by diabetes. He also suffered from asthma and autonomic neuropathy, and looked more frail than imposing, his eyes glassy and tired. Yet somehow, he still seemed vital, even unassailable, sitting there; though ravaged by time, pills and sickness, his craggy baritone reverberated with a mix of dignity, hunger and steadfastness that carried the same biblical freight as the man himself.

Indeed, the week before in Nashville, at the Americana Music Awards, he had accepted the first ever Spirit of Americana Free Speech Award for his unflagging commitment to people struggling on society's margins. He was also set to release the fourth album in his series of career-rejuvenating American Recordings with rap-metal producer Rick Rubin, and plans for a fifth project were already in the works. And he still had June, his partner and soul mate for the better part of four decades, at his side.

Cash pressed on after June's passing May 15, of complications from heart surgery; he even made public appearances and continued to record. But he was also in and out of the hospital, his final stay at Baptist ending with his death, from respiratory failure, shortly before dawn last Friday morning. People sensed it was coming; journalists had been updating their orbits since his health fell off precipitously after he was diagnosed—mistakenly, it turned out—with Parkinson's disease in the mid-'90s. It's one thing, though, to contemplate a world in which we'll never again hear him utter, "Hello, I'm Johnny Cash"; it's quite another to face the fact that, from now on, that salutation will merely echo in our memories.

Celebrities and public figures die all the time, but Cash, who was 71, was different: The figure he cut, the way he sounded and the things he stood for are etched into popular consciousness as ineradicably as the presidential countenances chiseled into Mt. Rushmore. Doubtless, some will find consolation in knowing that Johnny and June are somehow reunited, as they believed they would be—and as they sang in "Far Side Banks of Jordan." But for many who remain, Cash's passing is tantamount to losing a totem, an emotional and cultural compass the fixity and magnitude of which rival that of the North Star.

As emblematic and conflicted a figure as any in American popular culture, Johnny Cash was a singer, songwriter, actor, author, film-maker, historian and social activist who transcended categorization at nearly every turn. His music spanned country, folk, pop and rock, even as it influenced punk and rap. (He was the first person inducted into both the country music and rock 'n' roll halls of fame.) He was a doubter and a believer and could be hip as well as square, a rebel and a voice of reconciliation. He was an addict and an evangelist, a protestor of the war in Vietnam and a guest at the Nixon White House, a singer of grim odes to murder like "Delia's Gone" and an aficionado of clodhopper cornpone who married one of the funniest country comics ever. Unwilling to let any one thing define him, Cash could truly say, with Walt Whitman, "Do I contradict myself? Very well then, I contradict myself. I am large, I contain multitudes."

Which is why it's been so vexing in recent years to see the media, and especially the rock press, reduce Cash to a two-dimensional avatar of darkness, equal parts proto-punk and forerunner of the gangsta MC. This isn't to say that his dark side—his addictions, his hell-raising, his bouts of emotional turbulence—don't define a large part of his myth. Nor to deny that many people identify with the outlaw hero tradition of which that myth is an extension, particularly as epitomized by Cash's Man in Black persona. And neither is it to ignore the extent to which the prevailing fascination with the "bad-ass Cash"—the man who flipped off the camera at San Quentin and kicked out the footlights of the Grand Ole Opry stage—is a product of how the singer was marketed by his record label in the last decade.

Yet to tout his darker tendencies at the expense of the romantic, fun-loving and devotional sides of his character obscures the outsized spiritual journey that made Cash so heroic in the first place: his lifelong struggle—not nearly as easy as "I Walk the Line" admits—to remain true to his unruly heart. He wrote the song as a pledge of fidelity to his first wife, Vivian Liberto, but over the years, Cash's vow to keep the ends out for the ties that bind took on greater existential significance. He seemed to be confessing—his message driven home by the obdurate beat of the Tennessee Two—how desperately he wanted to unite the disparate strands of his conflicted self in hopes of subduing the beast within. It was through this hard-won multiplicity, and not by collapsing the tensions that dogged and defined him, that Cash achieved whatever transcendence he did.

That transcendence was considerable, and it's writ large in his music, beginning with the staggering catalog of songs he wrote: "Folsom Prison Blues" (flinty and class-conscious), "I Walk the Line" (definitive), "Big River" (Rabelaisian), "I Still Miss Someone" (a wrenching expression of Ralph Ellison's "blues impulse"), "Don't Take Your Guns to Town" (epic), "Daddy Sang Bass" (sentimental and devout), "Man in Black" (self-mythologizing), "The Man Comes Around" (apocalyptic). It's also evident in the way Cash sang these songs, and those of others—"Ballad of Ira Hayes" (patriotism at its radical best), "A Boy Named Sue" (serious fun), "Sunday Morning Coming Down" (spiritual abandonment on the brink)—his voice imperious, inimitable and, you'd swear, sui generis. And it's there in the boom-chicka-boom that drove it all, the inexorable, freight-train rhythm that Cash patented with Luther Perkins and Marshall Grant at Sun Records—a sound as enduring as Bo Diddley's hambone beat, Ray Price's 4/4 shuffle or the one-chord funk vamps of James Brown & the JBs.

That transcendence is likewise there in Cash's prodigious journey—in his rise from the cotton fields of Arkansas; in his perseverance and breakthrough with Sam Phillips at Sun; in his heady early days touring with Elvis, Jerry Lee, Roy Orbison and Carl Perkins; in his struggles with drugs, booze and self-doubt; and, finally, in his redemption by June Carter and her parents. "June and her family have kept me steadily on the course when the rudder was shaky," he told me in 1999. June might have written "Ring of Fire" (with Merle Kilgore) out of the trepidation she felt when she was falling hard for Johnny, but she proved to be even tougher than he was. She didn't just flush his pills down the toilet; she loved him with a fierceness that made their romance one of the great love stories of the 20th century.

Together, the Cashes blended two unwieldy broods, had one son of their own, toured the globe, starred on TV and in movies together and adopted all manner of singers, actors and ex-sons-in-law, seemingly drawing everyone into their fold. Indeed, few people have evinced Johnny and June's gift for attracting and uniting people of different stripes, from Bob Dylan and Kris Kristofferson to Billy Graham and Robert Duvall. And that's to say nothing of Johnny's wide-ranging taste in songwriters, including the likes of

Bruce Springsteen, Trent Reznor, Dorothy Love Coates and Beck. Nowhere was this ecumenism more dazzling than on his pioneering TV variety show, which during its run on ABC from 1969 to 1971 played host to such disparate icons as Dylan, Louis Armstrong, Mahalia Jackson and The Who. Making hillbilly culture hip to mainstream and even countercultural audiences, "The Johnny Cash Show" contributed as much to the Southernization of American culture as anything from its era.

Through it all, Cash remained attuned to issues of social class, and not just at arm's length. Born of the poverty he endured as a child, his vision of justice compelled him to stand, like a tree planted by the water, with oppressed people everywhere, be they in prison, on the streets, in hospital wards or otherwise on the margins of society. It was precisely this prophetic voice and stance—his ability to connect the dots between poverty and incarceration in "Folsom Prison Blues," or between racism and disenfranchisement in "Ballad of Ira Hayes"—that made him the Man in Black.

The meaning of that "blackness" has been masked by the recent gloom-as-fashion portrayals of Cash's persona—a persona born of his ability to envision a better world, to see a light that might dispel the darkness. Cash acknowledged as much, amid considerable talk of home and family, when I spoke with him at the Carter Fold a year ago. Yet he also admitted that despite his appreciation for—and embodiment of—the outlaw-hero mystique, he too had contributed to the increasingly narrow picture of his image and legacy. "I pigeonholed myself a lot," he said. "It's true that maybe I'm defining myself more as an artist, and maybe as a person, in these later years. I don't know. But looking back at myself, and at what I project out there, there seems to be a hardness and a bitterness and a coldness . . . and I'm not sure I'm too happy with that. I'm not sure that's the image I want to project, because I'm a pretty happy man."

Later that morning he asked me if I'd fix him a cup of coffee. He took it black, with three sweeteners.

ROBBIE FULKS

Sex, Heartbreak
and Blue Suede

One Saturday last summer, I went to Nashville to sing at the Grand Ole Opry. I rented a car at the airport, put the windows down and drove the five smoothly curving miles up Briley Parkway. The weather was transcendent, and I was feeling giddy. I switched on WSM 650—the AM radio station that got the Opry going seventy-seven years ago and has broadcast it every weekend since—and immediately heard a promo with my name amid a cluster of '50s pioneers and a few new Garth types. I had to laugh out loud. What was a pop-punk-hillbilly obscurity doing sullying country music's premier stage? It seemed like a cosmic error, but the mundane fact was that two of the show's regular stars, Gail Davies and Jean Shepard liked my music and had gradually worn down the gatekeepers on my behalf. No matter how I had arrived, it felt too fantastic to be true.

The sprawling suburban complex called Gaylord Opryland comprises a hotel, convention center, theater and mall. It sits in a U by the Cumberland River, northeast of downtown Nashville. The Grand Ole Opry House theater is a 147,000-square-foot brick-and-tile artifact of '70s high pastoral. Walking across the stone courtyard among vacationing families and T-shirted seniors, I saw Gail and her band setting up on an outdoor stage. Gail is a cheerful honky-tonk of a 55-year-old with an overlay of girl-power pizzazz. She wears her hair in a flapper cut and has a personality like a small rampage.

She strode over as I laid an arrangement of irises by her mike stand. "Gail, how can I ever thank you for this?"

"Well, listen. That's what we've got to do if it's going to be about the music," she explained, now heating up. "When I had five songs in the Top 10, do you think those guys running the Opry wanted Gail Davies? They didn't give a shit. Politics, just good-old-boy politics. Never forget, one artist needs to help another. God knows, those bastards"—she pointed vaguely to the sky somewhere above the Tower Records megastore—"never will."

The way she carried on, you'd have thought it was 1950, when the Grand Ole Opry was at the peak of its power, the top radio program in America, a king-maker. Back then, WSM's transmitter was a 50,000-watt 808-foot wand, transforming backwoods untouchables into wealthy superstars and primitive folk music into a showy and sharp-trimmed industry. Classic country was a peculiar kind of art, a demotic expression of savage emotion, deep-grained and bold, written with Flaubertian precision and performed with reckless humor and a ticking-clock focus. The Opry's weekly broadcast forged country's national image and presaged Nashville's emergence as its capital.

But since then, that city's Music Row—the source of the majority of country music as commonly and commercially understood—and the Opry have diverged, the one growing ever more pop-mimicking and machine-tooled, the Opry pretty much staying put. WSM and its flagship show are now Nashville's last sanctuary for hard country. This is why the Opry still matters very much to us fundamentalists—and should matter to anyone not immune to rough beauty nor completely infatuated with the present moment.

So how is the health of the church? The days when every true believer east of the Rockies tuned in for Saturday-night services are long gone. The contemporary Opry is a tourist-driven enterprise and, in recent years, an unsteady one. It offers little current-hit fare: The Faiths and Shanias would be loath to give up a weekend night for the few hundred dollars in union scale an appearance pays—even if their recycled rock didn't clash too bizarrely with the Porter

Wagoners and the Charlie Walkers. While many of these mid-century figures are still in good form, their ranks are rapidly thinning, and they have no obvious heirs. When they die, the Opry will die with them, unless it allies itself with fresh talent and somehow broadens its appeal without sacrificing its identity.

*   *   *

I was a teenager when I first visited Opryland, in 1977. After watching the Canadian singer Hank Snow ("I'm Movin' On") play an afternoon matinee, I went outside to the back of the building and jumped the low concrete barrier near the stage entrance, hoping to get his autograph. When the 63-year-old emerged, he was with a man-eater blond who sang in his show at the time; neither of them was amused to see me. Approaching the same door twenty-five years on, I still felt like a trespasser.

The Opry House's backstage is a drab grid of light brown tile and fluorescent lights, with a U-shaped locker-lined hallway curved around a greenroom. The place was as clean and charmless as a nursing home, at least until familiar forms started popping up and bringing it to life: Jumpin' Bill Carlisle, born in 1908, now hunched and trembling in a wheelchair, with seven decades of stage leaps, yodels and dirty novelty records behind him; and Jean Shepard, a protofeminist forerunner of Patsy Cline, belting a kick-ass "Crying Holy unto the Lord." Down the hall, Whispering Bill Anderson, singer of sentimental recitations, former TV-game-show host and pitch-perfect lyricist, was whipping his hair into a frizzy T. J. Hooker splendor. Each of them had been here for more than forty years.

I knocked tentatively on Whispering Bill's door. I had met him before but hadn't met his band, who were slipping into their lemon yellow sport coats. "Boys," said Bill, "This is Robbie. He's the one that wrote that song about Music Row. . . . Now, what was the title of that?"

"'Fuck This Town,'" I said. They laughed and pumped my hand. New friends!

Country's iconic zero-for-conduct types—Hank Williams, Elvis Presley, Johnny Cash (who drunkenly smashed the footlights here in 1965)—have tended not to prosper at the Opry. But the broader rank and file have been served well. For the singers elected to membership, the Opry is a sinecure, a fiercely protected institution and a dependable haven from hellish state-fair PA systems and sleepy casino crowds. For younger musicians like me, it's a place to commune with our betters: the old and the dead. Attire is therefore paramount.

"Some of these younger acts come on here like it's a bar gig," Gail told me. "The older people take it as disrespectful."

I do, too. For my big night, I had dropped $200 on a blue faux-suede western suit, which I wore with an American-flag necktie. Once I had changed and pomaded my flattop stiff, I felt lighter. I went to watch the show and wait my turn in the stage-right wing. Most of the house's 4,400 seats were full.

The WSM announcer, Hairl Hensley, stepped to the lectern to boom his opening lines. "Presenting the 3,989th consecutive edition of the world-famous Grand . . . Ole . . . Opry!" A fiddler named Hoot Hester kicked off a brisk two-step, accompanied by a troupe of cloggers; then Hensley introduced Little Jimmy Dickens, the host of the first segment. Dickens sang his hit "Sleepin' at the Foot of the Bed," following it with a few comic remarks about his no-frills upbringing ("Fifteen kids! Six boys, six girls and three others"). Then he reintroduced Hensley, who read some unctuous ad copy from segment sponsor Odom's Tennessee Pride, "The Real Country Sausage." Hensley then reintroduced Dickens, who introduced another act, and so on. . . .

As with any long-lived variety show, the format's the thing. The Opry shows—one on Friday and two on Saturday—are two and a half hours long and split into five segments, each with a dedicated sponsor and host, typically a veteran like Dickens. They bring out a few other acts (usually musical, but also some dancers and comedians) who hold the stage from four to twelve minutes each, depending on their market value.

I waited in the wings for a small eternity of subsegments. Finally Gail came on. Jean Shepard joined her, and the two of them introduced me. I was feeling no proper fright, but I couldn't stop bouncing on my heels and opening and closing my fists. The milling civilians eyed me, trying to determine if I was someone important—the suit was doing its work. Gail hit her final turnaround, and my legs tensed for the sprint into the lights. Just then a stagehand noticed the string ends jutting uncut from my turning pegs. "Want me to cut these off for you?" he asked pointedly.

"No thanks," I said. "It's a look."

He left, then reappeared a moment later with the world's largest pliers and took hold of my headstock.

"The Opry has a look, too," he explained.

Meanwhile, Jean and Gail were windily logrolling. "This woman is a legend!" cried Gail. "This woman ought to be in the Country Music Hall of Fame!"

Over the cheering, Jean snapped, "Do it before I die, y'all!"

Gail said a few words about me and asked Jean if she wanted to do the introduction. Jean fell silent for a second, then she simply said my name. I trotted on to very quiet applause.

When I crossed the line from the wings to the stage, a door closed behind me I could never again open. After many years of fanhood and close listening, I had come to feel intimate with Webb Pierce, George Jones, Jean Shepard and the rest. Their music had moved and calmed and shaped me. It had helped me through times of loneliness and despair. It had brought me to believe that the deepest truths dance perilously close to clichés like "times of loneliness and despair." In return for all this wisdom and comfort, I had given the music my unconditional love. But of course, fanhood is a childish idealization permitted only to observers in the wings. At that moment, I surrendered all that. I was still an obscurity, but I was in the club.

*   *   *

Five months later, Vince Gill and I were sitting on the back steps of the Ryman Auditorium, the restored nineteenth-century tabernacle that housed the Opry show from 1943 to 1974 and was once again serving as the show's base for its off-peak winter season. Vince had just finished his segment, which had not gone smoothly. His vocal mike had shocked him twice, and the star with the gentlest of public personae had cursed colorfully and well on the stage of the old church. But now he was himself again and in a reflective mood. "When the show went out to Opryland," Vince was saying, "it totally lost its alley vibe. And for a long time, downtown didn't have much going on. Now it's a place to be, havin' the Opry down here, and everybody slippin' back and forth and listenin' to music in the alley."

After the show fled to the suburbs in '74, the Ryman fell into disrepair, but the building was restored in the early '90s and finally outfitted with central air. Now the show was back, broadcasting during the winter season from the 2,038-seat smaller venue. The alley Vince had mentioned separated the Ryman's back doors from those of the honky-tonks on Nashville's lower Broadway, where rednecks played for tips into the small hours. A man in a ball cap spotted us. "Hey, Vince!" he yelled. "There's a great Tele picker over here!" He was motioning toward Tootsie's, the bar that once served as an after-hours salon for the likes of Hank Williams and Roger Miller. It was where Willie Nelson wrote "Crazy" for Patsy Cline.

"I know," Vince replied. "Johnny."

"Johnny!" The stranger nodded solemnly. "He's awesome."

"Amazing," Vince agreed. "I wanna go over and hear him." He turned back to me. "What I love about this place is, it has never done what pop culture does—find the next new thing and use it up and discard it."

Another passerby saw us and stopped his cell-phone conversation midsentence. "Oh, my God!" he said.

"Hi," said Vince.

"You're not going to believe this," the passerby said to the phone. Then, to Vince: "Can you just say hello? She's your biggest fan. It won't take long."

"You got that right," said the singer, rising to take the phone with weary forbearance.

At Opryland, country music dignifies the surroundings. At the Ryman, it strives to measure up to them. The auditorium is aesthetically and acoustically ravishing and perfectly embodies the best country music's depth of spirit and insistence on getting it right. And the backstage quarters—eight cramped dressing rooms and two narrow passages—reflect the music's communal humility. Singers and players stand clustered near the stage, laughing and talking about tractors and drywall, occasionally falling silent during a superior performance. The show itself seems like a bit of unreality that happens to take place between the wings.

In this atmosphere, you can better appreciate George D. Hay's characterization of his brainchild as a "good-natured riot." Hay came to Nashville in 1925, a mild-mannered 30-year-old Hoosier newspaper-and-radio man with a crush on rural culture and a back-ward-leaning imagination. He'd been hired as program director by the National Life and Accident Insurance Company, which was curious to see whether its month-old station (whose call letters abbreviated the slogan "We Shield Millions") could be useful for selling insurance policies beyond city limits. This experimental mating of commerce and sentiment was an instant success, and by 1939 the Opry had network coverage. By then, the musicians Hay had pulled from the Smoky Mountains—hard-drinking fiddlers and genteel family bands in overalls and felt hats—were giving way to canny popularizers in Stetsons and tailored suits with earsplitting embroidery.

This is the period, roughly between Pearl Harbor and "Heart-break Hotel"—the period of Hank senior's three-minute master-pieces, of raunchy hillbilly boogie and primitive pedal-steel pathos, of live analog recording whose elegance and dimensionality have yet to be surpassed—that many of us backward-leaners especially revere. Thus, I was curious to get a better sense of modern country's infancy, when connecting with fans was not as easy as picking up a cell phone.

To hear Jean Shepard tell it, before the interstate highway system, country stardom was like an interminable game of bumper cars, with intoxicants. "Three broken noses, twice in the same place; one broken kneecap," she said, pointing at the spots. I asked Bill Anderson if he could recall his longest drive between consecutive bookings. "British Columbia to New York City," he said. "We stopped to shower in Minneapolis." The itineraries were typically merciless: 2,500 miles a week in a crowded car, much of it done while tired or drunk or both, with an obligatory stop in Nashville to make a Saturday-night appearance on the Opry.

Sex is remembered with more evident amusement. On WSM one recent afternoon, a young singer traded tales with Jeannie Seely, the Opry's equivalent of Zsa Zsa Gabor. "On my last tour, I really learned what you older artists endured," the young singer said, "strugglin' to get on my hose before the show in the front seat of my car." Seely shot back: "That's funny. I seem to recall strugglin' to get them off—after the show, in the backseat."

My dreamy affection for a remote hillbilly Eden was not shared by all its old inhabitants. They had worked too hard to get the hell out of it. The wits of these single-minded people were honed by years of poverty and savage treatment. The hillbilly singer Stonewall Jackson told me that his earliest memory was of his step-father pausing in the middle of hacking up a car with an ax to lift him off the grass and spike him into the dirt "like you do a football." Hank Snow's father not only delivered brutal beatings to Hank and his baby sister but also sentenced his children to long shoeless lock-outs in the Nova Scotia snow. According to Jean, Hank (who died in 1999) broke a long estrangement to visit the old man, then in a nursing home, to grant him forgiveness. The father leaped from his wheelchair and snarled, "I don't want your goddamned forgiveness, you son of a bitch!"

Jan Howard's history trumps even these Dickensian memories: raped at 8 by a family acquaintance; married at 15 and a mother of three at 21; beaten by her first husband, abandoned by her second and serially betrayed by her third (the towering songwriter Harlan Howard, coauthor of "I Fall to Pieces"); one son killed in Vietnam, another a suicide. The writer V. S. Naipaul happened on Jan's bleak memoir, *Sunshine and Shadow*, while he was in Nashville doing leg-work for *A Turn in the South*. "It was hard to believe that anyone could live through all that and come up singing," he observed.

Sitting with her at a Cracker Barrel restaurant one afternoon, I asked Jan—still trim and pretty, wearing a white turtleneck—if music had been a balm during her ordeals.

Taking a drag off her Marlboro, she was all cold-eyed compo-sure. "No," she said emphatically. Her music career had begun at the kitchen sink, where husband Harlan overheard her singing one afternoon. Impressed, he badgered her into a studio date, and one thing quickly led to another. Jan had no experience performing and wasn't terribly interested in it, and she soon discovered that she suf-fered stage fright as a physical sickness. But she was nothing if not practical. "I was a bad secretary, and I made more money on the road in three days than I made in a month as a secretary. Well, I couldn't turn that down."

When we reentered the haunted places, the rhythm of her speech skipped and slowed. I wanted to know what she thought could explain to Naipaul and the rest of us how she could come up singing. "My philosophy on life is a very deep faith," she said. "I don't go around preaching it, but I do have a deep faith. Everything happens for a reason, and . . . I've gone through that period—yes, I have—of hate and bitterness. And I realized it was destroying me. It doesn't hurt the one you hate, because they don't care. I just try to hold on to the good things and . . ." Her eyes watered. "And put the bad things where they belong."

*   *   *

The Opry's ascent, paralleling country's, was fast and steady into the '50s, then halted with the emergence of the ultimate hillbilly celebrity. A framed photo of the usurper, taken when he made a surprise visit one December night, hangs on the wall near the back door of the Ryman. "I was in the dressing room," recalls Carole Lee Cooper, who now leads the Opry's in-house vocal backup quartet, "when word filtered in: 'Elvis is in the building, and some woman's already passed out in the hall!' Of course, being raised in the business, I wasn't as starstruck as that."

In 1957, Cooper was a 15-year-old eyeful who sang with her parents, the great Wilma Lee and Stoney Cooper. "Elvis had come to town to deliver a Christmas gift to Colonel Tom Parker, and Gordon Stoker from the Jordanaires suggested that they visit the Opry. Elvis thought he wasn't dressed for it, so he went out and bought a tux. I remember Bill Monroe was rehearsing when Elvis walked in and introduced himself. I remember him grabbing my hand and saying, 'Let's dance,' and the next thing I knew we were dancing to 'Blue Moon of Kentucky.' He was very polite—he had a lot of manners. After we danced, he came over to my dad and shook his hand and said, 'May I take her home?'"

"What did your dad say to that?" I asked.

"He just smiled and said, 'Not this time.' And then Elvis shook his hand again."

White rock 'n' roll decimated country's audience. In the '60s, the Opry followed Music Row to a softer musical paradigm and a more middle-aged demographic. Gradually, the edema set in. By the '90s, the good-natured riot was more a members-only gerontocracy.

Pete Fisher, the show's 40-year-old general manager, was hired in 1999 to turn things around. He quickly undertook essential reforms such as modernizing the decades-old set design and supplementing the show's distribution base with Sirius satellite radio and Internet coverage (opry.com). More controversially, Fisher and Steve Buchanan, then president of the Grand Ole Opry Group, moved to reverse the Opry's artistic sclerosis by aggressively pursuing current hitmakers, booking more *O Brother*–style acoustic fare and opening the stage to cool, even cultish, talents.

The controversy centers on the performers displaced by this agenda. Take Elizabeth Cook, a beautiful blond with stunning hard-country pipes and a single dud major-label CD to her credit. Each of the 130-plus times Fisher has booked her is seen by the show's second-rank veterans as a spot taken from one of them.

The bitterest of the old-timers is Stonewall Jackson. Formerly a chart-burning hunk of hillbilly sex drive—"like Garth Brooks," he told me—Stonewall is now a stout man of 71 with a wide, creased face. I met with him twice, once in his Ryman dressing room and once at a Shoney's restaurant; both times he spoke of almost nothing but the injustices done him by Fisher and Buchanan. They were eating him alive. "Buchanan told me a lot of hurtful things, like 'Stonewall, you're too old and too country, and you don't fit in here anymore. No one wants to see or hear you anymore.'" Moments after the phone call in which these verbal blows were delivered, Stonewall said, he suffered a heart attack.

I spent an hour with Fisher and found him affably low-key and emotionally opaque. On the question of the displaced veterans, though, he was forthright: The model of the Opry as a showcase for legends, as a repository of historical value, would no longer do. He continually stressed that the show's survival was at stake. "You don't want to be the guy managing the Opry when the lights went out," he said. "So I have no shortage of motivation to do what I feel is necessary for the Opry. This is too important to screw up."

The ambitious young suit sticking it to the faithful old company man is a squalid, familiar scenario. But there is no question that

Fisher has, on balance, been a boon to the show. After twenty years, listenership is finally rising as word spreads that the Opry is again reflecting country's full spectrum and taking risks. Truly, it is the best show in forty-five years. On a typical night, you might hear Porter Wagoner into Del McCoury into Alan Jackson into Gillian Welch; and if there's the occasional bit of cloying mass-appeal garbage, well, sorry, but that's country, too. The Opry's survival strategy is, finally, simple. It is to maintain a decent balance of big sellers and deep talent: commerce plus sentiment.

All of which still doesn't explain what I was doing singing at Opryland. Maybe a good slogan for the new Opry is "Big Sellers, Deep Talent and Robbie Fulks." While I can't admire the club for inviting me in, I'll always remember my eight minutes. After Jean's introduction, I trotted to center stage and flashed a wide grin at the flock. They looked politely skeptical. The drummer counted off, and I sang for all I was worth, concentrating on pitch and trying to secure myself by ignoring the scenic details—the screen behind me, grotesquely magnifying my pixilated yawping head, and the "sacred circle" beneath me, that patch of wood from the Ryman stage consecrated by the shoes of Roy Acuff and Hank Williams.

But when I was unexpectedly called back for an encore, I lifted anchor. The band broke into Webb Pierce's 1958 shuffle, "Tupelo County Jail," and Gail and Jean joined me in three-part harmony. During the solo, I looked at Jean. She had stood here long ago, in gingham and marcelled blond hair, cleansed of her dirt-poor Okie past and looking unblinkingly ahead to all the bright wild days to come, fast-flickering and overshadowed by tawdriness and loss. Now those days were done, but the soulful music that adorned them still stood, and so did she, tiny and smiling and silver-haired, bouncing in strict tempo and clapping her left hand against the mike in her right. Our voices swelled from the monitor wedges and carried through the room, the crowd sang and clapped along, and I drifted off somewhere far beyond the human burden, dreaming about dead times. Two minutes later, I was headed back to the dressing room to get into my jeans.

HOWARD HAMPTON

Let Us Now Kill White Elephants

The Short Life, Long Shadow,
and Enduring Brilliance of Lester Bangs

Sui generis critic and painter Manny Farber stated, "I can't imagine a more perfect art form, a more perfect career than criticism." Such a declaration must sound nuts if your points of reference pattern their careerism after such fast-growing fields as termite control, postmodern interior decorating ("This edgy Radiohead end table will perfectly complement your fabulous featherette Björk recliner"), and buzzword processing (every speck of expression forced through the finer-than-thou filters of a proper Esperanto machine). On the other hand (sporting half a *Night of the Hunter* tattoo), if you think of contentiously addictive voices from the past like the now-retired Farber or the late Lester Bangs, you may recall a time when such notions were self-evident. The fearless, heady, armor-piercing vernacular of "Carbonated Dyspepsia" or "Let Us Now Praise Famous Death Dwarves," "Hard Sell Cinema," or "James Taylor Marked for Death" amounted to more than off-the-rack jobbery, gushing politesse, consumer guidance counseling. Each new piece was an adventure in thought, language, feeling, and sensibility: meeting art and life on equal terms, it was the kind of writing that opened up whole underground vistas of tough-minded possibility.

"He was a romantic in the gravest, saddest, best, and most ridiculous sense of that worn-out word." So said Nick Tosches, no lightweight as a critic himself, eulogizing his friend and comrade Lester Bangs: romantic in a punk rock/*Naked Lunch* sense of the term, the kind who thought the only love worth having was one where all parties involved saw exactly what was on the end of every fork. He was the rock critic as simultaneous true believer and loyal apostate, someone who wanted to save rock 'n' roll, Blank Generation youth, and the world at large from themselves. His rambunctiously free-associating first-person prose has spawned a host of Lesteroids over the last few decades (less recognized is the way his insistence of the intimately personal as the political helped pave the way for more assertive, irreverent female voices in rock criticism). But as with Pauline Kael, his followers have tended to latch onto the more obvious and narrow aspects of his style, centering around no-bullshit attitude and an amped-up canon embracing the guilt-free pleasures of "trash." (Brian De Palma/Iggy and the Stooges serving as the standard-bearing yardsticks of their respective aesthetics, but instead of shaking up well-bred folks from within the venerable confines of *The New Yorker*, Bangs found his calling as writer and editor for *Creem* magazine—under his aegis, a cross between *Hit Parader*, *The National Lampoon*, and *The Partisan Review* if Susie Sontag had only been a glue-sniffing headbanger.)

Since his death in 1982 at age thirty-three, his notoriety and stature have gradually outgrown the strict insider status of rock cultdom: The posthumous 1987 collection *Psychotic Reactions and Carburetor Dung* (Knopf), edited by Greil Marcus, has become a modern touchstone that ranks with *I Lost It At the Movies*, *Negative Space*, *Mystery Train*, and *Studies in Classic American Literature*. Think of it as "Studies in Beautifully Unreasonable Noise," for "classic" is too stately a word for its Garageland environs and outlying districts, not merely launching pads for the best pure rock criticism as pure rock 'n' roll. That this hardy truism has become the bedrock cliché in the Legend of Lester—and no less accurate for it—has been helpfully nudged along by Jim DeRogatis's reverent but unflinchingly detailed keeper-of-the-flame Bangs biography *Let It Blurt* (2000) and in particular by Philip Seymour Hoffman's deeply affectionate portrayal of Bangs in Cameron Crowe's rapt valentine to early seventies rock, *Almost Famous*. The mystique of his writing and persona hasn't worn thin with the passing of time; that tightrope sense of writing without a safety net retains its capacity to move and amaze. Resolutely human-scale yet larger-than-life, Bangs's work had a warts-über-alles, kitchen-sink candor that made every tumultuous wrestling match with the high and low mucky-mucks of rock (right along with his own tag team of highly personalized demons) into a form of screwball heroism. A Shadows-of-Knight-errant Quixote and Sancho Panza rolled into one logorrheic typewriter junkie, he tilted at white elephants, sacred cows, boredom, and rampant mediocrity with a ravenous mixture of perception and bloodshot glee.

The publication of *Mainlines, Blood Feasts, and Bad Taste: A Lester Bangs Reader* (Anchor) finally provides the long overdue follow-up to *Psychotic Reactions*. The book positions itself as a logical extension of its predecessor, but as the slightly self-conscious title indicates, there's also a wish to play to the red-meat, Wild Man aspects of the Bangs myth-cum-brand-name. (Hey, Kids! It's the Amazing New Pocket Lester! Now with Extra Nova-Expressionism & Twice the Gonzo Scrubbing Bubbles of Hunter S. Thompson!) Given its bitter ruminations on the mortality of music as well as all things human, *Death May Be Your Santa Claus* might have been a better title, one belonging to a magnificent old Mott the Hoople rant (prevailing inarguable sentiment: "You're all too fuckin' slow") which Lester took for the headline of his exclusive 1976 interview with a very late Jimi Hendrix. ("Because one thing I learned while killing myself," Jimi ruminates from beyond the grave, "was that a hell of a lot of that shit was just sound and fury kicked up to disguise the fact that we were losing our emotions, or at least the ability to convey them.")

Mainlines features a good deal of corrosive material that can stand with the best of the earlier collection, along with a wider, more uneven spectrum of workaday pieces ranging from inspired to autopilot—entertaining to a few genuflecting, all-too-human duds. But even his much too solemn and dewy-eyed review of Patti Smith's *Horses* is a useful object lesson, a testament to the unavoidable occupational hazards of the profession: the awful, honest temptations of

hyperbole and needful thinking, especially in barren times like the
mid-seventies (or now), though many have made whole highly
respected careers out of far more egregious, uninspired treacle.
Compare this Joan of Art treatment to his "Jim Morrison: Bozo
Dionysus a Decade Later" about the great Doors Revival: It's not
that he was initially off the mark about Smith's soft parade of pent-
up ambitions and influences, only that he glossed over the half-
cocked, loony-tune tendencies which made Miss Smith as much the
provocateur-clown-headcase second cousin to Valerie Solanas as
noble heiress to Rimbaud or the Ronettes. (Of course, she was also a
friend he happened to have a hopeless crush on, but even factoring
that in this seems more a case of giving in to the savior fantasy: She
was a better conceptual fit for him than Bruce Springsteen, the
other big, street-angelic candidate for Rock Messiah circa 1975.)
Taken all in all, though some of editor John Morthland's choices
will doubtless be "heatedly debated," by encompassing the respective Babylons of Bob Marley and David Johansen, impassioned tes-
timonials on behalf of Black Sabbath ("Bring Your Mother to the
Gas Chamber!") and the Weimar-era Comedian Harmonists (take
the A train!), the undersea world of Eno and *The Marble Index* of
Nico, some inspired Dylan and Beatles debunking, plus naturally
more of his running battle with spiritual godfather Lou Reed, no
Bangs fan is going to feel cheated by *Mainlines.*

As the kind of incendiary book that could make a person want to
become a critic, or remind one why he became a critic in the first
place, it is also meant to separate the initiated from disinterested
observers and intellectual dilettantes. Like *Psychotic Reactions,* and in
the great cultural tradition of "Sister Ray," these *Mainlines* are dates
drawn in the sand: emphatically not nice little slices of music appreciation nor Dean's List honors seminaries nor funhouse slumming
for squeamish gentlefolk who require a formal introduction to *Raw
Power* ("I say, Jeeves, these Iggy and the Stooges characters really
are dashed clever fellows." "Indeed, sir?" "Just listen to this corker:
'I am the world's forgotten boy/The one who's searchin' to destroy.'"
"If you say so, sir.") Bangs practiced criticism as a hilarious form of
guerrilla class warfare, the revenge of the starving underclass (as
much in existential as economic terms) against the proudly oblivious
Overclass, the bourgeois-boho-yoyos, the Middle-C brows furrowed

in rigid anal-retentive concentration, and indeed the High ideals of Class itself, understood as a plumy nexus of ego-massaging rational-izations, humorless self-importance, affluent pretensions, good table manners, solid musicianship, starched professionalism, and an insa-tiable appetite for respectability at all costs. Discomfiting the com-fortable and afflicting the affected was what he lived for—"you cannot kick intentional cripples awake," but gee, Officer Krupke, it sure is fun to try anyway—but there was something more at stake than just being a gadfly freelancing boils or a chaotic court-jesting nuisance. (Dear me, what'll that darn Lester say next?!) The guiding suspicion behind his work was that the language of assurance and reassurance most art is crouched in was a way of insulating audi-ences from their own lives: By substituting overdetermined pseudo-emotions and numb freeze-dried ideas for precarious human exchange, the next thing you knew you'd wind up in a Keir Dullea pod, slippery-sloping into Kubrick's remake of *The Incredibly Strange Creatures Who Stopped Living and Became Mixed-Up Zombies*, with music by Kraftwerk and "emetic narcissism" by Stevie of Bel Air (a manicure worse than the disease). Hence Lester Bangs's writing contains more scar tissue and stealth vulnerability per square inch than anything this side of Mo Tucker singing "After Hours" to fin-ish the Velvet Underground's third LP: "Oh, but people look well in the dark."

Somewhere over the slough of despond, *Mainlines, Blood Feasts, and Bad Taste* includes his debut review for *Rolling Stone* in 1969, dis-missing the MC5's *Kick Out the Jams* (he later famously reversed himself on the album, but in Bangs such diametrical opinions weren't self-canceling: They were Polaroids of the running love-hate argument with music and life that constantly went on inside his head) and the Canned Heat review that got him bounced from its yellowed pages. Fittingly, too, there's the last piece published in his lifetime, "If Oi Were a Carpenter," sizing up minuscule punk off-shoots. The book starts with a few instructive chunks of wrought-up teenage angst, rites-of-passage pieces drawn from his unpublished autobiographical tome "Drug Punk": "A Quick Trip Through My Adolescence" et al. lay out a picture of early influences, tantrums, and formative traumas. In "Two Assassinations," William Burroughs looms larger than any of the other Beats as an influence (Kerouac would show up in his more fulsome and tender paeans). Young Lester incorporates a vintage naked lunchbox slogan—"Fuck 'em all, squares on both sides, I am the only complete man in the industry"—to serve as a nineteen-year-old hipster's holy grail, but the façade is already being undercut by his own grievous sense of estrangement, isolation, and doubt. When the kid from El Cajon gets cozy with the San Diego Hell's Angels and winds up as a passive, guilt-stricken bystander to one of their come-one-come-all rapes, the horror kind of takes the bloom off the whole outlaw-rebel pose for Lester. Hipster cool held an immense attraction for him, but his determination to break through that attitude of reptilian detachment and reach for some kind of human connection no matter what is what would ultimately make him an indelible writer.

There's also a tour through what *Mainlines* designates as the "Pantheon" (an I. M. Pious wax museum perhaps better left to Madams Sarris and Christgau) which includes four pieces on the Rolling Stones (about two and a half too many—dutifully forcing himself to muster a response to the supremely indifferent likes of *Black and Blue*) and a couple nice exercises in ambivalence devoted to Miles Davis's queasy-listening electric period ("Kind of Grim" and "Music for the Living Dead," funk in both senses of the word). A long profile of Captain Beefheart does veer off into awestruck, witch-doctor hagiography, but a good Kierkegaard-laced review of Public Image Ltd. (belying Bangs's anti-intellectual rep) counteracts such tendencies. There's achingly fervent, can-I-get-a-drowning-witness testimony on behalf of Nico's *The Marble Index*, as well as "Deaf Mute in a Telephone Booth" on Uncle Louie entering his Scrooge McFucked decline, and an epic, positively wistful evocation of Black Sabbath. Encountering Ozzy back in 1972, when *The Osbournes* was not even a gleam in the all-seeing TV Eye, the piece is at once a completely sincere, mostly convincing attempt to find the humanist impulses secreted in "War Pigs" and "Children of the Grave," and a disarming visit with a Prince of Darkness who already is halfway to his shrewdly befuddled husband-and-father persona, right down to the wholesome sitcom wackiness when Ozzy sans Harriet attempts to avoid the breathy clutches of a chick who calls herself the Blow Job Queen.

Here you catch a glimpse of the Lester Bangs who befriended a barely teenage Cameron Crowe and offered cranky encouragement to Crowe's alter ego in *Almost Famous:* While he positioned himself as the enemy of the whole scene-making "I am a Golden God" rockstar trip, Bangs had his own streak of wayward idealism and sentimental tenderness. It was more likely to express itself in a communing sing-along to "Ballerina" or "Beside You" rather than "Tiny Dancer," but so much of the rage and despair in his work came from a sense of possibilities betrayed, hope deferred or destroyed, good things turned into breathtaking travesties of themselves. (Crowe's adolescent chivalry towards beatific distressed damsels reflects an aspect of the romantic in Bangs as well.) It's not hard to imagine an alternate version of *Almost Famous* where Lester is the star, emerging from a far grungier, more stifling background, with a Jehovah's Witness mother and no prospects of an interesting, bearable life at all—his autobiography written in the albums he discovered and the books he found, which were signs not only of another world but another self he would construct from the traces they left. Music—and writing—was his deliverance, hence the desert island album essay included in *Psychotic Reactions* about Van Morrison's *Astral Weeks*:

It was particularly important to me because the fall of 1968 was such a terrible time. I was a physical and mental wreck, nerves shredded and ghosts and spiders looming and squatting across the mind. My social contacts had dwindled almost to none; the presence of other people made me nervous and paranoid. I spent endless days and nights sunk in an armchair in my bedroom, reading magazines, watching TV, listening to records, staring into space. I had no idea how to improve the situation, and probably wouldn't have done anything about it if I had.

The big epiphany voice-over would go something like this:

But in the condition I was in, it assumed at the time the quality of a beacon, a light on the far shores of the murk; what's more, it was proof that there was something left to express artistically besides nihilism and destruction. (My other big record of the day was *White*

Light/White Heat.) It sounded like the man who made *Astral Weeks* was
in terrible pain, pain most of Van Morrison's previous albums had
only suggested; but like the later albums by the Velvet Underground,
there was a redemptive element in the blackness, ultimate compassion for the suffering of others, and a swath of pure beauty and mystical awe that cut right through the heart of the work.

There was always that alternating current in him which oscillated
between destructive-nihilist character traits and the deep-seated
beauty-awe component, a tension that was easier and more salutary
to manage in writing than a life of self-mocking, self-medicating
excess. *Lester the Movie: Almost Bilious* would therefore traverse cir-
cumscribed beginnings handing out *The Watchtower* in El Cajon, his
humble start sending record reviews to *Rolling Stone (The Watchtower* redux), the glory days in Detroit as the conscience and soul of
Creem, his move to New York where he submerged himself in
CBGBs' burgeoning lemming-demimonde (Richard Hell and the
Voidoids more or less serving as his Stillwater) and freelanced for
the *Village Voice.* (Though in order to survive, he wrote for anyone
who'd take his byline: *Stereo Review, Musician, Rolling Stone* once
again, *New Wave, New York Rocker, Music and Sound Output, Con-
tempo Culture, Back Door Man*—publish or perish wasn't an idle
threat, but an imperative on several distinct levels.) The movie
would brim with obligatory romance and heartbreak up the wazoo
(cf. *Psychotic Reaction*'s love-as-absurdity classic "New Year's Eve"),
but Lester's most lasting lifelong relation outside of music was with
masturbation, so there'd have to be one of those gauzy memory
montages of the way we wanked: from early boyhood stirrings
before the telephone-book-sized Sears catalogue (ladies' undergar-
ments section) on to Hef's plasticine Playmates to Runways album
covers to the pastoral nostalgia of *Celebrity Skin.* But besides sentimental journeys, you'd get action 'n' adventure (remember "Jethro
Tull in Vietnam"?—our correspondent goes upriver to get the
skinny on a Kurtzian pied piper), rockin' intrigue (remember
"Screwing the System with Dick Clark"?—I see Michael Douglas
doing a perfect cameo as Mr. American Bandstand), and even
Lester's ingratiatingly mortifying attempt to become a singer him-

self (Andy Kaufman and the Blues Brothers had nothing on our boy).

Only the last reel would have to be rewritten: overdosing on Darvon after getting relatively straight and sober is by far the worst cliché he ever perpetrated and his one unforgivably corny stunt, going out in what he would have surely mocked as a shamelessly cheap career move. (The old die-and-become-immortal routine— the stalest joke in the book.) Maybe a *Twilight Zone* finish would be more in order: since Bangs has already entered cinema's nether realm of cultural fantasy alongside such luminaries as Sid & Nancy, Valerie & Andy, Charles Bukowski, *Naked Lunch's* William Lee, Jim Morrison, Hunter S. Thompson, Kaufman, John Belushi, and *24 Hour Party People's* Tony Wilson and Ian Curtis, why not convene a roundtable of the living and the dead, a meeting of the minds and the mindless. Have P. S. Hoffman's Lester and Lili Taylor's Val and the Thompson twins (Bill Murray and Johnny Depp) and the rest of 'em hash out the liberties taken by film biographies, the consolations of philosophy as spelled out in the Sex Pistols's version of "No Fun," the perils and ecstasies of nostalgia, and the nigh-unto-insurmountable task of not turning into the very thing you despised, especially once you've been projected onto the silver screen as some kind of suitably iconic/ridiculous figure. One minute you're the Elephant Man on stampede ("I am not an animal!") and the next you're another shiny white death-mask on display in a showroom window: smile, says the plastercaster, you're on *Candid Camera!* But Lester is unfazed: he goes into bemused Rod Serling mode and addresses the camera as a battle-of-the-stars melee erupts behind him (Andy has Val in a headlock, Bukowski's holding a pillow over Morrison's big mouth) and calmly intones, "Is there a happy ending? I don't think so." Roll credits as the mandolins play and Mott the Hoople's "I Wish I Was Your Mother" serenades you out of the theater humming a pretty epitaph.

No matter how you look at it, with all the exuberance and crazed comic poetry and hot/cold running insight of *Psychotic Reactions* and now *Mainlines*, there's an aura of sadness beyond simple untimely loss (as a wiseacre said to me, "Whaddayouwannaliveforever?"): the unremitting sense beneath all that beautifully overwrought manic desperation of how fragile and futile the constructs underpinning art and life really are, a rising awareness of the steep toll of all that persistent grappling with the inadmissible. No surprise then that Lester Bangs wrote some of the best obits in the business, his own dress rehearsals: for Elvis (whom he didn't much care for, and wrote all the more movingly about what that disconnection meant), Peter Laughner (a musician and writer who if he hadn't self-immolated trying to live out a fantasy camp version of alcoholic-druggie nihilist stupor might have grown up to surpass either Lou Reed or Bangs himself), "Bye, Bye, Sidney, Be Good" (for punk rock and all its slam-bam illusions, his own most of all). In addition, he invented the preventative obituary in his Lou Reed opuses and "Richard Hell: Death Means Never Having to Say You're Incomplete," bait-and-switch tracts which attempted to lure/jolt their subjects out of downward-spiraling self-hate with a carrot of praise or a cattle prod to their numb genitalia. (His answer to the Clash's "Ya need a little dose of electrical shockers," I expect.)

And then there were those reconnaissance flights that were hard to tell from kamikaze missions, diving into a record as he does on *Main-lines*'s "Your Shadow Is Scared of You: An Attempt Not to Be Fright-ened by Nico." Which is about trying to get past all the baggage of Pavlovian-dinnerbell art, chic dehumanization, over-weening signifi-cance, cheap thrills, working instead towards a definition of art as something as personal as the most intimate, wrenching flesh and blood encounter. Clearing away the distractions of secondhand fashion and vicarious kicks, he then elicits a long string of Joycean dictation from an old love over the phone, a séance which ends with the woman comparing doomstruck chanteuse Nico to "Beckett's play *Breath*, she's trying to find the last breath so she can negate breath, love, anything. A soft look would kill her." Then he hunkers down with the vast hosts of the dead he hears on the album:

> She's quite a rock critic, that old girlfriend of mine—sometimes she scares me even more than Nico. But then, I'm scared of everybody— I'm scared of *you*. My girlfriend's eloquence was one reason I loved her almost from first sight, but not why I had to get halfway around the geographical world to write a song that said how much I loved her. It was because of something obviously awry in me, perhaps healing, at

least now confronting itself, which is one way to perhaps not rot.
There's a ghost born every second, and if you let the ghosts take your
guts by sheer force of numbers you haven't got a chance though
probably no one has the right to judge you either. (Besides which, the
ghosts are probably as scared of you as you are of them.)

Now most critics, whether good, bad, or humdrum, are usually
doing their level best to suppress or deny such feelings, gloss over
the awkwardness, the groping, the fear which John Cale may have
said was a man's best friend but you wouldn't ever know it from
them. After all, that terror is weakness which in turn is a form of
need which is just a shade removed from psychic disintegration and
nervous breakdown—one slip on the stepping razor's edge there and
it's back to the bedroom armchair, counting the spiders and staring
into space forever, or worse. The difference between what Bangs is
doing here and an equally personal (albeit in a more baroquely literary manner) writer Camden Joy is doing in his latest collection *Lost
Joy* (TNI) comes down to risk. Not formal risk, idiosyncratic experimentation in structure and fantasy and syntax, which Joy's work has
in rhetorical abundance after a manner that suggests Fernando Pes-
soa's *Book of Disquiet* remodeled as rock fan's mash notes to his own
delicious sensibility. Bangs's work feels at risk in the same way the
work it lauds is—in danger of coming apart at the seams, devouring
its author and sucking its audience into the pit of disgust or hopelessness or fear with it. Joy's approach has a disembodied, art-project
halo: as though instead of listening to "The Greatest Record Album
Singer Ever" (Al Green) or "The Greatest Record Album Ever
Told" (Frank Black's *Teenager of the Year*) or "Greatest Record
Album Band That Ever Was" (Creedence Clearwater Revival), you
visited a gallery where they had been turned into ironic-obsessive-
compulsive installations. Everything (performer, music, album
jacket) becomes a pretext, each moved behind several layers of brilliant distancing devices; you marvel at the intricacy and thoroughness of every conceit, but they remain conceits, art for artifice's sake.
Bangs was convinced the only worthwhile purpose of music and
criticism was to break through that artifice. If it didn't implicate
you, as coconspirator or shamed silent partner, then it wasn't doing
its job: It was just providing a glass-bottom service to gawk at the

colorful creatures of the deep from a nice dry vantage point. The world as he saw it wasn't so much divided between the hip and the square ("Fuck 'em all!") or even the haves against the have-nots so much as between those who had to live in whatever drowned world they'd been consigned to or made for themselves (if it was even possible to tell the difference) and the tourists who watched the show and then put on their warm coats and went back home.

In *Mainlines*, there's a terrific 1976 piece called "Innocents in Babylon," on the lures and traps of such tourism, going to Jamaica in search of Natty Dread while waiting for Bob Marley's Godot at the Sheraton hotel. (The Clash could have cribbed notes for "Safe European Home" from it.) There's a glimmer of utopia that looks a little like prophecy:

> All the singles have an instrumental version on the B side, so the deejays can flip them over and improvise their own spaced-out harangues over the rhythm tracks. Since Jamaican radio plays so little reggae, most of the deejays come off the streets, where until recently you could find, periodically, roots discos set up. Out of these emerged deejay-stars like Big Youth and I-Roy, and along with producers like Lee Perry and Augustus "King Tubby" Pablo they have pioneered a fascinating technological folk art called dub. An album by I-Roy can thank six different producers on the back "for the use of their rhythms." Don't ask me where the publishing rights go. Don't ask anybody, in fact. And, don't ask how musicians might feel who play on one session for a flat rate, only to find it turn up on one or more other hit records. The key with dub is spontaneity, the enormous creative sculpting and grafting of whole new counterpoints on records already in existence. And this sense of the guy who plays the record as performer extends down into the record shops, where the clerks shift speakers, tracks, and volume levels with deft magicianly fingers as part of a highly intricate dance, creating sonic riot in the store and new productions in their minds: *I control the dials.*

But the reality beneath the pipe dream turned out to be predictably messier: exploitation, greed, racism, violence, lunacy, enough delusion to go around for everyone involved, the writing on the wall no one wanted to read.

The era Lester Bangs belonged to was unlike the present one in a key respect: A lot of people hadn't learned the rules of the game yet. All garage bands like the Count Five and the Troggs and uncounted no-hit wonders were too dumb to know any better: They didn't have a dainty neo-primitive paint-by-numbers instruction manual to work from. Punk was, briefly, a smarter free-for-all: anyone could join, and nobody had the slightest clue where it was going, oblivion or taking over the world as equally plausible consummations devoutly and simultaneously being wished. Then people internalized the rules or were assimilated by them—a process that was well underway before Bangs's death and so turns the later pieces in *Mainlines* into the sound of a man tired of losing the good fight, and certain that the worst was yet on its way. The book is Lester's Last Stand against the march of the lumbering artistic behemoths, Old Home Week back in the human wilderness: or as the girl on the phone once asked in the dead of night, "What good is music if it doesn't destroy you?"

JESSICA HOPPER

Emo

Where the Girls Aren't

A few months back, I was at a Strike Anywhere show. The band launched into "Refusal", a song offering solidarity with the feminist movement and bearing witness to the inherent struggle in women's lives. It is not a song of protection; there is no romantic undertow. It's a song about all people being equally important. Everyone was dancing, fanboys and girls at the lip of the stage screaming along—like so many shows at the Fireside. By the first chorus of the song, I was in tears. I have often been so moved to shed small wet tears at Strike shows, but this time was for AN entirely different reason—A mournful new awareness: *I am here, at the Fireside Bowl probably 75 times a year for the last five years. The numbers of times I have genuinely felt, or even sensed my reality or the reality of the women I know portrayed in a song sung by a male-fronted band—that number was at zero and holding.* The ratio of songs/shows/expressed sentiment-to-affirmation of feminist struggle/girldom is staggering. This song was the first.

No wonder most of my girlfriends and I have been growing increasingly alienated and distanced from our varying scenes, or have begun taking shelter from emo's pervasive stronghold in the cave-like recesses of electronic, DJ, or experimental music. No wonder girls I know are feeling dismissive and faithless towards music. No wonder I feel much more internal allegiance to MOP songs, as their tales of hood drama and jewelry theft FEELS far less offensive than yet another song from yet another all dude band giving us the 411 on his personal romantic holocaust. Because in 2003, as it stands, I simply cannot conjure the effort it takes to give a flying fuck about bands of boys yoked to their own wounding AKA the genre/plague that we know as E-M-O. Songs and scenes populated with myopic worldviews that do not extend beyond their velvet-lined rebel-trauma, their bodies, or their vans. Meanwhile, we're left wondering *how did we get here?*

As hardcore and political punk's charged sentiments became more cliché towards the end of the '80s—as we all soon settled in to the armchair comfort of the Clinton era—punk began stripping off its tuff skin and getting down to its squishy pulp heart. Forget bombs and the real impact of trickle down economics, it's all about elusive kisses and tender-yet-undeniably-masculine emotional outbursts. Mixtapes across America became soiled with the torrential anthems of hopeful boy hearts masted to sleeves, pillows soaked in tears, and relational eulogies. Romance of the self was on.

I think somewhere right around the release of the last Braid record is where we lost the map. Up until then, things seemed reasonable, encouraging, exciting—thus far we were sold on the vulnerability, there was something revivifying in the earnestness. New bands cast their entire micro-careers from bands we all liked: Jawbox, Jawbreaker, Sunny Day Real Estate, etc. In those bands, there were songs about women, but they were girls with names, with details to their lives, girls who weren't exclusively defined by their absence or lensed through romantic-spectre. Jawbox's most popular song, "Savory," was about recognizing male normative privilege, about the weight of sexualization on a woman ("see you feign surprise/that I'm all eyes"). In Jawbreaker songs women had leverage, had life, had animus and agency to them. Sometimes they were friends, or a sister, not always *girl to be bedded or pursued or dumped by.* They were accurate, and touched by reality.

And then something broke—And it wasn't Bob Nanna's or Mr. Dashboard's sensitive hearts. Records by a legion of done-wrong boys lined the record store shelves. Every record was a concept album about a breakup, damning the girl on the other side. Emo's contentious monologue—it's balled fist Peter Pan mash-note dilemmas—it's album length letters from pussy-jail—it's cathedral building

in ode to man-pain and Robert-Bly-isms—it's woman-induced misery has gone from being *descriptive* to being *prescriptive*. Emo was
just another forum where women were locked in a stasis outside
observation, observing ourselves through the eyes of others. The
prevalence of these bands, the omnipresence of emo's sweeping
sound and it's growing stronghold in the media and on the Billboard
chart *codified* emo as A SOUND, where previously there had been
diversity.

Girls in emo songs today do not have names. We are not identified. Our lives, our struggles, our day-to-day-to-day do not exist, we
do not get colored in. We span from coquettish to damned and back
again. We leave bruises on boy-hearts, but make no other mark.
Our existences, our actions are portrayed SOLELY through the
detailing of neurotic self-entanglements of the boy singer—our
region of personal power, simply, is our breadth of impact on his
romantic life. We are on a short leash in a filthy yard—we are mysteries to be unlocked, bodies to be groped, minimum wage earners
of fealty, harvesters of sorrow, repositories for scorn. Vessels
redeemed in the light of boy-love. On a pedestal, on our backs.
Muses at best. Cum rags or invisible at worst. Check out our pictures on the covers of records—we are sad-eyed and winsome and
well cleaved—Thank you Hod Rod Circuit, the Crush, Cursive,
Something Corporate—the fantasy girl you could take home and
comfort.

It is a genre made by and for adolescent and post-adolescent
boys, who make evident, in their lyrics and dominant aesthetic, that
their knowledge of actual living, breathing women is tiny enough to
fit in a shoebox. Emo's characteristic sensitive front is limited to
self-sensitivity, it runs in a fanciful maze of reflexive self-pity, rife
with a vulnerability that is infinitely self-serving. It is a high stakes
game of control—of "winning" or "losing" possession of the girl
(see Dashboard Confessional, Brand New, New Found Glory, and
Glassjaw albums for prime examples). Yet, in the vulnerability there
is no empathy, no peerage or parallelism. Emo's yearning is not to
identify with, or understand, but rather to enforce sexual hierarchy
and omit women's power via romanticide.

As Andy Greenwald notes in his forthcoming book about emo
culture *Nothing Feels Good: PUNK ROCK, TEENAGERS, AND*

EMO, lyrically, emo singers "revel in their misery and suffering to an almost ecstatic degree, but with a limited use of subtlety and language. It tends to come off like Rimbaud relocated to the Food Court." Women in emo songs are denied the dignity of humanization through both the language and narratives, we are omnipresent, but our only consequence is in romantic setting; denying any possibility or hope for outside the margins, where they express a free sexual, creative, or political will.

*   *   *

On a dance floor in Seattle, a boy I know decides to plumb the topic,
"I heard you're writing a column about how emo is sexist."
"I am."
"What do you mean 'emo is sexist'? Emo songs are no different than all of rock history, than Rolling Stones or Led Zeppelin."
"I know—I'd rather not get into it right now."
"How are songs about breaking up sexist though? Everyone breaks up. If you have a problem with emo, you have a problem with all of rock history!"
"I know. I do."
And to paraphrase words of Nixon sidekick H. R. Haldeman, "History is wack."
There must be some discussion, at least for context, about the well-worn narrative of *the travails of the boy rebel's broken heart* as exemplified in the last 50 years of blues-based music. There must be some base acknowledgment that in almost every band since the beginning of time, most songs are about loving and losing women. Granted, broken hearts are a part of human existence. Songs about women, but not written by women, practically define rock 'n' roll. And as a woman, as a music critic, as someone who lives and dies for music, there is a rift within, a struggle of how much deference you will allow, and how much you will ignore *because you like the music.*
Can you ignore the lyrical content of the Stones "Under my Thumb" because you like the song? Are you willing to? How much attention can you sacrifice to the cock-prance of Led Zeppelin or cheesy humpa-humpa metaphors of AC/DC or the heaping pile of dead or brutalized women that amasses in Big Black's discography?

Is emo exceptional in the scope of the rock canon in terms of treatment of women or in its continual rubbing salute to its own trouble-
boy cliché image? Is there anything that separates Dashboard
Confessional's condemnation of his bedhopping betrayer and makes
it any more damning than any woman/mother/whore/ex-girlfriend
showing up in songs of Jane's Addiction, Nick Cave, the Animals, or
Justin Timberlake? Can you compartmentalize and not judge the
woe towards women readily exemplified in most of the recorded
catalog of Zeppelin because the first eight bars of "Communication
Breakdown" is, as the parlance goes, total fucking godhead? Where
do you split? Do you bother to even care, because if yr going to try
and kick against it, you, as my dancing friend says "have a problem
with all of rock history," and because who, other than a petty, too
serious bitch dismisses Zeppelin?! Do you accept the circumstances
and phallocentricites of the last 50+ years of music, as it exists in
popular culture and in your "punk rock community" as simply *how it
is*?

Who do you excuse and why? Do you check your personality and
your politics at the door and just dance or just rock or just let side A
spin out? Can you ignore the marginalization of lady-lives that line
your record shelves, and give yrself where you can to where you
identify, bridging the sometimes massive gulf, because it's either
that or purge yr collection of everything but wordless free jazz/Ger-
man micro house 12"s and/or Mr. Lady Records releases.

It is almost too big of a question to ask. I start to ask this of
myself, to really start investigating, and stop, realizing full well that
if I get an answer I may just have to retire to an adobe hut on some
Italian mountainside and not take any visitors for a long time. Or
turn into the rock critical Andrea Dworkin, and report with ruthless
resignation that all male-manufactured music is in service of the
continual oppression and domination of women. Sometimes I feel
like every rock song I hear is a sexualized sucker punch towards us.
And I feel like no one takes the breadth of that impact seriously, or
even notices it most days.

My deepest concerns about the punishing effects of the emo-
tidal-wave is not so much for myself or for my immediate-peer lady
friends who can fend and snarl from the safety of our personal-
political platforms and deep crated record collections, but rather,

for the girls I see crowding front and center for the eem shows. The ones who are young, for whom this is likely their inaugural intro- duction to the underground, whose gateway may have been through Weezer or the Vagrant America tour or maybe Dashboard Confes- sional's *Unplugged* sesh on the MTV. The ones who are seeking music out, who are wanting to stake some claim to punk rock, or an underground avenue, for a way out, a way under, to sate the seem- ingly unquenchable, nameless need—the same need I know I came to punk rock with. It becomes a very particular concern because Emo *is the province of the young*, their foundation is fresh-laid, my concern is for people who have no other previous acquaintance with the underground aside from the shadowy doom and octave chords that the Vagrant Records roster hath wrought.

When I was that age, I too had a rabid hunger for a music that spoke a language I was just starting to decipher, music that affirmed my faith, my ninth grade fuck you values, and encouraged me to not allow my budding feminist ways to be bludgeoned by all the soul crushing weight of mainstream culture—I was lucky I was met at the door with things like the Bikini Kill demo, or Fugazi or the first Kill Rock Stars comp, or Babes in Toyland shows. I was met with polemics and respectful address. I was met with girl heroes in guitar squall, kicking out the jams under the stage lights. I was being hur- tled towards deeper rewards, records and bands were triggering ideas and wrenching open doors of interminable hope and inspira- tion. I acknowledge the importance of all of that because I know I would not be who I am now, doing what I do, 12 years down the line, if I had not had gotten those fundamentals, been presented with those ideas about what music, or moreover, what life can be about.

And so I watch these girls at emo shows more than I ever do the band. I watch them sing along, see what parts they freak out over. I wonder if this does it for them, if seeing these bands, these dudes on stage resonates and inspires them to want to pick up a guitar or drum sticks. Or if they just see this as something dudes do, because there are no girls, there is no *them* up there. I wonder if they are being thwarted by the FACT that there is no presentation of girls as participants, but rather, *only as consumers*—or if we reference the songs directly—*the consumed*. I wonder if this is where music will begin and end for them. If they can be radicalized in spite of this. If being denied keys to the clubhouse or airtime will spur them into action.

I know that, for me, as an auto-didactic teenaged bitch, who thought her every idea was a good idea worthy of expression and audience, it did not truly occur to me to start a band until I saw other women playing music (Babes in Toyland, early 1990). Up until then—seeing Bloodline chugga-chugga it up 97 times on local hardcore bills had not done it for me. Dinosaur Jr's hairwaving and soloing had not done it for me. The dozens of bands, bands whose records I knew all the words to, who were comprised of 25–30 year old dudes, with nothing much to say, did not feel like punk rock with its arms open wide to me. It took seeing Bikini Kill in an illegal basement venue to truly throw the lights, to show me that there was more than one place, one role, for women to occupy, and that our participation was important and vital—It was YOU MATTER writ large.

I don't want these front row girls to miss that. I don't want girls leaving clubs denied of encouragement and potential, quietly vexed and clad in the burka of emo's male dominance. Because as fucking lame as punk rock can be, as hollow as all of our self-serving claims ring—that punk rock's culture is something TRULY DIFFERENT (sic) than median society—at its gnarled foundations still exist the possibilities for connection, for exposure to radical notions, for punk rock to match up to the elaborate idea of what many kids dream, or hope for it to mean—for all of that to absolutely and totally exist—I believe—much of that hinges on the continual presence of radicalized women within the leagues, and those women being encouraged, given reasons to stay, to want to belong—rather than punished or diminished by the music which glues the various fractious communities together.

Us girls deserve more than one song. We deserve more than one pledge of solidarity. We deserve better songs than any boy will ever write about us.

T. R. HUMMER

The Mechanical Muse

A Poet Discusses His Inspiration

The scene is a run-down band room in a run-down school in east central Mississippi; the year is 1959. We are gathered here, we offspring and our parents, to honor the musical "aptitude" of the children—demonstrated by our having mastered, the previous year, a cheap plastic recorder known as the Flutophone. This instrument is capable of producing little more than a thin whistle, which, when multiplied in the inept hands of forty or so eight-year-olds, becomes a kind of teakettle of horror. But somehow we are chosen, and here we are, confronted by a roomful of brand new band instruments lying in state in their cases: clarinets, trombones, trumpets, flutes, French horns, drums, and the one I am about to choose: the saxophone.

Do not underestimate my ignorance at the age of nine. I am busy growing up on a farm in that distant white-boy Jim Crow Mississippi, a place where art generally and music particularly are not much noticed, no matter how many musicians have been engendered there. Music arrives on the radio, of course, and tinkles along in the background of our doings; it lives, too, in church. Guitars, pianos, pump organs, drums—these instruments are familiar, both to the eye and to the ear. But saxophones? At the age of nine, had I ever even *heard* one? Surely I must have registered some of those fat and bluesy rides from old late-night radio rock 'n' rollers, but I have never given it any thought. My exposure to the saxophone as a *voice* is certainly minimal.

But standing there in the crowded band room I fall suddenly and deeply in love with the saxophone as a *thing*.

It lies there in its case, a gold and nickel glitter. It *smells* wonderful—new instruments, or more likely their cases, have a terrific aroma, like new cats. I walk around the room with my parents in an obligatory kind of way: There the other instruments lie, in *their* cases, all a gold and nickel glitter. But it is the saxophone I want, a student model Conn alto, the Conn Director, its case dark blue with a powder-blue interior. I have never given a moment's thought to saxophones, but I take one look at it and the other instruments vanish.

Why the saxophone? Honestly, I have no idea. Why do you love your lover? What lightning strikes? Somehow, however dimly, I know that this is the instrument, and that this knowledge and this feeling are important.

The fact is, the instrument—the object, the thing—casts a kind of spell on me. In the months that follow, I receive only the barest instruction; our benighted little school has only one overworked band director for everyone, grades first through twelfth. But I want this, and I work at it. My fascination cannot be with the music I want to play, because I do not know what that should be. I am attending to, and being taught by, the instrument itself. It is years before I begin to study *music* with any real attention, and when I do, it is only because my horn finally insisted on it. It took years for me to learn to generalize about my obsession, and I began to do so only when my band director advised me to trade the Conn for a better one—then I saw that it was not *that* saxophone but *all* saxophones I loved. Music as such, like agape, waited at a distance with its face half turned away.

If this behavior sounds obsessive-compulsive or fetishistic, so perhaps are all children, so certainly are all artists. Because my saxophone is gold and curved and metallic and somehow distant, I come into its presence with respect. A farm boy in subtropical Mississippi, I will not approach the instrument when I am dirty (as I often am) or wearing short pants. I have to bathe and dress acceptably; otherwise, I am unworthy. I feel unworthy in any case. The instrument chastises, then chastens me. I will practice in the back hallway—

both for privacy and for the acoustics—where it so happened my mother's full-length mirror is attached to the bedroom door; I watch myself as I play, and know that I must stand up straight in the presence of my beloved—my posture has to be commensurate with my emotions; otherwise, I am unclean. There is a stance that is appropriate; there is a self-consciousness that is necessary. I did not have this language, but I felt these things, and that I feel them at all is extraordinary: nothing else in my life teaches me that I must have a stance, that an ethos was necessary. I learn decorum; I learn humility; I learn ecstasy. It so happens that I also begin, slowly, to learn music, which in the end demands an even more precise stance, an even more arduous ethos. At the age of nine, a white farm boy in the heart of the Jim Crow South, I cannot approach that power unmediated.

Every art and every artist has its instrument, for there is no unmediated art. And every artist-in-progress has teachers, whether present human ones, or book or canvas or stone or metal ones. In the place where I found myself, there were no artists, no human teachers. The very word *artist*, had you tried to apply it to me at the age of nine or ten or eleven, would have baffled and embarrassed me. Fortunately, the instrument itself taught me; the instrument, like the beloved, becomes a second self, a second nature.

In the end, the mystery remains a mystery—one for which I am almost abjectly grateful. The saxophone taught me, by inclination an inarticulate slumper, to stand up straight and to try to speak. Later it would teach me the value of a certain destructive connection to tradition, but that was after it led me to music, and thence to jazz, a process that took years. What is most important is that the saxophone, the thing itself, was my first passion, and my first exemplar. It terrifies me to think what I might have become without it, because it led me into my own life in the 1960s in a way that no other influence in my immediate world could have done.

It would be interesting to know how many poets of our generation are or have been musicians—whether practicing, failing, dabbling, wannabe, or ex—and how that proportion compares with the population at large. A survey might well reveal—as with the famous statistic about suicide—that even more dentists have tried it than poets. Ours is a music-saturated culture in which a certain kind of musician enjoys special status in the popular imagination. So many garages have begat so many decibels, so many high schools have encouraged so many out-of-tune choruses of trombone and violin, that you'd think everybody had been in a band at one time or another. Perhaps the attempt is an American rite of passage.

I became a poet. The hows and whys of that becoming belong to a longer story than this one. The point is, that it was the saxophone and the saxophone alone that brought me to art.

Why the saxophone? I ask again, as I have asked myself so many times before. All I can say with certainty is that there is something about it that suits me. Perhaps it is the ridiculous complexity of the object. Compared with the more elegant and mysterious-looking trumpet or French horn, the saxophone is a Rube Goldberg contraption; invented in the machine age, it is in fact the apotheosis of the musical instrument as machine—as the violin is the apotheosis of the musical instrument as furniture, or the pipe organ as architecture, or the trumpet that of the musical instrument as plumbing. I can look at certain of my poems in that light and see a similitude: complex machination, out of which issues a voice that is *almost* human.

In other circumstances, I might be asking, *Why the bagpipe, why the kalimba?* with equal gratitude. What is important is that, almost miraculously, I began to learn the discipline of instruments in the presence of a curved metal pipe; I began to be an artist under the tutelage of a golden machine. If this sounds like the story of a primitive who gains power and knowledge from a collection of soda cans and Styrofoam washed up on a beach, so be it; Mississippi was my island of exile, and I was its Caliban. It is a tribute to music, incarnated in a glorious cheap saxophone, that it could find me even there.

DAVID W. JOHNSON

Following the Valley Road to the Homeplace of American Music

Driving down the mountain ridge that divides Russell and Washington Counties in Virginia in the aftermath of a thunderstorm, I almost missed the small green sign that indicates the road to Mendota. I made the right turn faster than I wanted to and was not sure I was on the right road. I knew it only as "the Mendota road" and had never taken it before. Soon I found myself driving along a tranquil river valley—the north fork of the Holston—below soft green mountains where mist from the evaporating rain was rising. Rust-breasted barn swallows swooped over a field. Cows grazed in the meadow. The world had become bucolic and peaceful. I drove for miles at about 20 miles an hour, noticing the diverse structures along the side of the road—abandoned houses in states of collapse, single-wide and double-wide trailers, lovely homes on top of sloping hills, obsolete vehicles sitting in yards. Cows . . . many, many cows . . . and several bulls, including a big hump-backed brahma. There was a black dog playing with a stick and very few people. Some had posted signs on their property saying "NO TRAIL" to ward off hikers and bicyclists. Along about 20 miles of road there were half a dozen churches, if not more. Signs in front of churches

announced loyalty to Jesus Christ, and small signs in yards supported the United States and the pledge of allegiance.

A large electric sign at the side of the road advertised the Mount
Vernon Methodist Church. I had begun to read the biography of
southwestern Virginia's most famous musical family—the Carters—
and the church name sounded familiar. Had I known enough to take
the road to the right, I would have continued up a hill to the church
and might have found the cemetery that is the last resting place of A.
P. and Sara Carter—once husband and wife, who, with Sara's
cousin (and eventual sister-in-law) Maybelle, formed a trio that
continues to have an influence on American music. I was passing
through Maces Spring, from where the Carters journeyed on July
31, 1927, to Bristol, Tennessee, to record the next day for the man
from the Victor Talking Machine Company. Seventy-five years
later on August 1, 2002, at a low-key press conference in Bristol, a
British journalist asked A. P. and Sara's daughter, Janette, if she had
any recollection of her parents' emotions as they are about to make
the trip. "They were glad to try," said Janette. "They had played at
churches and schools. This was a new adventure." In Bristol that
evening 75 years ago, the Carters recorded for engineers directed
by freelance talent scout Ralph S. Peer, who had made an arrangement with Victor by which he would provide the company with
records to and he would keep the lion's share of the copyrights.
"These sessions were what started the company," said Ralph S.
Peer II at the same press conference. Revenue generated by the
Carter Family and an ambitious songwriter from Meridian, Mississippi, Jimmie Rodgers, quickly established Peer's Southern Music
Publishing Company—today a part of multinational peermusic—as
a most profitable enterprise.

Instead of stopping at the Mount Vernon Methodist Church, I
continued along the Mendota road until I saw a sign on my right
that said Carter Fold. More formally known as the Carter Family
Memorial Music Center, the fold consists of A. P. Carter's general
store, which he opened in 1945, and a 1,000-seat performance theater Janette Carter had built in 1976, with the help from siblings Joe
and Gladys, to keep her family's music alive. Separated for six years,
A. P. and Sara had divorced in 1939, continuing to perform and
record with Maybelle. In March 1943, when a final radio contract

expired, the original Carter Family disbanded. Sara returned to California, where she lived with her second husband, A. P.'s cousin Coy Bays. A. P. returned to southwestern Virginia to live with his daughter Gladys and her family in the homeplace he had purchased for the family. Maybelle, who was married to A. P.'s brother Ezra likewise returned to the valley with their three daughters—Helen, June, and Anita—soon moving north to Richmond and forming a second musical incarnation of the family: The Carter Sisters and Mother Maybelle. A. P. ran his one-room store and maintained an interest in music until his death in 1960. Sara retired from the music business except for making a reunion album in 1966 with Maybelle and Sara's son Joe, who sang A. P.'s parts. Performing with her daughters, solo, and with support from son-in-law Johnny Cash, who had married June, "Mother" Maybelle Carter became the first lady of traditional country music by the time of her death in November 1978. Still in California, Sara Carter died two months later. She had asked to be buried in the valley where she had been born and raised. Her funeral service took place at the Carter Fold. Her grave is two rows away from A. P.'s, marked by a headstone made of the same red granite as A. P.'s and bearing the same likeness of a 78 record and the words "Keep on the Sunny Side"—the title of one of the family's best-known songs.

When I reached the fold, I pulled over and parked between the store and the theater. No one seemed to be around. There were no other cars. I gingerly approached the store, in case it were a residence. I heard the sound of a motor and saw a man mowing on the hill above the store. He continued down the hill, oblivious to me. I stepped onto the porch of the store. The thought occurred that I was standing in a space trod many times by A. P. Carter, and possibly by Sara and Maybelle. His spirit seemed to occupy the place. I have a fondness for wood and noticed the somewhat askew wooden handle on the white-painted door. The handle was separate from a newer-looking doorknob. Surely A. P. and the family would have grasped this handle many times. I reached out and took hold of it, closing my eyes. After a few moments I felt close to something that was important to my own personal journey. Perhaps it was a sense of simplicity . . . of authenticity . . . of steadfastness in the face of a difficult life. For all the Carters' success in the music business, "Life was hard for them," said Norma Hite, one of four paid staff who operate the museum and gift shop of the Birthplace of Country Music Alliance in Bristol. Her family goes back 200 years in Washington County, adjacent to Scott County, where the Carters lived. Life was hard for anyone living in the region in the 19th and early 20th centuries, when people scraped out a living in a place with a very descriptive name: the Poor Valley. That is the valley that the Mendota road runs down. Before crossing the road, I entered the performance theater, which was silent except for the sound of a cat feeding. On the walls are pictures of A. P., Sara, and Maybelle Carter; the Carter Sisters, who were beautiful young women; a framed full-page of a newspaper covering the 1977 celebration of Sara and Maybelle's half century in music; and other memorabilia. I gazed at these with reverence, then took an uphill hike to the top of the theater to look down at the stage. On the sides of the theater, the seats are covered by carpet fragments. At the very top, a row of seats appears to have been taken from a bus.

When a phone rang somewhere inside the theater, I felt it was time to leave. I crossed the road and turned to soak in the feeling of the valley and the foothills to the mountains. The valley is now lush and green and the foothills are covered with trees. Norma Hite told me that in the 1800s the hills were bare because Poor Valley residents had logged them and farmed the cleared land. On this lovely late summer day afternoon, the valley was peaceful and quiet. Only an occasional car disturbed the singing of the birds. At some level, I began to understand how the Carters and their music had come from this valley. I noticed, across the street, that another vehicle was now in the parking lot and another car arrived as I watched. Wishing to introduce myself as a harmless sightseer, I walked across the Mendota road and waved to a woman who turned out to be Rita Forrester, Janette Carter's daughter. Apologetically, I said that I did not want to intrude and would leave soon. She assured me that I was not intruding and could stay as long as I wanted. "The fold is open," she said. "We're just working." That weekend was to be the 28th Carter Family festival, honoring the music of A. P., Sara, and Maybelle. Since the festival coincided with the 75th anniversary of the Bristol recordings, Janette was nervous about the possible size of the turnout. There was so much to do. I helped her and her friend Fern carry three large containers to an outbuilding that served as a concession stand. "Isn't it fortunate that there's always a nice man around to help you when you need it," said one of the women behind me. On that note of praise, I said goodbye, got back in my car, and drove through the town of Hiltons toward Bristol. As I drove along the winding two-lane highway that is Route 58, I wondered if this was the same road that the Carters had taken on July 31, 1927, on their way to make recordings that changed American music forever.

LYNNE D JOHNSON

Hip-Hop's Holy Trinity

"Shady Aftermath nigga, G-Unit, rap juggernauts of this shit, we takin' over"

—50 CENT, "DON'T PUSH ME," *GET RICH OR DIE TRYIN'*

"Take some Big and some Pac and you mix 'em up in a pot/Sprinkle a little Big L on top, what the fuck do you got?/You got the realest and illest killas tied up in a knot/The juggernauts of this rap shit, like it or not"

—EMINEM, "PATIENTLY WAITING," *GET RICH OR DIE TRYIN'*

Most great music, they say, is God inspired. Add to that adage, the recording industry's marketing machine, hype, and hip-hop's stamp of approval in the form of street credibility, and a rapper like 50 Cent (né Curtis Jackson) becomes what appears to be an overnight success. But of course, like any other mythical American dream sequence brought to life, there's more to this story.

Consider this parallel. When John Coltrane recorded "The Father, Son, and Holy Ghost" for his 1965 offering *Meditations*, he and Pharaoh Sanders communicated to one another through their intense tenors influencing one another's performance. After 'Trane's death, Albert Ayler claimed that with this movement 'Trane was expressing his discovery of a holy family in which 'Trane was the father, Sanders the son, and Ayler the Holy Ghost. All three musicians, no doubt, impacted each other's composition and improvisational styles, moving beyond the structures of bop toward free jazz.

If we believe in the scriptures, then the Holy Ghost or spirit of God is to inspire the new prophets as he inspired the prophets of the old law. Ayler would then have influenced both 'Trane and Sanders, which seems highly likely at this juncture in jazz's history. In following this train of thought, envision 50 Cent as hip-hop's holy ghost, both inspiring his mentors and provoking rappers, both old and new school, to step up their game.

That hip-hop would come to have its own holy trinity was inevitable. In Eminem (né Marshall Mathers), Andre "Dr. Dre" Young found what most music critics deem as hip-hop's great white hope, and together, in 50 Cent, they found the next Biggie and Tupac rolled into one. Their Shady/Aftermath/G-Unit stronghold in the music industry positions them as a certified holy trinity, with Dre as the father, Eminem as the son, and 50 as the Holy Ghost. Only four days after its official release *Get Rich Or Die Tryin'*, 50's major label debut, sold 872,000 copies. In its second and first full week, the CD sold another 822,000 copies. As of July, 5.3 million copies of *Get Rich Or Die Tryin'* were sold, with the album cushioning at #7 on *Billboard*'s 200 and #10 on its R&B/hip-hop chart respectively. The single, "In Da Club," received the most radio spins of any single, and became a remake magnet with Beyonce, Mary J. Blige, Bubba Sparxx, and many others turning out their own versions of the song.

No other black hip-hop artist had ever turned such tricks for the music industry before—that is sold anywhere near 1 million copies their first week of sales as a debut artist—and the only one who even came close was Snoop Doggy Dogg with his 1993 debut *Doggystyle* that was produced by Dr. Dre. Interestingly enough, Dr. Dre's protégé, Eminem, has been the greatest selling rapper of all time dominating with *The Eminem Show* and *The Marshall Mathers LP*. Both sold over 1 million units within their first week of being released. Rap juggernauts indeed, though many would neither find them holy or godly.

Although 50 was once signed to a major label deal with Columbia, it was his underground mixtape circuit tenacity that brought him to the attention of America's favorite, and best-selling rapper, Eminem. Their union exemplifies the old "pick yourself up by the bootstraps mentality," in that both worked hard in the underground trenches before someone more established in the game offered a hand to help them to rise up. A combination of record sales, radio spins, and video rotations for Eminem and 50 combined makes this triad appear unstoppable.

It would be too simplistic to signify 50's seeming meteoric rise to the *Billboard* charts, and ability to remain there for months, as merely America's fascination with outlaw culture. Certainly America loves its bad boys, just look at the opening weekend box office sales of $46.5 million for *Bad Boys II*, starring Will Smith and Martin Lawrence, and the 324,000 U.S. copies sold of the film's soundtrack its opening week. If being a bad boy is a blueprint for commercial success, then 50's bio reads like an up-from-the-gutter, serve-as-messenger for the gutter testament to it. But without the power of this union—with Dr. Dre and Eminem at the helm—would the story still read the same?

First there was the father. As the beatmaker behind the seminal gangster rap group NWA, Dr. Dre is credited with ushering in the G-Funk sound. With his slow-rolling sonics and NWA's villainous lyrical content, the era of party and bullshit rap, along with its political brother, was murdered. Dre later went on to form Death Row Records with Suge Knight, and with the Snoop Doggy Dogg collaborations on his own solo release *The Chronic*, and later as producer of Snoop's *Doggystyle*, he single-handedly altered the verve of hip-hop music. By 1996 Dre had severed his relationship with Death Row, declaring the death of gangster rap. But out on his own his influence on hip-hop began to wane. And so he sent us his son.

This is when the word became flesh. In the Bible, the first book of John, verse one reads: "In the beginning was the Word, and the Word was with God, and the Word was God." By verse 14, it reads: "And the Word was made flesh, and dwelt among us . . ." If Dre gets to play the role of God in this scenario, then certainly it follows that Eminem would star as his son—delivering his NWA days of violence and mayhem to the world.

Much like his role of Rabbit in the film *8 Mile*, Eminem came to the rap game via the battle circuit. But it wasn't until he created his alter ego Slim Shady that the controversial material he's best known for became commonplace. After Jimmy Iovine, Interscope label head, brought him to the attention of Dr. Dre, the unmitigated persona took off. Outlandish and brash in nature, criticizing the mainstream, and airing his dirty laundry, Eminem's word became one that disaffected youth, of all races and classes, could identify with. And while more shepherds continually entered the flock, which record sales and *8 Mile* viewership can attest to, Eminem began to feel that hip-hop was ready for a revival. "Right before *The Eminem Show* dropped, I said to a few different people that I was in a little bit of a slump as far as hip-hop was concerned. I was just bored. It was like the same artists were doing it consistently and nobody new was coming up," Eminem told Noah Callahan-Bever in a March 2003 *XXL* interview. And so the son declared, it was time for a new spirit in hip-hop. Enter 50 Cent, the Holy Ghost.

By now we all know 50's story. We'd have to be living in some third world country with no access to any form of media not to know it. Before his position was solidified with the trinity, though, 50 had already stirred up controversy in the rap game. His underground success, the '99 single "How to Rob," poked fun at celebrity rappers' successes and featured a how-to-rob them guide. With lyrics like, "I'd follow Fox in the drop for four blocks/ Plottin' to juice her for that rock Kurupt copped/ What Jigga just sold like 4 milli, got something to live for/ Don't want no nigga puttin' four thru that Bentley Coupe door," he definitely wasn't making industry friends. Not long after his recording industry debut, the rapper was shot nine times. Label heads, feeling he'd be too much of a burden, dropped him, but like the 1-million-dollar man that he is (Em and Dre are reported to have signed him for that much) he was rebuilt, both physically and artistically. The video for "In Da Club" is reminiscent of the wildly popular '70s TV show, *The Six Million Dollar Man.* Remember the opening narration: "We can rebuild him. We have the technology. We have the capability to make the world's first bionic man. Steve Austin will be that man. Better than he was before. Better, stronger, faster." Now watch the video again, and replace Steve Austin's name with 50 Cent. The video, displaying Dre and Eminem in white coats watching the doctors from above as they reengineer and reenergize 50 on the operation table not only symbolizes the gods watching down from the sky ideal, but also represents that in fact 50 Cent has posthuman qualities.

*   *   *

"I got God understand me tattooed in my skin/When I die and come back, I'ma do it again"

—50 CENT, "50 SHOT YA'," *GET RICH OR DIE TRYIN'*

Add to that bionic man/posthuman analogy 50's similarities with Tupac. Coincidentally, Dr. Dre served as primary producer on Tupac's projects when they were both at Death Row. And much like the charismatic certified gangster rapper, who was shot five times in the lobby of a New York recording studio and lived to tell it, 50 also survived such circumstances. Though Tupac was murdered in 1996, several albums containing never released before material have come out since. While Tupac's prolific output is a testament to his work ethic, it has otherwise convinced his most loyal devotees that he's still alive. 50 Cent likewise has an overwhelming amount of product, but it's mainly on the mixtape circuit. The most striking comparison that's being harped on between 50 and Tupac is that they both survived near death. 50 talks about it all the time.

This feeling of invincibility created by evading death is guaranteed to bring about a god-like complex in any mortal. "They say I walk around like got an 'S' on my chest," the rapper snarls on his single "What Up Gangsta?" Superman too has his Christ-like abilities. And though 50 follows up the opening line of the song with "Naw, that's a semi-auto, and a vest on my chest" the correlation has already been cast. Like Superman, 50 was also an orphan raised by his grandparents due to his mother's drug lifestyle and death when he was eight. Not that 50 directly fits the Superman archetype, but the battle gear he totes around and rides in (50 has had run-ins with the law for weapons possession and he wears a Kevlar vest, while riding around in a bullet proof SUV), for him, must serve as his superpowers. He not only feels he has no competition in the rap game—except Jay-Z and Nas—his near brush with death has also apparently convinced him that he is immortal, or at least all the paraphernalia will save him. In the DC Comics, Superman's mission was to save humanity, and if Eminem's rationale for signing 50 on the dotted line is to be extrapolated then 50 is here to save hip-hop from itself.

Befitting his post as Holy Ghost in the Aftermath/Shady/G-Unit Records triad, make that trinity, 50 embodies the divine messenger, as well as the breath of the spirit. In his role as messenger, he delivers the words of the gods, in other words "the greatest rappers of all time." On the mixtape circuit DJ Whoo Kid released 50 rapping duets with both the Notorious B.I.G and Tupac on "The Realest," and "The Realest Killas," respectively. That DJ Whoo Kid chose these slain rappers to team 50 up with fits comfortably within this scenario. In the words of many music critics, 50 Cent fills a void left by both slain rappers, so his collaborations with them appears to signify some sort of direct communication with the gods of rap. As inspirit incarnate—inspiring the prophets of the old law—50 has resurrected the spirit of the gangsta in hip-hop music. In the June 2003 issue of *GQ*, in an article entitled, "Can I Get a Thug?" Jon Caramanica wrote, *"Get Rich or Die Tryin'* is filled with morbid gangsta tales in which the sun never bothers to shine and weakness is rewarded with swift punishment. The 26-year-old 50 is hip-hop's first crossover boy in almost a decade to explicitly traffic in the sort of scar-tissue credibility that most rappers and fans see only on *Oz*. The thug has been mainstreamed anew, and a cavalcade of likely successors are readying their attack."

It's not only the new guard of rappers upholding the thug banner, first 50 got O. G. Snoop Dogg to trade lines with him on a remix of his single "P.I.M.P." Later he joined Jay-Z, probably the most successful black crossover hip-hop artist, on the cover of *Entertainment Weekly* touting their explosive "Rock the Mic" tour that began this summer. A Rock the Mic mixtape, featuring 50 and Jay-Z collabs, will soon follow. Clearly the old prophets recognize this newcomer's gangsta, and perhaps his Holy Ghost has also uplifted them.

Whether you believe there is an inkling of holiness emanating from 50 Cent or not, God is no stranger to him. In his lyrics for both "Many Men," and "U Not Like Me," he references talking to God every night. He and his G-Unit fam, including Lloyd Banks and Yayo, even put out a disc entitled *God's Plan*. On "U Not Like Me," he offers, "Everything that happened to us, was part of God's plan." Meanwhile, his God-like complex, as well as his own belief in his godliness, shines on the song when he boasts, "My songs belong in the Bible with King David/I teach niggaz sign language."

*"Don't think I'm crazy, 'cause I don't fear man/'Cause I feel when
I kill a man/God won't understand/I got a head full of evil
thoughts, am I satan"*

—50 CENT, "U NOT LIKE ME," *GET RICH OR DIE TRYIN'*

If 50 Cent is not here to save hip-hop music, there remains no
question that he has breathed new life into it. This idea holds true,
whether you consider his lyrics and persona disturbing, or not. Even
Eminem's delivery has raised up a few notches when he's beside his
hip-hop wunderkind on the stage and in the recording booth. The
honesty in all of this is that there hasn't been a rapper with this sort
of lyrical swagger in quite awhile. For that very reason, the comparisons to Tupac and the Notorious B.I.G are certainly not
unfounded. 50's brand of graphically violent reality rap, mixed with
sing-songy choruses, has unwittingly taken us back to the gangster
rap heyday—an era Dr. Dre is held responsible for creating—but his
talent for making catchy hooks imbue it a new twist. If nothing else,
at least 50's continuing the tradition of both his heavenly and
earthly forefathers. For like Dre and Em before him, he's managed
to achieve great earthly success by somehow speaking to and for
"the people." Though he's so far single-handedly boosted record
sales for 2003 and changed hip-hop's languishing direction, placing
it on a completely different track, it's still not clear whether he's its
definitive answer.

ROY KASTEN

Wild Is the Wind

The Fierce and Uncompromising
Nina Simone Could Never Be Contained

> *We always did prefer our iconic figures injured, stuck full of*
> *arrows or crucified upside-down; we need them flayed and naked;*
> *we want to watch their beauty crumble slowly and to observe their*
> *narcissistic grief. Not in spite of their faults but for their faults we*
> *adore them, worshipping their weaknesses, their pettinesses, their*
> *bad marriages, their substance abuse, their spite.*
>
> —SALMAN RUSHDIE

What has Nina Simone left us? The sound of struggle, the sound of a soul on fire. She was born in North Carolina, the sixth of eight children surrounded by desolation and music, Jim Crow and the holy dove. Her mother preached, and her father sang. Their brilliant child, Eunice Kathleen Waymon, played piano in churches before she could read. Trained at Juilliard in New York City, Eunice found her stage name in the endearment of a Hispanic boyfriend (he called her "niña") and a dreamland her father promised her, France (her invented last name was inspired by actress Simone Signoret). She found her music in a place female jazz singers weren't supposed to go: bad blood, violent sex, the wildness of unscripted discovery.

With the exception of a few live (and hard-to-find) recordings and the overly lush 1993 release *A Single Woman*, Simone's recording career effectively ended some twenty years ago. And like many jazz singers in their prime during the 1960s and '70s, Simone recorded too often, too quickly. Her catalog is a brambled field strewn with diamonds and cluster bombs. No anthology could clear a coherent path, though, taken together, Rhino's overview of her early Colpix career and 7-N's *Bittersweet: The Very Best of Nina Simone* come close. She claimed once that a label head locked her up in a studio and forced her to sing; her more erratic, even bizarre efforts sometimes sound that way. What she saw in Steely Dan's "Haitian Divorce" or Hall and Oates' "Rich Girl" is anyone's guess.

Simone was a commanding, uncompromising interpreter, but she never asserted her authority when it came to production and sequencing. She hated every label for which she recorded; too often she let those she detested have their way. But if we listen closely, with the imaginative freedom she demanded of herself and her musicians, we hear, in her willful, searing voice, the opening of sublime windows, glimpses of how much she, we and music might mean. "Power, Lord! Don't you know I need you," she moaned on "Sinner Man." Yet one need only listen to her many interpretations of Bob Dylan: Simone alone captured that irreducible strangeness, that shock of recognition in a truly free imagination.

"Mississippi Goddam" was darkly funny in the '60s, and it's funny today, but lest we forget, at the time she wrote and recorded the song, people were bombed or lynched for far less. "Everybody knows about Mississippi Gaaaaaaadddaaaaaaaammmnnn!" she wailed in a catharsis for those who were told "go slow," to be patient, for her brothers and sisters who chose nonviolent resistance to the deepest brutality. Simone sang what others repressed. "You thought I was kidding," she snarls at a liberal audience she feels might be enjoying their cocktails a bit too much. "We're having a good time now," she seems to hint. "But goddamn. I'm not kidding."

Vietnam, Attica, assassinations; brothers and sisters slandered, jailed and murdered; ghettos burning—the riot wasn't just going on in the streets. "When would the war stop?" Marvin Gaye asked, but he was talking about "the war inside my soul." The war never stopped; perhaps it never could. You hear that war in Nina Simone's most sublime performances, mostly onstage, in live testaments, which are her truest: the soft lulling, the jazzy insinuation into any self-satisfied mind and then the phrase or climax that cracks it all open. The bewilderment, the rage, the evil even in all that's repressed. It's there in one line, from her composition "Four Women": *My name is Peeeeaaaaccchhhiiiizzzzzzz!* At the height of the folk revival, she transformed the folk song "Cotton Eyed Joe" into a withering, even killing vision of impoverishment. Her voice meant more than her audience was willing to understand, more really than we can understand today.

Tagging Simone the "high priestess of soul" only proves how useless generic labels can be. She could sing anything she wanted, and she certainly did so with soul. She knew and appreciated R&B and influenced popular music in ways that are rarely remembered. She wrote and recorded "Don't Let Me Be Misunderstood" before the Animals, and Paul McCartney sang "Michelle" with her languid phrasing of "I Put a Spell on You" in his ears. Her underrated piano playing sounded with excited lyricism: as if at times she were guiding the instrument's birth, as if at times she were caressing the dying. And Simone was, when she so desired, as technically gifted as any opera singer, as pure and precise a singer as Sarah Vaughan or Mahalia Jackson. "They only compared us because we were black," she once complained. "They never compared me to Maria Callas, and I'm more of a diva like her than anybody else." She had few hits on the R&B charts—the one exception, "I Loves You Porgy," was pure jazz.

The U.S. Senate has declared 2003 the Year of the Blues. Seeing as how that aristocratic institution has done more than enough to inspire the blues, it's fitting that Simone, on April 21, at the age of 70, checked out. Her late years, a painful smear bordering on madness and paranoia, offer no redemption for her struggle. Her years adrift in Europe, the Middle East, the Caribbean and Africa brought no solace. Her lovers beat her and cheated on her, and she nearly overdosed on sleeping pills when one more affair curdled. She blasted noisy neighborhood kids with a shotgun, ran over motorcyclists, evaded taxes and alienated close friends and what few allies she had left in the business. She sang until her body gave out; in her exile, few heard.

She never forgave and never forgot. Save your talk of healing and letting go for Oprah and Dr. Phil. Nina Simone's music—her rage and glory, her talent and freedom, her visions and judgments—remains ours, dare we listen now without her.

CHUCK KLOSTERMAN

6,557 Miles to Nowhere

Death is part of life. Generally, it's the shortest part of life, usually occurring near the end. However, this is not necessarily true for rock stars; sometimes rock stars don't start living *until* they die.

I want to understand why that is.

I want to find out why the greatest career move any musician can make is to stop breathing. I want to find out why plane crashes and drug overdoses and shotgun suicides turn longhaired guitar players into messianic prophets. I want to walk the blood-soaked streets of rock 'n' roll and chat with the survivors who writhe in the gutters. This is my quest.

Now, to do this, I will need a rental car.

Death rides a pale horse, but I shall merely ride a silver Ford Taurus. Though I don't know it yet, I will drive this beast 6,557 miles, guided by a mind-expanding Global Positioning System that speaks to me in a soothing female voice, vaguely reminiscent of Meredith Baxter-Birney. This voice tells me when I need to exit the freeway, and how far I am from places like Missoula, and how to locate the nearest Cracker Barrel. I will drive down the eastern seaboard, across the Deep South, up the corn-covered spinal chord of the Midwest, and through the burning foothills of Montana, finally coming to rest on the cusp of the Pacific Ocean, underneath a bridge where Kurt Cobain never slept. In the course of this voyage, I will stand where 119 people have fallen, all of whom were unwilling victims of rock's glistening scythe. And this will teach me what I already knew.

New York, New York
(Wednesday, July 30, 3:46 P.M.)

When I walk into the Chelsea Hotel, I can't decide if this place is nicer or crappier than I anticipated. There are two men behind the reception desk: An older man with a beard, and a younger man who might be Hispanic. I ask the bearded man if anyone is staying in room 100, and if not, if I can see what it looks like.

"There is no room 100," he tells me. "They converted it into an apartment 18 years ago. But I know why you're asking."

For the next five minutes, these two gentlemen and I have a conversation about drug-addled Sex Pistols bassist Sid Vicious, mostly about the fact that he was an idiot. However, there are clearly lots of people who disagree with us: Patrons constantly come to this hotel with the hope of staying in the same place where an unlikable opportunist named Nancy Spungeon was (probably) murdered for no valid reason. "We hate it when people ask about this," says the younger employee. "Be sure you write that down: *We hate it when people ask us about this.*" I ask the elder man what kind of person aspires to stay in a hotel room that was once a crime scene.

"It tends to be younger people—the kind of people with colored hair," he says. "But we did have one guy come all the way from Japan, only to discover that room 100 doesn't even exist anymore. The thing is, Johnny Rotten was a musician; Sid Vicious was a loser. So maybe his fans want to be losers, too."

While we are having this discussion, an unabashedly annoyed man interjects himself into the conversation; his name is Stanley Bard, and he has been the manager of the Chelsea Hotel for more than 40 years. He does not want me talking to the hotel staff and asks me into his first-floor office. Bard is balding, swarthy, and serious, and he sternly tells me I should not include the Chelsea Hotel in this article.

"I understand what you think you're trying to do, but I do not want the Chelsea Hotel associated with this story," says Bard, his arms crossed as he sits behind a cluttered wooden desk. "Sid Vicious didn't die here. It was just his girlfriend, and she was of no consequence. The kind of person who wants to stay in room 100 is just a cultic follower. These are people who have nothing to do. If you want to understand what someone fascinated by Sid Vicious is looking for, go find *those* people. You will see that they are not serious-minded people. You will see that they are not trying to understand anything about death. They are looking for nothing."

At this point, he politely tells me to leave the Chelsea Hotel. We shake hands, and this is what I do.

West Warrick, Rhode Island
(Saturday, August 2, 5:25 P.M.)

For some reason, I assumed the plot of land where 100 people burned to death during a rock concert would look like a parking lot. I thought it would be leveled and obliterated, and there would be no sign of what happened on February 20, 2002, the night pyrotechnics from blues-metal dinosaurs Great White turned a club called the Station into a hell mouth. Small towns usually make sure their places of doom disappear. But not here: In West Warrick, what used to be a tavern is now an ad hoc cemetery—which is the same role taverns play in most to wns, really, but not so obviously as this.

When I pull into what used to be the Station's parking lot, I turn off my engine next to a red F–150 Ford pick-up with two dudes sitting in the cab. They get out and walk through a perimeter of primitive crosses that surround the ruins of the club; once inside, they sit on two folding chairs next to a pair of marble gravestones. They are James Farrell and his cousin Glenn Barnett; the two gravestones are for Farrell's uncle Tommy and Tommy's best friend, Jay; James aligned the gravestones where the beer taps used to be. The narrative they tell me is even worse than I would have anticipated: The week after Tommy died in the fire, Farrell's grandfather—Tommy's father—died from a stroke, exactly seven days and five minutes after his son was burned alive.

I realize that this story must sound horribly sad, but it doesn't seem that way when they tell it: Farrell and Barnett are both as happy as any two people I've ever met. Farrell is like a honey-gorged bear, and he reminds me of that guy who starred in *The Tao of Steve:* He's wearing a tie-dyed shirt and a knee brace. He comes here every single day.

"I will remember the night this place burned down forever," Farrell says. "I was in a tittie bar in Florida—I was living in Largo at the time. I looked up at the ceiling, and I noticed it was covered with black Styrofoam, just like this place always was. And I suddenly knew something was wrong. I could just feel it. Then my mom called me, and she told me what happened. I moved up here to help out my grandma. She obviously has been through a lot, what with losing her son and then her husband a week later. The doctor said my grandfather's stroke was completely stress-related. I mean, he stroked out a week after the fire, almost to the very minute. That was fucking spooky."

Farrell is 34; his uncle was just four years older, so they were actually more akin to brothers. Tommy, a longtime regular at the Station, didn't even want to see Great White the night they played in Rhode Island: He referred to them as "Not-So-Great White" and only went because someone gave him free tickets.

Farrell, Barnett, and two nameless lesbians built all of the Station's crosses in one night, a few months after the accident. The wood came from the Station's surviving floorboards. Originally, the crosses were blank; this is so someone could come to the site, pick one, and decorate it however he saw fit. There are only about five clean crosses remaining, but this is partially because some people have been memorialized accidentally multiple times.

As we talk, I find myself shocked by how jovial Farrell is. "I hide it pretty well," he tells me. "And between you and me, I just did a line. Do you wanna go do some blow?"

It turns out that this kind of behavior is not uncommon here: These grounds have fostered a community of both spirituality and decadence. Almost every night, mourners come to the Station cemetery to get high and talk about how they keep living in the wake of all this death.

"Nothing in West Warrick is the same," Farrell says later, as he paints his uncle's gravestone. "It changed everyone's personality. Everybody immediately started to be friendlier. For weeks after that show, if you wore a concert T-shirt into a gas station, everybody acted real nice to you. If they knew you were a rocker or a head, they immediately treated you better. It's that sense of community. It's kind of like the drug culture."

I ask him what he means.

"Well, okay—I just met you, but I would give you a ride any-where in the whole goddamn state of Rhode Island if you asked me, because I know you're a good guy. I have something on you, and you have something on me. It's like that here. The people who hang out here at night—it's definitely a community of people dealing with the same shit. I call it 'the fellowship.'"

A kid pulls into the parking lot and hauls an upright bass out of his vehicle, one of those seven-foot acoustic monsters that the Stray Cats used to play. He faces the grave markers, whips out a bow, and begins to play Eccles' "Sonata in G Minor." Either I am at the Station at the absolute perfect journalistic moment, or West Warrick is America's new *Twilight Zone*.

"Oh, I used to play at this club all the time," he says when I wander over. "I was in a band called Hawkins Rise, and I played upright bass through an amp. We were sort of like Zeppelin or the Who." He tells me his name is Jeff Richardson, that his is a 23-year-old jazz fanatic, and that he knew five of the people who died there. He was at least vaguely familiar with many of the other 95.

"The same people came here every night," Richardson says. "When a band like Great White or Warrant would come into town, all the same people would come out. There was never any preten-tiousness at this club. You wouldn't have to worry about some drunk guy yelling about how much your band sucked."

To me, that's what makes the Great White tragedy even sadder than it logically should be: One can safely assume that *none* of the 100 people who died at the Station were hanging out there to be cool. These were the blue-collar people trying to unironically experience rock 'n' roll that meant something to their lives when they were teenagers.

Tonight, I will go back to the graveyard at 11 P.M., and lots of their friends will pull up in Camaro IROCs and Chevy Cavaliers. They'll sit in the vortex of the crosses, smoking menthol cigarettes and marijuana, and they will talk about what happened that night. I will be told that the fire started during the first song ("Desert Moon" off 1991's *Hooked*). I will be told that the Station's ceiling was only 10 feet high and covered in synthetic foam, and that when the foam ignited, it (supposedly) released cyanide into the air. I will be told it took exactly 58 seconds before the whole building became a fireball. I will be told that a few fireman at the scene compared it to seeing napalm dropped on villages in Vietnam, because that was the only other time they ever saw skin *dripping* off of bone.

I will also be told (by just about everyone in the entire town) that Great White vocalist Jack Russell is a coward and a hypocrite, and that they will never forgive him (and the fact that a member of Russell's band died in said blaze doesn't seem to influence their opinion whatsoever). Around 1 A.M., Farrell will read me a poem he wrote about how much he despises Russell, and after he finishes, he will stare off into the night sky and say, "I would really like to hit him in the face." But he won't sound intimidating or vengeful when he says this; he will just sound profoundly sad. And it will strike me that this guy is a relentlessly sweet person with a heart like a mastodon, and I would completely trust him to drive me anywhere in the whole god-damn state of Rhode Island, even if he had never offered me drugs.

Magnolia, Mississippi
(Wednesday, August 6, 8:20 P.M.)

I'm semi-lost in rural Mississippi. And when I say "rural," I mean fucking *rural:* ten minutes ago, I almost drove into a cow that had meandered onto the road. This is especially amusing, because if I *had* driven into a cow, I would be only the second person in my immediate family to have done so. When my sister Teresa was in high school, she accidentally plowed into a cow with our father's

Chevy. Teresa hit it at 40 m.p.h., and the old, sleepy-eyed ungulate went down like a tree struck by lightning. Those were good times.

I am hunting for the site of the Lynyrd Skynyrd plane crash, which is supposed to be just west of Magnolia. It took forever to get to this town, and a few of the roads were unpaved. My first plan of action was to find a hotel, but there is no hotel in Magnolia. There is, however, a preponderance of signs promoting the consumption of butterfly shrimp, so I ate supper and started driving around aimlessly, looking for anyone who might know where Skynyrd's jet crashed into the wilderness in 1977, killing singer Ronnie Van Zant, guitarist Steve Gaines and Gaines' sister, back-up singer Cassie.

My initial plan was to ask someone at the local bar, but there doesn't seem to be one. All I find are churches. Near the outskirts of town, I spy a gas station. The auburn-haired woman working behind the counter doesn't know where the crash site is. However, there is a man buying a 12-pack of Bud Lite, and he can help. "My old lady can probably tell you for certain," he says. "She's waiting in my pick-up." We walk out to his extended cab 4x4 Ford, and his "old lady" (who looks about 25) instructs me to take the interstate south until I see a sign for West 568, and then follow that road for 10 miles until I see some chicken coops. There's one problem: There are a lot of goddamn chicken coops in Mississippi. It's getting dark, and I'm almost ready to give up. Then I see a sign by a gravel driveway for "mote-farms.com." This is the first time I've ever seen a farm that had its own web site, so I suspect it's more than just a chicken ranch. And I'm right, because when I pull into the yard, I'm immediately greeted by a shirtless fellow on a Kodiak four-wheeler.

John Daniel Mote is the 21-year-old son of the farm's owner. He is a remarkably handsome dude; he looks and talks like a young John Schneider, patiently waiting for Tom Wopat to get back from the Boar's Nest. "This is the right place," he says. "Follow me." We amble down a dirt road behind the chicken coops. I can hear the underbrush rubbing against the boom of the Taurus, and it sounds like John Bonham's drum fills from *Achilles Last Stand*.

He finally leads me to a landmark that his father constructed years ago: It's dominated by an archway with "Free Bird" painted across the top. There is a Confederate flag, of course, and a statue of an eagle. Mote says that if I were to walk through the "Free Bird" arch and 50 yards into the trees, I would find a tiny creek and some random airplane debris. I start to walk in that direction. He immediately stops me. "You don't want to go in there," he says. I ask him why. "Snakes. Cottonmouths. Very poisonous. Not a good idea." And then young John Daniel Mote drives away.

By now, the sky is as dark as Johnny Cash's closet. I am surrounded by fireflies. There is heat lightning to the east. Three hours ago, I passed an electronic sign that posted the temperature at 98 degrees. It feels like I'm trapped in the penultimate scene from *Raiders of the Lost Ark*, when Indiana Jones and Marion are tied to a stake while the Nazis try to open the Ark of the Covenant. Or maybe I'm just thinking of that movie because Mote mentioned the snakes.

Still, part of me really wants to see where this plane went down. I feel like an idiot for having driven 547 miles in one day only to be stopped five first downs from paydirt. I drive up to the mouth of the arch and shine the high beams into the blackness. I open the driver's side door and leave it open so that I can hear the radio; it's playing "Round and Round" by Ratt. The headlights don't help much; the trees swallow everything. I start to walk into the chasm. However, I don't make it 50 yards. In fact, I don't even make it 50 feet. I can't see anything, and the cicadas are so loud that they drown out Ratt. I will not find the spot where Ronnie Van Zant was driven into the earth. I turn around, and the cottonmouth snakes gimme three steps toward the door.

Memphis, Tennessee
(Friday, August 8, 3:14 P.M.)

So here is the big question: Is dying good for your career? Cynics assume that it is, but I'm not so sure anymore. And now that I've been to Memphis, I don't even know if I still care.

Memphis offers two key points of investigation for rock 'n' roll forensic experts. The first is Graceland, where Elvis Presley overdosed on a toilet. The second is Mud Island Harbor on the Mississippi River, where Jeff Buckley went for a swim and never came back. One could argue that both of these artists have significantly benefited from dying: Presley's life was collapsing when he died in 1977, so dying ended that slide and, in all likelihood, kept his legacy

from becoming a sad joke (it is virtually impossible to imagine a
"noble" 68-year-old Elvis, had Presley somehow lived into the present). Meanwhile, Buckley's death is precisely what made him into a
star; he was a well-regarded, but relatively unfamous, avant-garde
rock musician until he drowned on May 29, 1997. Almost instantly,
he became a Christlike figure (and his album *Grace* evolved from
"very good" to "totally classic").

I am typing this paragraph from the banks of the Mississippi,
presumably where Buckley disappeared into the depths. The water
is green and calm as a sheet of ice. I remember reading that Jeff
Buckley's mother believes there is a conspiracy surrounding her
son's death, because she insists that he was too strong a swimmer to
die in these waters. I don't know how I feel about this supposition,
as I cannot swim at all (I can't even float). The uber-calm Mississippi
looks plenty deadly to me; as far as I'm concerned, it may as well be
a river of hydrochloric acid. However, I must agree that the water is
not flowing very fast here in Mud Island Harbor. And though it certainly seems like a strange place to swim, it's hard to believe a guy
who (supposedly) wasn't drunk or high managed to disappear
beneath anything so tranquil.

But how or why Buckley died really doesn't matter at this point;
what matters is how his death is perceived by the world. And as far
as I can tell, Buckley's demise is viewed 100 percent positively (at
least from an artistic standpoint). There is an entire cult of disciples
(led, I believe, by Minnie Driver) who inject the knowledge of
Buckley's demise back into his work, and what they then hear on
songs like "Drown In My Own Tears" is something that could not
exist if he were alive. It's a simple equation: Buckley is dead, so *Grace*
is profound. But this is reverse engineering; this says more about the
people who like Buckley than it does about his music. Even when it's
merely an accident, dying somehow proves you weren't kidding.

Satan's Crossroads
(Friday, August 8, 4:33 P.M.)

Just north of Clarksdale, Mississippi, at the intersection of Highways 61 and 49, the soul of rock 'n' roll was spawned from Satan's
wheeling and dealing. You see, these are the "crossroads" where

Robert Johnson sold his soul to the devil in 1930, thereby accepting eternity in hell in exchange for the ability to play the guitar like no man before him. Satan's overpriced guitar lesson became the birth of the blues . . . and—by extension—the building blocks of every hard rock song ever recorded.

This, of course, never actually happened. Robert Johnson (poisoned to death at age 27) met the devil about as many times as Jimmy Page, King Diamond and Marilyn Manson did, which is to say "never." But this doesn't mean rock 'n' roll wasn't invented here. Rock 'n' roll is only superficially about guitar chords; it's really about myth. And the fact that people still like to pretend a young black male could become Lucifer's ninja on the back roads of Coahoma County (and then employ its demonic perversity through *music*) makes Johnson's bargain as real as his talent.

Unfortunately, this present-day highway to hell doesn't look like much: They look like (duh) two highways. There are fragments of spilled barley on the shoulder of each road, so this must be a thoroughfare for local grain trucks. The only thing marking the site is a billboard promoting microsurgical vasectomy reversal. What strikes me as most ironical is the fact that I was able to find Robert Johnson's crossroads with the Ford's GPS: Somehow, it seems like a satellite technology should not allow you to find the origin of America's most organic art form. You'd think the devil would have blown up my transmission or something.

Cedar Rapids, Iowa
(Saturday, August 9, 11:47 P.M.)

Four hours ago, I was looking for a motel. Then I heard something on the radio waves of rural Iowa: Just 36 miles away, Great White was performing a benefit concert in Cedar Rapids to raise money for the Station. Sometimes, you get lucky.

After turning around and driving to Cedar Rapids, I was faced with an immediate problem: I had no idea where this concert was going to happen. This is a bigger problem than one might anticipate, because the kind of bars that host Great White shows in 2003 are not exactly downtown establishments. I decide to just walk into a Hand-Mart gas station and ask the kid working the slushee machine if he knows where this show is; he does not. In fact, he didn't know it was even happening. "So, where do you think a band like Great White would play in Cedar Rapids?" I ask. He guesses the Cabo Sports Bar, a new place right next to the shopping mall. His guess is completely fucking right.

The show is outside on the club's sand volleyball courts. It's $15 to get inside, and the profits are going to the Station Family Fund. When I get there, the opening band—Skin Candy—is doing a cover of Tesla's "Modern Day Cowboy." There's maybe 1,000 people waiting for Great White, and it's a rough crowd: When you look into the eyes of this audience, you can see the hardness of their lives. More than a few of them are complaining that 16-ounce Budweisers cost $3.50. This is exactly what the crowd in West Warrick must have looked like.

I get backstage (which is really just the other side of the parking lot) and find Great White vocalist Jack Russell; he's wearing a sleeveless T-shirt and pants with an inordinate number of zippers, and he's got quite the little paunch. Somebody walks by and stealthily hands him a handful of tablets, but it turns out they're merely Halls cough drops.

I ask him what he remembers about the fire in Rhode Island, but he balks. "I can't talk about any of that stuff, because there is an ongoing investigation and I don't want to interfere with anything the attorney general is doing." This is understandable, but I ask him the same question again. "Well, it changed my life. Of course it changed my life," he says the second time around. "But I had to make a choice between sitting in my house and moping forever, or doing the one thing I know how to do."

Russell tells me he can't talk any further. However, guitarist Mark Kendall is less reticent. He's wearing Bono sunglasses and a black do-rag, and he fingers his axe throughout the duration of the conversation. He seems considerably less concerned about the Rhode Island attorney general. "That night was just really confusing," Kendall says. "I was totally numb. I didn't know what was going on. I had my sunglasses on, so I couldn't really see what was happening."

I tell him that there are people in Rhode Island who will never forgive him for what happened.

"Oh, I totally understand that," Kendall says. "That is a completely understandable reaction on their behalf. I mean, I've never
gotten over losing my grandfather, and he died 15 years ago. On the
day of that show, I met five different people during the day who
ended up dying that night. I feel really, really bad about what happened. But no blame should be cast."

Supposedly, Great White now donates almost all of their tour
revenue to charity. I ask Kendall how they can do that and still
afford to live. "Well, we did sell over 12 million records," he says
with mild annoyance. Twenty minutes later, the band opens with
"Red Light," and—much to my surprise—they sound pretty great.
After the first song, Russell asks for 100 seconds of silence to com-
memorate the victims. It works for maybe a minute, but then some
jackass in front of me holds up a Japanese import CD and screams,
"Great White rules!"

Minneapolis, Minnesota
(Monday, August 11, 1:30 P.M.)

There are a lot of disenfranchised cool kids in downtown Minneapolis, and a lot of them have a general idea of where Replace-
ments guitarist Bob Stinson drank himself to death in December of
1995. They all know it was the 800 block of West Lake Street, and
they all seem to think it was next to a bowling alley called Bryant
Lake Bowl. These hipsters are correct; Stinson died in a dilapidated
upstairs apartment, situated above a small-time leather shop and
directly across from Bryant Lake lanes.

I knock on the apartment door. No answer. I knock again. Again,
no answer. This is strange, because I know (for certain) that somebody is in this apartment: As I walked around to the back stairs, I
saw a pudgy white arm ashing a cigarette out of the window.
Granted, I don't really have a plan here—I'm not exactly sure what I
would ask this person if and when he opens the door. But I feel like I
should at least see the inside of this apartment (or something), so I
keep knocking. And knocking. I knock for 10 minutes. No one ever
comes out. I try to peep into the same window where I witnessed
"the cigarette incident," but now the shade is down, and I'm starting

to feel like a stalker. I ultimately decide to simply walk away, having learned zero about a dead musician I really knew nothing about to begin with.

Seattle, Washington
(Saturday, August 16, 2:12 P.M.)

Lots of dead people here. If rock musicians were 16-ton ivory-bearing pachyderms, Seattle would be America's elephant graveyard. First you have Mia Zapata, the female punk who represented liberation and self-reliance before being abducted by a sociopath, raped, and strangled to death with the string of her sweatshirt. There is Kristen Pfaff, the Hole bassist and smack addict who overdosed in her bathtub. You have Scott Jernigan, drummer for Karp and The Whip (not really a rock "star," I realize), who died this past June; his liver exploded after a bizarre boating accident on the dock of Union Bay. And one cannot forget the (entirely predictable) demise of Alice in Chains singer Layne Staley, a man who OD'd in perhaps the least rock 'n' roll spot in all of Washington: a generic, five-story teal condo in an area of town widely considered to be Seattle's least cool neighborhood (it's one block from a Petco). Perhaps you are wondering how I knew where all these people perished; the truth is that I did not. The guided Seattle death tour was provided by Hannah Levin, a rock writer for that city's alternative newspaper *The Stranger* and a freewheeling expert on local tragedies. And, of course, all these aforementioned deaths were really just a precursor to the Citizen Kane of modern rock deaths: The mighty K.C. This is what Levin and I discuss as we maneuver the long and winding Lake Washington Boulevard, finally arriving in what used to be Kurt Cobain's backyard.

"In the weeks before he killed himself, there was this litany of rumors about local singers dying," Levin says. Back in '94, she worked at Planned Parenthood but was already engulfed in the grunge culture. "There was a rumor that Chris Cornell had died, and then there was a rumor that Eddie Vedder had died. So even though a bunch of my friends called me at work that day and said Kurt was dead, I didn't really believe them. That kind of shit happened

constantly. But then I went out to my car at lunch to smoke cigarettes and listen to the radio. My radio was on 107.7 The End,
which was Seattle's conventional 'modern rock' station. And as soon
as I turned the ignition key back, I heard the song 'Something in the
Way.' That's when I knew it was true, because The End would have
never fucking played that song otherwise. It wasn't even a single."

The greenhouse where Cobain swallowed a shotgun shell was
torn down in 1996; now it's just a garden. One especially tall sunflower appears to signify where the Nirvana frontman died, but that
might be coincidence. When we arrive at the site, there are four
guys staring at the sunflower. One of them is a goateed 24-year-old
musician named Brant Colella; he's wearing a Glassjaw sweatshirt,
and it has been a long time since I've met someone this earnest.
Colella makes Chris Carrabba seem like Jack Black.

"I'm from New York, but I moved to Portland to make music.
I'm a solo artist. I used to be in a band, but my band didn't have it in
them to go all the way, and that's where I'm going," he says, and
then looks longingly toward the sunflower. "His heart is here. My
heart is here, too. I wanted to see where Kurt lived and hung out. I
wanted to see where he was normal. The night before he died, I had
a dream where Kurt came to me and told me that he was passing the
torch on to me. Then we played some music together."

Colella was 15 when Cobain died on April 5, 1994. Last night, he
and his three friends attended a Mariners game—Ichiro hit a grand
slam to beat the BoSox—but Colella wants to make it *very* clear that
seeing Cobain's house was his primary motivation for visiting Seattle. He also wanted to make it very clear that (A) he hates people
who wear Abercrombie and Fitch; and (B) that Kurt probably didn't
kill himself.

"There are some people who assume he was completely suicide-
driven, but he wasn't like that," Colella says. "I don't want to stir up
waves and get killed myself, but the information that indicates Kurt
was murdered actually makes way more sense than the concept of
him committing suicide. But I'm not here to point fingers and say
Courtney Love did it. Only God knows the answer to this question.
And I realize there are people who want to believe Kurt Cobain
committed suicide. People are kind of broken into two factions:
There are right-wingers who want to use his death to point out that

this is what happens when you listen to rock 'n' roll, and there are also all his crazy fans who want to glorify depression and have Kurt be their icon forever."

When Colella first said this to me, I thought it reductionist, simplistic, immature, and quite frankly, pretty stupid. But the more I think it over the more I suspect he's completely right. Except maybe about the murdering.

Aberdeen, Washington
(Monday, August 18, noon)

Kurt Cobain's hometown can be described with one syllable: *bleak.* Everything appears belted by sea air; the buildings look like they're suffering from hangovers. Just being here makes me feel tired.

In the early 1990s, the suicide rate in Aberdeen was roughly twice as high as the national average. This does not surprise me. It's also a hard-drinking town, and that doesn't surprise me, either: There are actually road signs that inform drivers that the Washington DUI limit is .08 (although it would seem that seeing said signs *while you are actually driving your vehicle* is like closing the barn door after the cows are already in the corn).

I notice these roadside markers as I drive around looking for a bridge that does not exist.

What I am looking for is the bridge on the Wishkah river that Kurt Cobain never slept under. He liked to *claim* that he did (the last official track on *Nevermind,* "Something in the Way," is the supposed story of this nonexperience), and it's quite possible he hung out down there, since hanging out under bridges is something lots of bored, stoned high school kids are wont to do. But Cobain didn't really live under any bridge; he just said he did to be cool, which is a totally acceptable thing to do, considering what Kurt did for a living. Being cool was more or less his whole job.

There are a lot of bridges in Aberdeen—this would be a wonderful community for trolls. I walk under several of these bridges, and I come to a striking conclusion: They all pretty much look the same, at least when you're beneath them. And it doesn't matter if Kurt Cobain slept underneath any of them; what matters is that people *believe* he did, and that is something they want to believe. Maybe it's something they *need* to believe, because if they don't, they will be struck with the mildly depressing revelation that dead people are simply dead. Everything else is human construction; everything else has nothing to do with the individual who died and everything to do with the people who are left behind (and who might even wish those roles were somehow reversed).

As I walk back to my car and prepare to drive back to the world of the living, I think back to the conversation I had with the unabashedly annoyed man who runs the Chelsea Hotel. It turns out that he was right all along: I am not a serious person. I do not have any understanding of death. And I am looking for nothing.

ADAM MANSBACH

Hip-Hop Intellectuals

A Radical Generation Comes of Age

50 Cent's "Get Rich or Die Tryin'" has been topping the charts for two straight months. Eminem's *8 Mile* set an opening-week record for an R-rated movie last winter, hip-hop mogul Russell Simmons took his Def Poetry Jam to Broadway and won a Tony and Ali G, the white-gangsta-rapper persona of British comedian Sacha Baron Cohen, is a hit on American cable.

In ever-evolving forms, hip-hop rules planet Earth, or at least the global entertainment economy from Japan to Cuba. But is there something deeper going on than the flash of 50 Cent's platinum chains and Eminem's silver tongue? Where is hip-hop's artistic vanguard, its intelligentsia? Wasn't this $1.6 billion-a-year industry once rooted in resistance?

It was, and if you know where to look, it still is. Many of today's most vibrant young artists—from rapper Jay-Z to solo performer Sarah Jones to novelist Zadie Smith—can best be understood through the matrix of hip-hop. Just as the jazz aesthetic birthed nonmusicians such as novelist Ralph Ellison, poet Amiri Baraka, photographer Roy Decarava and painter Romare Bearden, hip-hop has produced its own school of thinkers and artists. Call them hip-hop intellectuals: folks who derive their basic artistic, intellectual and political strategies from the tenets of the musical form itself—collage, reclamation of public space, the repurposing of technology—even if they're not kicking rhymes or scratching records.

165

Hip-hop was born in the Bronx, sprouting up in the margins to which people of color had been relegated in the early '70s. Graffiti, rap music and break dancing were assembled from spare parts, ingeniously and in public. Paint cans refitted with oven-cleaner nozzles transformed subway trains into mobile art galleries. Playgrounds and parks became nightclubs; turntables and records became instruments. Scraps of linoleum and cardboard were made into dance floors. Verbal and manual dexterity turned kids into stars, and today's artists grew up listening to the first strains of the musical form.

Today's 25–35 set is hip-hop's second generation—not the pioneers who invented it, but the crew who shepherded the culture into global prominence, political importance, artistic fullness. They were the first to study its history, to strive to "keep it real." This group got involved before hip-hop was a fully mass-mediated form, back when rap radio shows aired at two in the morning and "Yo! MTV Raps" was a thing of the future, not of the past.

"Our generation is a different breed, intellectually," says Jeff Chang, author of "Can't Stop, Won't Stop," a political history of hip-hop due out from St. Martin's Press in 2004. "We've grown up with multiculturalism, grown up in a world where pop culture has always mediated how we analyze the world. We're not afraid of the media anymore; there's a constant dialogue in hip-hop about the gaps between our reality and the ways we're represented. We're naturally interdisciplinary; we mix signifiers, we break everything down to bits and bytes and rebuild something new."

Stitching It All Together

Collage, as Chang suggests, is fundamental to hip-hop, and has been since the beginning. The DJ was the central figure in the culture's early days; his job (at least early on, DJs were all male) was to rock the crowd with whatever worked, which meant digging for sonic snippets anywhere and everywhere and recontextualizing them with seamless spontaneity into a danceable mix. The very sound system on which he played was a pastiche of homemade, self-modified and repurposed equipment. The DJ was a circuit board, receiving, reviewing and cataloging information and retransmitting only the best of the best.

Today's hip-hop intellectual collages ideas with the same democratic, genre-crossing, do-it-yourself attitude. In any poem by Paul Beatty, for example (he's now primarily a novelist—see the review of "Tuff" by Ishamel Reed), one of the first poets to be dubbed "hip-hop" after winning the 1993 Nuyorican Poets' Cafe Slam and still regarded as a leading voice—one finds a field of reference that obliterates high-culture/low-culture distinctions: He rhymes African nationalist Jomo Kenyatta's name with that of white boxing great Jake LaMotta and moves seamlessly from Martin Luther King Jr. to Saturday-morning cartoons.

Hip-hop theater artists such as the pioneering Danny Hoch and Hanifah Walidah ("Straight Black Folks' Guide to Gay Black Folks") cobble together underrepresented voices, taking on multiple identities in their one-person shows to create a fluid new paradigm. In his award-winning "Jails, Hospitals and Hip-Hop," for example, Hoch, 31, embodies 10 characters—from an inmate with AIDS to a Montana rapper to New York street kids—with a sociolinguistic dexterity that comes straight from his roots in multicultural Queens.

The fiction of writers such as Touré ("The Portable Promised Land"), Zadie Smith ("White Teeth"), Junot Diaz ("Drown") and Oakland native Danyel Smith ("More Like Wrestling") crackles with cross-stitched rhythms and multicultural wordplay. And hip-hop activists such as William Upski Wimsatt—who mixed marketing with graffiti in the advertising campaign for his book "Bomb the Suburbs," writing the title on sidewalks nationwide and selling 30,000 copies, unheard-of for a self-published work—have begun to take the notion of uniting and amplifying disparate voices to a political level. Wimsatt's new project is an attempt to create a national voting bloc of young people hungry for change. Using hip-hop as a common language, he hopes to network his generation politically, create voter guides and force candidates to "take our power seriously."

"A hip-hop mind state is an eager, hungry mind state," says Wimsatt. "Kids of my era who got into hip-hop wanted to know everything about it, wanted to master it. The same way I wanted to be the best graffiti writer in Chicago when I was young—and was willing to go out all night and find the spots no one else knew about and paint them—I'm now trying to find the people no one has mobilized politically and bring them together."

Seizing Space

Such attempts to take back public space are a historical part of hip-hop. The musical collages old-school DJs such as Grandmaster Flash, Afrika Bambaataa and Kool Herc created were for the enjoyment of crowds assembled, as often as not, in the playgrounds of the Bronx. The electricity needed to power the sound systems was supplied by jimmying open lampposts and plugging in—a literal reclamation of power from the city, and an early indication of hip-hop's investment in building community and staking out ground by means of creative challenges to uncaring authorities.

Graffiti writers, similarly, reclaimed the urban subterrain, painting elaborate murals on subway trains and eluding capture despite the $250 million the city of New York spent between 1973 and 1988 in its "War on Graffiti" (i.e., its war on young, poor people of color—from the beginning, political attacks on hip-hop had coded meanings).

Today, hip-hop intellectuals are still staking out public space—not only in the arts but also in education and journalism.

University classes on hip-hop have proliferated in the past decade; there are now more than 100 being taught around the country, some by such noted scholars as Tricia Rose (author of the seminal hip-hop text "Black Noise: Rap Music and Black Culture in Contemporary America") and prolific author and University of Pennsylvania Professor Michael Eric Dyson. Alternative high schools such as New York City's El Puente base entire curricula around hip-hop, and nonprofit groups such as Youth Speaks in San Francisco indoctrinate young people into the culture of writing by throwing poetry slams that attract audiences in the thousands.

"In the beginning, we went out with no money and took over classrooms and theaters," says James Kass, Youth Speaks' executive director. "That's hip-hop right there. The idea is to give young folks the space to do what they want to do, to approach writing in ways that are relevant to their daily lives. By the time Youth Speaks started, hip-hop had already laid the foundation for multiracial communication, so we built on that. What people always say about Youth Speaks is that we make poetry cool. Hip-hop is the only place that tells kids it's cool to be creative and smart—the more clever lines you put in your poem, the more response you get."

Even the industry devoted to covering hip-hop culture can be seen as a source of resistance. "Hip-hop journalism works between two worlds," says Chang. "It fights the old-boy rock-critic network and also the highbrow world of cultural criticism—both traditionally very white—by developing an indigenous cultural criticism." The fight Chang describes is taking place not only within the pages of magazines such as the Source, XXL and Stress, which are devoted entirely to the culture. Hip-hop journalists such as Chang, Jon Caramanica, Kalefah Sennah, Oliver Wang and Joan Morgan are also bringing it to the pages of the New York Times, The Nation, Spin and even GQ.

"Ego Trip's Big Book of Racism" (HarperCollins, 2002) is another product of the sensibility Chang describes. A collection of some 200 lists and short articles, ranging from "Movie-Franchise Stereotypes" to "Riot On! The Best of Twentieth-Century Civil Unrest" to "10 Items Found in Every Asian Home Not Worth Stealing," the book blends reportage and opinion, seriousness and absurdity, insight and provocation, into a compulsively readable collage of race trivia. Written by the former editors of the '90s indie magazine Ego Trip—all of whom have moved on to editorial positions at other publications since their brainchild's demise—the "Big Book" pushes boundaries and buttons like the most provocative rappers do: to convey a message, but also for the sheer thrill of getting a response.

An embodiment of the strategies hip-hop intellectuals derive from rappers, the "Big Book" gives rap fans what they look for in MCs: innovation, humor, dexterity, confrontation and fearlessness. The authors engage their readers in call-and-response, blurring the line between performer and audience just like the stage routines old-school rappers developed to engage their crowds: the nature of list making is to invite additions, deletions and arguments, and the nature of provocation (an art the Ego Trip crew has mastered) is to solicit a reply. Articles such as "Six Steps to Interracial Dating Perfection" and "Why Latin Dudes Love Going Downtown" practically beg for a comeback.

Though a palpable hip-hop sensibility runs through the work, there is barely a word in the "Big Book" about beats, rhymes, break dancing or graffiti. This omission illuminates a further point about the hip-hop mind state: Once in place, it maintains no topical allegiance to hip-hop itself. Because hip-hop is a culture that is constantly synthesizing, evolving and testing out new notions, it can survive higher education, wider experience, even the process of growing up. A hip-hopper can be bored to death with every rapper in the world and still consider herself hip-hop.

A Critical Moment, a Lasting Sensibility

In fact, the current class of hip-hop intellectuals is largely fed up with what hip-hop has become—sick of rap's minute attention span, disorganization, violence, misogyny, cynicism, self-obsession, arrogance, machismo, homophobia and materialism. 50 Cent's hedonistic club anthems, Nelly's odes to his Nike Air Force Ones and Missy Elliot's goofy expressions of sexual bravado might be worldwide hits, but they sound hollow to a generation reared on KRS-One's "You Must Learn," Public Enemy's "Fight the Power" and the Jungle Brothers' "Acknowledge Your History"—righteous directives that passed as song titles in the late '80s.

Circa 1988–1990, the zeitgeist years for hip-hop's second generation, rap was going to be The Revolution. Those three groups mentioned above, plus X-Clan, Brand Nubian and Queen Latifah, were articulating the hypocrisy of American life. They railed against police brutality and racial profiling, called for multicultural education, gave their own history lessons.

The music spoke with passion and urgency, reconnected militancy with cool. It opened lines of communication in black youth culture; for the next 10 years after he said it in 1988, nobody could write an article about hip-hop without including Public Enemy front man Chuck D's identification of rap as "the black CNN." And, as has always been the case with black American music, hip-hop articulated something so universal and revelatory that white kids wanted (to listen) in. Some even began to question the skin privilege into which they had been born. Rap was beginning to break down the doors barring access to the mainstream, exploding onto radio and TV with its politics intact.

"When [Public Enemy] hit in '89, they focused a lot of issues that were urgent, from ethnic studies to racism in education to affirmative action to college admissions," says Chang. "It seemed like an incredibly energized period to me. Intellectually, it was all of a piece, from 'Fight the Power' down to how to actualize that in activism and journalism. And if you shift the details, the context is still there for a lot of folks."

But, as Chang notes, "art never produces coherent politics." While deeply oriented to social justice, this generation of young entertainers didn't have the fully conceived agendas, or access to resources, or experience in coalition building, to lead a movement.

By 1991, the market had swung away from consciousness and hip-hop moved into its next phases: gangsta rap, crossover success, worldwide diffusion. KRS-One and Chuck D gave way to Ludacris and the Cash Money Millionaires, and "hip-hop" devolved into a marketing term. But by this time, the hip-hop intellectuals had started to earn their advanced degrees, land book deals, establish their nonprofit organizations and influence literature and theater. In the face of massive commercialization, they were the ones who suddenly found themselves as the experts, the torchbearers, keeping the spirit of hip-hop alive.

*   *   *

At one of Hanifah Walidah's performances of her debut one-woman show, "A Straight Black Folks' Guide to Gay Black Folks," at the Black Box Theater in Oakland last December, the range and insight of one hip-hop intellectual was powerfully on display.

Before an audience that ran the gamut from teen activists to sextegenarian college professors, Walidah gave a commanding, nuanced performance of her multi-character play that deals with gay people being ostracized within the black community. As she transformed herself from a preacher to incense-salesman to undercover angel—all residents of what she calls "Anyblock, USA"—the audience watched raptly, sometimes perfectly hushed and other times exploding into raucous laughter.

For some, the show was a confirmation of their own existence, a chance to see people and perspectives they knew well given the spotlight. For others, Walidah provided a glimpse of an unfamiliar world. But whatever the audience's points of entry, the point of exit was universal: they rose in a standing ovation. Hip-hop—courtesy of a playwright and actress who used to be an MC and a poet, a woman named Hanifah Walidah who used to call herself Sha-Key—had expanded its scope and vision once again.

"People's understanding of hip hop can be really close-minded. You have to talk 'ghetto' or about hip-hop specifically to be hip-hop theater," Walidah told the Chronicle. "I'm like you can talk about anything . . . It's using theater to reflect the end result of your generation."

Or, as Wimsatt puts it, "In '88, we were talking about changing the world. Now we're doing it—through community organizing, electoral politics, business, media, art and philanthropy. Hip-hop gave us the tools, and now we're trying to build the house."

MICHAELANGELO MATOS

69 (Years of) Love Songs

Who wrote the book of love? No one's ever answered that, but we do know who composed love's soundtrack: Damn near everyone.

To prove it, I've put together a kind of audio box of chocolates—inspired equally by Gary Giddins' "Post-War Jazz: An Arbitrary Road Map" and the Magnetic Fields' *69 Love Songs*—of some of the many things love can be. It's not a smoochfest. Betrayal and heartbreak both loom large, and the latter applied to making of the list as well: I've heard (and expect to hear) more about what I've left off than what I've included. (As one friend put it, "What do you mean there's no Sam Cooke or 'Stardust'? Are you *insane*?" My doing this to begin with apparently hadn't convinced her.) Still, as the Magnetic Fields crooned, "The book of love is long and boring/But I love when you read it to me." Singing, as it turns out, works even better.

1934: Pinky Tomlin: "The Object of My Affection."   Appropriately, we begin with schmaltz. Vocally, Tomlin, who wrote this chestnut, was something like Louis Prima minus the buoyancy—lithe, a little winsome, and totally charming. Love is human scale.

1935: Patsy Montana & Prairie Ramblers: "I Want to Be a Cowboy's Sweetheart."   Believe it or not, this record changed everything. It was the first record by a woman to sell a million copies, and made Montana the first female country megastar. Though the subtext of her first hit was later made explicit by the more forward "I Wanna Be a Western Cowgirl," she gives it everything she has, yodeling until—you bet I'm going to say it—the cows come home.

1936: Red Norvo featuring Mildred Bailey: "A Porter's Love Song to a Chambermaid." Housework as foreplay: "I will be your dustpan," Bailey winks over Norvo's good-humored swing, "If you'll be my broom/We could work together/All around the room." Just imagine what they might have accomplished with a Mini-Vac.

1937: Fred Astaire: "(I've Got) Beginner's Luck." Astaire sang like he danced, so suave he convinced you he really had fallen in love for the first time, and was sort of mystified by it: "That's what I've always heard/And always thought absurd/But now I believe every word." Doubly impressive given that it was from his seventh movie with Ginger Rogers.

1938: Robert Johnson: "Love in Vain." The cold, hard facts of life, recited like a fatalist weather report.

1939: Coleman Hawkins: "Body and Soul." Self-explanatory. The way Hawkins fusses over the melody is one of pop music's great acts of love, even if the way he extended it—and extended it, and extended it some more—made him seem something of a libertine.

1940: Duke Ellington: "Me and You." It don't mean a thing if it ain't got that swing, and this does, hard, with a bit more sauce than usual, which with Ellington during this period is saying something. The words are straight-up courtship, while the music invites . . . more.

1941: Ernest Tubb: "Walking the Floor Over You." Stoicism is a country singer's best friend—after heartache, that is.

1942: Billie Holiday: "Trav'lin' Light." Cutting through the perfect, gauzy, orchestration like a fingernail through tissue paper, the queen of heartbreak whistles while she walks away from her latest heartache, swinging her arms by her sides.

1943: Louis Jordan: "Is You Is or Is You Ain't My Baby?"   Jordan's usual comic gait serves as the undertone here—only he's not being funny, which deepens it. Not quite the tears of a clown, just the uncertainty of whether his baby's found somebody new or not, which makes him even more vulnerable—and appealing.

1944: The Ink Spots & Ella Fitzgerald: "I'm Making Believe."   World War II saw a surge of sentimental I'll-be-home ballads, most famously "White Christmas," that captured the country's mood. This is one of the loveliest, matching lead Ink Spot Bill Kenney's Victorian prissiness with Ella's palpable put-a-good-face-on-it ache.

1945: Spike Jones & His City Slickers: "You Always Hurt the One You Love."   Love is farcical, so who better than the auteur of "Der Fuhrer's Face" to soothe a nation's wounds by simultaneously clowning on the Ink Spots and Mills Brothers? When the basso profundo intones, "Honey lamb, honey face, uh-honey piiie," nothing is safe—which doesn't necessarily prepare you for the screams and gunshots to come, but it helps.

1946: Lennie Tristano: "What Is This Thing Called Love?"   Love is modern—or in this case, modernist. Tristano was one of the first jazz musicians to record fully improvised pieces, but he was just as free with standards, as on this solo recording: turning the melody sideways, lurching the rhythm, but keeping a keen sense of play throughout.

1947: Charles Brown & Johnny Moore's Three Blazers: "Merry Christmas Baby."   The definition of insouciant, and—appropriately, given that it's set on December 25th—the ultimate morning-after song.

1948: The Orioles: "It's Too Soon to Know."   An R&B quartet from Baltimore, led by the shivering-timbred Sonny Til, crooning a lament that made the Ink Spots sound like a Shriners Convention and the radio seem like a haunted house. Few records have ever conveyed male desire so poignantly; it spawned a thousand imitators, most of them after birds or cars, and kicked off the doo-wop craze—and maybe all of rock and roll.

1949: Hank Williams: "I'm So Lonesome I Could Cry." Country music's archetypal lament, everybody's covered it, and for good reason: that swooping melody is a singer's dream, and line-for-line, it's probably the most quotable pop song ever, poetry made into everyday speech, and twice as breathtaking for it.

1950: Hank Snow: "I'm Movin' On."   "You've switched your engine, now I ain't got time/For a triflin' woman on my main line . . . I warned you twice, now you can settle the price/'Cause I'm movin' on." In short, more attitude than the state of New Jersey— no wonder it spent three months atop the country charts.

1951: The Larks: "My Reverie."   Love is classic—or in this case, classical, since the gorgeous melody was adapted from Debussy. Lead singer Eugene Mumford, having served 29 months in prison on a false rape charge, sounds both woeful and ecstatic, going out on an impossible high note that seems to freeze the song in midflight, even as the piano and backing dum-dum-dums resolve quietly underneath.

1952: The "5" Royales: "Baby Don't Do It."   A sextet despite their name, these former and future gospel harmonizers chase the secular dollar: "If you leave me pretty baby/I'll have bread without no meat," Johnny Tanner sings, church far behind him. For songwriter-guitarist Lowman Pauling, it began a string of classics that culminated with "Think" and "Dedicated to the One I Love," which not even James Brown or the Shirelles performed better.

1953: The Harp-Tones featuring Willie Winfield: "A Sunday Kind of Love."   Love is religious. What Winfield wants is a relationship that gives him the peace of mind he gets from attending church; the organ and vocal harmonies illustrate his desire without pushing it too far toward the secular, and without making it sound like a drag—a miracle you can believe in.

1954: Chet Baker: "My Funny Valentine." Simultaneously ecstatic and menacing, cuddly and frightening, impressionistic and prophetic, pinprick evil and sexier than hell, harrowing and totally androgynous, this registers as an unanswered prayer for an escape from the slow death of his heroin addiction. It also makes it sound inevitable.

1955: Frankie Lymon & the Teenagers: "Why Do Fools Fall in Love?" For God's sake, people, he was 12 years old! When I was 12 I could barely form a coherent sentence!

1956: James Brown: "Please Please Please." Before concocting the parts of modern music not invented in Jamaica, James Brown was the rawest and most inventive ballad singer this side of Ray Charles. This feral debut single so infuriated King Records president Syd Nathan ("It only has one word!" he exclaimed) that Nathan dropped Brown and fired Ralph Bass, who'd signed him. Then the record shot to number one, and Brown and Bass got their jobs back.

1957: Elmore James: "It Hurts Me Too." There were "blues shouters," but James was a blues screamer, from his cut-glass voice to his night-shivers guitar. Here he begs a woman to leave her man out of simple friendship, though the forthright carnality that infuses all his work is certainly a factor. Sensitive, sure, but every bit as primal, pained, and fearsomely loud as everything else he cut.

1958: Frank Sinatra: "Angel Eyes." Dressed up for the abyss, as usual, Frank hails the last call, also as usual. I don't hear him whispering "Ava" at the song's close the way others swear he does, but the way he utters "You happy people" near the end, all hope drained from his voice, comes close enough.

1959: The Flamingos: "I Only Have Eyes for You." This Chicago quintet were experts at making records that felt both overwhelming and full of room, of which this is the ultimate example—a transformation of a dapper '30s number into a slow, gorgeous epiphany with a hint of fatalism lingering underneath. The ultimate doo-wop record.

1960: The Shirelles: "Will You Love Me Tomorrow?"   The ultimate girl-group record, and never was teenage (or adult) love's ultimate question stated better: "Is this a lasting treasure/Or just a moment's pleasure?" I hereby apologize for every time I've opted for a moment's pleasure over a lasting treasure. Not that I'm taking any of it back, but still.

1961: Elvis Presley: "Can't Help Falling in Love."   "Wise men say/Only fools rush in," so naturally this is his most relaxed record ever, and who could resist his guileless sincerity, the anthemically swooping melody, the backup vocals of the Jordanaires? OK, maybe not the Jordanaires, but still.

1962: Patsy Cline: "Why Can't He Be You?"   The most pained of Cline's not-especially-cheerful ballads—the way her voice cracks on "I hear it all the time" says it all. But when the most passionately sung line in the song is "But his kisses leave me cold," is her predicament cause or effect?

1963: The Ronettes: "Be My Baby."   The opening drumbeat is fixed in the heart of everyone who's heard it—a box set could be made of songs that ripped it off—but it's the way Ronnie Spector declares "For every kiss you give me/I'll give you three" that makes this eternal. Love is ungainly, and sexier than hell for it. Now give her a great big kiss.

1964: Dionne Warwick: "Walk on By."   The most quietly devastating record ever made; when the piano enters, quiet but hard, the bottom drops out as surely as the blast of distortion opens up "Smells Like Teen Spirit." It's so perfect it'll even make you forgive that corny-ass trumpet riff.

1965: Pamelo Mounk'a et Les Bantous de la Capitale: "Amen Maria." Congolese singer-guitarist Mounk'a was never as iconic a figure as his rivals Franco or Tabu Ley Rochereau, but this might be the best record any of them made. The melody unfurls for what seems like forever, carrying you along with it—until two minutes in, when the lead guitar steps forward, lifts the proceedings off the ground, and then the horns send it into the air. Of all the songs on this list you aren't familiar with, find this first.

1966: The Marvelettes: "The Hunter Gets Captured by the Game." The ultimate relationship metaphor, courtesy of, who else, Smokey Robinson, with Wanda Young, usually one of the Marvelettes' secondary singers, delivering the most offhandedly sexy Motown vocal of the '60s. The Marvelettes' greatest hit—and Motown's.

1967: The Rolling Stones: "Let's Spend the Night Together." The Stones at their most open: Mick Jagger actually sounds like he believes that "We could have fun just fooling around," and like he's genuinely overwhelmed on the "And round and round and oh, my, my" that follows. If "This doesn't happen to me everyday" sounds disingenuous coming from '60s rock's biggest sex symbol, figure it's his way of being generous, just like "I'll satisfy your every need," whose corollary, "And I know you will satisfy me," is—he's Mick Jagger—a foregone conclusion.

1968: Tammy Wynette: "Stand By Your Man." The lyrics are such rank male chauvinism, and Wynette's voice breaks so often, you've got to wonder how much she actually means it. Then she hits the chorus—part plea, part willful bravado—and you get your answer: as much as she needs to, which is probably too much.

1969: Serge Gainsbourg & Jane Birkin: "Je T'aime . . . Moi Non Plus." The most (ahem) climatic pop song ever made to that point, Gainsbourg originally recorded this long faked orgasm in 1967, with then-paramour Brigitte Bardot. It's probably best, though, he waited until a more appropriate calendar year to (ahem) do it again, this time with British starlet Birkin, whom he'd met on a movie set. Number one in the UK, it peaked on the American charts at, I kid you not, number 69. (Did he pay *Billboard* off, or what?)

1970: Al Green: "Tired of Being Alone."   Soul's most deeply eccentric, deeply enigmatic figure, this is where Green struck the synthesis that would make him the premier male singer of the '70s. He sings of being tired, so he feigns exhaustion; he sings of loneliness, so he backs his voice into a corner and wails forlornly. Alongside the unstoppable pulse of veteran Memphis soul drummer Al Jackson, Jr., he could have sold cake to a baker.

1971: The Temptations: "Just My Imagination (Running Away with Me)."   An answer record to the Kinks' "Waterloo Sunset," with Ray Davies' impassive observer replaced by Eddie Kendricks' unrequited lover, that surpasses its model in every way, devastated alienation included: the only reason it doesn't sound like a suicide note is that five people are singing it.

1972: The Spinners: "I'll Be Around."   Love is gracious: not only does Phillipe Wynne promise to stay friends with his ex, he even cops to his ongoing attraction to her without sounding like a manipulative jerk. You'd be in a forgiving mood, too, if you had that guitar part behind you.

1973: Marvin Gaye: "Let's Get It On."   You were expecting maybe "You Sure Love to Ball"?

1974: Ken Boothe: "Everything I Own."   Love is transfiguring. Take this cover, in which Bread's dippy soft-rock original is made over into rock-solid reggae soul: the lithe arrangement opens the door, and Boothe's disarmingly sincere vocal brings you all the way in. A number one hit in England that might have done as well in America had it been released here.

1975: 10cc: "I'm Not in Love."   A cushion of sound with a shockingly hard center: the guy's a total prick ("Don't tell your friends about the two of us," yeah stuff it you immature control freak), but the music exposes every word as a lie.

1976: Diana Ross: "Love Hangover."   Disco was derided as mechanical, and once the beat kicks in you can set your watch to it, but the way Miss Ross hisses the lines "Don't call the preacher— *NO!*—I don't need it" will deregulate your breathing in a hurry.

1977: Donna Summer: "I Feel Love."   On second thought, maybe disco *was* mechanical—like this robotic maze of synthesizers and sequencers, over which Summer moans a grand total of 18 words—and maybe that's exactly what's sexy about it.

1978: Buzzcocks: "Ever Fallen in Love."   Opting to leave the state-smashing to the Sex Pistols and the Clash, the Buzzcocks instead discovered how effective punk rock was for gnashing out your personal problems. Here they gnashed so hard it was a wonder they had any teeth left when it was finished.

1979: Prince: "I Wanna Be Your Lover."   The Minneapolis child prodigy's first euphoric burst, a saucily good humored come-on that climaxes with the blunt, "I wanna be the only one you come for." Cute calling card, the world thought; maybe he'll stick around. By 1980's *Dirty Mind*, a scant year later, he'd stop showing quite so much fucking propriety.

1980: George Jones: "He Stopped Loving Her Today."   A true story: the first time I heard this greatest of all country records, I was so distracted by it I had to stop making out with the girl I was with until the song was finished. I don't know whether that makes me any better off than the poor fucker Possum's singing about, but there's no way I'm worse, because most of the song takes place at a funeral—his.

1981: Taana Gardner: "Heartbeat."   Love is obsessive. So is this bassline, which digs the deepest groove in disco history. When New York DJ Larry Levan first heard this record, which he'd pro-vide the definitive remix of, he played it at his club, the Paradise

Garage, and cleared the floor. So he played something else, got the floor back—and kept putting it on again and again until his dancers got the message. Sampled by everyone from De La Soul to Bounty Killer, two club-going generations they still do later.

1982: Gregory Isaacs: "Night Nurse."   In the year Marvin Gaye came back with "Sexual Healing," this mirror-image record emerged from Jamaica: bubbling synth lines, insinuating beats, totally assured begging that nobody but these guys this smooth could possibly get away with. They even both have nurses—Isaacs just put them in the song instead of the video. Weird.

1983: Loose Joints: "Tell You (Today)."   Kitchen-sink disco, with cherry-sour horns, a whistled hook, and piano-led dynamic shifts that sound like a comet knocking down a telephone booth over a nervous, knuckle-hard groove. Brought to you by the late Arthur Russell, who'd worked with Allen Ginsberg, Laurie Anderson, Ali Akbar Khan, and Larry Levan, and sang the lyric like he was giving directions to a tourist.

1984: Thompson Twins: "Hold Me Now."   "Warm my heart," these Limey fops moan—and then they do! Vocative speech lives!

1985: Chaba Fadela & Cheb Sahraoui: "N'sel Fik."   Love and marriage go together like a house and fire, at least on this Algerian record, the Arab world's biggest hit of the mid-'80s. The title means "You Are Mine," and wife Fadela and husband Sahraoui aren't kidding—over a fierce rai groove, they're as devoted as Marvin & Tammi, and as eyeball-to-eyeball desperate as John & Exene. They couldn't sound more intense if they were quarreling over what color to paint the bedroom.

1986: New Order: "Bizarre Love Triangle (Shep Pettibone Remix)."   On the original, Bernard Sumner sings, "Every time I think of you/I feel a shock right through like a bolt of blue." Pettibone's remix illustrates that shock—only his quick edits and warm synth build-ups turn that shock every color of the spectrum.

1987: Guns N' Roses: "Sweet Child o' Mine." Claims that bloat got the better of them are exaggerated: they were bombastic even when they were lean and hungry. But at their best, their grandiosity was justified—sometimes big emotions demand big production, big guitar sounds, big vocals, all teetering on overkill, all staying on the right side.

1988: Lucinda Williams: "I Just Wanted to See You So Bad." Long before becoming Starbucks Nation's agony aunt, Williams' cult was tiny but fierce. These 27 perfect lines, 12 of which are the title, that add up to the most accurate song about a long-distance relationship ever written, not to mention the roadhouse-perfect guitar and organ licks that accompany them, are a good indication why.

1989: De La Soul: "Eye Know." In a genre as brag-heavy as hip-hop, any artists confident enough to promise, as Posdnous and Trugoy do here, that "My peak of love for you is brought to an apex/Sex is a mere molecule" is clearly a catch. Not to mention quite possibly being the first rappers to use the term "by golly gee."

1990: L.L. Cool J: "Around the Way Girl." Hip-hop's greatest personal ad: "I want a girl with extensions in her hair/Bamboo earrings, at least two pair/Fendi bag and a bad attitude/That's all I need to get me in a good mood." Well, that's not *all*, but you get the idea.

1991: Matthew Sweet: "Evangeline." Love is dorky. Actually, this one probably doesn't count: Sweet only *thinks* he loves Evangeline, and says so in the chorus. Mostly he just wants to fuck her. She's a comic book character. And he's a power-pop singer. *Perfect*.

1992: Baby D: "Let Me Be Your Fantasy." Love is cheesy, nowhere more agreeably than this archetypal rave anthem, as much a paean to ecstasy-a.k.a.-MDMA as ecstasy-as-post-orgasmic sensation or other human beings—not that anyone is complaining.

1993: Bikini Kill: "Rebel Girl." "That girl thinks she's the queen of the neighborhood/I've got news for you/*She is!*" This was probably inspired by Joan Jett, so it's only fitting that of the three versions Bikini Kill recorded of their greatest song, the one I'm choosing (available on *The Singles*) is the one Jett herself provides guitar and backing vocals for.

1994: M People: "Excited." This perfectly constructed, utterly irresistible house music ode to sexual freedom, sung by deep-voiced Heather Small backed by a butch male chorus, pivots on the second verse: "So climb right on in/You know our love's not a sin/You can kiss all of me/'Cos you're my ecstasy." (She probably doesn't mean MDMA either.) Love is never having to say you're sorry, and reveling in it.

1995: James Carter: "You Never Told Me That You Care." The greatest of jazz's mid-'90s young lions purrs. He also moons, hollers, shows off, cajoles, plays real purty, swings slow, and makes every note count.

1996: Amy Rigby: "Beer & Kisses." Love is worth saving. Even if the couch you used to make out on is now where you sleep after yet another fight. The details are heartbreaking and the resolution hopeful—a rare combination—you'll root for them, even if you suspect it's too late.

1997: Yo La Tengo: "Autumn Sweater." The low hum of Converse-shod boys and girls: organ wash, fuzz-bomb bass, and the funkiest drumbeat in all of indie rock, complete with conga breaks. Ira Kaplan's murmur is so awestruck-devotional you'd be amazed if he and the drummer *weren't* married.

1998: Aaliyah: "Are You That Somebody?" The greatest record ever by the subtlest female R&B singer of her generation. But as fabulous as Aaliyah's performance is, this belongs to producer Timbaland, who pushed an already terrific song over the top with the most eccentric production to hit mainstream radio since approximately "I Am the Walrus"—before he and Missy Elliott discovered Bollywood on "Get Ur Freak On," that is.

1999: Armand Van Helden featuring Roland Clark: "Flowerz." An aural iris shot, focused through a red lens: limpid garage-house bassline, dewy guitars and strings, and Clark's love-struck falsetto, so wet it threatens to dissolve completely, so feverish it can give you tunnel vision.

2000: Future Bible Heroes: "I'm Lonely (And I Love It)." Stephin Merritt's definitive moment, an antiheartbreak anthem released a year after *69 Love Songs*: "I'm as lonely as an eagle and I'm crazy as a loon/Who would ever think I could get over you so soon? . . . If that's how it feels to get your heart broken/Break my heart again."

2001: Daft Punk: "Digital Love." The Stay-Puft Marshmallow Man pours his sweet, sticky heart out while Giorgio Moroder rewrites the "Layla" riff in the background. Some people swore they were being ironic, but I believe every single word and bleep.

2002: Kylie Minogue: "Love at First Sight." As spangly and dizzy with grace notes as "Digital Love" (love that bongo loop), only with the Euro-Madonna riding the disco groove for all it's worth. She conflates seeing and hearing ("It was love at first sight/Baby when I heard you for the first time I knew/We were meant to be as one") like a born MTV product. And speaking of which: sexiest video *ever*, with no excess flesh displayed.

BARRY MAZOR

Same Shabby Dress

The Legacy of Little Miss Cornshucks

Almost everyone knows the song "Try a Little Tenderness." Most remember it as the soul ballad nailed by Otis Redding in 1966—based, he always said, on ideas heard in performances by Sam Cooke and Aretha Franklin a few years before. Some recall its origins as a sentimental number recorded by Bing Crosby, Ruth Etting and others in the early 1930s.

But almost *no one* remembers how the song first jumped from crooners to modern soul—transformed by a diminutive singer dressed as some down-home bumpkin just come to town, sitting on the edge of a stage barefoot and weary, actually *wearing* that "shabby dress" of the lyric, and just letting it wail.

On the forgotten 1951 recording by *that* singer, the song cuts across the space from microphone to speakers, and then across the years, with an almost embarrassing intimacy, an intimacy never to be forgotten by those who have heard it. The record begins with a low sax moan, and her singing builds to a heart-rending, pleading ending: "*Awww-oh* . . . oh, it's so easy—try a little . . . *tenderness!*" It sets the pattern for all the famous versions which followed.

Today, most people have never heard of that powerful performer, let along had the chance to hear her music. That's as large a distortion in the American musical record as the now-corrected neglect of "Lovesick Blues" songster Emmett Miller.

She was called Little Miss Cornshucks.

Miss Cornshucks was, above all, a unique *live* performer. She riveted audiences from Los Angeles to Chicago to New York in the post-World War II years, the "after-hours blues" era between swing and rock 'n' roll, when the break between jazz and popular R&B was not yet a chasm.

She was not a back-country singer of acoustic folk blues. She did not fit the scat-singing "Great Lady with precision vocal instrument" model favored by jazz critics and historians. Neither did she provide the cool rebel or dead-by-25 personal story often sought by those looking for the proto-rock romance. Thus, she's fallen between the card files of chroniclers of all forms.

Little Miss Cornshucks has merited but a line or two in any available reference work, with not even basic facts—her birth and recent death dates, her married name—accurately reflected. But she *has* been mentioned repeatedly in the memoirs of R&B, jazz and vaudeville performers alike, as a personal favorite and as a singular influence.

Ahmet Ertegun, the storied chief and co-founder of Atlantic Records, chose to begin *What'd I Say*, his recent memoir of the label's rise to dominance in soul, jazz and rock 'n' roll, by remembering Miss Cornshucks as "the best blues singer" he's *ever* heard, "to this day." She was the first performer he was moved to record, privately, when he was awed by her appearance at a Washington, D.C., nightclub in 1943.

As he recently shared a new listen to "Tenderness" and the 30 other sides Miss Cornshucks recorded (most over 50 years ago, and virtually all unavailable since), Ertegun's eyes welled up. "*That*," he said, surrounded by his memorabilia of Ray Charles and the Rolling Stones and Led Zeppelin, "was the reason I got into this business in the first place."

"Little Miss Cornshucks was the most important voice that I'd heard," says Ruth Brown, the hugely successful singer who helped transform R&B into rock 'n' roll in the '50s, "and, I'm proud to say, she was a *big* influence for me. There was something really deep in her *meaning*. That was the kind of stylist that I wanted to be; closing your eyes, you could say *just* what her meaning was."

By the late '40s, Little Miss Cornshucks' unique style was already a powerful bridge between generations of singing—combining the emotional wallop and clarity Brown recalls, predicting the best soul music of the 1960s—while keeping alive the undiluted sentiment of 1920s Ethel Waters-era vaudeville and torch singing, and working the phrasing and rhythm smarts of 1940s Billie Holiday-era swing for good measure. The continuing shock of that synthesis is a key source of Cornshucks' power as a vocalist.

"There were three singers of that era who were the *best*," Ertegun reflected. "Miss Cornshucks, Dinah Washington, and Little Esther Phillips. But Cornshucks was just so . . . *soulful.*"

Little Esther is anthologized; Dinah Washington is even memorialized on a postage stamp. But the story of Little Miss Cornshucks has been a blank postcard in the dead letter office.

The story began in Ohio. By her own testimony to the only one who seems to have asked, the late liner-notes author and *Ebony* magazine reporter Marc Crawford, Cornshucks was born Mildred Cummings in Dayton, Ohio, "learned to sing at her mother's knee, and got a great big soul in church."

Federal records show that she was, in fact, born May 26, 1923. Her own daughter, Francey, adds that Mildred was the smallest, youngest child in a large musical family; she regularly sang spiritual-style gospel with her sisters around Dayton, in a popular local act billed as the Cummings Sisters. A brother was a working musician as well

As a teenager in the 1930s, Francey said, Mildred was already stepping out at amateur shows or performing for the family as a single. A lover of poignant, torchy ballads, she began to adopt heart-tugging, down-and-out tramp costumes when she sang them. Briefly, she tried an outfit that presaged street hip-hop gear by decades, but found that her largely black audiences, which consisted of many rural southerners who had migrated to northern towns, seemed to respond best to a touch of country style.

That meant donning a plaid shirt at first, then more, much in the way Charlie Chaplin found his "Little Tramp" character's suit—piece by piece. Mildred's mother finally made her the first of the full pantaloons-and-gingham-dress outfits that would be a key part of her emerging Little Miss Cornshucks stage persona. Never finding shoes that seemed quite right, she started taking to the stage barefoot.

A woman who had been promoting gospel acts around Dayton (her name thus far unrecalled) first brought Mildred to Chicago in 1940, solo. Chorus girl Eloise Williams Hughes, now 87, remembers Mildred's first arrival at Chicago's famed 1,000-seat Club DeLisa the following year.

"The dance orchestra at that time was Red Saunders'. We just looked up one day and she was there"—with her stage character set and practiced, and an act that quickly grabbed attention. "And she was in love—*madly* in love with a young man! I mean, as things got going good for her, she bought *him* a Cadillac, which was *something*, back in those days. It was the talk of the club!"

The young man, just six months older than Mildred, was Cornelius Jorman, whom she'd met and married back in Ohio, at a very young age. Ertegun remembers him at this stage as a short young fellow in a Wilberforce College sweatshirt; he was from an Indianapolis family that had briefly been living in Dayton.

"She was very conservative at that time; she was in love; she had a kid," recalls orchestrator Riley Hampton, then an alto sax player with Red Saunders' popular big band. "When we were at the DeLisa, her husband was always there. He'd have that car out in the alley, and he kept their baby out there."

That would have been their first child, Francey; two more arrived soon after—daughter Phyllis (whom some at the DeLisa called "Cornshucks Junior"), then son Chauncey. The children were only rarely seen in public, generally staying with the Cummings family in Ohio, particularly as Cornshucks' husband joined her on the road as her personal manager. Mildred was already soloing in smaller black clubs around the country when Ruth Brown saw her perform at the Big Track Diner in Norfolk, Virginia.

It was on that same 1943 mini-tour that Ahmet Ertegun recorded Cornshucks in Washington, privately, backed by some visiting musicians from Kansas City, including pianist Johnny Malachi, who later worked with Sarah Vaughan. Results of that amateur recording session, Ertegun regrets, are permanently lost.

"When I first saw her," he recalled, "she sang pretty much the same sorts of things as Dinah Washington—'Kansas City,' for instance—but then she also had that song, 'So Long.'"

Originally the closing theme for bandleader Russ Morgan's radio show, "So Long" is a ballad of loss and parting that had in 1940 been turned into a modest Ink Spots-style hit by the Dayton-born Charioteers vocal group. By '43, they were regulars on Bing Crosby's radio show, and heroes back home. Cornshucks adopted their song and hushed crowds with it.

Little Miss Cornshucks was not just a name Mildred took to match a costume, but a character role she filled. She'd arrive on stage barefoot, her close-cropped but pigtailed wig topped by a little girl ribbon or a frayed, wide-brimmed Huck Finn straw hat, and wearing that ragged, country girl's make-do dress—usually bolstered by what a Chicago *Defender* columnist would term "thirtieth century bloomers." She'd bring a straw basket with her, place it gently at the side of the stage, and watch it get filled with cash as she sang. Sometimes, multiple observers pointed out, it would take two baskets to hold it all.

Her stage manner was summed up smartly in a 1947 ad for Chicago's famed Regal Theater: *The Dynamic Blues Sensation Little Miss Cornshucks, the Bashful, Barefoot Girl with Blues*. She was often described not just as a "blues warbler" but as a top "rustic comedienne," reporters invoking a term then more associated with Minnie Pearl at the Grand Ole Opry than with any jazz/blues act.

Fan Charles Margerum, who much later on would briefly manage her, says, "It's not so much that she was *clowning*, or telling jokes, but she did comic things onstage. You know how Fanny Brice would *be* 'Baby Snooks'? Cornshucks did that sort of thing."

She might dance the latest steps out front of the orchestra and chorus girls. "Bashfully" poking her cheek, she might "accidentally" lift her skirt to reveal a pair of famously great legs. She might even stand there picking her nose, "forgetting" where she was. But from that distracted, unkempt little girl would come this no-joke woman's voice. Riveted audiences would simply not know what was coming next.

Along with modern blues numbers, she'd mix in old torch songs such as "Time After Time" or "Why Was I Born?", written by Kern and Hammerstein for a 1929 Broadway show. The latter song came to be associated with singers such as Judy Garland (when she donned *her* down-and-lonely hobo street urchin characters), or Carol Burnett (as that lonely late-night cleaning lady). These sentimental, comic personifications reached the global stage, and owed more than a little to the "special audience" Cornshucks original.

If, in the wake of those big-time show business performers, the Little Miss Cornshucks character may seem less fresh now, the act was essentially one-of-a-kind in its era. Black women in vaudeville and clubs, even the comics, had almost always emphasized glamour.

There were other startling connections to those later "mainstream" acts as well. "From the time I first saw her, she sat down on the edge of the stage and sang right to you, *all of that*, long before Judy Garland did it," Ruth Brown points out.

Garland would adopt the same stage tactic at her famed concert at the New York Palace theater in 1951, and reprise it in the film *A Star Is Born*—which, provocatively, also featured her in a Cornshucks-like country street girl outfit dancing along with black kids. (Garland had frequented the very clubs where Mildred appeared in the '40s, and they eventually shared a number of direct Hollywood ties.)

"Cornshucks' schtick was trying to *get* to you," Margerum recalls. "She could just *mesmerize* a certain type of crowd." That type of crowd was most prevalent in northern cities, especially in Chicago, where masses of rural southern Afro-Americans had migrated, searching for work, beyond the reach of segregation by statute.

Many in her urbane, largely black club audience had some far-from-urban memories, whether firsthand or received from parents—memories reawakened by performances of a shy, funny, but vulnerable country woman-child you wanted to protect, who, like Garland or French street heroine Edith Piaf, had somehow been badly hurt.

By 1945, in that town, Little Miss Cornshucks was becoming a star.

Cornshucks was featured at Chicago's posh Rhumboogie Club, owned by heavyweight champ Joe Louis, where jazz band conductor and arranger Marl Young worked with the likes of T-Bone Walker (on guitar) and Charlie Parker (on sax). When Young moved over to the top-of-the crop Club DeLisa to conduct the Fletcher Henderson Orchestra there, that already familiar haunt became Cornshucks' regular home base, for years to come.

The DeLisa was nearly as famed in its day as New York's Cotton Club, but with an audience that, by the '40s, was more racially integrated. There are photos of everyone from Gene Autry and Louis Armstrong to John Barrymore hanging out there. Since the price of admission was as little as the cost of "set ups" (glasses and ice, maybe with a mixer) and you could choose to bring your own, the sophisticated street really did mingle with the elite—black and white. For many, it was also the sort of place where, as it's often put, "you could buy *anything* you wanted."

In 1945, seasonal themed revues at the DeLisa would run all night, featuring celebrated dancers such as the Step Brothers or Cozy Cole, comics such as George Kirby, and top-line orchestras. One who played behind Cornshucks regularly in the Fletcher Henderson Orchestra, keyboardist Sonny Blount, would have the ongoing chance to observe these extravaganzas and Mildred's character-based headline act closely. He must have learned a lot: He eventually produced more modernist revues of his own and transformed himself into the character called Sun Ra.

Cornshucks regularly delivered the rhythm numbers the times demanded; raucous jump blues was king. But it wasn't everything.

"Mike DeLisa, the club owner, wanted her to do *those* blues, but we had that slow ballad 'So Long' that she did, and I would call the number," Marl Young remembers. "He'd come rushing up the aisle to say, *'Don't do it!'* and I'd just turn my head like I didn't hear him. When she took that stage, boy—that was it! Everybody stopped and was quiet, listening and *looking*."

By the following year, Young and his brothers were running a short-lived record label, Sunbeam, among the earliest to have been black-owned, with Miss Cornshucks as their star act. The half-dozen sides she cut there in 1946 document a varied, experimental recording act in the making.

If some of these first records, though skilled, are very much of their moment, with noticeable Billie Holiday influences, others startle.

"When Mommy Sings A Lullaby" shows Cornshucks' character-ization skills, sounding alternatively like the joyous remembrance of the child and of an assuring mother—on the same record. Margerum accurately describes that chameleon-like quality cap-tured on these lavishly orchestrated 78s: "She had a good voice—but not *only* a good voice; it didn't always *show* the same way."

Her affecting signature tune "So Long" was a regional hit, Sun-beam's largest; poet Langston Hughes would cite this orchestral version as among his favorite jazz recordings of all time. Arguably, the number would work even better on a simpler 1951 Coral Records version.

The most remarkable of the Sunbeam sides is "I Don't Love You Any More," a swinging upbeat blues co-written by Cornshucks and Young. The lyrics and music taunt the abusive man who has tossed her out into the street, left her drifting door to door—and Corn-shucks turns it, in a moment of self-discovery of newfound freedom, into a triumph of female independence.

In her own life, however, Mildred Cummings Jorman's blues were not so handily beaten.

She suffered from growths in her nasal cavity, leaving the impres-sion on several recordings that she may have had a bad cold. She received regular injections to treat them, fearing that having the growths removed would alter her inimitable voice. She also suffered from severe asthma; there were times they had to rush her from dusty stages right to a hospital, because she simply couldn't breathe.

Back in Ohio, other aspiring performers in the Cummings family were increasingly jealous of young Mildred's growing success, even as she was essentially supporting them with whatever money she earned, daughter Francey says: "They were taking advantage of her—and they weren't the only ones."

Meanwhile, the once-proud husband Cornelius, functioning as her manager, was described by some who met him first in the mid-'40s as someone "to be avoided." More than one observer present at that time suggests strongly that, like many around the 1940s night-club scene, he'd become involved with drugs on some level. Friends of Mildred from Chicago state flatly that he'd been unfaithful, and was now "just showing up to take some money and go."

Their daughter Francey does not dispute that scenario. "Well, they were very young people—and flighty. Just *out* there," she says, "and he was even *more* out there than she was! He was just young and wild, that's all. And they were very off and on with each other."

As Eloise Hughes, the last surviving DeLisa chorus girl, put it, "She'd been *so* much in love with him, and he was womanizing. I think his cheating on her was what set her on her downfall."

With the marriage over for most practical purposes, Cornelius returned to Indianapolis. Under the pressure, even friendly observers suggest, Mildred began to drink too much.

"She began to turn," says arranger Hampton. "It had to do with her family and the divorce from her husband. She was drinking a lot and lost control of herself."

The immediate family says that people exaggerated Mildred's state; that she never, for instance, really suffered from what a common street diagnosis termed "mental problems," that these experiences even toughened her. In any case, it was in this troubled context, ironically, that the most prominent phase of Little Miss Cornshucks' professional life bloomed.

While the fledgling Sunbeam label had to be sold off in less than a year, the records cut there added to her fame nationally. With Cornelius moving to the background, Arthur Bryson, described at the time as "the one Negro full-time theatrical agent on Broadway," became her working manager. A 1948 report in *Color* magazine says Cornshucks had already "had a telling effect" on Bryson's growing business, and shows her autographing new reissues of her Sunbeam sides on the Old SwingMaster label, as fans—black and white—await their copies.

Mid-'40s reviews report smash shows in Detroit, where she replaced jump blues star Wynonie Harris at the Frolics Bar; success in New York City clubs such as the Baby Grand; and across the whole so-called "Around the World" tour of major urban black theaters: the Washington Howard, the Philadelphia Earle, the Chicago Regal, the New York Apollo.

As Lee Magid, producer at key jazz and R&B label Savoy Records, told Arnold Shaw for his 1978 book *Honkers and Shouters*, "that little black chick with two buckets and pigtails would come out in the Apollo Theater—in *rags*—and sing her ass off."

It was on one of these trips to Detroit, show dancer Henry "Henny" Ramsey says, that he and Miss Cornshucks met and began traveling together for several years. The children remained with her family in Dayton. Ramsey describes their relationship as a brief, *de facto* marriage. A good amount of their time was spent in her new home-away-from-home, the bustling, lively, late-'40s jazz and R&B scene around Los Angeles' Central Avenue.

Cornshucks headlined at the Last Word Room, played one-nighters with acts such as the Joe Lutcher Jump Band and Joe Liggins, and starred at the top Central Avenue venue, the Club Alabam, along with T-Bone Walker and Wynonie Harris, and comedians Redd Foxx and Moms Mabley. The music, built on honking saxes and electric guitars, sparked hot new dances and attracted Hollywood stars who came to take in the moves.

L.A. jump king Johnny Otis has described the Club Alabam scene thusly: When two main bands, his own and Harlan Leonard's Kansas City Rockers, backed singers such as Cornshucks, you "could see the music that was to be named 'rhythm and blues' taking shape."

Cornshucks' live performance peak was a set of shows in early 1948 in downtown Los Angeles at the elaborate, 2,200-seat Million Dollar Theater, a former movie palace then hosting acts such as Nat King Cole and Artie Shaw. Cornshucks was advertised as "the new look in comedy" and referred to in an L.A. *Sentinel* report as "a rustic comedienne as good as Judy Canova." Comparisons to Canova—popular, energetic white country girl entertainer—were usually reserved for Minnie Pearl. Cornshucks' stand at the Million Dollar Theater set house records.

Her reputation as a comedienne bore additional fruit when in November 1947 she was cast in *Campus Sleuth*, a B-movie made at Monogram Pictures, home of the Bowery Boys and Charlie Chan. One in a series of cheap, hour-long musical mysteries involving the Teen Agers (a set of young, adventuring friends including Freddie Stewart, June Preisser, and the future Lois Lane of TV's 1950s "Superman" series, Noel Neill), this forgotten film also featured swing band leader Bobby Sherwood, Judy Garland's brother-in-law.

The film, released later in 1948, has proven impossible, thus far, to find, missing even from the Library of Congress and university

Monogram Pictures archives. But a shooting script shows that Mildred Jorman (billed as playing the *character* Little Miss Cornshucks) appeared later in the picture, running a haywagon ride on a campus reunion weekend with her "boyfriend," singer Jimmy Grissom. (Grissom, who, like Mildred, recorded for Miltone records at that time, would eventually sing with the Duke Ellington Orchestra.)

Cornshucks, in full character regalia, has comedy bits, cries when the boy hides from her in the woods (her daughter recalls that she could cry "on a dime"), then sings (a handwritten note on the script indicates) a new self-penned number she would soon record, "Cornshucks Blues."

Meanwhile, her own dramas had hardly ended under the California sunshine. They took her, once, to the outskirts of a still obscure Las Vegas, Nevada.

"Her husband kidnapped her out of there one time," Henny Ramsey says. "I was sitting at home waiting for her to come home from the movie studio, and when 6 o'clock come, I said, 'Where's Shucks?' The phone rang, and she was saying, 'Baby . . . Cornelius just said "Get in the car," and drove me clean to Las Vegas! . . . And he put me out and took the money and the car.' He just left her in the mountains out there . . . in the desert."

Inevitably, with her rising fame, new recording opportunities followed, all in Los Angeles.

The first sessions, in May 1948, were at that little Miltone label, under the direction of tenor sax player Maxwell Davis. Today, Davis is called the father of west coast R&B, the man behind hits by Percy Mayfield and B. B. King as well as early recordings of Charles Mingus. He cut nine sides at Miltone with Cornshucks—including the memorable ballad "In the Rain" (later covered by Ruth Brown), a sweet turn on the standard "He's Funny That Way," and excursions into straight blues, such as the "Cornshucks Blues" number from the *Campus Sleuth* movie.

The Miltone 78s show Cornshucks in complete command vocally. In light of the senseless "divamatic" oversinging so prevalent in pop, country and R&B today, it's downright bracing to hear the ease and simplicity with which she can make clear both acceptance of love *and* its loss.

On these sides she sings soft and slow, without frills, painting a picture of the situation, until—just at the right moment—there's a sudden cry or a stern warning, completing the emotional picture and bringing us along. Her ability to hold and then stun listeners in a single number, which mesmerized live audiences, is detectable on record as well.

The Miltone singles were credited to "Little Miss Cornshucks with The Blenders"—the Blenders being a house band built around musicians who played with Roy Milton's hit-making Solid Senders. At least one side, the ballad "Keep Your Hand On Your Heart," was arranged by pianist Calvin Jackson, who would later ghost-orchestrate more than a dozen movie scores for MGM, including *Meet Me In St. Louis*, starring Judy Garland.

Cornshucks' homecomings to Chicago were triumphs now. *Defender* columnist Lou Swarz gushed, after the Million Dollar Theater triumph, that agent Arthur Bryson was "being offered heap much" for her to make a return engagement to an unspecified Chicago venue: "No wonder," he added, "with her act being so unique. Watch the climb to stardom of Little Miss Cornshucks!"

Ramsey remembers a series of unchronicled shows Cornshucks did out on the road around this time with the old vaudevillian and bandleader Ted "Is everybody *happy?*" Lewis, including a show at the upscale Los Angeles club Ciro's. "She had them white people cryin' out there, every time she sang," he says.

Such a racially integrated act would have been unusual. It's also suggestive that Lewis frequently sang "She's Funny That Way" himself, and that he had been an early performer of a number Corn-shucks soon adopted to extraordinary effect: "Try a Little Tender-ness."

Back in California, at Aladdin Records in 1949, she waxed a couple of new tunes as Miss Cornshucks & Her All-Stars. "Waiting In Vain" is among her most expressive recordings, featuring close vocal give-and-take with a deep, aching sax that is very likely Maxwell Davis' again; he was the key producer there.

Cornshucks' exemplary emotional and vocal control is also evident on "(Now That I'm Free) You Turned Your Back On Me," in which she pulls off a challenging feat: She rides the upbeat feeling of just getting free, but still cues us in on the pain she feels when spurned by the second lover supposedly waiting for this moment.

The song may or may not reflect the fact that her relationship with Henny Ramsey was about over. Young daughter Francey, home in Dayton, was unaware of it at the time, but in retrospect is surprised it lasted even that long, since after her marriage troubles, "Mom never got that close to *anybody*," Francey says.

Ramsey's own perspective: "Well, she started drinking that whiskey, and I couldn't live with it. If she'd see me even talkin' to a woman, she would come up and start fighting. I had to stand at the end of the stage until she got off, so she could see me! She was so sweet when I first met her—but it was that *whiskey*, man."

In the summer of 1950, Cornshucks was featured in an *Ebony* magazine cover story that focused on how popular jump blues had become. She was included right along with the biggest names of the era—Arthur Crudup, Ivory Joe Hunter, Roy Brown and Amos Milburn. Professionally, at least, things were rolling.

The small-group approach used effectively at Aladdin set the stage for sessions at Coral Records in 1950 that featured the best backing band she'd ever have, under the direction of swing legend Benny Carter.

"Papa Tree Top Blues," among the first sides Cornshucks cut with Carter at Coral, is one of her most striking extended blues turns. They also recorded, with bright, positive results, Carter's pre-rock composition "Rock Me To Sleep"; it's probably the best uptempo number in her catalogue.

Union contract records show that the previously unnamed jazz musicians on these sides, whom even Benny Carter himself can no longer identify by ear or memory, included such busy Central Avenue talents as Bumps Meyer, Que Martyn and Charles Waller on saxes, Eddie Beal on piano, and Mingus' teacher Billy Hadnott on bass.

Recorded at Coral's state-of-the-art studio on Melrose Avenue, these sides show just what Little Miss Cornshucks could be— singing like one smooth, vibrating violin, then suddenly shaking you like a horn. These, and the follow-up singles cut there in 1951, for which no session notes survive, were the best records she ever made.

They included the definitive recording of "So Long"—never more rueful, full of surprising syllable bends, stretches and trills, yet utterly direct; the blues "I Lost My Helping Hand," in which she handles great vocal and emotional ranges in tandem with Carter's honking sax; and, so notably, that record which introduced "Try a Little Tenderness" to the world of soul.

But if this was the working peak for Mildred Cummings Jorman and her Little Miss Cornshucks show, a series of circumstances and limitations would make 1951–52 the *de facto* end of her near stardom.

Back in Chicago, Delores Williams, a young niece of blues legend Memphis Minnie, was dressed up, by owners of clubs that Cornshucks had played, in an outfit indistinguishable from hers—and billed as "Miss Sharecropper." Confusion was inevitable, and deliberate. Miss Sharecropper's handlers even recorded "So Long" with *her* for National Records in 1950.

In New York, Ahmet Ertegun and Herb Abrahamson had started up Atlantic Records in 1948, on a $500 loan. While they remembered Cornshucks fondly, as Ertegun explains now, "We didn't know then even where to *find* her. And at that time, we didn't have money for things like finding people!"

They did know a young singer in town named Ruth Brown, who would deliver such a string of early hits with them that Atlantic is often called "the House that Ruth built." What's generally forgotten is that Miss Cornshucks provided some of the blueprint for that house, since the first, key smash hit was an outright copy of Cornshucks.

"You've heard Ruth Brown's record of 'So Long'?" Ertegun asks. "Well, that doesn't even sound like Ruth; she sounds like a different singer! And it doesn't sound like any other recording she made ever after, either. We signed her at first *because* she could sound like Cornshucks!"

Brown, charming in her candor, is even more blunt: "I *stole* that from her! It was a big hit for me—and it should have been hers."

Not one of the labels that handles Miss Cornshucks ever furnished the kind of ongoing support someone who could be so delicate surely required.

Coral/Decca didn't back her for long, but she was contracted there just long enough to miss a potentially bigger opportunity. In 1951, she was singing with Maurice King's band at the Detroit Flame Show Bar when Okeh/Columbia Records producer Danny

Kessler caught her act. He'd tell *Honkers and Shouters* author Arnold
Shaw, "I *flipped* over her, but found that she was unavailable."

A white boy who had seen Cornshucks perform in Chicago, and
had developed a similarly dramatic way with a ballad, followed her
onstage that night. Kessler signed *him* instead, and they would be
pushing out hit after national hit together just a few months later.
The boy's name was Johnny Ray. (Legendary San Francisco critic
Ralph J. Gleason later underscored that Ray's famed rock-predicting
emotional style was, in fact, influenced heavily by Cornshucks.)

Mildred's own recently burgeoning career then took a series of
hard hits in rapid succession.

Miltone's Warr Perkins and William Reed put out some sweet
78s with amusing cartoon labels that collectors love, but they were
more interested in selling off record rights than in actually pushing
discs. The Miltone sides were delayed, then sold to Aladdin,
Gotham *and* Deluxe Records—in some cases to all three, practically
at once. These labels began stepping on each other's release dates, as
announcements in *Billboard* indicate. The generally positive *Billboard* previews of the records were not enough to help. And Cornshucks would not have been paid for those resold sides at all.

A would-be "manager," claiming to represent Cornshucks, put
come-on announcements in the trade papers and Afro-American
weeklies, detailing an enticing upcoming tour of Latin America that
never occurred.

Marl Young, who had moved to California and become a successful conduit of reconsolidation and racial integration of the Los
Angeles musicians' unions, calls the parties from Miltone "crooked
S.O.B.s." Trade papers reported that these parties were being sued
by Miltone founder Roy Milton for record bootlegging, even as
Mildred began recording. Young adds, "She was not a sophisticated,
educated woman; she was having all sorts of trouble then, being
taken advantage of."

It got worse. A telltale sign is the noticeable downturn in her
appearances during 1951–52. Just as the multi-label records were
tumbling out, background personal stress was coming to the foreground. Word got around that the rising star had suffered a "nervous breakdown." Ertegun recalls, for instance, in explaining why

Atlantic never signed Cornshucks: "Well, *then* we heard that she had mental problems."

In 1953, Atlantic instead signed the rival known as Miss Sharecropper, a talented singer who was eager to drop the imitative persona. She proceeded to record under a new name—LaVern Baker—and subsequently became the first rock 'n' roll queen, with hits such as "Tweedlee Dee" and "Jim Dandy to the Rescue."

Rather suddenly, there was not much interest in performers who didn't fit this new "rock 'n' roller" model; old-style nightclubs were closing. This shift could only have added to Little Miss Cornshucks' consternation.

"With her type of entertainer, performing's a spiritual thing," Charles Margerum suggests. "When they're at their peak, it's like a high—and when they shut down, they don't understand that it's *really* shut down. The times changed, and she wasn't really akin to that new style coming in."

Mildred Jorman was 39. Some who began to lose track of her amid the emergence of rock 'n' roll have long believed that she quit show business at this point, debilitated and frustrated. But that's just not so.

Mildred did get out of Chicago; her daughter Francey confirms that she moved to nearby Kenosha, Wisconsin. She stopped touring, and no one was recording her. But frequent ads in the Chicago *Defender* and elsewhere verify that she regularly returned for appearances.

The venues were smaller, but, not at all bad. She appeared in Chicago at Little Joe's High Hat Lounge, at the Flame Show Lounge with Singer Jo Jo Adams (who reportedly was briefly her boyfriend), and even back at the fading DeLisa. On one occasion, she sent Francey, then a teenager, out in the Cornshucks costume to confuse the regulars; both mother and daughter wound up onstage together, along with a visiting Pearl Bailey.

She appeared in revues at the Crown Propeller Lounge hosted by beloved Chicago DJ McKie Fitzhugh, sometimes sharing stages with blues shouter Joe Williams. There was a notable stand in 1956 at the Budland club with the King Kolax band and the Delta Rhythm Boys; Cornshucks also appeared at Budland in a "Battle of the Blues" with two fine Texas bluesmen—pianist Floyd Dixon and guitarist Clarence Gatemouth Brown.

There were also, increasingly, unscheduled "bad day" appearances that were a little bizarre. Denizens of South Side clubs remember Miss Cornshucks showing up where she *wasn't* booked and wandering onstage singing, interrupting ongoing acts.

"We'd be in a place, playing, and she'd come by and do some nutty things," musician and local historian Charles Walton recalls. "First thing she'd do is throw her wig at you. She'd take her dress over her head . . . all *kinds* of nutty things."

Ruth Brown recalls another mid-'50s incident. "I was playing in Chicago at the Crown Propeller. We'd been friends, but she came in and sat down at the bar, and just for that moment she got real angry at me, because I'd sung her song 'So Long'—and she just twirled her wig on her finger and threw it right at me!"

In 1958, Cornshucks showed up back in Los Angeles, when a new turn for her career looked possible. Old backer and friend Marl Young was now an arranger/conductor at the Desilu studio and was soon to become musical director for Lucille Ball's TV show. They brought Miss Cornshucks there for a possible non-musical movie role, and called in Young to work with her.

"She was supposed to speak some lines, but she had trouble memorizing them. They thought I could help, because she trusted me. It didn't help, though—and I never saw her again after that."

Soon after, "drifting blues" master Charles Brown, blacklisted from major venues by the union for "skipping a gig," found work outside of Cincinnati and brought Mildred along.

"I had to go to Newport, Kentucky, and work with the gangsters there; that kept me going!" he told a *Cincinnati Post* interviewer. "I had in Little Miss Cornshucks, and Amos Milburn. I was bringing in all the people who were having a hard time."

But just a little later, in 1960, times for Miss Cornshucks suddenly looked a whole lot better.

As she had done in many places before, Cornshucks wandered into Chicago's spacious Roberts Show Lounge one night. Charles Margerum, who was temporarily managing shows there under contract, recalls, "She was all screwed up drinking, getting into crying jags. She just walked up on the stage, unannounced, but people *knew* her—and she hushed that crowd!"

This time, instead of tossing her out, they booked her for a week, in a show with young comic Dick Gregory as MC. On the last night, as both Margerum and the late writer Marc Crawford related, among the curious who showed up to see her most publicized show in nine years was Rock and Roll Hall of Famer Ralph Bass.

Bass had known Cornshucks back on Central Avenue in her Los Angeles days, and had since become a major record producer—he was the hipster who signed James Brown to King Records.

"She was sitting there on the edge of the stage singing, and Ralph said she still sounded good," recalls Margerum who was now representing Cornshucks despite misgivings about her condition. He suggested to Bass that it might be really interesting to try recording her with strings.

That must have struck a chord. Ray Charles' "Georgia On My Mind" was a string-laden hit that year, RCA was trying out strings with Sam Cooke, and they had just started experimenting with strings where Bass was now musical director—the core Chicago blues label, Chess Records.

Word that Cornshucks was going to record again caused a considerable stir in Chicago jazz and R&B circles. Working singers such as Lorez Alexandria showed up at the October and November 1960 sessions just to watch and listen. Bass set about re-recording some of Cornshucks' most celebrated numbers in an updated context, with strings, adding a handful of R&B numbers from the rocking '50s style she had essentially missed.

Miss Cornshucks told liner-notes author Crawford about confronting that "new music" in a revealing direct quote:

> "I was nervous and scared the day I walked into the recording studio . . . I'm no rock and roll singer. Would the people like me? It took a while to get straightened out. Finally, I decided just to go on and sing what I felt, do the best I could . . . What else was there to do?"

According to Margerum, who was present at the sessions, technicians loved the voice they heard, finding they didn't have to adjust controls when she performed—nearly alone with a microphone. Neither the group—piano, guitar, bass and drums, located elsewhere in the studio—nor anyone else (none of the string session players) were there to interact with Miss Cornshucks at all, even for her to hear.

Bass was using the newfangled technique of adding on the strings later—no doubt strange for a nervous returning singer of the '40s who'd worked best with close audience and musician contact. The strings were actually arranged by the same Riley Hampton who had played behind her at the DeLisa years before.

"I had rhythm and strings on her session, as best I can remember!" Hampton says now, from retirement in Little Rock. "At that time, I used from seven to nine strings—violins, and two violas and a cello. I did a lot of that stuff with Etta James, too." One famed example, recorded not long after these sessions and patterned after them, was James' classic *At Last*.

The resulting Cornshucks LP, *The Loneliest Gal In Town*, was released in mono on Chess in early 1961. In the big color cover photo, Miss Cornshucks sits on a railway trunk in full character regalia, screaming red dress, straw hat, pantaloons and all.

The songs with strings are all bunched together on one side, with the small group numbers on the other. The album includes re-recorded versions of "So Long," "Try a Little Tenderness," "Why Was I Born?" and "You Turned Your Back On Me." (The remakes, it must be noted, are inconsistent.)

Her phrasing and attack are still there, sometimes touchingly so, despite the perceptible aging. The voice has coarsened and lowered; you can catch her struggling to reach some notes, and there are oddly strained enunciations and tics in phrasing—perhaps an effort to simulate some of rock 'n' roll's more mannered styles, in a sort of "Little Anthony" mode.

The best cut on the LP may well be "The Lonesomest Girl In Town," a slow old Tin Pan Alley tune that shows the singer's acceptance of her own obituary, in a dramatic, desolate, half-talked reading. Some of the new R&B numbers actually fare relatively well, too—a version of Johnny Ace's "Never Let Me Go," and "No Teasing Around," which clearly anticipates soul ballads still up the road. The "Tenderness" remake approaches outright crying, ending in a dramatic "try a little . . . *try* a little" build that specifically predicts later Stax-Volt drama.

"After the record was made," says Margerum, flatly, "I sent her to a couple of places, but I would have had to go with her and monitor her all of the time. She couldn't make it on her own. Wherever she would go, she'd get some booze, and once she got into booze—well, I had other clients."

Chess put a couple of the new R&B songs on a single—"No Teasing Around," penned by Billy the Kid Emerson, backed with "It Do Me So Good," by Emerson and Willie Dixon—but the 45 didn't click. Some months later, Margerum was sure he heard a *different* Cornshucks single on the radio.

"This new record of 'Try a Little Tenderness' came out, with strings, and I thought, 'Yeah; there it *was!*' The guy on the radio said, 'You've got to hear this!' And he just played it over and over. And then he said, "That, ladies and gentlemen—was *Aretha Franklin*."

Aretha's string-laden version of "Tenderness," lavishly produced by Bob Mersey in April 1962 and among a handful of Franklin singles released by Columbia Records that year, shows Cornshucks influences that are hard to miss—from the opening "*I* may be weary," to the mannered enunciation of many of the phrases, to the emphasis on certain emotional points. It got heard then—it reached the Billboard pop charts—and has been in print most of the time since. And it overshadowed what had come before.

There was no new Cornshucks "Tenderness" single from Chess. Nothing much happened with her only LP, and the disappointment must have been overwhelming.

Mildred Jorman would now truly begin to disappear.

Dancer Lester Goodman, returning to Chicago after years on the road with the traveling Ted Steele Revue, renewed his friendship with Cornshucks at this time. Goodman says she had just about stopped performing late in 1961, not that long after the Chess LP's release. After a while she moved back to Chicago, staying at a theatrically-oriented South Side hotel.

Her last advertised appearances included a July 1963 show at jazz room McKie's Lounge—side by side with Ruth Brown, now some years past her hits herself, and well ahead of an eventual comeback.

A Halloween show at the Golden Peacock in 1966 put Corn-shucks on the bill, very possibly for the final time anywhere, with West Side guitar stylist Eddie C. Campbell and his band. She employed a last vocal turn that sounds like an extension of some rhythmic talk heard on the Chess LP—perhaps borrowing a tactic from Ted Lewis, who'd always used dramatic patter.

"She was a very sweet lady. She would sing a little bit and then she would talk a little bit—just like poetry," Campbell recalls. "Was she good? Yes, she *was*; she had that beat and was good and all— even though her voice wasn't there."

Campbell and Cornshucks were both being handled, Campbell notes, by Jay Banks Delano, who ran the tiny R&B labels Delano and Hawaii and also specialized in booking acts "who'd lost a lot of their money," Campbell says. Campbell recorded for them; Corn-shucks evidently didn't.

Lester Goodman ran into her a while later: "She told me that she'd then gone into the church, was singing *only* in a church, and couldn't be hired anymore."

Daughter Francey simply says that her mother didn't perform again, anywhere, save for the funerals of friends. But a curious Cornshucks coda occurred in 1975.

The late Jimmy Walker, a fabled boogie-woogie pianist very much up in years, but still active, was in a South Side supermarket when he spotted Cornshucks, shopping for groceries. He had instant visions of setting her up for a comeback—live appearances, even recording again. He invited her to his nearby basement rehearsal space to see what could happen.

Bassist/engineer Twist Turner recalls: "The following week, Miss Cornshucks showed up at our rehearsal, wearing regular street clothes. She brought a bottle of white port and a package of Bugs Bunny brand lemon flavor Kool-Aid in her purse. We played a couple songs while she and a friend stood around and drank the port.

"I was really interested to hear her sing, excited about being a part of her comeback. Jimmy gave her the mike, but the next thing I knew she just snatched off her wig and threw it on the ground. She did sing a little, baldheaded, but she just couldn't get it together to perform."

Mildred did show up again, with a startling effect, at the 1980 Chicago wake for the famed "sepia" dance troupe producer Larry Steele, with whom she had appeared years before. Much of the black show business community had gathered to memorialize Steele; the A. A. Raynor Funeral Home was packed. Lester Goodman relates what happened.

"She just walked in, from the back—already singing. She came all the way up the side aisle, singing. It could have been her song 'So Long' . . . "

"So long, hope we'll meet again someday . . . "

". . . and she finished it just as she reached the funeral bier at the front. The place was hushed. It was such a surprise that she was there; she had faded out, you know."

Longtime *Living Blues* magazine editor and Chicago resident Jim O'Neal ran into Little Miss Cornshucks face-to-face in March 1980, while visiting the same South Kenwood Avenue apartment building in which she lived. He tried to arrange an interview, but it never materialized. The generally reliable *Living Blues* erroneously reported the death of Little Miss Cornshucks, in passing reference, in 1985, apparently based on someone's misunderstanding of a report that she was now "gone" from the city. Around that time, Lester Goodman attempted to reach her at the Chicago resident hotel where she'd last stayed; he, too, was told she was "gone"—perhaps back to Dayton.

And that, her family confirms, was the sad-enough truth: Mildred Jorman continued to live alone in Dayton for many years, unrecognized, doing "not very much."

In the early 1990s, after suffering a stroke, Mildred moved closer to Francey and surviving Jorman relatives in Indianapolis. (Cornelius had passed on in the '70s.) Her health worsened, and further strokes followed. She joined other family members in taking Bible study classes with the Jehovah's Witnesses; she was taking a class over the phone when she suffered a final stroke, and her last words came during that conversation.

She was, in those last years, Francey reports, saddened to be forgotten, resentful that others had capitalized on musical breakthroughs she

knew she had made. She died in Indianapolis, at the age of 76, on
what in her day they had called Armistice Day—November 11,
1999.

It went unnoted.

ND contributing editor Barry Mazor thanks the dozens of direct witnesses,
record collectors and period specialists who helped make this report possible, over the more than two years that it's been in the making—especially fellow music researchers Nadine Cohodas, Robert Pruter, Charles Walton and
Alan Balfour, who suggested directions that proved especially important.

ANDY McLENON AND GRANT ALDEN

Branded Man

> *Do I contradict myself?*
> *Very well then I contradict myself*
> *(I am huge, I contain multitudes.)*
>
> —WALT WHITMAN ("SONG OF MYSELF")

It says here that Merle Haggard is our greatest living singer and songwriter. Country singer and songwriter, if you must limit him.

Just do not argue the point.

We are not in the mood. Johnny Cash is newly buried, George Jones doesn't write his own material, Willie Nelson and Ray Price, Billy Joe Shaver and Bob Dylan are astonishing, towering figures. Dolly Parton comes darn close, there's that.

But if you can listen to "Sing Me Back Home," "If We Make It Through December," and, say, "I Hate To See It Go" (from Haggard's new album) without being moved to the core of your soul . . . well, you're beyond our repair.

Depending upon where you took your meals during the winter of 1969, that may prove a difficult pill to swallow. Those not yet born may have a hard time understanding what all the fuss was (and is) about: A generation later we're still arguing about "Okie from Muskogee," either the most or least important of Haggard's 38 #1 country hits, and the most famous song he will ever write.

"Okie" made Merle Haggard the darling of Spiro T. Agnew's silent majority and a lightning rod for the new left. It suggested a southern strategy to the Republican party that dramatically changed the political landscape. And it cemented the chasm separating country from rock, made that divide seem as impenetrable as the Berlin Wall. (It wasn't, not even that permanent; Waylon, Willie, and a five-leafed weed eased tensions only a few years later.)

Already a major country star, Haggard became a household name, and, like *Uncle Tom's Cabin* more than a century earlier, "Okie" clove that house in two. So politically charged were the times that even chitchat around the dinner table, ordinarily useful to keep family values on track, could erupt into screaming matches. Nightly. America was, then as now, in the midst of a bitter cultural war, and everything got serious when names like Richard Nixon, Martin Luther King, and Abbie Hoffman came up in conversation. Haggard's song inserted him into the middle of that discussion.

By the winter of 1969 there was no middle ground, and where you stood on "Okie" firmly established which side you were on, whether you wore sandals or boots, whether you thought hippies deserved to be beaten or honored for their opposition to the Vietnam War. Haggard's next single, the patriotically charged "Fightin' Side of Me," made clear where he stood.

No, it didn't, actually.

The reaction to his latest single, "That's the News," smartly selected from his latest record, *Like Never Before* (on his own Hag Records imprint), suggests just how complex and mercurial a figure Merle Haggard has always been. And what a gifted artist he remains.

Sad truth to tell, Haggard has been old news for a while, at least in the pop culture wars. His last #1 country hit, "Twinkle, Twinkle Lucky Star," charted in 1987. As with many of his peers, he was consigned to greatest hits packages and casino tours. And, like a gratifying number of his contemporaries, he rose from the slumber of premature retirement and proved to have rather more to offer, if to a smaller and more discerning audience.

Haggard's 2000 release of *If I Could Only Fly*, the first of his two albums for Epitaph . . . wait. Think about that: 31 years after

"Okie," Haggard was finally, unexpectedly embraced not simply by the rock world, but by one of its foremost punk labels.

The first record he gave Epitaph revealed a newly self-aware, mature, still brutally honest singer, a man still willing to write songs that cut precisely to the marrow of his own bones, an artist easy with his own legacy. The *If I Could Only Fly* record managed little of the commercial impact of Johnny Cash's four American albums. Nor did *Roots* (its 2001 follow-up), nor did *The Peer Sessions*, a sparkling homage (his latest among many) to his musical ancestors (released in 2002 on Audium). The work, however, was first-rate, and suddenly Haggard was back among us as a functioning artist.

And yet so potent is the memory of his celebrity, so deeply rooted is Haggard's place on the right wing of our cultural imagination, that the fairly mild anti-administration protest of "That's the News" landed him on the national news. Which only amplified the point of his song, though the talking heads ignored the obvious irony.

"Politicians do all the talking, soldiers pay the dues," Haggard sings in his calm, resonant, world-worn voice. "Suddenly the war's over, that's the news." That, combined with an editorial he posted on the website defending the Dixie Chicks (while simultaneously praising Toby Keith), led to great concern among certain of his longtime fans.

The first post on CMT's message board reads: "I just saw Merle Haggard on Fox News discussing his new song . . . which is anti-Iraq war and will give great aid and comfort to the Sadamites who are killing our troops every day."

And so it began.

Controversy sells. Or at least secures airtime. "I'm totally happy with what's gone down so far," Haggard says, over the phone from his office in Northern California. "I've had twelve television major news anchor kind of people ask me to come on: Letterman, Leno, every show that matters wants me, and television is powerful."

Why should the political views of a 67-year-old country singer be newsworthy? It was more than a little disconcerting to see Hag displayed in the same context with images of dead Americans in Iraq, shots of bombed buses in Israel, Scott Peterson and his attorneys looking like emotionless druids, and hourly reports on the status of Ben and J-Lo's wedding plans.

"Maybe I'm a media critic," Haggard suggests mildly. "With music. But I'm in the business of information myself, and I'm a poet and a singer and I have a platform to sing from. I think sometimes it's necessary to write certain songs. I think that song ['That's the News'] was necessary, and I'm really glad that it's causing the controversy it's caused."

Haggard's new single is a fairly mild rebuke, even by today's standards. In conversation, his criticisms become substantially more pointed.

"I'm trying to say, 'This is me now,'" he says. "I think we are living in a terrible, paranoid condition. We have troops that we should be proud of, but are we getting the straight story, do we have all the facts, or are we short of information like the President?"

He is less kind a few moments later. "You know, George Sr. calls me and wishes me a happy birthday," he says. "Hell, I want to see George W. Bush do good. I just think he's been disingenuous. I think if he would step up now and say, 'OK, we're gonna cut the crap. This is what the deal is: We want to build this pipeline from somewhere to somewhere else and there's two assholes over there that need to be taken out anyway, and we need to be the ones to remove them, nobody else in the world can.' I just believe that's the honest truth and if he'd done that, all the people would rally around him and jump up and he'd be more popular than Abe Lincoln."

(Forgetting, for the moment, that Lincoln was assassinated.)

Anyway, Haggard's critique of President Bush seems to have as much to do with California environmental issues as with the endlessly convoluted politics of the Middle East. "The right that the President has given to cut down these big trees out here on the West Coast needs to be brought up," he says. "He's also given the right to drill for oil off the coast of California. Well, it's obvious that he doesn't give a shit about California. That happens to be where I live.

"I don't understand how we can be so stupid to [not] realize that we have to have the lungs of the earth, the earth has to breathe. And if we do away with the trees . . . We have to quit burning things. We have the mentality of a firecracker, you know? We're still in the woods lighting fires."

In his own way, Haggard's still lighting fires. Just when it seems safe to suggest he's revealed himself as an evolved liberal, conversation turns to the recent flap over a granite monument to the Ten Commandments placed in the Alabama Supreme Court.

"I called my booking agent and asked if we could go down there and set up and play on the steps of that Alabama courthouse," he says. "Or do something in defense of the Ten Commandments. It didn't work out where we could do anything; they moved them back and hid them someplace before we could get it together. But that's a terrible infringement on American rights, I believe."

But it's the song "Yellow Ribbons" on his new album that properly sets the pot boiling. Ostensibly an ode to a longstanding tradition ("There used to be a time when soldiers went to war and folks at home would tie yellow ribbons everywhere," he states matter-of-factly in the liner notes), it's hard not to wonder whether Haggard has another meaning in mind when he sings, "Go tie a yellow ribbon in your hair/So folks around the world will know you really care."

His explanation doesn't settle the matter. "It's just part of my intention to let people know for sure that I haven't changed my views about the red, white, and blue," he says. "There again, were we being given all the information? But while we wait and wonder, we have a patriotic duty to the soldiers, and to the people engaged in war."

Ah, but aren't you being a little cynical, a little sarcastic in that song?

"I can't, with all honesty, say that you might be a little bit right," he acknowledges. "You know, 'God bless America for doing what we dare' is [the line] you're talking about. I'm holding my breath, as I think every conscious American should be, on what is our next move, what do we do in the global community, how do we regain our stature? How do we get 150 countries to quit hating us?"

Let's dispense with "Okie," shall we? Everybody now knows that Haggard became, at least in part, one of the figures the song seems to mock. Most now realize that the hippies and outlaws of that era had more in common with Haggard's restless spirit than did the flag-waving hard-hats who made up much of his audience back then. Today, crowds at his shows, regardless of persuasion, whoop it up when he sings that first line: "We don't smoke marijuana in Muskogee . . . "

Haggard seems at peace with all that. "I had different views in the '70s," he says, selecting his words slowly. "As a human being, I've learned [more]. I have more culture now. I was dumb as a rock when I wrote 'Okie from Muskogee'. That's being honest with you at the moment, and a lot of things that I said [then] I sing with a different intention now.

"My views on marijuana have totally changed. I think we were brainwashed and I think anybody that doesn't know that needs to get up and read and look around, get their own information. It's a cooperative government project to make us think marijuana should be outlawed."

But note it's only that first line with which he takes issue. He swept the CMA awards in 1970, played the Nixon White House in 1973, was pardoned by California Governor Ronald Reagan, and never got a real shot at rock or pop radio. All largely on the strength of what he said, and who he said it to, in that one song.

Times have changed. "What was one side years ago is not the same deal now," he muses. "I mean, what was a Democrat in 1960 doesn't apply now."

As has often been pointed out—particularly by Haggard's liberal apologists—his career might have played out far differently had Capitol Records exec Ken Nelson granted Haggard's wish to follow "Okie" with "Irma Jackson," a song about an interracial romance. Instead, the next single was "Fightin' Side of Me".

"It wasn't exactly what they had in mind," he says, a faint chuckle at the edge of his voice. "They figured it might be a problem. They had been awful good to me and allowed me to have my own head and everything on sessions. That was the only time they ever squelched anything I wanted to do, so I didn't really argue with them. I just . . . 'OK, can we put on an album?' And they said, 'Well, yeah.' But they said, 'I don't think it'd be best for you to do that at this time, put it on a single.' Whatever you say, Mr. Nelson. So I didn't think no more about it."

Ken Nelson had brought Haggard to Capitol—and had produced his records with a clean, sympathetic sound—along with Hank Thompson, Merle Travis, Jean Shepard, and Buck Owens. That is, he'd earned Haggard's trust.

"Over the years it became an issue, because people found out they wouldn't let me do that," Haggard continues. "So, hindsight being 20/20, it probably did more good them not wanting it out and people finally finding out about it, than me putting it out anyway."

But, no, he hardly repudiates "Fightin' Side of Me." "I was a redneck to some degree, because I had just got out of the joint and I really had been somewhere where the mat was jerked out from underneath your feet," Haggard says. (So powerful is his memory of prison that, though he wrote "Fightin' Side" almost a decade after his release, the memory of San Quentin still haunts his thoughts.) "It destroyed my career in a certain way because people just said, 'Ah, bullshit, if he feels that way then the hell with him.' It destroyed a pop career for me for a period of time. *But*—the force works in mysterious ways and it may come back. It's working in my favor now."

And for a little cultural context, remember that Haggard showed up during that winter of 1969 to play "Okie" on the proudly left-leaning "Smothers Brothers Show," lip-syncing while a field of waving flags was projected behind him, with the nearest thing to a hound dog slumped to his left. Haggard always seemed to thrive on the idea that this simple song could get so many people so worked up.

It's also worth noting that Haggard sandwiched the flurry of releases capitalizing on "Okie" and "Fightin' Side" with 1969's *Same Train, A Different Time: Merle Haggard Sings the Great Songs of Jimmie Rodgers* and 1970's *A Tribute to the Best Damn Fiddle Player in the World (Or My Salute to Bob Wills)*.

In the end, that will do for summation of Haggard, for his songs are deeply personal, and deeply felt. Notice his connection to the soldier in Iraq his latest single seeks to refocus our attention upon. "The only people that realize what's really going on is the soldier," he says. "He's the only guy out there that's catching the human torment from it." Human torment, that's something Merle Haggard understands.

Toss that handful of political songs aside, and a very different—a richer, more eloquent, more enduring—Merle Haggard emerges. As a child of the late depression (born April 6, 1937), his instincts, like those of one of his mentors, Johnny Cash, have always been to sing for and about those in the margins: the working poor, the imprisoned, the love-torn.

The roots of his raising have made for easy cliché. His family joined the migration from Oklahoma to California, where his father found work near Bakersfield as a carpenter for the railroad. Company housing was a converted boxcar, a fact that shows up in even the shortest biographical essay because it explains his fascination with Jimmie Rodgers and several albums of train songs.

By the standards of the late 1930s, that boxcar may not have been such a bad place—probably a good bit nicer than the migrant housing down the road, and no less primitive than the simple homes small farmers had built across the San Joaquin Valley. Still, listen to him sing that opening line from the mostly autobiographical "Mama Tried": "The first thing I remember knowin' was a lonesome whistle blowin'."

His father died when Merle was nine, and his mother took work as a bookkeeper. Merle shortly went wild, beginning a long run to and from government custody (seven escapes, all told), and pursuing a career in petty crime legendary for its ineptitude. An older brother and a younger sister made other choices.

Like many gifted songwriters, Haggard soon found he was suited to no other career, not even a life of crime. As the story goes, he and a friend were drunk and broke (and presumably operating without a watch) when they decided to break into a club and take the night's receipts. They were discovered trying to pry open the back door at an hour patrons were still walking through the front.

Haggard slipped away from jail and returned to the hotel room where his first wife was waiting. It proved an expensive visit, for the escape was what caused him to be sentenced to San Quentin. And so it was that Johnny Cash, on January 1, 1958—nearly a decade before he would record "A Boy Named Sue" there—headlined an eight-hour variety show at San Quentin, giving Merle Haggard a glimpse of a different future.

Not that Haggard hadn't previously considered music as a career. "I got onstage when I was 14," Haggard says. "I guess I had my sights already set then, I just didn't realize that I was adamant about it. When I saw Johnny Cash, I'd already formed an opinion about the whole scene of music, and wasn't really a terrifically big Johnny Cash fan, wasn't really a fan of Johnny Cash at all.

"I just knew who he was, and I played lead guitar, so I played Luther's licks because they were nice licks. A lot of people kinda laughed at us country boys that they figured liked him. Well, when he came, he didn't have a voice. He'd sung his voice off the night before in San Francisco. And he just stood up there and totally waxed that audience, without much more than a whisper."

Haggard was paroled from San Quentin in 1960. He dug ditches for his brother's electrical contracting business, then found a better job playing bass for Wynn Stewart. Two years later, following an introduction from Buck and Bonnie Owens, he cut his first singles for Fuzzy Owens' Talley Records. The fifth single, "(My Friends Are Gonna Be) Strangers," went top-10 in 1965, Ken Nelson came calling from Capitol, and a star was born.

Johnny Cash knew who Merle Haggard was the next time they were in the same room. "It was 1964, or '63, maybe," as Haggard remembers things. "I went to do a show in Chicago with multiple artists on it, a gang of people. He was on it, I was on it, and we met in the restroom, down below the Chicago studios where we were doing a television show. He offered me a double dot, a little old green Dexedrine pill, and a drink of wine. He had this flask underneath his big black coat.

"That was back in the days where everybody was taking those little pills, everybody from the church lady to the truck driver. So there wasn't nothin' thought about it, but that was the first time I met him. We went on to be extremely close friends. I think he would have knocked somebody down had they badmouthed me, and vice versa."

Enough of politics, of lurid legends and oft-told stories, for they only serve to obscure the real work. Haggard's greatest gift is a knack for vividly exploring the forces that can bring people together, and dramatizing what tears them apart.

Consider the simple, eloquent dignity of "If We Make It Through December." Haggard is the poet laureate of the broken-hearted, able to articulate feelings of total hopelessness with an honestly and crippling regret in his voice that not even Hank Williams could conjure from his pathetic, lonely life.

This side of Hag is not for the fragile. Listen well, but if you aren't careful you may catch a glimpse of something within your own soul that you imagined long forgotten and well buried. No matter how dark your darkest night was, Hag's was darker. Heart broken? No contest. Just hear the man sing, "What Am I Going To Do (With the Rest of My Life)?"

"I'm a man that goes through . . . I have terrible mood swings," he says, picking through his words before he speaks. "I'm like other people that I have read about that are . . . gifted in some way and have the capability or mentality to be crazy, to be deeply depressed. I have all those problems to deal with."

Haggard has met those problems with frightening honesty throughout his best songs. "Some of it is dramatized in order to make the songs work, of course," he says, "But it's like 'Mama Tried,' I wasn't doing life but I was in prison and I did turn 21 there. For the most part it's 98 percent fact, and the rest of it's to shape the song right. I get my enjoyment or appreciation out of all music I'm totally honest about it. 'Footlights' is probably my honest attempt at my own self-descriptions."

Then something in his voice changes; one can almost hear his spine straighten. "Life is a tiger, and it's no easier for any of us," he says. "I think Willie said it in 'Nobody Slides'—life is going to deal its misery to all of us."

And its good as well. Haggard's fifth marriage has produced a second batch of children; they figure prominently in the emotional underpinning of *Like Never Before*, and throughout his conversation.

"To have children late in life is, in some ways, the greatest gift God could offer one man," he says. "I would have thought the direct opposite. In fact, I was fixing to retire an old single country music star, partying my way out, on a houseboat. But these children were given and it just changed my life, changed my values, made a different person out of me." That houseboat is now for sale on his website, the kids are almost teenagers, and his first batch of children has produced 13 grandchildren.

Not so fast. He is asked the old campfire question, if a UFO landed tonight and offers you a one-way ride, do you climb on?

"Yessir," he answers quickly. "I'll jump off this island if I get a chance." He chuckles. This is a man who does not like to fly.

In the winter of his years, Johnny Cash found another layer of fame, his ears ever open to the work of songwriters with whom most folks would've figured he had nothing in common. Merle Haggard, too, has found his pen again, wielding it as casually and as topically as Woody Guthrie once did.

They are—Merle and Cash, Dolly and Dylan—the rarest of beings, entertainers who are simultaneously artists. Singers whose songs are inextricably linked to the lore of their private lives. Songwriters of subtlety and great substance.

"All I'm trying to do is entertain, be unpredictable and maintain honesty," Haggard demurs, and then stops talking for a long moment.

His future is not to resemble Cash's immediate past. The new album appears on his own Hag label, an enterprise with which he seems to hope to take control of his own legacy.

"I just sorta figured my big record-selling days were over," he says, without rancor, "and I think a lot of other people agreed with me, because I couldn't get a lot of money for a record deal. I just thought, hell, I'll start my little ol' company and do my own stuff. It's sorta took on legs of its own and it's jumping up here and acting like it might really be something. I know as much about the music business as most of those young kids who are trying to run the big companies."

His new label is also bolstered by the recent reversion of his MCA masters from the late-'70s and '80s to his control. "That immediately makes my little Hag Records worth a lot more money," he says with evident satisfaction. "Little by little I'm going to get control, if I can, of all the music. Somebody said, if you want to make God laugh, tell him your plans." He laughs.

Complementing the ten new original tunes on *Like Never Before* is a glorious duet with Willie Nelson of Woody Guthrie's "Philadelphia

Lawyer." It's a cowboy song, not a political number, but still a revealing choice.

"It's hard to find songs for two men to sing together," he begins. "And it was a Woody Guthrie tune, and it was written the year I was born, and it was given to Rose Maddox, who recorded it, I think, first (or next after Woody, at least). And it had a long history of being a song that had been around me that I'd never cut, and Willie has never cut it, and that's sorta odd because between the two of us we've cut the Bible, you know?"

(Bonnie Owens sang the song on Haggard's 1970 live album, *The Fighting Side of Me;* Nelson cut a version on the 1988 Folkways tribute, *A Vision Shared,* but no matter.)

Haggard's rationale gives a hint of the deep, passionate, probing nature of his musical curiosity. A question about the relative obscurity of western swing pioneer Milton Brown brings a cackle of delight. "I'm glad [Brown's music isn't often recorded] because I'm fixin' to record a bunch of it. I've got a tape in my truck as we speak of Milton's stuff, and I just told a couple of people in my staff to find everything they could find on him. I'm going to do a study like I've never done before, and it's just the most enjoyable study I've ever got into."

There it is. Far more than "Okie" and even fame, it's the music that still speaks to Haggard. Just watch him close his eyes onstage when the band hits it right. "Some artists—I won't mention any names—wouldn't tell you who they admired, if their life depended on it," he says. "There's something arrogant about that I don't like; I like people that are not too big to talk about who they like."

Another question, suggesting he phrased a bit like Maurice Chevalier on "I Hate To See It Go," elicits a more revealing correction. "You know, I have a problem with that," he says. "I have a habit, and we are characters of habit. I've always enjoyed impersonations, and when I tell stories, I fall in and out of characters. When I sing songs, sometimes certain characters will just jump and appear at the moment. That's my attempt at Satch. It just sounded like Louis Armstrong ought to be [singing] 'He's just like you.' I don't know if we ever meant that to be the final vocal, but it came off good. That's probably a little bit of Louis Armstrong trying to come out there. He was probably sitting there in the studio and tickled me on the neck or something."

Though he is not writing songs at the clip he once did, Haggard seems to have entered into a newly fertile stage, and to be moving forward with fresh urgency. He has become a man with abundant plans for his future.

"We have a swing album we're keeping as a release if we don't have a new Merle Haggard record, which we may have," he says. "I write sporadically, and it'll probably be something that I haven't cut yet. I kept a couple songs back that was maybe current-event related to September 11. For example, I have a song called 'Flight 93' that's going to be on the next album. And I have a song, it's about feelings on Iraq and where we're at—why don't we take a look around and recognize some of the problems in California and Oregon?"

But his response to news of the death of his old friend, Johnny Cash, which arrived in the midst of a battery of interviews for his new album, is most telling. "I think when the next Bible's written he'll be something like Moses," Haggard says.

"I didn't want to face it anymore than anybody else did. I did around twenty interviews that morning, and when I got loose I just went out in the studio and I didn't want to sing anything except Johnny Cash songs. And I thought, you know, I don't want to forget something here, so me and my wife recorded a really good track on 'Jackson.' I don't know, I might do a really extensive album to Johnny Cash."

MARK ANTHONY NEAL

The Tortured Soul of
Marvin Gaye and R. Kelly

The music of R. Kelly has always been rife with blatant contradictions. It has often been difficult to reconcile the man responsible for the 1990s motivational anthem "I Believe I Can Fly" with the man responsible for songs like "Sex Me," "Bump and Grind," and "Feelin' on Your Booty." Taken as a whole, these songs are clearly the musings of a thoughtful, passionate, and openly sexual individual. But Kelly, like many African-Americans raised in the bosom of the black Christian experience, has likely felt shamed and constrained by that experience, which at times has openly aimed to deny the full expression of black sexuality, not only within the walls of the church, but within those public, civic, commercial, and private spheres where the Black Church holds sway. One can only wonder if the often absurd and surreal sexual narratives Kelly has produced (including his illegal propensity for under-aged girls) is a product—a response—to the sexual repression of the Black Church and its institutional satellites (what'cha y'all think the sex scandals among Catholic priests are about?).

A close listen to Kelly's formidable body of work suggests that of a tortured soul—a literally Tortured Soul. Kelly has at times been linked to the Soul Man tradition—a tradition that has produced a litany of talented, even brilliant, men who often lived tragic and tortured lives. When one thinks of the lives and deaths of figures like Sam Cooke, Donny Hathaway, Walter Jackson, or the tragic-comic dramas of Al Green, Teddy Pendergrass, Rick James, and Wilson Pickett, to name just a few, there seems a clear pattern. Many have suggested that these men, all products of black church culture, paid a price for their willingness to sell their gifts from "God" to the highest bidders, be they record companies or adoring female fans. None of these men can match the impassioned contradictions that were Marvin Gaye—a preacher boy at odds with all forms of authority, including that which he felt was imposed by the women in his life and the father who eventually took his life, who shamelessly and shamefully explored the intersections of sex and spirituality with a clarity rarely achieved in any form of expressive art during the 20th century. While R. Kelly is no Marvin Gaye, the recent releases of Gaye's *I Want You (Deluxe Edition)* and Kelly's *The R. in R&B Collection (Volume 1)* place their tortured Soul in striking proximity with each other.

Janis Hunter was a 16-year-old high school sophomore when she walked into a Los Angeles studio in March of 1973 with her mother Barbara and was introduced to a then 33-year-old Marvin Gaye. Gaye was recording his 1973 classic *Let's Get It On* and by all reports was immediately smitten with the mature *teen-age* girl. Hunter's full impact on Gaye can be heard on the deluxe edition of Gaye's *Let's Get It On* (2001), which contains versions of the title track recorded before and after Gaye's initial meeting with Hunter. It is the post-Hunter version of the song that has become the classic ode to soulful ecstasy. By the time Gaye released *I Want You* (a sexual ode to Ms. Hunter) in mid-March of 1976, he had fathered two children with Hunter: Nona (born in September of 1974) and Frankie Gaye. The duo would finally marry a year later, once Gaye's divorce to Anna Gordy Gaye (sister of Berry) was finalized.

Throughout his career Gaye escaped intense scrutiny of his relationship with Hunter, which began while he was still married to, though estranged from, his first wife—the kind of scrutiny that has dogged Kelly since his marriage to the late Aaliyah Houghton in 1993. Granted, Gaye was never implicated in acts of child pornography and—unlike Kelly—he didn't have to confront a 24–7 media glare. There was no Electronic Urban Report (EUR), Tom Joyner

in the Morning Show, BET, or Wendy Williams for Gaye to contend with, only *Jet Magazine*, the still ghetto-fabulous digest of
choice in many black homes. But there's no denying that he was sexually involved with an under-aged woman-child, 17 years his junior,
when he sang lovingly in 1974 on "Jan" (from *Marvin Gaye Live*),
"Janis is my girl, in all the world, there no one as lovely . . . "

The most striking thing about *I Want You* when it was first
released (the single "I Want You" dropped shortly after the album)
was the cover art, which featured a painting by Ernie Barnes. "Sugar
Shack" (perhaps the first visual celebration of the bootyliscious aesthetic) was well known to some audiences, as a version of the painting was featured at the end of the opening credits of the television
series *Good Times*. The painting embodies what Thelma Golden,
curator of the Studio Museum in Harlem, would call the "Black
Romantic"—a style of painting that Natalie Hopkinson of the
Washington Post describes as the "visual-art equivalent of the Chitlin
Circuit." The hip-hop group Camp Lo paid tribute to Barnes'
painting on their 1997 release *Uptown Saturday Night*, which featured a hip-hop remix of the painting by Dr. Revolt. Gaye was initially introduced to Barnes by Barbara Hunter, eventually buying
eight Barnes originals, including "Sugar Shack." For the album
cover, Barnes added references to Gaye's new release, "I Want You,"
much the way CD stickers currently highlight the hoped-to-be new
singles.

When the single "I Want You" finally dropped on April Fool's
day (exactly eight years before Gaye's murder), Gaye was trying to
compete in an arena that he was largely responsible for creating:
hyper-sexualized Soul. In the aftermath of *Let's Get It On*, a bunch of
cats had changed up their flow, including Smokey Robinson (who
dropped his definitive solo release, *Quiet Storm*) and vocalist Major
Harris (who broke from the Delfonics and recorded 1975's classic
"Love Won't Let Me Wait"). "Love Won't Let Me Wait" gained
some notoriety because of the female vocalist who feigns a rather
impressive orgasm in the background. That same year, Leon Ware
produced "Come Inside My Love" for Minnie Riperton, using the
same strategy featured on the Harris recording. Ware broke
through as a songwriter a few years earlier, co-writing (with T-Boy
Ross) Michael Jackson's "I Wanna Be Where You Are" (1972) and

writing the title track to Quincy Jones' *Body Heat* (1974). Gaye was being chased by the demons of his relationship with Jan, his failed marriage, and the IRS, and resisted going into the studio to follow-up *Let's Get It On*, but it was Ware who was largely responsible for getting Gaye focused again.

Virtually all of the tracks on *I Want You* were co-written by Ware with T-Boy Ross (Ms. Di's brother) and Gaye. Most of the songs were intended for Ware's album *Musical Message* and a debut project for Ross, but after Gaye heard versions of "I Want You," he asked Ware to produce a whole album for him. Like many of Gaye's most classic albums, *I Want You* was a collaborative effort, but part of Gaye's genius was that those albums always seemed to be the product of his own tempestuous burden. If Gaye only co-wrote some of these songs, he surely was the single author of their emotional power.

Nowhere is this more apparent than on songs like "I Wanna Be Where You Are" and "All the Way Around" (both written by Ware and Ross), and "Since I Had You" (written by Ware and Gaye). "I Wanna Be Where You Are" seems like an afterthought, as Gaye improvises for little more than a minute over the melody that Ware and Ross first wrote for a teen-age Michael Jackson. But it's in the closing moment of Gaye's riff that you realize the song is simply a night-time whisper to his children ("Good-night little Frankie/Nona/Night little Marvin") and to his lover ("I'll always love you Janis"). The alternative version of the song clocks in at over six minutes, though much of it remains an instrumental groove, but you can't listen to it without imagining Gaye riding on a tour bus or airplane looking out the window and thinking longingly about his family.

Both "All the Way Around" and "Since I Had You" seem songs less about Gaye's budding romance with Jan Hunter and more about some sort of reconciliation with wife Anna, which at the point of his recording *I Want You* would have been highly unlikely. But "Since I Had You" also seems to suggest an unraveling drama between Gaye and Jan Hunter, one that might have necessitated the recording of an album like *I Want You* in the first place. Though they finally married in 1977, Janis Gaye filed for divorce in 1979, even as Gaye was settling up financially with his first wife Anna

Gordy Gaye. One of his best performances on the album, "Since I Had You," is about a man stepping to a former lovely years later at "a neighborhood" dance where they "got that old feeling again." The song is legendary among some critics, who have for more than twenty years tried to decipher the song's bridge: "Big Daddy Rucker is sho' nuff getting down . . . ooh baby I haven't seen you in such a long time/Remember how I use to do this to you/In" at which point Gaye's vocals become inaudible as his vocals are mixed down and background vocalist Gwenda Hambrick's feigned orgasm is mixed louder. The alternate mix offers little relief to the mystery.

But so much of *I Want You* is less about romance and romance-revisited, but the nuts and bolts (no pun intended) of hot sweaty sex. "Come Live with Me Angel" (written by Ware and Jacqueline Hilliard), "Feel All My Love Inside," and "Soon I'll Be Loving You Again"—all explicitly sexual tracks that Gaye performed full of the obsession that he seemed to carry for his new love. Gaye sings the refrain, "I wanna be your lover/At least three times a day" through-out "Come Live with Me Angel." On "Feel All My Love Inside," Gaye gleeful describes, "I'll be stoking you/In and out/Up and down/All around/I love to hear you make those sounds . . ." while Hambrick "responds" accordingly. The alternative version of the song features a post-coital musical release (more tasteful than, say, Art of Noise's "Moment in Love" or Lil' Louis' "French Kiss") that functions as a sledge hammer for those who had somehow missed the point of the song. But it is the exquisite "Soon I'll Be Loving You" that ranks as the most sexually explicit song in Gaye's oeuvre. The tension begins at the beginning of the second verse, where Gaye sings in a straight falsetto, "Oh, no I never gave up no head" while his layered tenor affirms "I never did that before," referencing his first trip "downtown" with the object of his affection. An enjoy-able experience, apparently, as the song's closing refrain finds Gaye singing "give you some head baby/I'm gonna lock you right up woman . . . I want to give you some h-e-a-d . . . oooh I love to get it/'Cause I know just what to do with it" as he closes the song with a whispered "Soon I'll be lovin' you, oh Janis. . . . " The alternative version features Gaye in what can only be described as an extended orgasmic fit.

It's hard to believe that R. Kelly didn't have "Soon I'll Be Loving You Again" in mind when he playfully sings "boot-e-e, b-o-o-t-e-e" over and over on the remix of his song "Feelin' on Your Booty," and yet the fact remains that Kelly has never recorded *anything* as sexually explicit as Gaye's "Soon I'll Be Loving You Again." R. Kelly's notoriety has really had less to do with his music, but really the conflation of his celebrity persona, extralegal exploits, and the overtly sexual themes of his most popular songs. Understand, Kelly deserves all the scrutiny and scorn that he has received in recent years, but his music doesn't place him outside of a tradition—as many pundits would like us to believe—but as the most exemplary example of that tradition since Marvin Gaye's death in 1984. And yes, titles like "Bump N' Grind" and "Sex Me" (both featured on *The R. in R&B*) and "Feelin' on Your Booty" are perverse, but very much representative of hip-hop generation colloquialisms about sex and sexuality and thus no different than colloquialisms like "Jellyroll," "Roll with Me," or "Make Me a Pallet on the Floor" exchanged by earlier generations.

To truly understand R. Kelly is to listen closely to the songs that don't ask you to shake your ass or to get your "Bump & Grind" on. There is that critical moment in "I Wish" (in my mind his most brilliant performance) where Kelly sings "instead of y'all throwing them stones at me/Somebody pray for me"—"*Somebody Pray for Me*"—and while Kelly admits to nothing in that lyric, he admits to *everything*, trying to find solace in the one place he always expected would forgive him for his sins. The aforementioned lyric is immediately followed by the closing chorus in which Kelly very consciously echoes the voice of Sam Cooke as he sings, "I'm up at the crossroads/Of my, my, my, my, my life." The Sam Cooke echo is crucial because Cooke was the first successful Gospel artist to break ranks with the "Church" and sing of the "flesh" instead of the spirit. Up until his death in 1964, Cooke was stung by criticism for his move to secular music and by the "Church's" refusal to embrace him, once he literally crossed-over.

The mystical meaning of the "Cross Roads" is also important here, as Kelly's reference to it speaks to his acceptance of the fact that he is going to have to own up to his sins. This theme (including the Cooke references) is also echoed in Kelly's "Turn Back the Hands of Time," which was originally featured on his 1998 double-CD, *R*. "I Wish" is largely a song about loss, as Kelly acknowledges the loss of friends and families, including his estranged siblings and his mother Joann Kelly, whose death (in 1993) had a dramatic impact on Kelly. Kelly is ostensibly reaching out to friends, family, and the grave—a man grasping to make sense of his wealth, his celebrity, and the utter misery of his life.

There's a 10-minute version of Kelly's "I Believe I Can Fly" (currently unavailable commercially) which delves even deeper into Kelly's chaos. Midway through the performance, Kelly acts out an exchange with the "Church" as he knocks on its doors ("I'm sorry for all of the wrong that I've done/So can you please forgive me and deliver me from my way") only to have the Church's figurehead—presumably the minister—openly reject him: "you are a heartless thug and we don't want you here . . . any man that is of the world won't be accepted here, go away." After his rejection in the song, Kelly is rhetorically embraced by both his deceased mother and the "king of kings." Taken at face value, the performance suggests that Kelly had in fact attempted to reach out for help in the past, but had likely been rebuffed by folks who could only see his celebrity and perceived reputation.

Kelly is a product of an era when the private and the intimate in black life and culture came into the full view of the marketplace, a process that had already begun when Gaye, Major Harris, and Minnie Riperton recorded songs with feigned orgasms in the background. For Kelly, part of that new terrain meant sharing not only his perceived sexual exploits, but the demons that have haunted him as a young black man coming of age in the full view of the public in a way that has only been experienced by young black male athletes, singers, actors, etc., who have come of age in the era of MTV, ESPN, CNN, and AOL-Time Warner. For all of the political significance and cultural weight attached to figures like Jack Johnson, Jesse Owens, Joe Louis, Sammy Davis, Jr., Jack Robinson, Wilt Chamberlain, and Nat King Cole, none of them—with the exception of Ali—lived in the constant media glare that even second-rate rappers and third-string point guards often face today. This doesn't excuse Iverson with a gun or Kelly with under-age girls, but places their indiscretions in a broader context than "what's wrong with the hip-hop generation?" Imagine the media coverage today if a prominent rapper or R&B artist was murdered and one of his boys—his protégé—married his widow months after the murder, as was the case when Bobby Womack married the widow of Sam Cooke months after his murder.

While it is admittedly unfair to compare the obvious mourning process of Womack and Barbara Campbell (who were dealing with complicated feelings of longing and loss) alongside those of Kelly or anyone in the Hip-Hop Generation, my point is not to compare "sins" but to highlight how contemporary culture's coverage of those sins unfairly depicts the sins of the "sons" (and daughters) as worse than those of the "father" (and daughter). R. Kelly is no Marvin Gaye, nor should he be. But R. Kelly is a Soul Man, who seemingly for lack of any other recourse, has chosen to share his demons with us through his music as so many tortured Soul Men of the past have.

ALEX ROSS

Rock 101

Academia Tunes In

Duke Ellington once had to field a barrage of questions from an Icelandic music student who was determined to penetrate to the heart of the genius of jazz. At one point, Ellington was asked whether he ever felt an affinity for the music of Bach, and, before answering, he made a show of unwrapping a pork chop that he had stowed in his pocket. "Bach and myself," he said, taking a bite from the chop, "both write with individual performers in mind." Richard O. Boyer captured the moment in a Profile entitled "The Hot Bach," which appeared in this magazine in 1944. You can sense in that exquisitely timed pork-chop maneuver Ellington's bemused response to the European notions of genius that were constantly being foisted on him. He said on another occasion, "To attempt to elevate the status of the jazz musician by forcing the level of his best work into comparisons with classical music is to deny him his rightful share of originality." Jazz was a new language, and the critic would have to respond to it with a new poetry of praise.

Now Ellington is himself a classic, the subject of painstaking analytical studies. He occupies a Bachian position in an emergent popular pantheon, which is certain to look different from the marble-faced, bewigged classical pantheons that preceded it. The very idea of a canon of geniuses may be falling by the wayside; it makes more sense to talk about the flickering brilliance of a group, a place, or a people. In the future, it seems, everyone will be a genius for fifteen minutes. The past decade has seen the rise of pop-music studies, which is dedicated to the idea that Ellington, Hank Williams, and the Velvet Underground were created equal and deserve the same sort of scholarly scrutiny that used to be bestowed only on Bach and sons. Pop-music courses draw crowds of students on college campuses, and academic presses are putting out such portentous titles as "Instruments of Desire: The Electric Guitar and the Shaping of Musical Experience," "Rock Over the Edge: Transformations in Popular Music Culture," and "Running with the Devil: Power, Gender, and Madness in Heavy Metal Music."

Pop-music professors, especially those who specialize in rock, are caught in an obvious paradox, which their students probably point out to them on the first day of class. Namely, it's not very rock and roll to intellectualize rock and roll. When Pink Floyd sang, "We don't need no education," they could not have foreseen the advent of research projects with titles like "Another Book in the Wall?: A Cultural History of Pink Floyd's Stage Performance and the Rise of Audiovisual *Gesamtkunstwerk*, 1965–1994." (That comes from Finland.) Ever since Ellington, Armstrong, and Jelly Roll Morton struck up the soundtrack to the bawdy, boozy twenties, popular music has been the high-speed vehicle for youth rebellion, sexual liberation, and chemical experimentation, none of which yield willingly to the academic mind. The pop scholar is forever doomed to sounding like the square kid at the cool kids' party, killing their buzz with sentences like this: "From the start, hip-hop's samples ran the gamut of genres, defying anyone who would delimit hip-hop's palette."

Then again, maybe it's not a problem that so much pop-music scholarship sounds conspicuously uncool. For decades, jazz rhapsodists and rock poets were so intent on projecting attitude that they never got around to saying much about the music itself. The pioneering rock critics of the sixties, such as Lester Bangs and Greil Marcus, wanted to mimic the music in their prose, and they had enough style to pull it off. Bangs, whose writings have been collected in a new anthology from Anchor Books, lived the life of a rock star, or at least died the death of one. But his writings are a better guide to the mentality of smart people who went to rock shows in the sixties and seventies than they are a reliable record of music and musicians. Discussing the Rolling Stones in 1974, Bangs wrote, "If you think I'm going to review the new 'It's Only Rock 'n' Roll' album right now, you are crazy. But I am going to swim in it." Between prose poetry and academic cant there has to be a middle ground, and pop-music studies is searching it out.

Interrogating Bruce's Butt

One weekend last spring, a few hundred scholars, journalists, musicians, and onlookers arrived in downtown Seattle for Pop Conference 2003, entitled "Skip a Beat: Rewriting the Story of Popular Music." The Pop Conference was created two years ago by Eric Weisbard, a former *Village Voice* rock critic, and Daniel Cavicchi, an assistant professor of American Studies at the Rhode Island School of Design. The decision to bring scholars and journalists together was unusual. It gave the critics an opportunity to drop arcane allusions instead of having to pretend to sound like teen-agers, while the academics could loosen up a little. Weisbard and Cavicchi hope that the two worlds can cross-pollinate each other, breeding a sensibility that is scholarly but not stuffy, stylish but not frivolous.

The conference took place within the wavy-gravy walls of the Experience Music Project, a Frank Gehry culture palace, housing artifacts and bric-a-brac from a century of pop. The dress code was diverse to the point of incoherence: some of the older academics showed up in business attire, while younger ones wore T-shirts and jeans. (The divergence of styles became especially dissonant when sixties-generation scholars espoused radical political agendas while Gen X doctoral students sounded a neo-formalist, let's-just-talk-about-the-music tone.) For three days, participants hawked their wares in a tight twenty-minute format, taking persnickety questions afterward. At any given time, there were three different panels running in the various rooms of the E.M.P., meaning that the curious onlooker had to choose among equally tempting offerings. In order to attend the Bob Dylan panel—entitled The Dylan—you had to skip panels on art music (one paper was "Changing the System: Brian Eno, Sonic Youth, and the Combination of Rock and Experimental Music") and contemporary R. & B. ("Supa Dupa Fly: Styles of Subversion in Black Women's Hip-Hop").

Some of the presentations, a few too many for comfort, lapsed into the familiar contortions of modern pedagogy. Likewise, in the many pop-music books now in circulation, post-structuralist, post-Marxist, post-colonialist, and post-grammatical buzzwords crop up on page after page. There is a whole lot of problematizing, interrogating, and appropriating goin' on. Walter Benjamin's name is dropped at least as often as the Notorious B.I.G.'s. The French sociologist Pierre Bourdieu gets more props than Dr. Dre. At the Pop Conference, I made it a rule to move to a different room the minute I heard someone use the word "interrogate" in a non-detective context or cite any of the theorists of the Frankfurt School. Thus, I ducked out of a talk on Grace Jones's "Slave to the Rhythm" album when I heard a sentence that began with the phrase "Invoking Walter Benjamin." And I bailed on a lecture entitled "Bruce's Butt"—Bruce Springsteen's butt, as seen on the cover of "Born in the U.S.A."—when the speaker began to interrogate the image of the butt, which, under sharp questioning, wouldn't give anything away.

Scholars of this type always want to see pop music as the emanation of an entity called popular culture, rather than as music that happens to have become popular. As a result songs and bands become fungible commodities in the intellectual marketplace. In the anthology "Popular Music Studies," the hip-hop scholar Ian Maxwell asks the significant question "How can our analyses avoid reducing the objects of those analyses to desiccated cadavers on a slab?" His solution—a "more rigorous understanding of what an ethnographically informed approach might offer the study of popular music, nuancing that approach through Bourdieu's reflexive criticality"—gets us only so far.

Roger Beebe, one of the editors of the "Rock Over the Edge" anthology, even looks at music as purely a media phenomenon, inseparable from image and marketing. Analyzing Kurt Cobain's appearances on television, he says that Cobain mattered to his fans mainly as a disembodied entity, not as an individual with a voice, and that he exemplified something called "the post-modern *dispositif.*" Such McLuhanesque musings have been rendered obsolete as

MTV has more or less stopped showing videos in favor of frat-house documentaries. Meanwhile, the Internet has become the main avenue for the spread of music. The mania for downloading music may be wreaking havoc with artists' careers, but it is interesting to see how the ear trumps the eye when the computer takes over. Music is being consumed with no images attached—no videos, no TV appearances, not even album jackets. In the nineteenth century, the Viennese critic Eduard Hanslick dreamed of a world "purely musical," beyond politics and personality. Such a world now exists in the form of the MP3.

The Mathematics of "Superbad"

Despite minor infestations of Benjaminites, there was no shortage of up-close musical discussion at the Pop Conference. I often had the happy experience of being held hostage by an informed fanatic who convinced me that whatever he or she was discussing was the most important music on earth. The presenters tended to avoid obvious mainstream figures—there was nothing on Elvis, the Beatles, or the Rolling Stones—focusing, instead, on the margins and subtexts of pop history. There were papers on the lo-fi ideology of nineties indie rock, the Filipino d.j. scene in San Francisco, and the trailblazing transsexual punk of Wayne/Jayne County, among a hundred others. You got a sense of music as a world of jostling subcultures, each with its resident inventors and masters, its purists and populists. The conference conjured up the everlasting complexity of how songs are made, heard, and remembered.

Rock and roll has generated more self-serving myths than any other genre, and scholars have been busy dismantling them. Too often, pop history has been written as a march forward to a handful of utopian moments in the late fifties and the sixties: Chuck Berry recording "Maybellene," Elvis appearing on Ed Sullivan, the Beatles appearing on Ed Sullivan, and Bob Dylan plugging in his guitar at the Newport Folk Festival. These events have acquired an exaggerated importance, mostly because they had sentimental value for the baby-boom generation that dominated early pop-music writing. Younger writers are especially impatient with the rock narrative—

the "rockist paradigm," they call it—and delight in cataloguing its contradictions and omissions. Consider Dylan's famous rebellion against the folkies. At the Pop Conference, the historian Michael J. Kramer presented a paper in which he defended the folk-music movement from the stereotype that prevails in Dylan studies—the image of humorless fanatics rejecting the visionary in their midst. Kramer pointed out that the singer took a great deal of his mocking, critical voice—"humorous impurity," he called it—from the very movement that he was supposed to have renounced. In a similar vein, Franklin Bruno, a doctoral student in philosophy who writes quirky, literate pop songs, noted that Dylan in his electric period relied heavily on the tricks of Tin Pan Alley songwriting, precisely the sort of mom-and-dad music that the singer was supposed to have left behind. "Blonde on Blonde," Bruno said, was "a head-first dive into pop-song formalism." Everybody must get stoned, but not before the bridge and the modulation.

Again and again, popular music has been described as a story of youth rebellion, in which each generation breaks free of the oppressive mediocrity of its predecessor. When you place these rebellion narratives end to end, they cancel each other out. Whatever is considered edgy and liberating in one generation is dismissed as bland and confining for the next. An aging genre invariably becomes a straw man against which a new genre defines itself. Dylan "plugged in" and defied the folkies. Chuck Berry sang "Roll Over Beethoven" to get the original rock-and-roll revolution under way, using classical music as a foil. The Beatles were said to have swept aside the prefab pop of the early sixties, which happened to include some of the great early Motown songs. Punk sneered at disco. Why should the love of one kind of music necessitate the knocking down of another? Schopenhauer may have had the answer when he observed that the listener is always fighting battles in his head which he can never win in life. "We like to hear in its language the secret history of our will and of all its stirrings and strivings," the philosopher said. Music at its most potent creates the feeling that the world is about to undergo a vague but tremendous change, which is how political energies become attached to it. When the world fails to change as promised, however, the music becomes an object of ridicule.

The ultimate pop-music myth is the one that scholars file under the rubric "authenticity," according to which only the rudest, rawest music—the primal scream of the outcast—qualifies as "real." African-American music is usually expected to supply the perfume of the primitive. Since the nineteen-twenties, white teen-agers have used black music as the Muzak of their pubescence. Some pop historians still perpetuate this mythology, but others make a point of celebrating all that is rigorous, complex, and exalted in the African-American tradition. One of my favorite passages in pop-music studies appears in "Instruments of Desire," an erudite paean to the electric guitar, by Steve Waksman, of Smith College. It describes how Bo Diddley came to invent his tremolando sound. "Tremolo involved an oscillation of the electronic signal," Waksman writes, "transmitted from the guitar to the amplifier so that the volume level would fluctuate at regular intervals between extreme loudness and virtual silence." I don't really know what this means, but it certainly puts Diddley's "bump-a-bump bump" in a new light. Likewise, David Brackett, the author of "Interpreting Popular Music," lost me when he began to expound on James Brown's "Superbad" by way of the mathematical proportions of the Golden Section, positing that various parts of the song relate to each other by a ratio of 0.618 to 1. Bach has long been subject to this sort of arcane analysis, and there is no reason that the hardest-working man in show business shouldn't get the same treatment.

In a less pedantic vein, a paper by Portia K. Maultsby, who teaches in the department of Folklore and Ethnomusicology at Indiana University, dismantled the clichés attached to Motown's "hit factory," which for a long time was accused of purveying what critics called a "diluted blackness." She stressed Motown's profound connections with the African-American tradition, especially jazz, gospel, and rhythm and blues: James Jamerson's restless, all-over bass lines are electric bebop. Maultsby's paper went hand in hand with an essay by John Sheinbaum in the "Rock Over the Edge" anthology—a devastating account of how white rockers are routinely celebrated as enigmatic artists while their African-American counterparts are made out to be simpleminded conduits of energy and fun. "The Rolling Stone Illustrated History of Rock and Roll" once described Motown as a "wholly mechanical style and sound." The Beatles, by contrast, were hailed as mop-top Beethovens immediately after releasing "I Want to Hold Your Hand." The Beatles were great, but they did not save music from oblivion when they arrived in America in 1964. In fact, as Keir Keightley notes in "The Cambridge Companion to Pop and Rock," the blues-besotted British Invasion had the effect of putting a great many African-American session musicians out of work.

The Crucifixion Mambo

By common consent, the tour de force of the Pop Conference was a lecture by the Cuban music scholar and producer Ned Sublette, which took place at the not very funky hour of 9:30 A.M. In the space of twenty minutes or so, Sublette conjured up the sweeping influence of Cuban music and Caribbean traditions on almost every popular form of the twentieth century. It was not so much a lecture as an all-out performance: Sublette, who also leads a Latin-country fusion band, sang, tapped, and danced the Cuban rhythms that have insinuated themselves into every breakthrough moment in American music, including ragtime (Scott Joplin's "The Entertainer" uses the *danzón* rhythm), New Orleans jazz, bebop, rock and roll (Bo Diddley's "hambone" beat is similar to the Cuban clave), and funk. Sublette called Cuban music "the elephant in the kitchen that pop-music historians have failed to see"; it was, he insisted, the site of the original marriage of African rhythm and European harmony.

By installing Cuban music as "the other great tradition," Sublette did the unthinkable: he questioned the primacy of African-Americans in pop history. There were murmurs of unease when he announced that African-American music was not originally polyrhythmic. Robert Christgau, the fiercely informed critic of the *Village Voice*, said in the question-and-answer period that blues singers implied polyrhythm in the interplay of voice and guitar. In a way, though, Sublette's Cubacentric reading—the book version of which will be published next year—relieves African-Americans of the burden of being the primitives of American music; they become the appropriators rather than the appropriated.

Sublette mentioned, in passing, the fascinating history of two old Spanish-American dances, the *zarabanda* and the *chacona*, which probably stemmed from the Afro-Caribbean melting pot. They spread to Europe in the sixteenth and seventeenth centuries and helped shape some of the masterpieces of the Baroque. In Seattle, I got to thinking about the tangled history of the *chacona*, or cha-conne, which has appeared in so many diverse places in the past five hundred years that it could be considered one of the iconic images of the universal language. It is identifiable by its bass line: a con-stantly repeating, often downward-plunging figure, over which higher instruments and voices play variations. "A dance in the way of the mulatto's," Cervantes called it. The lyrics were bawdy and irreverent; the music was said to have been invented by the Devil. Once it reached Europe, it slowed down and took on more solemn connotations. In the hands of Monteverdi it led to the "Lamento" bass, which was well suited to the dying utterances of operatic hero-ines. In its most striking form, the "Lamento" proceeded down a grand, chilly staircase of semitones, or chromatic steps. You can hear this version of it in the heart-stopping final lament of Purcell's "Dido and Aeneas," and in the "Crucifixus" from Bach's Mass in B Minor.

At the beginning of the twentieth century, a *chacona*-style figure reappeared in the hands of African-American musicians in New Orleans, Chicago, and, notably, the Mississippi Delta, where the Devil was again said to be active. It sounded obsessively in Skip James's "I'm So Glad," one of the greatest of the Delta blues, and can be heard rumbling beneath Ellington's "Reminiscing in Tempo." Descending chromatic basses gave a slow-marching power to some of the more ambitious rock songs of the sixties and seven-ties—Dylan's "Ballad of a Thin Man" and "Simple Twist of Fate," Led Zeppelin's "Dazed and Confused" and "Stairway to Heaven." Somehow, four centuries after the lamenting bass surfaced, its meaning remained the same. It summoned up the dark comfort of heartbreak and depression: the heart descending step by step to the bottom and going back up to repeat the journey.

Universal figures such as the *chacona*—"memes," as musicologists call them, borrowing from sociobiology—reveal the interconnectedness of all musical experience. If you could bring together a few seventeenth-century Afro-Cuban musicians, a continuo section led by the Master Bach, and players from Ellington's 1929 band, and then ask John Paul Jones to start them off with the bass line of "Dazed and Confused," they would, after a minute or two, find common ground. And very interesting music it would be, too. Purists of all genres can never stand the fact that the genealogy of music is one long string of miscegenations and mutations.

The Timberlake Perplex

When, in 1943, Ellington presented his symphonic masterpiece "Black, Brown, and Beige" at Carnegie Hall, he spoke of it in the first-person plural, including his band in the creative process. Scholars often point out that African-American genres, like their West African antecedents, resist the European cult of personality: they tend to take the form of a collective ritual, not of a declamation by a charismatic star to a passive crowd. The problem with the "genius" model is that it puts up a wall between performer and audience; this is surely why so many pop musicians reject it, even as they feed on the adulation that creates it. They look warily on the archivists and commentators who crowd around any long-lasting genre. If, as another old German dude said, the owl of Minerva flies at dusk, rock critics are Minerva's vultures: when enough of them take flight, it means that something is dying.

Still, we listeners want to talk about genius. We want a language that articulates and perpetuates our passions. What's bedeviling about pop music is that while we sense greatness in a song we have trouble saying where it comes from. It is often difficult to say who even wrote the thing in the first place. Some performers exert such a powerful presence—Billie Holiday, Sinatra, Elvis—that they seem to become the authors of songs that were actually the work of schlumpy men in the Brill Building. Then there are the rock songs that were written by committee, often in the middle of the night, and under the influence of something other than the muse Euterpe. Composers have the advantage of being shrouded in myth: we can project fantasies of omniscience upon them. Pop stars torment us with their inconvenient humanness—their tax problems, their noisome politics, their pornography collections, their unwanted comebacks. No wonder the greatest legends are the artists who die young.

Call this the Timberlake predicament. In the past year, rock critics found themselves in the faintly embarrassing position of having to hail Justin Timberlake's "Justified" as one of the better records of the year. Timberlake, for those who have let their subscriptions to *Teen People* lapse, is the blond, curly-haired twenty-two-year-old lead singer of 'N Sync. Encomiums from certifiably heterosexual male critics such as Christgau have demonstrated that Timberlake was not getting praised for his pretty face alone. Granted, cynics may see all this as a rationalization on the part of writers who can't admit that music keeps getting worse; they eat a Hostess Twinkie and call it a gourmet meal. But it shouldn't be forgotten that many of the most impossible achievements in pop history had their origins in ditsy teenybopper fads. The Beatles were once a boy band, too. What happened to them in the middle and late sixties was a mysterious transfer of energy, in which disposable fame was transmuted into artistic power. The band found fame first, then it found greatness. So it would be foolish to write Timberlake off too quickly.

In any case, the songs on "Justified" aren't really Timberlake's. A dozen names appear in the credits, and it's anyone's guess how much of a song like "Cry Me a River," the album's best track, actually came from Timberlake's pen, if he owns one. Every bit of the song shows the fingerprints of the hip-hop producer Tim Mosley, a.k.a. Timbaland, who is the éminence grise behind half of what is great in the Top Forty these days. He has sampled every genre under the sun, from world music to austere electronica. He likes to leave yawning gaps of silence between his speaker-puncturing beats, which inspire new kinds of vehemence on the dance floor. (As Virgil Thomson observed long ago, we dance to syncopated music because our bodies like to fill in the missing beats.) Modernist ideology accustoms us to think that experimentation can take place on the margins of a culture, but hip-hop production is the site of some of the weirdest, wittiest thinking in pop music today.

"Cry Me a River" has no apparent relation to the 1955 standard made famous by Julie London, although a future analysis of internal structural ratios may show otherwise. The vocals are plaintive to the point of whining, but the inner voices have a cool, contrapuntal flow, creating the sort of muscular melancholy so characteristic of postwar rhythm and blues. There are at least seven layers of simultaneous activity in the song—it's as if Timbaland wanted to see how much he could pile on without creating atonality. First there is an arpeggiated keyboard figure, followed by male voices singing a bit of Gregorian-style chant. Next comes a steady, somber pattern that sounds a little like the minor-key vamp in Ellington's "East St. Louis Toodle-Oo." Below it are four bass notes, recurring in *chacona* style. Now the angelic Timberlake enters, together with a more nasty-minded rhythm section, a vaguely Indian-sounding synthesized string orchestra, and, finally, sped-up versions of all of the above.

In sum, "Cry Me a River" may be the most polyphonically complex teeny-bopper ballad in history. At the very least, it's not something that any idiot could have done. It has the inward delight of a song that is better than it needs to be. Popular music is full of this sort of mad tinkering; in the background of even the most ostentatiously numskulled acts may be a music geek who stays up all night trying to find a single chord. Pop-music scholars spend a lot of time describing the messages that become attached to songs, and this is a necessary part of the history of listening. Yet, when music passes from one generation to another, it leaves most of its social significance peeling off dorm-room walls, and its persistence is best explained with reference to beats, chords, and raw emotion. Which is why pop writers have to find a new way to describe musical events, and not just by offering dopey imitations of classical musicology. No one would give much credence to a style of art criticism that alluded to paintings without mentioning their shapes and colors, or an architecture criticism that refused to say whether buildings were made of stone or metal.

It was disappointing to hear from attendees at the Pop Conference that they are still viewed with intense suspicion by their colleagues in classical musicology. Increasingly, leading colleges and universities have full-time pop specialists; the musicology department at U.C.L.A. is headed by Robert Walser, the author of books on jazz and heavy metal. Given the vast quantities of obscurantism that classical musicologists have churned out in the past fifty years—the impenetrable tautologies of Schenkerian analysis, the higher-math delirium of pitch-class set theory—classical scholars have no right to dismiss their pop counterparts as anything less than serious. They probably picture themselves fighting a last stand against the armies of ignorance, but any mode of teaching that promotes close, histori-cally attuned listening can't be a bad thing. And those of us who write on classical music have a lot to learn from pop studies. It exposes the hard realities of how music is made, how it is paid for, and how it is consumed. To understand music only as art and not as entertainment, as classical scholars tend to do, is to dehumanize the past. For all we know, Bach may well have rolled his eyes and munched on a pork chop whenever someone asked him about his relationship with Palestrina.

Pop music is music stripped bare. It is like the haphazard funeral portrayed in Wallace Stevens's "Emperor of Ice Cream": a woman laid out with all her flaws intact, covered with a sheet from a chest of drawers that is missing three knobs, her horny feet protruding. Boys bring flowers in last month's newspapers, but she is noble to look upon. Twentieth-century music, the empire of ice cream, lies before us in all its damaged majesty.

CARL HANCOCK RUX

Eminem

The New White Negro

*"From the Negro we take only the magical-liturgical
bits, and only the antithesis makes them
interesting to us."*

—HUGO BALL

*"There is a zone of non-being,
An extraordinary sterile and arid region,
An utterly naked declivity
Where an authentic upheaval can be born.
In most cases the Black man lacks the advantage
Of being able to accomplish this descent
Into a real hell."*

—FRANTZ FANON, FROM "BLACK SKIN, WHITE MASKS"

Revenge of Pentheus

Pentheus, the protagonist of Euripides' *The Bacchae*, was a young
moralist and anarchical warrior who sought to abolish the worship
of Dionysus (god of tradition, or perhaps better said, god of the re-
cyclical, who causes the loss of individual identity in the uncontrol-
lable, chaotic eruption of ritualistic possession). When Pentheus
sets out to infiltrate the world of the Bacchae and explore the mysteries of savage lore, his intention is to save the possessed women of
Thebes (from themselves), who engage in hedonistic practices
somewhere high in the mountains. Dionysus derails the young warrior's lofty mission by titillating his sexual curiosity (inviting him to

take a quick glimpse of the drunken women as they revel in their lesbian orgy). In order to witness firsthand the necromancy of the inhumane, Pentheus must disguise himself as *one of* the inhumane. Ultimately the young moralist's disguise mirrors the appearance of Dionysus, the very god he seeks to subjugate. The transformed soldier, now possessed by the spirit of his nemesis, is set on the highest branch of a fir tree, elevated above all and visible to none—or so he is led to believe. Pentheus' disguise is as transparent as his voyeuristic fetish, and it is because of this very visible elevated space he inhabits that he is brutally dismembered by the gang of possessed women on the mountain (led by his own mother), who see him for what he is.

Historically, academics have neatly interpreted the characters of *The Bacchae* as belonging to themes of good versus evil, rational versus reason, nobility versus paganism. In the casual study of classical realism, Pentheus is noble in his efforts to eradicate paganism, and Dionysus is an all-powerful demonic and *immoral* force. But in more careful study (or at least, an alternate one), we may learn that Dionysus is a traditional Olympian god, neither good nor bad. His powers are *amoral*; they are powers informed only by the powers that control human existence. Real life—death, sex, grief, joy, etc.— in its entire splendor. Dionysus and his worshipers cannot be controlled or converted. Their humanity *has been perceived as* inhumane, and in defense of their right to preserve an identity and a culture for themselves, an extreme cruelty befitting of inhumanity is enacted. The mother's murder of her son is a necessary *evil*; we accept the death of Pentheus as the inevitable defeat of his judgmental and moral idealism, but because this act of brutality is performed by the mother of its victim, we also question the value of human existence above the existence of humanity (couldn't she have just given him a slap on the hand and a good talking-to and said, "Baby, some people live differently than others, but ain't nobody better than the rest . . . "?). Perhaps the moral of the story is: The identity of the individual is most often sacrificed for the identity of the collective, so we must now all live and speak in broad familiar terms and forsake our sons and daughters for the ultimate good of humanity as we see it. The evolution of human existence is pro-

pelled by a constant narcissism; a struggle to negotiate one's perception of self and one's perception of the other, and some of the
most (historically) flawed (though pervasive) acts of negotiating a
collective identity are politicized oppression and cultural mimicry
of the other—both of which seek agreement. Inevitably, collective
agreement regarding identity produces a common design for
humanity, or a morality relative to the perceptions of a particular
group. Hierarchical notions of humanity are formed, and, eventually, once the tracks are laid, people will have to pitch their tents on
either side. Conflict. War. Somebody (or bodies) in opposition to
the populace will have to be dismembered so that new orders of
identity can be formed.

Fast-forward a few thousand years to a more contemporary but parallel heroic-antiheroic protagonist—Eminem, the platinum-domed,
Caesar-haircut, pop-prince bad-boy superstar of late-twentieth/early-
twenty-first-century postmodern hip-hop culture. Like Pentheus, he
dresses himself in the garments of the outcasts, has learned their language, their songs and rituals. But unlike Pentheus, Eminem is no
moralist martyr with a secret desire to objectify. The real Slim Shady
does not make the mistake of re-creating the Theban soldier's vain
attempt to destroy the god of mass appeal. He accepts the unholy
ghost as his personal savior, and with a slight flip of the Greek
tragedy script (with hip-hop flare), introduces us to his first sacrifice—his own mother, whom he publicly debases and strips of all
garments of integrity, drags nude into the spotlight, and ritualisti-
cally murders hit single after hit single. Though savagery is
expected to call for misogyny of magnanimous proportions,
Eminem's humiliation of the maternal figure is not just limited to
his *own* mother, but extends itself to she who is also the mother of
his own child (or in ghetto fabulous vernacular, his *baby mama*). In
one of his first award-winning acts of hit-single hedonism, the real
Slim Shady murders his baby mama right in front of his baby (for
our entertainment pleasure)—and later, in his sophomore phase,
morphs into a fan of himself who is inspired to do the same. A continuum, thereby raising the inhumane status of outcast culture to
new bacchanalian heights.

The postmodern pop-culture icon of the new outlaw is complete and to be carried into the new millennium; Eminem does not *seek* to know pagan lore—he was *born* into it, has always spoken the language of it, has always danced to the music of it, has always dressed himself in the latest pagan wear, has never used this language, this music, or this apparel to *disguise* his true identity or to disguise his race, and he has never tried to dissociate himself from the source of his performance, the black male outlaw or outcast of hip-hop fame. Rappers Big Boi and Dre may go by the moniker Outkast, but Eminem proves that a *real* outcast has got to do more than make *Miss Jackson*'s daughter cry—you got to fuck the bitch, kill the bitch, dump the bitch's dead body in the river, and not apologize for any of it.

Eminem's politically incorrect vaudeville routine (an oxymoron) is not to be attempted by everyone. Even his protégés, D-12, failed miserably as horror rappers on their debut album *Devil's Night* (if poor record sales and bad reviews are any indication). With boasts of slapping around handicapped women, gorging pills, and sodomizing their grandmothers, the effect is less tongue-in-cheek than tongue-in-toilet. And, when old-school mack daddy of hip-hop cool, Slick Rick, made a cameo appearance on the recently released Morcheeba album, *Charango*, derivatively flowing à la Eminem style ("Woman Lose Weight") about murdering his overweight wife in order to hook up with his sexy blond secretary, MTV did not come-a-calling. The result is derivative at best. Incidentally, not long after the Morcheeba album release, Slick Rick found himself arrested by the INS and awaiting deportation from this country (because somebody *just* found out that he has been an illegal resident for over thirty years). Not to suggest that his penal consequences are the direct result of imitating Eminem, but so far, only Eminem gets away with *being* Eminem, perhaps because he uses his visors and disguises to disguise his split personality as undisguised—raising the questions, who is the real outcast, who is the real Slim Shady, what has he inherited from culture to achieve his bad-boy, outcast minstrel, rebel superstar status, and *exactly* what identity crisis is being performed?

Fanon Had a (Semantic) Dream

Frantz Fanon tells us that the oppressed must identify an oppressive archetype in order to overcome historical oppression. But before the oppressed can achieve acts of true upheaval, they must first realize that they have yet to achieve "non-being" status. The oppressed may have attempted prior acts of resistance, but have never actually "descended into a real hell" that will scorch into the very nature of seeing an *effective* upheaval that brings the non-being into being. For now, the oppressed continue to live in the dream of identity, the dream that (in reality) the oppressed are, in fact, Negro, Colored, Black, Minority, Afro or African American, Hispanic, Oriental, Dykes, Queers, Bitches, Hos, Niggaz. All accepted as real identities. The acceptance of these identities further compels a performance of these identities, whether compliant or rebellious.

The oppressed identity performance relies upon a collective agreement informed by a historical narrative that either supports the validity of, or opposes the construct of, these identities. Before a revisionist identity can be forged, there was an inheritance and an acceptance of a construct—thus, even when the oppressed think they are revising their identities, updating the language of their identities, or endeavoring to better the circumstances of their identities, they are not—not completely and not actually—because no language in the American polyglot has ever been subscribed to by the collective that points to the very nature of human identity beyond elementary categorizations, and no accurate language regarding race-identity exists in our collective agreement. We are comfortable with vague concepts of identity, and the ghettos and empires these concepts create.

What the oppressed figure in America has been working with as an identity is actually an archetypal construct born out of a dream (as in aspirations and imaginings) belonging to an oppressive figure who is not only the architect of the dream that oppresses us, but is also the Dionysian-like landlord of our realities—both good and bad—neither real nor unreal, and completely exempt from being vanquished from our realities. We inhabit an oppressive dream, and until that descent into Fanon's "real hell," the oppressed will continue to pay a high price to rent substandard space in the dream that we call *race* in America.

Eminem, the Other White Meat

". . . If all the Niggers
Started calling eachother Nigger,
Not only among themselves . . . but among Ofays . . .
Nigger wouldn't mean anymore than 'Good night,'
'God bless you,' or 'I promise to tell the whole truth
And nothing but the whole truth so help me God' . . .
When that beautiful day comes,
You'll never see another Nigger kid
Come home from school crying
Because some Ofay motherfucker called him Nigger."
　　　—LENNY BRUCE

Eminem, a.k.a Marshall Mathers, was born in St. Joseph, Missouri (near Kansas City), spending the better part of his impoverished childhood in Detroit, Michigan—which, by the way, is about 90 percent *ethnic minority* and has one of the highest concentrations of African Americans in the nation, at 83 percent, while non-Latino whites comprise only 12 percent of the city's population. Detroit's recent dip below one million is largely attributed to continuing *white flight*, and 10 percent of the state's population has lived in poverty for more than twenty years (a family of three with an income of a little more than $9,300 earns too much to qualify for welfare in Michigan—but is about $4,000 below the federal poverty guideline), according to the American Community Survey released by the U.S. Census Bureau. Translation: Eminem may have been born *white* but he was socialized as *black*, in the proverbial hood—and the music of the proverbial hood in America for the last twenty-five years has been hip-hop music. The same inner-city struggles and impoverished circumstances that brought us blues, jazz, rhythm and blues, doo-wop, and soul, brought us hip-hop music—it began as a form of identity-boosting vocal scatting over pulsating beats and progressed to become a means of expressing the social realities of African-American urbanity. By the time it became a major moneymaker in the music industry, the genre of hip-hop transformed into a bodacious representation of gangsta life and gangsta obsessions replete with murder, money, sex, alcohol and drug consumption—and, when this got tired, narrowed itself down and preoccupied itself with the glam of capital gain.

The legend of Eminem, a.k.a. Slim Shady, a.k.a. Marshall Mathers (and his psychotic nasal slapstick trips of alienation) begins with his Detroit exposure to rap, performing it at the age of fourteen and later earning notoriety as a member of the Motor City duo Soul Intent. The legend is that he dropped out of high school, worked minimum-wage jobs, practiced beat boxing and freestyling his lyrics on home recordings, and worshipped rap groups like NWA—he admits he "wanted to be Dr. Dre and Ice Cube," wore big sunglasses while "lip-synching to their records in the mirror." He also honed his style in the company of five black Detroit MC's (D-12). Together, the racially integrated posse decided that each of them would have an alter ego, thus the six MC's were to be thought of as twelve MC's—dubbing themselves, the Dirty Dozen. When Eminem emerged as a solo artist in 1996 with the independent release *Infinite*, he was accused of trying to sound "too much like Nas," so he perfected a nasal white-boy, horror-rap cadence, following *Infinite* with *The Slim Shady LP*, which led the hip-hop underground to dub him hip-hop's "great white hope."

The legend of his discovery varies. Allegedly, Dr. Dre discovered Eminem's demo tape on the floor of Interscope label chief Jimmy Iovine's garage. Another story goes that Dre first heard him on the radio and said, "Find that kid whoever he is! I'm gonna make him a star!" Either way, not until Eminem took second place (who won first?) in the freestyle category at 1997's Rap Olympics MC Battle in Los Angeles did Dre agree to sign him, producing the best-selling triple platinum *Slim Shady LP* in early 1999. With controversial yet undeniable talent (the right mix for stardom of any kind), Eminem became the white-boy cartoon god of surreal white-trash humor and graphic violence, a stratum of Roseanne Barr–meets–Quentin Tarrentino–meets–Mickey Mouse Club–cum Snoop Dogg and beatnik Dobie Gillis. *The Marshall Mathers LP* followed and sold close to two million copies in its first week of release, making it one of the fastest-selling rap albums of all time, and his latest album, *The Eminem Show*, was the first album since 'N Sync's *Celebrity* and the September 11 terrorist attacks to sell over one million copies in its debut week. To top it all off, Eminem's roman à clef feature film debut, *8 Mile*, is described as a story about "the boundaries that define our lives and a young man's struggle to find the strength and courage to transcend them." In his greatest struggle to transcend boundaries, the surrealist rap icon has also managed two weapons charges, an assault charge, a lawsuit from his mother for humiliating her in his lyrics, and his baby mama's attempted suicide—all to keep it real, as they say.

But Eminem does not offer us real, he offers the *surreal*—several alter egos further immersing our bacchanalian notions of race-inclusive hip-hop lore. We all want to be Bacchus or Dionysus. Especially black people, especially Niggaz, who have invented the alter ego of a New Savage God—a gun-toting nationalist radical with supreme sexual prowess and unsurpassable talent to counter Bill Cosby's 1980s middle-class Negrodum. We, who are members of the so-called ethnic minority and belong to a hip-hop generation, have inherited an imposition and elaborated on it until it has become an opportunity, borrowing our new black character from a relevant history of slavery, reconstruction, ghetto realism, black civil rights, arts and radical movements, and mythic Blaxploitation heroes like Shaft and Foxy Brown. But lest we get high-minded about it all, the badass thug and gangsta bitch are not purely the inventions of inner-city urban imagination. They are also products of Hollywood's imaginary American heroes: second-generation immigrants turned Depression-era gangster moguls, as portrayed by Edward G. Robinson, James Cagney, Humphrey Bogart; John Wayne's cocky cowboy; Sean Connery's hyper-heterosexual sci-fi upper-class guy, "James Bond."

Hip-hop inventors have grown up with these archetypes on their television screens, and incorporated them into a contemporary gothic myth set in the housing projects they know America to be. In order for this merger of white and black icons to evolve, there had to be in place a basic understanding of race among a contemporary generation. The new power brokers of culture had to inherit an inherited concept of race and form vaguely similar ways of seeing the construct of race. If it appears that the history of race in America means less to the new generation of pop-music icons and their fans—socially, politically, and psychologically—than the performance of class and outlaw status, it is because a race-inclusive product for the American cultural marketplace demands short-term memory.

What has emerged from an old system of cultural supremacy and inferiority is a new superpower contingent upon our informed (and uninformed) race perception. The final incarnations of the black male figure in a century that began with sharecroppers and first-generation free peoples trying to avoid the hanging tree are their gun-toting, dick-slinging capitalist descendants. The black male outlaw identity is a commodifiable character open to all who would like to perform it. In order for the oppressed figure's dream of attaining ostentatious wealth and fame while defying conventional structures of morality to come into fruition, the dream *had to* be race-inclusive, race-accessible, and dangerous enough to pose an idealistic threat to a conservative society—translation: like jazz, white people had to like it, buy it, invest in it, and benefit from it, and above all, identify with it too. And the seduction had to appeal to a fascination with and fear of a complex figure they'd been taught to disdain. Not unlike Pentheus' objectifying curiosity, white culture watched the evolution of the hip-hop character from afar before the hip-hop character knew they were watching at all. Thus, hip-hop culture has evolved into another classic ready-to-wear American original, like rock 'n' roll—except this time, the black hip-hop artist participates in the profit and control of the industry (to some extent) more so than ever before. But it is still an outsider culture, perpetuating its own outsider mythology, and if there are non-black, economically privileged teenagers who wear their oversized jeans pulled down around their knees and sleep beneath posters of self-proclaimed rapists, gang members, and murderers with record deals, it is because every generation of youth culture since Socrates has identified with outsider/outcast/radicalism, and typically pursued some kind of participation in it. Because radicalism, whether political or not, is a multicultural and universal sentiment.

Some may contend that white artists who pioneer their way into so-called black music forms take the privilege of being allowed to do so seriously and pursue lofty goals of destroying race barriers, thereby bridging gaps of new race perception in America. But others may contend that race *inclusivity* [*sic*] diminishes the organic intention of race music [*sic*] until it simplifies into yet another popular entertainment form in the marketplace, where its inventor will compete for a right to exist (i.e., if Eric Clapton, Bonnie Raitt, or Lyle Lovett stopped playing the blues, what would it mean to B. B. King or Keb' Mo's pop chart eligibility?).

Race performance in America—however guilty we all are of it (and we *all* are guilty of it)—has suffered an uneven exchange. There are allowances made for some to a greater degree than others. From jazz to rock 'n' roll, white representation in black music forms is completely acceptable and rarely questioned (even if contemporary black representation in rock, alternative rock, or any kind of rock warrants front page *New York Times* explanations), but some have questioned whether or not white representation in black music ultimately diminishes the sentiment of black music, or distracts a critical audience from narrowly perceiving black music innovations *as* black music. Whom does music or race belong to? Whether or not race is to stake its claim in music, race performance prevails as much now as it did in the good ol' Al Jolson days. One can easily see a careful study in the color-line cross-over iconography of artists like Vanilla Ice, the first popular hip-hop "wigger" to top the charts, who cooked his character with the main ingredients of authentic angry black male aggression, by promising dope hits and throat slits (from *"Livin'"*), further validating himself with essential sociopolitical blues lamentations of existential thug life, screaming his hatred at society (from *A.D.D.*), and offering us some insight to the familial dysfunction of ghetto life that produced his incredulity, blaming an abusive father and excusing his mother from all responsibility for his compulsive and unexplainable brain-blasting (from *Scars*).

But Vanilla Ice's middle-class white-childhood reality emerged and ruined the authenticity of his performance—though his hip-hop icon still left an indelible mark on hip-hop culture. As with all great rock stars or rock-star hopefuls, it is the image of these icons and their proclamations of themselves that reach beyond them, creating a mass of followers who are inspired by their belief in the performance, not the person. In this way, those few artists fortunate enough to achieve superstar status become ancient, distant archetypes that appeal to our psychic dispositions, like Jesus or Gatsby— the icon we believe in helps us validate what we believe about ourselves and the world as we see it, whether it's real or not.

The Good, the Bad, and the Nigga

"It's not right to start penalizing good people . . .
We need a humane monitoring system to
search out the good and bad."

—SLICK RICK, WHILE AWAITING DEPORTATION
IN A FLORIDA DETENTION FACILITY

Both Eminem and Vanilla Ice take their cues from a savage model, and it is this savage model that has informed everyone from the Surrealists to the Bohemians. If there is an eternal plan, it is a primitive one with no bearing on virtue. Their performances are rooted in a supposed realism. Realism places God in heaven, makes distinct social classes where moral law distinguishes between good and evil—an orderly world with gradual changes: wars, revolutions, inventions, etc. One can belong to the outcasts of this world, and still be a realist. It's all in the style of your performance. Style becomes the only authentic instrument of classic realism, and an important elemental style of hip-hop realism involves daily mortal danger. However, within one's own existence, one is influenced not only by the current circumstances of life but by the style of life where we are experiencing it. Style both replicates reality and takes us away from our reality. Style also heightens and produces a counterbalance to the realism of life (i.e., your hip-hop icon du jour may live with a sense of daily mortal danger—like you do—but unlike you, he drives a Mercedes jeep, wears diamonds and furs, and maintains a harem of scantily clad women with bodies endowed according to his fickle fetish fantasies).

Those of us who choose to deny that we now live in a society psychically impacted by hip-hop realism may still embrace the changing styles of hip-hop realism because it removes us from our actual reality (as all good forms of entertainment should). If the edict of early hip-hop lore shifted its weight from the innocence of Sugarhill Gang's party babble to Public Enemy's urban radicalism and political consciousness, it seemed to be a call to arms—an insistence that the oppressed figure recognize something about his status-elevation potential. If hip-hop again shifted its weight from Suge Knight's heyday of East Coast/West Coast rivalry and gang-banging to Puffy's epoch of Versace gear, Cristal champagne, and Harry Winston diamond-encrusted platinum jewelry, it read as an attempt to break from the tradition that celebrated the kind of violence that produced the sudden and actual deaths of Biggie Smalls and Tupac Shakur—an attempt to make a gradual transference from ghetto realism toward escaping conventions of death. An oppressed capitalist's bargaining with life.

The antisymbolic nature of the savage archetype from which Eminem creates his character is different from Vanilla Ice's invention. Vanilla's performance is classic in nature—a form of modern realism where human truth was more important than the poetry of words. Eminem's eminence rarely attempts to address serious social or political ills, nor is it obsessed with hypercapitalism. Eminem does not attempt to perform the authentic Nigga as much as he performs a New White Nigga. He maintains his whiteness with quirky vocal Jerry Lewis–like phrasing and a bright Greek-god bleached-blonde buzz cut; and the classic hip-hop realism he was initially influenced by when he first studied the style of Naughty by Nature and Nas has been replaced by his own brand of contemporary Surrealism that abstracts and exaggerates hip-hop lore more so than any of his authentic heroes or contemporaries dare try.

Eminem's lyrics speak to the wayward descendants of Fanon's Negroes: Niggaz. Niggaz hear him and Niggaz understand him; still, he comes as a representative of what Niggaz have produced in their dreams—someone who is not them but worships them and belongs to them and, by virtue of socialization, is one of them. He confounds Niggaz and white people alike in the multicultural schoolyard with his mastering of Nigga language and assumption of

Nigga style. His presentation is not overtly authentic, but infused with authenticity because he has lived in Nigga neighborhoods and listened to Nigga music and learned Nigga culture—and the integrity of his performance does not overtly attempt mimicry, like those culture bandits who came before him, after him, or share pop-chart status with him. He frowns at white people like Moby, Christina Aguilera, Fred Durst, and Everlast, who poorly adapt yet successfully co-opt the aesthetics, ideologies, and style of Niggaz. He comes already revered by relevant society of new and old royalty—Dr. Dre who discovered him, Busta Rymes who once dubbed him "the baddest rapper out there," Madonna and Elton John who have knighted him their heir apparent. But before we give him the NAACP Image Award, it should remain clear that Eminem's race performance is not (solely) intended to impress the oppressed. He's already done that and moved on.

Eminem takes the mythology of the oppressed—identifying himself as impervious, armed and dangerous, sexually superior, economically privileged, radical—and turns this dream on its head. Makes it a macabre comedy of internal warfare. We must laugh at our anger and still be angry, he says. We must be offensive and still be funny, he says. Our enemy is not race . . . our enemy is everybody and anybody who is not "us," and "us" is defined as outsiders who have grown up disenfranchised with strange, irreverent dreams—the problem with "us" Niggaz is we don't take our irreverence far enough, lyrically speaking. We talk about killing each other and celebrate our daily drug and alcohol consumption, but we still get up at the MTV awards and *thank and praise my Lord and Savior Jesus Christ* for small favors like best rap video. We aspire to make millions of dollars any way we can, to get rich quick and stay rich forever, but as soon as we sign our souls to a record contract, we take our advance to the nearest check-cashing place, lay away sneakers with diamond soles, slam a deposit on any house Cher once owned, (equipped with gold-leaf toilet paper) and wait for *MTV Cribs* to drop by. (At least Eve promises to buy herself a Warhol every year for her birthday.)

Niggaz may talk bad about bitches and they baby's mama—Eminem brutally murders his. Niggaz may have issues regarding absent fathers or dysfunctional mothers—Eminem comically exposes their dysfunctions, and hangs his mother's pussy high up on a wall for all the world to see. Niggaz may be misogynist, may boast of sexual superiority and sexual indiscretions with a multitude of women, may commonly relegate women to just another piece of ass prime for taking status—but Eminem drugs the bitch, fucks the bitch, moves on to the next bitch. This horror-rapping member of the oppressed nation has won. He has proven to the oppressed that he is not one of us, but he is down for us—and he has proven to the oppressor that he is not one of them, but he is the product of their extreme idea of "us"—and, by virtue of neutralizing the nebulous medium, Eminem becomes us with supernatural powers beyond us. Ultimately, he replaces us, paying homage to an old abstract idea.

The New Surrealist Manifesto

The early-twentieth-century European movement of white male artists who attempted to perform a poetic, political, revolt by way of anti-cortical [*sic*] understanding, insisted that there was to be no distinction made between what they considered to be abstract and what they considered to be real. In "Surrealist and Existentialist Humanism," Ferdinand Alquie wrote, "To claim that reason is man's essence is already to cut man in two, and the classical tradition has never failed to do so. It has drawn a distinction between what is rational in man (which by that sole fact is considered truly human); and what is not rational (instincts and feelings) which consequently appears unworthy of man." Freud also spoke of the mortal danger incurred for man by this split, this schism between the forces of reason and deep-seated passions—which seem destined to remain unaware of each other. Surrealism wanted to save impulses and desires from repression.

Like Eminem, the Surrealists borrowed the sinister dreams of the oppressed—aspirations for economic success outside of traditional structures; achieved narcissism born to overwhelm self-loathing and inherent existentialism; illusions of grandeur used to counter inescapable depressed circumstances; dismissal of history in order to fashion a new reality in the present tense.

The Surrealist as well as the early Modernist movements fashioned themselves after their associations with the outcasts of society—in most cases, the outcasts were either of Spanish or African descent, and in all cases, the outcasts (or savages) were economically and socially disenfranchised. Gautier and Alexander Dumas traveled through Spain and wore gypsy costumes as if to make their willed identification more real, and this escape into the exotic became the trend of many pre– and post–World War II European writers, artists, and autodidacts, or White Negroes.

It was Verlaine who first coined the phrase "White Negro" when describing Rimbaud, calling him "the splendidly civilized, carelessly civilizing savage," though the origin of the phrase is usually ascribed to the title of a Norman Mailer essay, in which he attempts to explain the impulse of the white man who dares to live with danger by attempting the art of the primitive.

"The White Negro," written in 1959, was Mailer's response to William Faulkner on the topic of school segregation, and the relationship between blacks and whites. He insists, "Whites resist integration and the prospect of equality" because whites secretly know "the Negro already enjoys sensual superiority . . . The Negro has had his sexual supremacy and the White had his white supremacy." Mailer further identified himself as a "near-Beat adventurer" who identified with Negroes and "urban adventurers," those who "drifted out at night looking for action with a Black man's code to fit their facts." "The hipster," he said, "had absorbed the existentialist synopsis of the Negro and could be considered a White Negro" because "any Negro who wishes to live must live with danger from his first day . . . the Negro knew life was war . . . The Negro could rarely afford the sophisticated inhibitions of civilization, and so he kept for survival the art of the primitive. The Black man lived in the enormous present, he subsisted for his Saturday night kicks, relinquishing the pleasures of the mind for the more obligatory pleasures of the body, and in his music he gave voice to the character and quality of his existence, to his rage and the infinite variations of joy, lust . . . and despair of his orgasm . . . "

Mailer's pronouncement of Beat culture (a mid-century replication of Bohemian culture) as "the essence of hip" further emphasized that "the source of hip is the Negro," for he "has been living on the margin between totalitarianism and democracy for two centuries . . . the Bohemian and the juvenile delinquent came face to face with the Negro . . . the child was the language of hip, for its argot gave expression to abstract states of feeling." James Baldwin countered Mailer's racist and myopic views in his essay "The Black Boy Looks at the White Boy," calling Mailer's sentiments "so antique a vision of the Blacks at this late hour." But countering Baldwin, Eldridge Cleaver called Mailer's view "prophetic and penetrating in its understanding of the psychology involved in the accelerating confrontation of Black and White in America."

Fifty years before Mailer's ethnographic fantasy, Flaubert traveled to Egypt out of a desire for a "visionary alternative," for something "in contrast to the grayish tonality of the French provincial landscape"—resulting in his "labored reconstruction of the other." Baudelaire said true civilization was comprised of ". . . hunters, farmers, and even cannibals—all these . . . superior by reasons of their energy and their personal dignity to our western races." Gautier (whose best friend was a Negro from Guadeloupe, Alexandre Privat d'Anglemont) when commenting on the Algerian influence on turn-of-the-century French fashion, said, "Our women already wear scarves which have served the harem slaves . . . hashish is taking the place of champagne . . . so superior is primitive life to our so-called civilization." Before Josephine Baker reared her beautiful black ass in Paris in the 1920s, European Bohemia was already fascinated with their perceptions of Negroes, and as explained by Firmin Maillard, Bohemians were "philosophers who couldn't have cared less what their philosophy was based on . . . [they were] brave searchers for infinity, impudent peddlers of dreams . . ." And Erich Muhasm admitted, "It emerged that all of us without single exception were apostates, had rejected our origins, were wayward sons." Maurice de Vlaminck was already collecting African art as early as 1904, and Picasso ennobled the command of African sculpture on his own work by stating, "I understood what the Negroes used their sculpture for . . . to help people avoid coming under the influence of spirits again."

In 1916, Hugo Ball, founder of the Dada movement, opened a cabaret in the red-light district of Zurich, called the Café Voltaire, where prostitutes and Africans commingled freely with starving European artists, like Jean Arp, Tristan Tzara, and Walter Serner, who became infamous for their illogical simultaneous poems—explained by them to be "elegiac, humorous, bizarre." They wore black cowls and played a variety of exotic drums, titling their performance the "Chant Nègres." Ten years later, in Paris, Surrealist artists Robert Desnos and André de la Rivière moved into studio apartments next door to the Bal Nègre, a bar frequented by Negroes who lived in hostels on the same street. Hugo Ball explained, "We drape ourselves like medicine men in their insignia and their essences but we want to ignore the path whereby they reached these bits of cult and parade."

These "bits of cult and parade," co-opted by European Bohemians, leaked into the mass culture of modernity, much in the same way hip-hop and R&B have produced Eminem, Britney Spears, and 'N Sync. The result is not associated with race as much as it is associated with an abstraction of culture. Alfred Jarry (author of the infamous nineteenth-century French play *Ubu*) also re-created himself as an avant, but the invention was so abstract that it could not directly be linked to the Negro—Jarry lived in a room with nothing except a bed and a plaster cast of a huge penis (his ode to both poverty and the wealth of hypersexuality). He perfected a staccato speech for himself, a Negro slang of sorts, without directly impersonating the Negro. He publicly performed the fictional character he'd invented for himself by walking up and down the boulevards or attending the opera in white clown masks, cycling clothes, or dirty white suits and shirts made of paper on which he had drawn a tie—demanding outcast inclusion in a formal world. Heseltine, a writer who possessed a sweet, boyish face and closely cropped blonde hair, was described by D. H. Lawrence (in *Women in Love*) as "degenerate," "corrupt," married to the beautiful Puma (who eventually committed suicide—much like Em's baby mama has tried to do—an ode to the tragic *grisette*, or working girl, of Paris who loved the self-indulgent Bohemian savage artist), and composed music under the nom de plume Peter Warlock. Heseltine was also known to smoke a lot of weed, and delve into the occult. Eventually, he gassed himself to death—death by suicide translated into immortality for most existentialist Bohemians, much like death by driveby once meant the same for hip-hop dons.

Fifty years or so after the European Bohemian era, the Beat generation invented itself with Jack Kerouac, Allen Ginsberg, Neal Cassidy, and William Burroughs at its forefront (LeRoi Jones is often omitted from the history of insurgent Beat culture—most likely because any true Beat poet is to be remembered as a *performer* of savagery, not an *actual* savage). When a young Allen Ginsberg admitted in an interview that while growing up he "developed a tremendous tolerance for chaos," and described the world as "absolutely real and final and ultimate and at the same time, absolutely unreal and transitory and of the nature of dreams . . . without contradiction," he easily validated Verlaine and Norman Mailer's theoretical view of the Negro and their psychological profile of the White Negro.

Like hip-hop culture, Beat culture emerged in an era of economic prosperity and political paranoia. If the mid-twentieth-century American White Negro emerged in a postwar era of convention, in which hip and cool Negro icons created a counterculture of style, immorality, and self-destruction, the latter twentieth-century American New White Negro patterned himself after hip-hop culture's era of rebellion, taking him on an uncharted journey prone to danger. Ronald Reagan and Rodney King were good reasons to re-create a new generation of Charlie Parkers and Billie Hollidays—undeniably gifted icons of artistic genius, personal style, and self-destruction. If the Negro hipster lived without a definable past or future, the hip-hopster never let you forget his past and elaborately decorated his present with excess in anticipation of a life without a future—which elevated him to the status of potential martyr. He (or she) emulated Robert De Niro (in *Taxi Driver*) or, the hip-hop favorite, Al Pacino (in *Scarface*)—an outlaw feared for his enormous ferocity, and survival skills, or revered for his unsurpassable stolen wealth, and for living daily with the threat of assassination or mutiny. Beat culture produced popular icons that offered a more abstract version of the White Negro. Its superstar, Jack Kerouac, was a Dionysian figure whose impulses toward the primitive conflicted with his tendency toward culture, education, and ego.

Ultimately, Jack was not as interested in being an outlaw as he was interested in being a star—the celebrity that white status could afford him. And as Baldwin pointed out, the Beat hipster could, at the end of the day, "return to being white." The threat of daily living could never mean as much to him as it did the Negro because the hipster's was an avant-garde performance of cool. Vanilla Ice has returned to the beach, has formed a heavy-metal band, and reflects on the days when Suge Knight hung him by his ankles over a balcony railing—Ice has escaped the danger of hip-hop lore by maintaining fundamental whiteness. Eminem escapes the actual danger of hip-hop lore by maintaining fundamental whiteness in the context of comical blackness. As Sir Elton John assuaged us all, we mustn't "take him seriously."

Living in the Dream

(Types & Tropes, Symbols & Signs)

In the reality that is our daily human existence, Eminem does not exist. He never did. But he is a real product of the American dream—a character born out of our nation's collective unconscious, our inborn predilection to produce parallel images or identical psychic shapes common to all men. He is conjured from what we think of ourselves and what we think of others. He is born out of *The Jerry Springer Show*, *South Park*, Jack Kerouac, Carl Van Vechten—all part of a dream, and within this dream there is a dream. Singling out Eminem as an archetype of race perception and performance in America is a shallow undertaking—the composition of his character has its history within the context of the American dream, which is now a conundrum of dreams within dreams. Dreams may be difficult to interpret—because they are, after all, indistinct metaphors and allegories of fantasy—but the dream of race and its performance in American culture is not difficult to track. It has a history, and that history comes with presupposed rules and presupposed character traits that are familiar to us all.

In the dream that is identity, there are archetypal conflicts between the free will of the human maker (his savage creative impulses—an unconscious state of being) and what is the human thinker's intellect (culture, and historical perspective—a conscious state of being). The landscape of democracy and freedom for all men is also the invention of a dream—a utopian impulse, a way of

perceiving an eternal plan in the contingencies of time; a creation of
the human will born out of fiction where there is no transcendental
dimension or registration of the infinite "I am."

Race is a recent historical invention used to make a distinction
between people for purposes of colonization. C. Loring Brace, professor of anthropology at the University of Michigan, explains that
the concept of race "does not appear until the Trans-Atlantic voy-
ages of the Renaissance." But the prevalence of race as a concept—
and its relationship to appearance, human status, and identity
formation—is actually more significant today than it ever was. Our
obsession with race is surpassed only by our seemingly polite and
progressive neutrality regarding race. The Racial Privacy Initiative,
a ballot promoted by black businessman Ward Connelly (who also
successfully ended affirmative action in the state of California), is
designed to obliterate the "race box" on school and government
forms because it forces us to "pay attention to immutable and mean-
ingless characteristics like skin color and ancestry" ("When Color
Should Count," Glenn C. Loury, *New York Times*). But even if race
does not accurately identify a people, the concept is firmly in place
and forces a social dynamic as well as pinpoints a social perception
of a people. We don't see each other as one in the same. Never did.
Never will. The perceived image of race is based on individual (or
collective) sight, which has been re-created and reproduced. It is an
appearance, or a set of appearances, which has been detached from
the place and time in which it first made its appearance and pre-
served (in language and colloquialism) for a few moments or a few
centuries. Once we are aware that we can see, we are aware that we
can be seen, and "the eye of the other combines with our own eye,"
. . . we are always looking at the relation between things and ourselves . . . our perception of what we see depends on our way of seeing. Images, for instance, were first made to conjure up the
appearance of something that was absent. Gradually, it becomes evident that an image can outlast what it once represented, but the ver-
balized perception of image arrests the object in a perceived context
for as long as the perception and the original language for the perception are upheld (*Ways of Seeing* by John Berger). In the case of
race in America, it is physiology and the historical perceptions of

and common terminology used to describe physiology that most often informs the individual's sense of defining race.

The dream of race as identity is born only in a perceived land of diversity (or difference). Race is a regenerated fantasy owing its genesis to neurosis (or as Freud said, "some early trauma repressed") and our need to achieve psychic balance. What is actual is what we produce from our dreams—symbols and signs of our expressions and intuitive perceptions. Our response to what we *think* we see. Identity. Race. Identity is an invented thing. Race is an invented thing. They are not real, but they are *actual*. Race and identity are based on perception and performance and are relative only to the perceptions and performances of the individual and the collective understanding of existence and the activity of being within the context of the dream. These symbols and signs cannot be expressed differently by us or better said by us. Language fails us—and the individual or collective mind is forced into overdrive in order to invent language and behaviors for archetypes of identity. Apertures into nonordinary reality.

It is therefore less significant that Eminem, easily identified as "white" (a nonspecific race term for people of European descent), identifies himself with "black" culture (a nonspecific race term for people of African descent, "black culture" being that which is socially produced by the collective of people of African descent). That is not what makes his archetype of nonordinary reality a significant landmark in the landscape of the American dream. Rather, it is how he has refashioned an old symbol that appeals to popular culture and its boilerplate concepts of race, class, and identity, to fit a new generation in a new yet strangely redundant way—and how that old symbol has transmogrified in the last one hundred years, owing its present-day existence not to the historical performance of *blackness* but to the historical performance of *whiteness* and the ingenuity of human dreams.

There is something called *black* in America and there is something called *white* in America and I know them when I see them, but I will forever be unable to explain the meaning of them, because they are not real even though they have a very real place in my daily way of seeing, a fundamental relationship to my ever-evolving understanding of history, and a critical place in my interactive relationship to humanity. If one believes in the existence of race, it is because one needs to believe in the existence of self (within a culture that relies on race as an important variable of human existence). One needs to believe in culture, and the products of culture that define identity and inform history. The concept of race has long been one of the most vital sources of cultural product (as well as cultural conflict) because race has as its square root a hierarchical structure of being expressed in symbolism. A semiotics of identity that has yet to be solved. These tropes and signs are produced from the unconscious in revelation. The collective unconscious creates them in order to survive (by confrontation) the present archetypal structure. Conveniently forgotten in our race sentimentality are the ever-changing faces of race. Whiteness *became* something one had to attain in America. Being of Nordic or European ancestry did not automatically translate into whiteness. Whiteness had more to do with class privilege than some notion of nationality or physiology (and class is a better definition). Whiteness was purchased and fought for by Jews, Catholics, the Irish, Italians, Polish, indentured servants . . . all considered to be, at one time or another in America, non-white (and even today, depending on whose definition of whiteness you subscribe to). Blackness was never something one had to attain, at least not outside Bohemian circles. Today, it seems . . . it is.

If we look to Eminem's archetype to appeal to what we know about ourselves now, we do it without referring to what we know about the identity of the other. The Eminem show is supposed to make us forget about race and think about how rigid this society is. How we have never really loosened up, and just had barnyard fun with our sacred cows. He uses the vernacular of black hip-hop culture, as well as the psychoanalytical vernacular of the white intellectual—and this invention of character is transferable to any race. The old White Negro may have worn cork and Afro wigs, soaked up Harlem culture and delivered the talented tenth to the mainstream, given race music a haircut, tuxedo jacket, and orchestration, may have learned to shake his narrow white hips in the snakelike manner of the Negro, thereby creating just enough soul to gain Hollywood movie-star musical status, and may have heroicized Negro jazz musicians in his literature, proudly proclaiming to have actually shared a joint or some smack with one or two at the height of a Bohemian subculture's race mixing—but the new White Negro—like Eminem—has not *arrived* at black culture . . . He has *arrived* at white culture with an authentic performance of whiteness, influenced by a historical concept of blackness.

And there is a difference . . . ?

Selected Bibliography

Arrowsmith, William. "Introduction to *The Bacchae.*" In *Euripides V: Three Tragedies*, edited by David Grene and Richard Lattimore. Chicago: University of Chicago Press, 1969.

Berger, John. *Ways of Seeing.* New York: Viking Press, 1995.

Wilson, Elizabeth. *Bohemians: The Glamorous Outcasts.* New Brunswick, N.J.: Rutgers University Press, 2001.

GENE SANTORO

Willie Nelson at 70

On April 30, Willie Nelson turned 70, celebrating with the release of his latest greatest-hits collection. *The Essential Willie Nelson* (Columbia/Legacy), a two-CD set, has an intriguing 1970s-vintage cover shot that sets exactly the right tone for forty years of selective tracks. Nelson's unkempt long red hair and scraggly beard frame his thin, almost Bob Hope nose. His mouth twists slightly, a smile just short of a sneer, in sardonic, knowing reaction to the world behind the camera. His eyes, couched in wrinkles and bags, stare straight and deep into the lens, and suggest hard-to-fathom distances and recessions at the same time as they focus you into connecting. This interaction, evasive, seemingly casual, direct and subtle, represents the essence of Nelson's sly, almost unobtrusive art.

The Essential Willie Nelson demonstrates once again that the Red-Headed Stranger's nonchalant, gospel-flavored, jazz-inflected voice and guitar have remained essentially themselves for decades despite a wild variety of musical backdrops: bare-bones string bands, sleekly glossy Nashville productions, twangy 1970s Outlaw country-rock, jazzy standards with strings, gospel-laced soul.

Maybe that breadth helps explain why Nelson's recurrent duets with Ray Charles are almost always so charged—and so much fun. After all, only Charles and Bob Dylan have traveled as sure-footedly across as far-flung a constellation of genres and expectations as Nelson has and still remained themselves; Charles and Nelson have

long shared material and appearances. (A 1984 show at the Austin
Opera House, captured on *The Willie Nelson Special* [Rhino Home
Video], features excellent versions of "Georgia on My Mind," "I
Can't Stop Loving You" and the old hillbilly fave "Mountain Dew.")
Part of this odd couple's magnetism stems from the fact that they
represent opposite poles of the American spectrum. Charles, the
consummate besuited black professional trained in the tough world
of low-rent, postwar r&b, whose nonpareil voice influenced countless singers, is a hard-bitten recluse who heads a thriving business
dynamo and a drilled band. Nelson, the white country-music renegade who tried pig farming for a while when his career soured,
comes onstage in hippie-cowboy-Indian costume, calls his band
Family and is the epicenter of the self-consciously laid-back Austin
music scene (his disciples include Townes Van Zandt, Lyle Lovett,
Joe Ely, Jimmie Dale Gilmore and alt-country outfits like Uncle
Tupelo) he helped seed and feed for the thirty years since he first
strode onstage at Armadillo World Headquarters. Even on an off
night, Charles can suddenly burst whatever frames the ragged,
churchy elasticity of his scuffed and soaring trademark voice. Nelson stays introspective: Lacking Charles's explosive interpolations,
he subsumes his surroundings, enticing the audience into his voice's
unexpected contours.

Think of Charles as Louis Armstrong's direct descendant, and
Nelson as a cross between Bing Crosby, Jimmie Rodgers and
Woody Guthrie. Their duets are like oil and vinegar, always about
to separate if not stirred up, delicious because they don't. Thanks
to the gospel-jazz core of their artistic personalities, their encompassing self-assurance in their craft's portability of application,
they make singing symbolic of existential struggle. It helps that
they both love what Charlie Parker loved most about country
music—storytelling.

Like Charles, Nelson absorbed the breadth of American music
by living it. Born in poor Texas cotton country, Nelson and his sister
Bobbie, who still plays piano for him, were raised by their grandparents, devout people and gospel-music fans who encouraged their
grandchildren to pick up instruments. By the time the boy was 7 he
was writing songs. "I was raised and worked in the cotton fields
around Abbott," he has said, "with a lot of African-Americans and a

lot of Mexican-Americans, and we listened to their music all the time." So blues and Mexican ballads underpin Nelson's phrasing and narratives, along with the hillbilly and Western swing (13-year-old Willie once duetted with Western swing founder Bob Wills) that his radio picked up from Nashville and the border. Following a quick hitch in the Air Force and a tempestuous marriage to a Native American woman, Nelson moved in 1953 to Fort Worth, became a country deejay and played bars, mixing honky-tonk and preaching. (Nelson's longtime drummer Paul English originally played with the Salvation Army.) In 1956 in Vancouver Nelson made his first record; it sold 3,000 copies. Then he wrote and sold a couple of hits, which got him a publishing contract and brought him to Nashville.

Producers there had little interest in demos of his nasal voice with its eccentric phrasing, and capitalized instead on Nelson's songwriting. And yet now that those demos have surfaced on various reissues, they actually outline a central portion of Nelson's work, since most made the Top 20 country charts, though almost always as performed by others. The low-key style of his bare-bones demos, however, grants Nelson's lithe voice more space for embellishment, pauses and inflection than his released 1960s Nashville recordings, while showcasing his off-kilter lyrics, which refashion clichés from unexpected angles, on tunes like "Hello Walls" or "Crazy." One outstanding example is "I Never Cared for You," whose opening lines cleverly subvert Tin Pan Alley macrocosm/microcosm imagery: The sun never shines, the rain doesn't fall and I never cared for you. In the liner notes to *The Essential Willie Nelson*, Emmylou Harris's longtime collaborator, Rodney Crowell, recalls the song's effect when he heard it over the radio in the mid-1960s: "A voice rivaling Bob Dylan's in authenticity delivered the fantastically ironic lyric to a weird-sounding gut-string accompaniment."

Ray Price was the first star to cover Nelson's tunes; for a while Nelson played bass in Price's band and wrote hits for Faron Young ("Hello Walls"), Billy Walker ("Funny How Time Slips Away") and Patsy Cline ("Crazy"). But Nelson the singer suffered: His first label closed, and he kept being wedged into the curtain of syrupy strings that defined Nashville countrypolitan—a very 1950s sonic confection spun by producer Owen Bradley, modeled after the bland but influential approach to contemporary pop that Mitch Miller had fashioned as A&R head at Columbia. Countrypolitan gave the likes of Cline crossover appeal while trying to erase the singing rube/cowboy image that, via earlier movie and radio stars like Jimmie Rodgers and Gene Autry, first brought hillbilly music into mainstream markets. Nelson, who stubbornly resisted conforming, was a problem child.

He scored a couple of middling hits, but even though he joined the Grand Ole Opry and signed with RCA in 1965, he spent the next several years in limbo as a performer. The then-pudgy Nelson's idiosyncratic, limber vocalizing and nonconformity, his insistence that his songs could sell themselves and his unwillingness to glitz up his act led to a constant, debilitating battle. Still, in the midst of a few blandly uneven countrypolitan discs, he managed to cut one of country music's first concept albums, *Yesterday's Wine* (RCA), a dazzling song cycle about a life from cradle to grave that demonstrated what he could do given his head.

By 1972 Nelson had quit Nashville and moved to Austin, where he noticed that young rock fans were turned on by honky-tonk and folk. (His way had been prepared, in part, by friend and colleague Johnny Cash's eclectic 1970s TV show, showcasing the Man in Black, who had been performing at folk-music festivals for years, with folk-revival stars from Dylan to the Carter family.) Shrewdly, Nelson resurrected the country-folk-rock style that Nashville had rejected, enhanced by his lengthening hair, cowboy-Indian duds and hippie-crossover ideas. His old Music Row pals thought he'd killed what was left of his career. In fact, he had finally found his audience, post-1960s types who thought rock was too corporate and responded to Guthrie-esque storytelling minus the whiny self-indulgence of James Taylor, Carly Simon and Carole King—the same crowd Emmylou Harris would wow and Bruce Springsteen would tap with *Nebraska* and *The Ghost of Tom Joad*.

After an abortive stab at his own indie label, Nelson recorded with Atlantic, by then a major label that had mostly jettisoned r&b and jazz for the Rolling Stones and Led Zeppelin. With soul-music producer Arif Mardin and his own band (including pianist Leon Russell), Nelson cut killers like "Shotgun Willie," which crossed funky soul back into country and rock, laced with the introspective touches and wry phrase-turnings that Nashville had scorned. In 1974, "Bloody Mary Morning," a Texas-swing smoothie with characteristic witty lines ("It's a bloody Mary morning baby left me without warning sometime in the night"), hit No. 14 on the country charts. At 41, Willie Nelson was finally hitting his stride.

One of my Austin-based colleagues comments with bemused affection, "Willie is the Buddha. He's also a duet whore." In terms of consistent quality, he's right, but Nelson's duets, which have included outings with Charles, Cash and Dylan as well as U2 and Julio Iglesias, if nothing else do reveal Nelson's prismatic musical curiosity. Two classics ("Good Hearted Woman" and "Mammas Don't Let Your Babies Grow Up to Be Cowboys") boast Waylon Jennings, that other Outlaw who, with Nelson, launched the 1970s back-to-the-roots country movement, its revisionist rock, rockabilly and folk ingredients contrasting sharply with contemporary countrypolitan productions. Merle Haggard, another perpetual Nashville outsider, shows up for Townes Van Zandt's evocative border ballad "Pancho and Lefty," where Nelson's nuance nicely plays off Haggard's swagger while making clear that Haggard, whose band, the Strangers, routinely improvises, is among the few country singers whose jazzy phrasing—the dancing rhythms that infiltrated the best American singing after Louis Armstrong—compares to Nelson's.

Red Headed Stranger (Columbia) in 1975 marked a pinnacle, Nelson's *John Wesley Harding*, an artistic restatement of purpose in the guise of an Americana concept album about an Old West preacher who loved women; its brilliantly sparse, country-folk production features his voice and trademark nylon-stringed guitar. "Blue Eyes Crying in the Rain" shot to the top of the charts to make him a star. RCA, tailgating his success, compiled an album of Nelson, Jennings and others called *Wanted! The Outlaws* (RCA), the first country album to go platinum, thanks to "Good Hearted Woman." A movement begun as a rejection of the Nashville music business became the business's newest stack of chips in the hit-making casino.

Nelson hit No. 1 again with Lefty Frizzell's sardonic "If You've Got the Money (I've Got the Time)" then cut a fine album of

Frizzell tunes. When Bing Crosby died, to his label's dismay Nelson abandoned what corporate types saw as a winning formula and zagged into the unsure turf of jazz-pop standards; he scored again: 1978's *Stardust* (Columbia), arranged and produced by the MGs' Booker T. Jones, triumphed with slow tempos and strings, as if Nelson had internalized Nashville and subtly refocused it. His jaunty phrasing genially enlivened classics like "Georgia on my Mind," "Someone to Watch Over Me" and the title track. The album hung on the country charts for almost a decade.

Nelson never played it safe, as in career-building, and so success, like failure, didn't stop his eclectic wanderings: a jam-based feel (*Willie and Family Live*, Columbia); covers of another renegade songwriter (*Sings Kris Kristofferson*, Columbia); pallid reprises of *Stardust* (*Somewhere Over the Rainbow* and *Always on My Mind*, both Columbia); reunions with Price (*San Antonio Rose*, Columbia) and Russell (*One for the Road*, Columbia). By 1985, however, old-timers like Nelson had begun to be swept away by New Country, the latest Nashville formula, brewed from reheated George Jones and Buck Owens. That year, Nelson founded Farm Aid, which lured performers like Dylan. Nelson also joined forces with Cash, Jennings and Kristofferson in The Highwaymen, a band of Nashville misfits who revivified the roots of country music and expanded the genre's possibilities—and in the process extended its reach to the post-Eagles rock audience, eventually helping to make country music pop's bestselling style with the widest radio play. In 1990 the IRS whacked Nelson for nearly $17 million in back taxes and seized practically all he owned. *Who'll Buy My Memories* (Columbia), a twenty-five-cut compilation of Nelson-only demos, outtakes and keepers, was issued in 1992 to help pay off the debt; it remains one of Nelson's most effective and affecting albums. The following year, he was solvent.

A collapsed lung, a pot bust, induction into the Country Music Hall of Fame, an ersatz acting career (*The Electric Horseman, Thief, Wag the Dog, Austin Powers: The Spy Who Shagged Me*)—Nelson is now legend enough to have songs written about him. Like Charles and Dylan, he's grown so powerful and centered in his artistry that even his lesser efforts outgun the best of others.

Dungeon Family Tree

Cast of Characters

Andre *(aka Andre Benjamin, Dre, Andre 3000): OutKast*
Big Boi *(aka Antwan Patton, Twan): OutKast*
Big Rube *(aka Ruben Bailey): Society of Soul, guest rapper/poet*
Cee-Lo *(aka Thomas Calloway, Thomas Burton, Cee-Lo Green): Goodie Mob, now solo artist*
Cool Breeze *(aka Freddie Calhoun): solo rapper*
Gipp *(aka Big Gipp, Cameron Gipp): Goodie Mob*
Khujo *(aka William Knighton, Jo): Goodie Mob*
Mr. DJ *(aka David Sheats): OutKast DJ, Earthtone III producer*
Ray *(aka Ray Murray): Organized Noize producer*
Rico *(aka Rico Wade, Ric): Organized Noize producer, Dungeon studio owner*
Sleepy *(aka Patrick Brown, Sleepy Brown): Organized Noize producer and vocalist*
T-Mo *(aka Robert Terrence Barnett): Goodie Mob*

Late September 1993: Atlanta's LaFace Records, interested in grooming young talent, asks local production team Organized Noize to do a song for the label's upcoming Christmas album. LaFace head L.A. Reid wants the track to feature Organized's new protégés, OutKast, the teenaged duo that Reid is considering signing to LaFace. The song, "Player's Ball," with its laid-back groove, razor-sharp rhymes and old-school soul melody, kicks off a new era for Southern hip-hop.

Late September 2003: Southern hip-hop hits flood the radio. Arista Records President L.A. Reid is one of the most powerful men in the music industry. And OutKast, the flagship of Organized Noize's Dungeon Family crew, has sold more than 10 million albums worldwide.

But in the three years since the group's previous studio album, *Stankonia*, much has changed. The rest of the Dungeon Family struggles to regain momentum after a string of commercial disappointments, and OutKast seems to be pulling apart at the seams. Their much-anticipated new album, *Speakerboxxx/The Love Below*, arrives this week in the form of two separate solo albums packaged together as a double disc.

Here's the rest of the story . . .

Fade in: Southwest Atlanta, 1980s

ANDRE: I grew up in the ghetto just like everybody else, right across the street from the projects. But my mom bussed me to schools like Sarah Smith [Elementary] and Sutton [Middle School], right in the middle of Buckhead. So by me going to school with a lot of white kids, I got into skateboarding and the music and everything. I'd come home and I might hear Eric B. & Rakim or Too Short, then go to school and hear another thing.

CEE-LO: I've known Andre since the third grade. We were good friends in elementary school. I don't think our artistic nature was cultivated back in the third grade, but I think a lot of my artistic energy came out in moments of misbehavior. I remember a moment when Dre's mother came and had to chastise him in front of the class.

BIG BOI: [Dre and I] were new to the high school [Tri-Cities High in East Point]; this was 10th grade, 1989 or '90. The first time Dre and I really talked was on the way back from Lenox mall; me and my little brother rode back with him. We just got to kickin' it, and I found this cat was cool. So we went back to his crib in East Point. We talked about music and girls and shit.

ANDRE: We listened to the same types of music. We both loved De La Soul, A Tribe Called Quest. I had stopped going to Tri-Cities and started going to an alternative school, because I was skipping class and got kicked out.

BIG BOI: We used to steal cars off of Old National Highway. We tried selling dope, but we'd get some and smoke the shit before we could sell it. So that's when we knew we had to get us some jobs at the shoe stores.

CEE-LO: Dre and I didn't see each other again until about the 11th grade. We were at an alternative school called Frank McClaren for dropouts and teen mothers and individuals who have to work a job and were trying to come in and get their GED.

*   *   *

SLEEPY: My dad [Jimmy Brown] was in a band called Brick, and they had some hits. I would go to concerts and be backstage and get to see all the funk bands—Cameo, Bar-Kays, Commodores, Parliament-Funkadelic.

RICO: Lamonte was just a black man who owned a business [Lamonte's Beauty Supply in East Point's Delowe Shopping Center]. I got the job with him when I was about 13, just going around saying, "Can I take your trash out? Can I sweep your carpet?" By the time OutKast came around, I was like 19, and I was the manager there.

GIPP: Ray Murray was the first guy I had been around who kept a drum machine. Ray introduced me to the graffiti thing, kind of took me under his wing. He really hipped me to hip-hop. I met Khujo and T-Mo once I started going to Mays High School. The first time I met Cee-Lo, he came over to my house with his cousin. That's when they used to call him Chickenhead.

RAY: I moved into the Greenbrier area in 1987. That's when I met Gipp and Khujo and all of them. They all went to high school together at Benjamin E. Mays.

*   *   *

BIG BOI: We were sitting at my aunt's house. Dre had made some rhymes, and I had some. And I would start where he ended.

ANDRE: Me and Big Boi were a group by that time named 2 Shades Deep. We both had jobs at shoe stores. One day, Big Boi couldn't get off of work and I had set up our first shot to perform—on this cable access show. So Cee-Lo went with me. So we performed, and some guy called in and said, "I just wanted to let you know y'all sounded like *shit!*" To this day, me and Cee-Lo never can forget that.

BIG BOI: Cee-Lo was damn near about to be in the group for a minute. Me, Dre and Cee-Lo would go back to my auntie's house. We used to make loops on the tape deck, and Cee-Lo would have beats on tape that were so fucking funky it was retarded.

ANDRE: The first live performance was at this club called Club Fritz in the West End. We went, and Big Boi's uncle gave us weed. We smoked it in a napkin, so it was burning all wrong. So then we got on the mic and just crunked it up. We was on one mic, passing it back and forth, busting each other in the lip.

BIG BOI: We were 2 Shades Deep, but there was a group called Four Shades Deep. We were going to do Misfits, but there was already a group called the Misfits. So we went down till we found OutKast, which meant what we wanted.

*   *   *

SLEEPY: I met Rico through a girl I was dating at the time. She was good friends with him and T-Boz [of TLC]. Me and Rico started out in a singing group, the Uboys. At the time, when T-Boz got with TLC, she told Pebbles [TLC's manager, then married to L.A. Reid] about us. Pebbles liked our music, but vocally we weren't that great. So she just flat-out told us, "I like y'all's beats; I think you should get more into production."

RICO: I can't sing, though I was just fly—like a local celebrity. I had a car, girls liked me, I had a perm. I danced and I looked like I sang.

RAY: Me and Gipp had been a group, Sixth Sense. The Gulf War was going on, and we recorded a song called "Pray for Peace." We had talked to NBC's *Today Show* and we were going to perform, but the war stopped.

BIG RUBE: This guy Joe Carne—his mother was the singer Jean Carne. He had some musical equipment over his house, so we

[Rico, Sleepy, Rube] were going over there working on stuff. And that's how we met Ray. But working with Joe was getting kind of hard, so then we decided to branch off on our own. We got a little setup in Rico's apartment in Delowe Gardens. And it was 24/7 after that.

RAY: Jellybeans [skate rink] was an institution; that's where everybody went. In 1990, we had a studio up there. There was an office and we had converted it into a live performance room. There was no ventilation, so if you were in there for 15–20 minutes, you'd be in a complete sweat. We were the producers for [rap group] P.A. After they got the deal with Pebbles, that's when we officially became Organized Noize. The name comes from a singing girl group Rico and Sleepy put together, but we couldn't find the girls for it. So we said, "That's a fly ass name. Fuck the girls."

*   *   *

RICO: A friend of mine knew [former Atlanta police chief] Eldrin Bell, and he owned a house in Lakewood that he was renting out. We had the apartment at Delowe and a studio at the skate rink, and I couldn't afford to pay rent at both places, so we moved to the house and made everything one.

RAY: The Dungeon was under the kitchen floor at Rico's house. It's a dirt floor. We had a table and chairs set up, an MPC with dust all over it, keyboards, records all over. When the shit flooded, we had to pick up, take the shit upstairs, because it warps. The vibes down there were otherworldly. Sometimes we'd be sitting down there writing, then the drum machine would go on. Because of the moisture in the machine, it used to go haywire. It would trigger samples, crazy shit.

BIG RUBE: The whole idea of calling it the Dungeon came from the way the basement looked. There were red clay walls, pipes over your head, like a boiler room or something. People didn't leave. You'd go over there and you basically was living there, so it was almost like you was held captive. So it just fit perfectly.

*   *   *

ANDRE: We had started to perfect our craft, meet after school and trade rhymes in Big Boi's auntie's kitchen. We had two meetings set up. One was with a manager called Don Ray, he's Cody Chestnu TT's manager now. But we met Rico first that day. He worked at the beauty supply store right up the street from Big Boi's aunt's house, so we just walked.

RAY: Me and Rico were at this hair products store that Rico worked at. We were having some creative differences with P.A., and we were saying to ourselves, "Man, we need two fly-ass young MCs that we can really get with and help shine, help nurture." Right as we said that, these two dudes came walking over the hill.

RICO: I was like, "What y'all got? Y'all got songs?" Then they put in [A Tribe Called Quest's] "Scenario"—the seven-minute instrumental version—and they went back to back until the tape stopped. No hooks, no errors. As soon as one finished the other one came up right behind.

GIPP: I played the tape in my Isuzu Trooper. They could really spit like an up-North rapper.

SLEEPY: They had bald heads, and that was kind of crazy; nobody was into that yet. When they first rapped for us, I just thought they rapped long as hell. Each one had a rap for like 15, 20 minutes. I was just standing there, like, "Damn, when you gonna end?"

RICO: They reminded me of myself. One of them had on cut-off jeans; they had thermals, sweatshirts, some huaraches on. They were fresh; they weren't no ghetto Atlanta niggas—no gold teeth. They were hip-hop.

ANDRE: The first thing Rico said was, "That's dope, come to my house tonight." Rico was the hustler, the mouthpiece of Organized Noize. He would say stuff like, "Yeah, we can get you a deal next week." And we believed him. So we went to the Dungeon.

BIG RUBE: It's funny, because the personalities were already there. Dre had the kind of quiet personality, Big Boi had this reputation for not giving a fuck—talking about you right in your face even if he don't know you.

BIG BOI: I thought it was going on over there. Ten, 15 people in the studio downstairs. Niggas just writing on pads everywhere, smoking their herb, 40 ounces. The atmosphere said, "Damn, this is where we need to be."

RAY: We didn't have anything. We used to scrape money together to go buy cigarettes. Everybody would eat off of a $3 basket from Church's. Ten, 15 niggas in the room, on the wood floor with blankets rolled up as beds.

RICO: Every day after school they'd come to the Dungeon, spend the night, go to school from the Dungeon sometimes, stay over on weekends. It was to the point where it started to get ugly. Andre's momma was just so concerned, like, "What the fuck is going on?" That's when she started making crazy comments, like calling my momma and asking me some really disrespectful shit, like, "What, you gay or something? Why they want to be around you?" She turned around years later and became the most important person in his career. She's a great person, so I don't fault her for nothing.

*   *   *

CEE-LO: We happened to be in Greenbriar Mall one day, and my homeboy was telling Marqueze [Etheridge, Organized Noize associate who co-wrote TLC's "Waterfalls" with them] that I sing. He was going over to the Dungeon, so we decided to give him a ride. We went over there, and I sung for Sleepy Brown. At the time, Rico, Dre and Big Boi had rode off to get something to eat. They came back and saw me sitting there and Dre got excited, like, "That's my homeboy Cee-Lo I was telling you about. He can rhyme, he can sing." That particular day, T-Mo and Khujo and Gipp walked in the door—I knew them from high school. When I saw their familiar faces, I was immediately comfortable.

KHUJO: Me and T-Mo started fucking with them Crown Royal liquor bags, the purple and gold bags. We used to strap them on our belts and have goodies in them—weed, a couple dollars. Just a little bag we used to walk around with, and it would swing on the side. We'd say, "It's the goodie bag, man."

Late 1992: OutKast makes its first recorded appearance on an Organized Noize-produced remix of TLC's "What About Your Friends."

ANDRE: Organized Noize had a relationship with L.A., so L.A. said he'd check us out. He called in the entire staff of LaFace and says, "Go." I'm nervous, but Rico puts in the DAT and we start rapping. I don't think L.A. got it, but he said he wanted us to do a showcase. After that, he told Rico he didn't like it. At that point, I decided I didn't want to do it anymore. Big Boi was like, "We came this far; we can't stop now." We kept on, and the buzz started going around town. Polygram had us showcase for them. I think L.A. got wind, and that helped us get another showcase for him. He gave us a single deal to put a song on their Christmas album. We decided to keep it real—talk about what Christmas was about to us. "Player's Ball" changed OutKast's sound. We were rhyming in a way that was melodic and funky.

SLEEPY: Ray had a beat that I thought was incredible. He said, "It would be fly if we could find somebody to sing it kind of like Curtis." I was like, "I can do that." It was like 5 in the morning, and I just went in there and did it. After, I was like, "That's kind of funky, I may need to mess with that a little more." I was just trying to sing like what Curtis Mayfield would've sung.

ANDRE: Puffy [Sean Combs, aka P. Diddy] was the new flavor man at Arista [LaFace's parent company]. He loved "Player's Ball" and wanted to direct the video. So he comes down to shoot the video with Rico. And Puffy was the first person who brought us out of Atlanta to a show at Howard University, opening for Biggie. Then the video comes out and people are loving the song, so L.A. was like, "You have to record an album."

April 1994: OutKast debuts with the acclaimed, platinum-selling *Southernplayalisticadillacmuzik*.

RICO: We knew 'Kast was good enough. They could rap. But we knew we had to flip the beats. We couldn't let them rap over the same New York beats or L.A. beats, we had to come with something new. That's why we called the first album *Southernplayalisticadillac-muzik*: We had to get into who we were.

RAY: Down-South music had always been fast. We slowed it down to make you listen to the MC, make the MCs be rapid fire. And that was OutKast.

ANDRE: It was a family event. You had Goodie Mob on there, pretty much every one who came through the Dungeon. If you had something to say, you did it. On "Git Up, Git Out," Cee-Lo came and laid the verse and set the tone.

BIG RUBE: The first record left a bad taste in my mouth. You look at the first OutKast record, my name ain't nowhere on it. Not even for the shit that I said. Somebody just dropped the ball in terms of making sure everybody got credit. I never got any publishing [royalties], and it would've been a lot because basically me and Sleepy and Rico wrote all their hooks.

*   *   *

BIG BOI: Our first taste of performing in front of an audience was the Howard University homecoming. That was my first ride on an airplane, and I was terrified. But I knew if this was my career, I had to get used to it. We weren't even old enough, but we was drinking. We came out and we performed and they clapped when we came off.

ANDRE: Freaknik was still around, so we made these snippet cassettes with dice and incense. We passed them out and everyone from all over the country came to town and went back home with our sounds.

BIG RUBE: The first OutKast album was like the whole energy and chi of the whole South. It represented all our asses. When OutKast came out, young kids had something to look up to that wasn't necessarily gangsta. Because *The Chronic* was like the bible of rap at the time, and people were associating the gangbang style with hip-hop. So it was like putting a fire extinguisher on a fire that was starting.

November 1995: The Dungeon Family's second album, *Goodie Mob's Soul Food*, is released and eventually goes gold (500,000 copies sold).

RAY: L.A. came to us and said, "What you guys got next?" And we said, "This is what we feel: Goodie Mob." We had never recorded any songs with all four of them together until they got their deal.

CEE-LO: Goodie Mob as a collective was more or less the brainchild of Rico Wade. And me, Gipp, T and Khujo were all familiar with each other, so it was nothing to say, "Yeah, let's do an album together." The first Goodie Mob record was supposed to be a compilation of sorts, but we stumbled upon a magic of our own.

GIPP: *Soul Food* was a fun record because it was all about ideas. Didn't nobody really have shit. I remember when we first signed to LaFace, we got a check for $20,000—$5,000 a piece.

GIPP: We just really felt like, OK, people know us on the street through OutKast. What about the political side, the real historical side of Atlanta that everyone doesn't really talk about?

RICO: Cool Breeze came up with the term "Dirty South" [guesting on *Soul Food*'s track, "Dirty South"].

CEE-LO: My mother passed during the recording of *Soul Food*. I was able to stop it in time to dedicate the record to my mother.

April 1996: A third Dungeon group, Society of Soul, debuts with the album *Brainchild*.

BIG RUBE: Me and Sleepy worked so well together, with him doing melodies and me coming up with lyrics, it was like, "We oughta put a group together." When we did the Society of Soul album, we were actually working out of Curtom, Curtis Mayfield's studio. We were working on Society of Soul, Goodie Mob's first album and some OutKast stuff. Everything was feeling pretty good, like everyone was going to have what they needed.

RAY: We did "Waterfalls" [TLC's biggest hit] while we were doing the Society of Soul record. After we did "Waterfalls," we wanted to put that sound onto Society of Soul.

Summer 1996: OutKast's second album, *ATLiens*, arrives. It goes platinum as well.

RAY: Dre went through a metamorphosis when they came with *ATLiens*. I don't know if it was the introduction to celebrity, or just wanting to have more control of your life. He became more introverted, more expressionist. He became more of an individual. Big has also changed, but not so much artistically—more inside. After the first record, Dre started taking it seriously. He stopped smoking, stopped drinking, stopped doing a whole lot of shit that we were all doing.

BIG RUBE: They started understanding the power they had in their music—particularly Dre. He started getting a lot more brave as far as saying what he felt. They started showing a swagger that certain artists have—the ones that are stars.

ANDRE: I had an interest in producing, so I started buying equipment, trying out stuff. And I ended up doing a lot of songs on *ATLiens*. The first single I did was "Elevators." I started going around Atlanta looking for records. I liked 411 Records, Wax N Facts and pawnshops.

Early 1997: Organized Noize severs its ties with LaFace Records and signs a label deal with Interscope Records.

RAY: Society of Soul, OutKast and Goodie Mob were signed through Organized Noize Productions for their first album because we had the relationship with L.A. Once he saw that the acts were viable, we didn't need to be in the middle of the situation. There was friction between us and LaFace, and that was turning into friction between us and the artists. Once we alleviated that, we didn't have a deal with LaFace anymore. After that, we did the deal with Interscope.

BIG RUBE: Around the time of the deal with Interscope, that's when the new Dungeon [Rico's new home studio in the Cascade area] came into play. The studio was paid for with the money from Interscope. My only problem with the Interscope thing was that the first artist released was Kilo. He wasn't DF, and I knew Kilo wasn't going to blow up nationally; it was regional booty-shake music. I think it put a damper on the Interscope deal. It wasn't what they were looking for. The Cool Breeze record could've been really great, but it took him about two or three years to write his record. Organized Noize got the reputation for just being the fuck-offs that had the talent but weren't exactly on top of their game as far as business. And Little Will's record never hit the shelves. They just pulled their money, I guess.

RICO: [Interscope] took care of us. They're the reason why we got a studio. All of us got houses. But we didn't get enough numbers for the kind of deal we were in.

April 1998: Goodie Mob releases its second album, *Still Standing*; it goes gold. September 1998: OutKast's third album, *Aquemini*, arrives and goes on to sell more than 3 million copies.

GIPP: With *Still Standing*, we knew we had something. Our first tour we went out with the Roots and the Fugees—three live bands back-to-back, all really breaking ground. After that tour, we knew we could do things other hip-hop artists couldn't. We knew we had a voice.

RAY: It's a dark album; that was the vibe. It was a dark time. 'Pac and Biggie had died. We had been with both. That's why we called the record *Still Standing*. Goodie Mob had just come from the West Coast; they were about to record some stuff with 'Pac.

CEE-LO: We traveled to Helen, Ga., and got a cabin in the woods and sat and talked about concepts—just the four of us. I did the bulk of my writing for that album after I had my tonsils out. I had about two weeks to just write and be quiet and reflect.

*   *   *

RAY: By *Aquemini*, it was running on its own. Where we might have been worried [about Dre's direction], that died down. We understood a lot better what he was doing. At first, I took it as kind of personal when he switched up. We felt like [*Southernplayalistic*] was their best expression of themselves. True indeed, how can somebody else tell you how to express yourself? But I didn't think it called for putting on the headwrap, you know, being non-smoking, non-drinking. But with *Aquemini*, when he changed up, I could see clearly that it was more of a growth.

SLEEPY: I always thought our crew was like the Parliament of hip-hop, but I never thought anyone would be willing to go there with it. The first time Dre started dressing that way, we were doing the "Skew it on the Bar-B" video at the Tabernacle. I was backstage, and he came out in that white feather suit. I was like, "Wow, either the crowd is going to laugh at you, or they're going to be with you." He had the white wig on, the shades. He jumped up on stage and the crowd went bananas.

MR. DJ: Dre, Big and me started trying to produce from watching Rico and them. And Big Boi and Dre came to me and said, "Hey, why don't we start a production company together?" I was no longer DJing for them, but I was still an OutKast fan. And we had good chemistry together. So we formed Earthtone III.

BIG RUBE: Organized Noize still did some tracks on *Aquemini*, but I think it was out of respect. OutKast was getting to the point where they could produce their own stuff.

ANDRE: Things were really about me and Big at the time, and I liked the way *Aquemini* [combining their astrological signs, Aquarius and Gemini] sounded. It meant something really smooth, the coming together of two forces.

MR. DJ: *Aquemini* was right when everybody was starting to deal with adult-type things. Right around that time Big's aunt passed, and Dre had his relationship with Erykah [Badu]. Everyone was really finding themselves, and you can hear it in the music.

RICO: When *The Source* gave *Aquemini* five mics [its highest rating], we knew we had world supremacy. We were given respect by the industry, by our peers, and by the public.

Last week of 1999: Goodie Mob releases its third album, *World Party*, which many view as a departure from the group's grittier, more outspoken earlier records.

October 2000: OutKast releases its fourth album, *Stankonia*, recorded in the group's new West Atlanta studio, also called Stankonia.

CEE-LO: Gipp initiated the whole change of direction. *World Party* was unconscious—it's so simple to speak ignorantly. I plead temporary insanity because of what we went through, being the ones who helped to kick down the door and not reaped the same benefits as the rest of Southern [hip-hop]. I don't think it was whack, but after we set such a bar, it was regression. We were ahead of our time and turned our space ship around to come back to earth to simply fit in. The market was congested with bling-bling, and people were waiting on Goodie Mob. If anybody's going to keep it real, Goodie Mob will. And we didn't. We failed the people.

GIPP: We were on our third album; we had been through the ropes, starting to get tired. We put together what we thought people wanted to hear.

BIG RUBE: I think they got a little scared they weren't selling as many records as OutKast. They were going gold, though. Just one more time without changing what they were doing [and] they would've gone platinum. Sometimes you drop the ball right before you get to the end zone.

*   *   *

BIG BOI: Bobby Brown came to see our show. He was drunk as hell and telling us his studio, Bosstown, was for sale. He was like, "Really, y'all can have the studio. I'd rather y'all have it than someone else get it." But it came up that the IRS had it for sale; we bought it from them and just revamped it. That was the studio where we recorded the first album, so there's a lot of good vibes in there.

ANDRE: Before there was any lyric or hook on "Bombs Over Baghdad," we knew it was going to be the first single. Just that tempo alone, we knew that this go around, we just want to be in the business of blowing people's minds. I'm always with stretching it, so when this song came out, it had guitar solos and everything. Even the record company was like, "I don't know if radio's going to play it." They actually told us to take the guitar out, and I was really mad about that.

BIG BOI: We'd be in the studio, and then go to the strip club afterward. So instead of going back and forth, I figured if we put the [stripper's] pole in the Boom Boom Room [Big Boi's den/home studio], that could inspire some more shit. So I put the pole over there. Soon as a chick walks in, they want to get on it just to show they can set that bitch off.

MR. DJ: Big is more of the street-savvy rapper. And Dre is more of the ghetto-poetic one. But when we're in the studio, you wouldn't even think there were lines between them. They think the same creatively. The differences come in their personal lives.

_____

2001: The entire crew comes together to work on a long-planned Dungeon Family record.

November 2001: *Even in Darkness* **comes out on Arista, which also releases an OutKast anthology,** *Big Boi and Dre Present . . . OutKast* **the same month.**

BIG RUBE: We had been wanting to do a family record since the beginning, but something inspired Big Boi to want to do it—and he had some power with L.A. [Reid]. I was kind of apprehensive to be on Arista, but it had to go there because the most powerful group, OutKast, was on Arista. Everybody who had tracks to submit, we all listened to them. And everybody who wanted to get on those tracks got on them. That's how we did it at first.

RICO: Certain tracks we had a concept, like, "Man, it would be great if we could get Andre and Cee-Lo, or we can get Khujo and T-Mo to do a song together, like the old Lumberjacks group." "Six Minutes" went down just how it was supposed to; it was a dream. Ray did a hot beat; Big came over, he busted. Big had the hook idea, Sleepy stacked the hook. Gipp wanted to come next; he wrote a verse, and everybody else came up behind.

BIG RUBE: We're in a meeting at the Dungeon, upstairs. The whole DF. L.A. [Reid] is on speakerphone. Everything's sounding great, like it always does in those initial meetings. Everybody's going to get an equal split of the budget money. But then Arista was like, "We're going to pay our artists [OutKast, Goodie Mob] more." Which is completely negating the whole thing—DF was supposed to come before what label you're on. The whole point was to bring the guys who were in a slump out of it. So then you got one guy who might get $5,000 and the motherfuckers that were already rich getting $50,000 to $100,000.

RAY: It was almost like a return to the old days, but it didn't really get to fruition. There was so much politics. It just didn't get no support from Arista. As soon as the OutKast album [*Big Boi and Dre Present . . . OutKast*] dropped, you don't hear shit about the Dungeon Family record. Nothing.

BIG RUBE: We did a promo tour. We start hitting a couple of cities. We're thinking, "OK, if this starts taking off, we can do a real Dungeon Family tour; it would be like we always wanted." But, you know, there's a lot of different attitudes by now. This isn't nine years ago. On the road, we had Dungeon Family posters. But they'll have even bigger [*Big Boi and Dre Present*] posters. I'm not saying it's OutKast's fault, but it ain't like they put up no major fight either.

CEE-LO: The album was long overdue. I'm not certain the world was waiting on the Dungeon Family album after all that time. OutKast was in the midst of doing their greatest hits album, and I was working on my solo album at the time. So we were juggling, trying to make it all happen—and it wasn't as organic as it should have been.

April 2002: Cee-Lo releases his first solo album, the acclaimed *Cee-Lo Green and His Perfect Imperfections*.

June 2002: Khujo is involved in a car accident that results in the loss of his lower leg.

CEE-LO: Goodie Mob toured with the Fugees and Lauryn [Hill] was always a kindred spirit to me. So she called on me to sing on ["Do You Like the Way," on Santana's *Supernatural* album]. The Santana project empowered me. It's the first time I'd ever sung a full-fledged vocal. It was empowering in monetary terms as well. But in just being a part of something so phenomenal as that album, it did have a great effect on me.

GIPP: After he came back from doing the Santana thing, I knew there was no turning back. Because of the acceptance he got from being part of such a great album. He was around a lot of people who had broke ground. We started doing shows, and he starting calling saying he's not coming out for the shows.

CEE-LO: My first solo album represents liberation. A very exciting and challenging time, to take the reins of an entire album. It's not disconnected from Goodie Mob; it's a continuation of the same revolutionary spirit we always have reveled in.

*   *   *

KHUJO: I was leaving from the Dungeon; it was probably about 4 in the morning. Lots of people fall asleep at the wheel, but I guess it was just my time. Folks came through to say what's up to me, and then everybody went about their business. Everybody making records, making bread, so I had to heal on up and get back with it.

Dre came down [to the hospital] and gave me a bass guitar, trying to keep my mind off what I was going through. That was greatly appreciated. And Big came down, so I felt love. Cee-Lo came through too. After that, I haven't heard nothing else from him. At the time, L.A. Reid wanted to know what would it take for us to get back in the studio together. But Cee-Lo declined; he didn't want to do it.

GIPP: When this shit started, Cee-Lo was 17. We damn-near raised this kid. So to a certain degree, it's about respect. When you have something as tragic as a car accident happen to a man [Khujo] who was out here trying to feed his family, because his brother [Cee-Lo] decided he didn't want to tour anymore, it's like your own group member tearing down what you gave all your sweat and love into.

CEE-LO: My separation from the group was not intended to be permanent. It was agreed that we venture out for solo endeavors to make the net worth of Goodie Mob more viable. But I've been depicted as some cutthroat individual who left the guys out to dry. None of us are getting any younger. So it was about attaining stability, being as I had a son on the way and a mortgage and a wife and a whole family.

KHUJO: I didn't know Goodie Mob was dropped from Arista until late last year, when we started working on a new Goodie Mob record. They had put it in a magazine. I was like, "For real? Shit." I was just naïve. Cee-Lo didn't really want to fuck with us. So we started solidifying the Goodie Mob Records deal [with Koch].

GIPP: The name [of the forthcoming Goodie Mob album, without Cee-Lo] is *One Monkey Don't Stop No Show.* It's not against him. But motherfuckers are not going to tell us Goodie Mob are not going to be, because Cee-Lo's not in the group. My man Khujo got his leg amputated and he's still out there on stage yelling Goodie Mob. That's real.

September 2003: OutKast's sixth album, *Speakerboxxx/The Love Below*, arrives this week.

BIG BOI: After *Stankonia*, we were working on our solo albums and an OutKast record. But then we realized both our records are Out-Kast records, so we'd just give them two sides of it.

ANDRE: I had been doing songs at home, and I wanted to make a departure from the same OutKast thing. I was writing a lot of melodic songs; I hadn't written raps in so long, and I started seeing a theme come along with these songs. So I said maybe it would be cool if I put out this singing album. And I wanted to make a movie. I told Big Boi about these plans. I had him and my manager on the phone, and they didn't think it was a good time because the record company would be expecting to cash in on the next OutKast album. We had just won Grammys, after "Ms. Jackson" and "The Whole World." That's when I had to put the movie on hold and we decided to make the double album.

MR. DJ: I worked with Big on four tracks on his side of the record. Most of the time, Dre was in L.A. Earthtone III expired a year ago. Dre decided we should probably have our own production companies. He said he kind of wanted to do his own thing and we should all have our own entities.

ANDRE: I'm pretty much focusing on playing the background, producing and writing for people. I'm campaigning to branch out, do other music, start a band, do movies. I'm living in California now, but I think I want to move to New York. Seems like good energy there. But this is definitely not the last album.

BIG BOI: The biggest thing that's changed is that we're not in the same place at the same time. But we both learned how to write, produce, do the melodic funk thing together. So we can trust each other to come correct. With this album, it's about saying you've got Big Boi and Andre3000—just get more acquainted with the members of the group. And we got the next three records planned out. The next record will be the soundtrack to the movie we're doing for HBO. After that, I can't tell you because it's top secret. And the one after that we've got sewed up, too. You're gonna get some more OutKast records.

Other Dungeon Family projects in the works: Rico Wade's new group, Da Connect, featuring "DF second generation" rappers, and a Sleepy Brown solo album, both to be released on DreamWorks Records. Ray Murray is working on the Dungeon East (his studio) compilation. Goodie Mob (minus Cee-Lo) has a new record on its own Goodie Mob Records coming late this year. Khujo and Cee-Lo have solo albums on the way as well. In addition, Big Boi and Sleepy have launched a project called West Savannah.

BIG BOI: We lived in the same house together. We scraped up money together to go buy one plate of the spaghetti special at the Citgo. All of us would eat off one plate—I'm talking about cutting the meatballs in half. So when you kick and scratch, and put blood, sweat and tears in one house, that keeps people together.

CEE-LO: I won't say it's the same. We're not kids who can sit around for hours watching TV and playing PlayStation. But Dungeon Family is tattooed in my left forearm; it's in my skin permanently. You move on and you hold on, and you try to meet halfway.

STEVIE WONDER

Berry Gordy Jr., already living in Los Angeles, came back to Detroit to host a 21st birthday party for Stevie Wonder at the Gordy Manor. The next day he flew back to California to find a letter waiting on his desk from a lawyer representing the former child star, informing the Motown Records founder that Stevie Wonder was disaffirming his recording, publishing and management contracts with Gordy and demanding to be paid in full.

Gordy immediately picked up the phone and called Wonder at home. His wife, Syreeta Wright, a former Motown secretary who married Wonder the previous September, answered the phone and told Gordy she couldn't imagine what he was talking about. She would have Stevie call, she told Gordy. It took about six months for Stevie to return the call.

Within days after his birthday, Wonder pulled into New York City, where he holed up at the distinctly unglamorous Holiday Inn on the west side of bustling midtown Manhattan. He was a man on a mission.

It was Memorial Day weekend 1971 when Malcolm Cecil looked out of his third floor apartment above Media Sound, the 57th Street studio where he served as chief engineer. He saw his friend Ronnie Blanco, a bass player Cecil knew since his first night in New York two years earlier. Standing with Blanco was someone Cecil didn't recognize wearing a pistachio green jump suit with an album under his arm. The second man turned out to be Stevie Wonder.

"Stevie turned 21 on the 13th of May," said Cecil. "When you turn 21 in this country, any contracts you made prior are now null and void because you're no longer a minor. So Stevie's contracts with Motown and his publishing contract with Jobete (Motown's song publishing arm) were now null and void. Stevie knew he didn't have his publishing. Since he was 18 years old, he had been saving songs in his head because he knew if he played them, Jobete would get 100 percent of them. He had been holding off on them for three years. He had not played them to anyone. They were bursting out of him."

The album under Wonder's arm was "Zero Time" by Tonto's Expanding Head Band, a 1970 record made by Cecil and his partner Bob Margouleff on the cobbled-together set of primitive synthesizers and sequencers that made the pair pioneers in the rarified early days of analog synthesizers. They called it TONTO—The Original Neo-Timbral Orchestra—and they had forged ahead into the unknown on an electronic instrument still in its infancy with an album released on a label run by jazzman Herbie Mann. "As far as their concept, their level of complication, in terms of how it was executed, their album was way beyond anything in the analog synthesizer world at that point," said Bernie Krause, another early synthesizer pathfinder who recorded the landmark "In a Wild Sanctuary" with partner Paul Beaver in 1970.

"You did this on one instrument?" Wonder asked. "I gotta see this."

They did not come out of the studio all weekend. When they did emerge, they had recorded 17 songs. In one quick, unexpected weekend, Cecil and Margouleff's lives went into lunar orbit and Stevie Wonder had launched one of the most extraordinary outbursts of creativity in popular music history—a four-year, four-album run that would be unprecedented and, as yet, unsurpassed both in terms of the level of artistic achievement and the widespread popular acclaim. He went into that room Little Stevie Wonder, the blind harmonica-playing 12-year-old who sang "Fingertips Pt. II" on "The Ed Sullivan Show." He came out his own man. Before long, his music would be heard in every corner of the globe, forever changing the way pop music was made and played. He brought together the worlds of rock and soul and, for a moment, made the whole world color blind. It was an extraordinary explosion of talent and determination by man who would be remarkable by any measure, let alone a blind black kid who grew up poor in Saginaw, Michigan.

Gordy allowed Wonder to produce his 1970 album, "Singed, Sealed, Delivered," and he and Syreeta co-wrote all the songs for his most recent LP, "Where I'm Coming From." He had always strained at the Motown factory formula, at least co-writing his own songs as far back as his 1965 Top 10 hit, "Uptight (Everything's Alright)." He watched carefully as Marvin Gaye battled Gordy for his creative freedom the previous fall over "What's Goin' On." He was absorbing all the fabulous music coming from outside Motown—the Beatles, Sly Stone, Burt Bacharach, Jimi Hendrix—and he felt his day of reckoning draw near.

Margouleff and Cecil moved TONTO downtown to Electric Ladyland, Hendrix's up-to-date studios in Greenwich Village. Wonder relocated his entourage to nearby Fifth Avenue Hotel around the corner, a block from Washington Square. The three of them began recording in earnest. They worked interchangeably in the studio. Wonder would noodle on keyboards, developing the songs, while Margouleff and Cecil programmed sounds under earphones. Either Margouleff or Cecil ran the recording equipment. Wonder played drums. When it came time to make a pass, it could take all six hands to navigate TONTO's cumbersome, bewildering forest of patch bays, knobs and switches. Sometimes Stevie's people were around—girlfriends, his brothers, his assistant, Ira Tucker Jr.—sometimes it was just he three of them alone. Sessions often started past midnight and lasted through the following day. They quickly lost track of time. They had done 40 songs "when we looked up," said Cecil.

Wonder wanted to tap the energy of the thriving, vibrant contemporary rock scene. He started putting together his new road band, Wonderlove, with musicians from the recently disbanded Paul Butterfield Blues Band—guitarist Buzzy Feiten, horn players Trevor Lawrence, Steve Madaio and David Sanborn. His new interracial group was not instantly well received in Motown circles. "It was rough going for a while," said Sanborn. "The audience was expecting Little Stevie Wonder and we were all these scraggly hippies. It was a whole different image than they were expecting. We were free-forming it a little bit. In Chicago with Gladys Knight and the Pips, we almost got booed off the stage. It was humiliating."

Margouleff and Cecil mentioned attorney Johanan Vigoda to him. A longtime music business attorney who cut Jimi Hendrix's first U.S. record deal and handled Richie Havens, Vigoda was a long-haired maverick who looked like hell, but was as sharp as they come ("Forget the fucking costume," one of his opponents once warned, "Vigoda's a shark."). He first met with Wonder in his Holiday Inn room, where Wonder told him about prospective representation that was asking for about 25 percent of his earnings across the board; records, songs performances. "To me, it sounded nuts," said Vigoda.

It would be up to Vigoda to solve Wonder's problems with his somewhat tyrannical, usually inflexible record company. While Vigoda briefly entertained offers from other labels, Wonder always felt an allegiance to Motown and never seriously considered leaving the label, Vigoda said. Of course, Motown had never before granted any artist the kind of control over his career that Wonder was demanding.

Before long, Vigoda found himself in California, trying to hammer out a satisfactory agreement with Motown Records president Ewart Abner, whom Vigoda used to represent when he ran Vee Jay Records. "They basically surrounded me with lawyers," Vigoda said. "Every six hours, they would bring in another two lawyers with a fresh draft, around the clock. Berry hired all these outside law firms to cover me. They would have all these fancy lawyers in their suits with their yellow pads and I showed up in jeans, bandana and cowboy boots. I would do yoga, stand on my head, to deal with it."

While Motown's lawyers waited for Vigoda and Wonder to sign the finalized agreement, Vigoda realized that they had worn him down to where he gave away some crucial procedural points and, at the last minute, advised Stevie against signing the document. After a long, restful sleep, Vigoda re-read the entire 240-page contract, making semi-legible handwritten changes with a felt-tipped magic marker. He delivered the dog-eared, scrawled-over contract to

Motown with Wonder's signature and told them they had 48 hours to return this exact document signed or the deal was off. They brought it back signed in six hours.

Vigoda won unprecedented concessions from Motown. Wonder earned the total creative control he sought. Motown was required to release the records he delivered "as is," said Vigoda. Wonder had complete command of cover art. The company retained only the right to pick the singles. Wonder not only won half of all his future publishing for his own Black Bull Music, but he won back half of the publishing to his previous work. "He needed the freedom," said Vigoda. "He needed the money, basically, to fund the freedom. He made more on the initial advance than he netted the entire previous 10 years."

Wonder ran up studio bills in excess of $250,000 of his own money. By the time an album release neared, Motown had to send out someone to straighten out all the paperwork and administrative details that had been ignored.

With the contract he needed in place, Wonder gave the label his first new album, "Music of My Mind." Released in March 1972, everything about the album—from the title to the fine print on the back of the cover—"This album is virtually the work of one man"—declared it the personal statement of the artist, now a man completely in control of his destiny. His overdubbed vocals criss-cross and bounce off each other with the exuberant joy of the freedom.

"I had all the instruments set up in the studio in a circle—the piano, the clavinet, the Rhodes, the Moog, everything," said associate producer Bob Margouleff. "Stevie could go, just like Braille, from one instrument to the next. They were all plugged in all the time. It was like a huge, instantaneous recording media. We fixed a lot of the instruments, modified our sound. We were using guitar boxes on the Rhodes, doing all kinds of experimental things."

"We didn't make albums," said Cecil. "We made songs." At the same time they were piling up tracks that would become "Music of My Mind," they were also recording an album with Syreeta, even though the marriage was breaking up after a year and a half. Cecil and Wonder came to London to add string parts, simultaneously, to both Syreeta and Stevie Wonder tracks. Eric Clapton sat in on a session, but couldn't cut it, according to Cecil. "All he could play was the blues," he said. "He was out of it."

Jeff Beck, on the other hand, showed up at Electric Ladyland in June 1972, ready and eager to dump a guitar part on a couple of Wonder's tracks (horns and guitars were the only instruments Wonder didn't play on the records himself). The record labels arranged this summit meeting and, in exchange for his guitar playing, Wonder was supposed to write a song for the rock guitarist. Beck and his band heard "Maybe Your Baby" at the studio, but were told there were already plans for that song when they asked about it. Later, Beck was sitting at a drum kit, pounding out a simple, mundane tattoo, just goofing around, when out of nowhere came this monster riff from Wonder behind the clavinet. Wonder scratched out some quick lyrics and Beck left the studio with a dub copy of the track, called, at the time, "Very Superstitious." Although he tried to cut the song with his musicians at Ladyland, Beck fired the entire band as soon as they returned to England (the bass player took a swing at Beck during the Wonder sessions). He didn't get around to recording the number for several months, by which time Wonder's version was already shooting up the charts. Beck made some snide comments to the music press.

"But I did promise him the song," Wonder told *Rolling Stone* later that year, "and I'm sorry it happened and that he came out with some of the arrogant statements he came out with. I will get another tune to him that I think is as exciting, and if he wants to do it, cool."

(Beck would have a 1973 worldwide hit with an instrumental cover of Wonder's "'Cause We've Ended as Lovers" from the second Syreeta album.)

Beck wasn't the only key Wonder tried to unlock the white rock audience. He hired a New York-based publicity firm, Wartoke Concern, to court the rock crowd (they also, oddly enough, booked Wonder for appearances on TV game shows "I've Got a Secret" and "What's My Line"). But the breakthrough came when he landed the plum assignment opening shows on the 1972 summer U.S. tour by the Rolling Stones, the most popular rock band in the world at the moment. "That Stones tour crossed him over to a white audience," said Margouleff.

"I hope it will do just that—make more people aware where I'm coming from," Wonder told this writer at the time between Stones shows in San Francisco. "I think the brothers know me—I just want more people. When you begin as a young artist, certain problems develop. You know, like 'little' becomes your first name or middle name or something like that.

"Fortunately I did do a lot of my own writing. The character of my tunes did express where I was coming from. Now I've just got to get to more people."

Beck finally got around to cutting "Superstition" with Beck, Bogart and Appice in December 1972, a month after Motown released the song as the first single off Wonder's new album, "Talking Book." "Superstition" blasted its way to No. 1 in February 1973. As powerful as his version sounded, it would be impossible to blame Wonder for using the track (he nevertheless always pointed out that it was the label that picked the singles from his albums). The track just went off like a grenade on the radio. The groundswell the Stones tour stirred up for Wonder on the rock scene paid off with instant attention on the newly powerful FM rock stations across the country.

But it was the album's second consecutive No. 1 single, "You Are the Sunshine of My Life," the song that launched a thousand bad lounge versions, that galvanized his sudden ascent into the stratosphere. Wonder didn't even sing on the track until the chorus—background vocalists Gloria Barley and Jim Gilstrap handle lead vocals on the opening verse. The recording had been sitting around finished for more than a year. Wonder originally passed over the song, written under the euphoria of a burgeoning romance with background vocalist Barley, because he didn't think it fit the mood of "Music of My Mind," which, with darker cornerstone pieces like "Superwoman" or "Keep On Running," felt more like a meditation on the dissolution of his marriage.

Margouleff and Cecil considered themselves true collaborators on the new album. Not only did they work on every second of music on the album, but Margouleff took the candid cover photo that showed Wonder without dark glasses. Cecil even accidentally came up with the title, he said, arguing with Wonder about the large number of tracks Wonder wanted to stuff on the two album sides.

"It's an album," he said, "not a talking book." For two years, they had lived in Stevie Wonderland, where clocks don't count and days turn into nights, nights into days. "It was a star-crossed couple of years," said Margouleff. "Day and night, we worked for Stevie Wonder. That's what we did."

"Stevie Wonder can't see, so everything is round-the-clock craziness," said guitarist Ray Parker Jr., a teenager who was playing in the house band at Detroit's Twenty Grand Club (and sitting in on the occasional Motown session) when Wonder summoned him to New York to join the band. "He's not on the same time schedule as the rest of the planet."

With "Talking Book" hovering near the top of the charts, Wonder headlined baseball stadiums that summer with the Kool Jazz Festival. He made it clear to the feverish audiences, however, that he was moving on—his sets concentrated on material from the as-yet unreleased, unfinished "Innervisions." He wrote and recorded "Higher Ground" in a three-hour blitz in May and was featuring as many as seven new songs in the hour-long sets. Most of the new album was being recorded at Record Plant in Los Angeles, where Wonder had switched the center of his operations. Malcolm and Cecil packed up TONTO, dutifully moved all the gear across the country and continued their work, credited as "associate producers." Up to the last minute, Cecil was arguing with Wonder about the length of the album, complaining that anything over 18 minutes per side would mean sacrificing volume level. He found a brand new mastering suite and somehow managed to cram more than 22 minutes on each side.

It was long past midnight August 6, 1973, and John Harris, Stevie's cousin, was driving through deep forests in the heart of the Carolina tobacco belt on Interstate 85. Wonder was asleep in the passenger's seat. They had played a concert earlier in Greenville, South Carolina, and were zooming through the night to Durham, North Carolina, for a benefit the next night at Duke University. "Innervisions" was just leaving the pressing plants for the record stores. A logging truck in front of them was weaving and rolling. Harris decided to pass. As he accelerated into the passing lane, the truck lurched and braked suddenly. Giant logs spilled off the truck and smashed into their windshield. The sleeping Stevie Wonder, seat-belted in place, took the blow right in his face.

He was rushed to nearby Rowan Memorial Hospital in Salisbury, N.C., and lay in a coma in intensive care for three days, his head swollen like a watermelon. Diagnosed with severe brain contusion, he was transferred to the neurological center at Baptist Hospital in Winston-Salem, where he stayed in a semi-coma for seven more days. It was Ira Tucker Jr., his longtime associate, who got him to tap his finger in time while Tucker sang "Higher Ground" into Wonder's ear. Two weeks after the crash, he was flown out to UCLA Hospital in Los Angeles, where he gave Associated Press a brief interview.

"The only thing I know," Wonder said, "is that I was unconscious and that, for a few days, I was definitely in a much better spiritual place that made me aware of a lot of things that concern my life and my future and what I have to do to reach another higher ground."

Four months later, as Elton John settled back for a brief flight from New York to Boston on his private jet, the Starship, he was surprised to discover the pianist in the plane's lounge was none other than Stevie Wonder. He joined Elton John that night at the Boston Gardens for a duet encore of "Honky Tonk Woman" and then led the band in a rousing "Superstition" to frenzied emotional applause. It wasn't Wonder's first public appearance since the accident—he had been jamming briefly earlier with Edgar Winter at a Greenwich Village nightclub, the Bottom Line—but it set the stage for an extraordinary series of comeback appearances.

In January 1974, he tested the waters with a pair of European appearances. He played the Rainbow Theater in London before all of England's reigning rock royalty—Paul and Linda McCartney, Ringo Starr, Pete Townshend, Eric Clapton, David Bowie. Still he whipped out brand new songs—"The Bumblebee of Love," "Sky Blue Afternoon" and the instrumental, "Contusion." He traveled to France to appear before a tuxedo-clad audience of industry executives at a music business conference in Cannes.

Nominated for six Grammy Awards, Wonder arrived at the televised ceremony at Los Angeles' Shrine Auditorium March 2 on the arm of his mother, Lula Hardaway. He dedicated the first Grammy to her (also mentioning his brother, Calvin Hardaway, who pulled him from the car wreck). By the end of the night, he won an historic five Grammys—stretching across both of the previous year's albums. He won awards for both "Superstition" and "Sunshine of My Life" from "Talking Book" and "Innervisions" was named Album of the Year. He gave his Best Engineered Album award to Margouleff and Cecil. He made his mother accompany him to the stage to accept the final award, waved it over his head and then gave it to her.

A week later, Wonder held a press conference in Los Angeles and announced he planned to move to Africa. He said he had already made contacts with people in Ghana and that he planned to complete the move within two years. He hoped to work with the underprivileged in Africa, particularly blind children. He allowed he would probably conduct a nationwide tour before leaving to raise money for African charities. He also said his next album would be released in a month.

The next week, he walked onstage before a capacity crowd at New York's Madison Square Garden, pointed dramatically heavenward and then pointed at his own battered forehead. The place went nuts. For the finale, he held hands with Roberta Flack, Sly Stone, Eddie Kendricks of the Temptations—a representative pantheon of the day's soul Olympians—while they all sang "Superstition."

The next album wasn't finished for six months (Wonder also dropped his plans to move to Africa). When the album was done, he titled it "Fulfillingness' First Finale." "Fulfillingness" was his name for Malcolm Cecil. It was the last album Margouleff and Cecil would make with Stevie Wonder.

"After four albums, we had gone to all the creative places we were going to go to," said Margouleff, "and we were starting to repeat ourselves. I think Stevie had said all he was going to say for a while. I think he went on to imitate the style of those records for another record or two, but they were never as successful, in my eyes, as those four albums."

Even during the album's production, the "associate producers" were drifting away from Wonder, who they found even more remote since the accident, surrounded by yet greater labyrinthian entourages and inaccessible in new ways. They were chafing at being kept in the shadow of Stevie Wonder—"His credits kept getting larger and ours kept getting smaller," said Margouleff—and their lawyers were unable to wrest any royalties out of Wonder for their participation as "associate producers." The Isley Brothers were calling and the pair found themselves jetting between Teaneck, N.J., and "Fight the Power" and the Record Plant in Los Angeles and "Boogie on Reggae Woman." Cecil was getting so angry, he stopped showing up for the sessions.

"After the accident, that's when the changes occurred," said Cecil. "Stevie became more black-oriented in terms of the people around him. He didn't want anybody who didn't absolutely have to be there who wasn't black."

"He was never quite the same person," said Margouleff. "Stevie became much more controlling and less free with himself. I think he began to realize he was mortal. I think he took a lot of medication after the accident because it was very severe. I think it gave him a very different perspective on his life. He became more and more famous and we became less and less important."

To Johanan Vigoda, it is not so simple. He thinks everybody grows and changes, that you can only spend so much time with people like Coretta Scott King or Jesse Jackson before it begins to effect how you see yourself. He thinks a 24 year-old man, at the top of the world after surviving a brush with death, is a very different animal than a 21 year-old man freshly emancipated, looking to make his own mark. He remembered talking to Wonder backstage at the Rainbow Theater before he went out to play his first show anywhere since this disfiguring accident in front of every famous rock musician who was in London that night. "Aren't you afraid?" Vigoda asked his client.

"What do you mean afraid?" Wonder said.

JEFF SHARLET

Big World

How Clear Channel Programs America

On July 17, 2002, as a band called the Boils was preparing to play, seven men with badges, police officers and agents of Philadelphia's Department of Licenses and Inspections, walked into the basement of the First Unitarian Church at Chestnut and Van Pelt. Nobody knows who tipped them off, but it was clear that someone wanted the Church, as the club in the basement was called, shut down. The show's promoter, Sean Agnew, had been booking acts there for six years, but before the night when the inspectors appeared his shows had not warranted a single official complaint. A tall, lean twenty-four-year-old with a stubbled undertaker's jaw and long, dark eyelashes, Agnew almost always wore a black mesh cap, with DORM SLUT scrawled on it graffiti style in silver Sharpie, crammed over thick black hair. He was known locally, and in little music magazines around the country, as "DJR500." Agnew's shows were "straight-edge," which meant that drugs and alcohol were not welcome. A local paper had recently named him a man of the year, alongside 76ers guard Allen Iverson.

The Department of Licenses and Inspections does not keep records of complaints. All the deputy commissioner could tell Agnew was that someone had gone down to City Hall, pulled the Church's permit, and discovered that the Church was not zoned to hold gatherings for entertainment purposes. No bingo, no swing dancing, and definitely no Boils. The inspectors gave Agnew a red-

and-white-striped "Cease Work/Operations" sticker to affix to the Church's door and declared the concert over.

Agnew got on stage and told everyone to go home; his friends circulated through the crowd, whispering that the show was moving to West Philadelphia, to a theater called The Rotunda. Soon Agnew cut a deal to produce all his concerts there, but he was able to put on only one more show before the Department of Licenses and Inspections shut that operation down as well. Someone had gone down to City Hall, pulled the theater's permit, and discovered that it was zoned for drama only. Then inspectors visited the record shop where Agnew sold his tickets, with the news that someone had gone down to City Hall, pulled the shop's permit, and found out that it wasn't zoned for selling tickets. A few days later the inspectors were back at the shop, looking for a box under the counter in which the store kept Agnew's mail—another violation, reported by yet another concerned citizen.

Although he had no evidence, Agnew's suspicions fell on Clear Channel Communications. Clear Channel controls almost every concert venue in and around Philadelphia—from the Theater of the Living Arts on South Street to the Tweeter Center in Camden—as well as six radio stations and nearly 700 billboards. The company's local viceroy, a man named Larry Magid, once ran the city's live-music scene as a private fiefdom. Now, since Clear Channel bought him out in 2000, he manages it as a corporate franchise. Clear Channel maintains a similar chokehold on live music in almost every major city in America, as well as in most of the small ones. Agnew, who had managed to book bands that could have made far more money playing Clear Channel theaters, suspected that he was grit in the machine.

"Four or five years ago," Agnew told me one day in the record shop, where he also works as a clerk, "there were a lot more people aware of corporate power." Now, he said, money so dominated the music scene that a lot of younger kids didn't even know what "selling out" meant. When I asked him what had kept him in business, he corrected me: "I don't consider what I got into a 'business.'" Many Philadelphia music fans had rallied to his defense, he explained. After the closures, Agnew sent out word to his email list, 8,000 people who had attended at least one of his shows, and within days 1,000 of them had written to City Hall. He rented a paid mail-box. He persuaded a lawyer to represent the Church pro bono, and soon the Church had a dance-hall permit, the record shop had a ticket-selling permit, and Agnew had more events scheduled than before he was shut down.

Whoever was behind the attempt to close the Church, nearly every concertgoer I talked to blamed Clear Channel. They adored Agnew for "standing up to the evil empire," as one musician put it. Agnew, a vegetarian who lives with a cat and thousands of obses-sively organized records, is now the most authentic rock and roller in the city. When he walks down the street, people nod and smile and pat him on the back. DJR500 is huge, and one day soon Clear Channel might make him an offer.

Some people complain about Clear Channel because they miss their old, independent stations, some because Clear Channel stations shrink playlists and recycle an ever smaller number of songs. Musi-cians say touring has become a cross-country hopscotch from one Clear Channel venue to another, each more sterile than the last; their agents and managers say that if artists don't play when and where Clear Channel says, they will suffer less airplay or none. As journalists point out, Clear Channel has made commercial radio nearly reporting-free, believing that its syndication of Rush Lim-baugh to as many stations as possible fulfills its mandate to provide news and political diversity. Evangelical Christians are distressed about radio firsts pioneered by Clear Channel DJs, such as torturing and killing live animals on the air (a chicken in Denver, a pig in Florida), but this can happen only where there's a DJ: Clear Chan-nel has put hundreds of radio veterans out of work, replacing them with canned broadcasts tailored to sound local and live. Consumer advocates argue that such robot radio is the only efficiency Clear Channel has passed along to the public. In the last several years, they point out, the cost of "free" radio—in terms of time spent enduring ads—has spiked. Concert tickets have jumped from an average of $25 to more than $40, and radio advertising rates have risen by two thirds, pricing small businesses off the airwaves.

Clear Channel says that its enemies snipe simply because it's big, and this is probably true. No one had imagined that a radio company could *get* so big. When Clear Channel was founded in 1972, with one station bought by a San Antonio investment banker named L. Lowry Mays, federal law forbade a company from owning more than seven FM stations and seven AMs. By the 1990s, that cap had crept up to forty stations nationwide, no more than two per market. Then, in 1996, Congress passed the Telecommunications Act. Up to eight stations per market would be allowed, and as many overall as a company could digest. Within less than a year more than 1,000 mergers occurred; by 2000 four behemoths dominated the business. Today, Clear Channel rules.

Z-100 in New York? Clear Channel. K-BIG in L.A.? Clear Channel. KISS in Chicago? Clear Channel. KISS, POWER, the FOX, and the ZONE are all Clear Channel brands, and the dozens of radio stations nationwide that bear one of those names take their orders from San Antonio, where Clear Channel's headquarters remain, in an unassuming limestone box next to a golf course. Rush Limbaugh is Clear Channel, and so are Dr. Laura, Casey Kasem, and Glenn Beck, the rising star of rant radio who organized the "Rally for America" prowar demonstrations.

Last June, when the FCC raised the caps on how much access to the American public any one media company could control—a move too crassly reminiscent of the days of robber barons for even the Republican-controlled House of Representatives, which voted 400–21 to roll it back—the one media company the commission hinted might actually be too big was Clear Channel. The recent debate in Congress over television ownership has focused on two numbers: 35 percent, which is the portion of American viewers to which a single TV-station owner can currently broadcast, and 45 percent, which strikes media giants as a more reasonable number. Clear Channel, meanwhile, reaches roughly 200 million people, or more than 70 percent of the American public. It owns 1,225 stations within the United States, or around 11 percent overall, and greater portions in major markets. It broadcasts from at least 200 more stations abroad, many clustered just south of the border like radio maquiladoras, and it owns or controls more live-music venues than any other company. In the first six months of 2003, Clear Channel sold more tickets than the forty-nine next largest promoters combined; in 2001, it claimed 70 percent of the total live-music take.

The billboards that ring the stadiums, line the highways, clutter the skyline? Clear Channel owns most of those too.

As a business enterprise, Clear Channel is an experiment. It is giant and potentially unstable, more reliant on muscle than on financial finesse, and to date only moderately profitable. A sort of Frankenstein's monster, it was built from the parts of once-dying industries and jolted into life by the 1996 Telecommunications Act. Supporters of the law say there was no choice; at the time, more than half the stations in the country were losing money. Opponents retort that Clear Channel is hardly a democratic solution. "I don't think there was anybody in Washington in 1996 who could have imagined that a few years later there'd be one company owning 1,200 stations," says Michael Copps, one of the two commissioners on the FCC's five-person board who opposed raising ownership caps. "We should never give anybody the ability to have that much power."

When I asked to interview Clear Channel's executives, a P.R. rep for the company told me that Clear Channel wouldn't talk to me, because it no longer needs the media: a Zen koan of consolidation. After the company learned that several underlings had talked nevertheless, radio CEO John Hogan agreed to speak with me on the phone. An amiable, forty-six-year-old former radio-ad salesman, he told me that "the key to radio is that it's a very personal, intimate medium." Hogan's first executive role was as the general manager of WPCH, a fully automated station in Atlanta known as "the Peach." Hogan made running the station sound like changing a diaper. "It was a 'beautiful music' station," he said. "You didn't have to make any decisions. All you did was put the tape on in the morning and you let it run for twenty-four hours and then you changed it the next day. There were no decisions to make, they were made for you. It was nice, you know, it was easy."

His idea of what radio is and can be does not seem to have changed since his days at the Peach. "People use radio 'cause it works," he told me. "If it stops working for 'em, they stop it." The "they" he was referring to were the advertisers. "For the first time ever, we can talk to advertisers about a true national radio footprint," he told me. "If you have a younger, female-skewing advertiser who wants access to that audience, we can give them stations in, you know, Boston and New York and Miami and Chicago, literally across the country. Los Angeles, San Francisco . . . We can take outdoor [ads] and radio, and drive people to live events and concerts and capture the excitement, the real visceral experience." The goal? "A different kind of advertising opportunity."

Hogan was promoted to radio CEO just over a year ago. He has tried to soften the company's image after several years of brutal acquisitions under the leadership of Randy Michaels, the former disc jockey who now manages the company's new-technologies division. Clear Channel wouldn't let me talk with Michaels, but not long after he left the radio division he gave a trade publication called *Radio Ink* an even blunter rationale for the company's push to dominate live music as it does radio. "People attending a concert are experiencing something with tremendous emotion," he said. "They're . . . vulnerable."

Across town from the Church, in a little club called the Khyber Pass, I went to see a show booked by Clear Channel's man in Philadelphia, The headliner was a band called the Dragons, best known for their album *Rock Like Fuck*, but the night belonged to the opening act, the Riverboat Gamblers, or, rather, to their singer, Teko. Tall, skinny, gruesomely pretty, he vibrated across the two-foot-high stage, shouting loud and hard. No one was there to see the bands; the crowd, maybe a hundred strong, was there to get drunk, or to take someone home. But everyone in the room—a cigar box painted matte black from top to bottom, beer on the floor and loose wiring dangling from the ceiling—pressed forward, chins bobbing, drunken eyes widening. Near the end of a song called "Hey, Hey, Hey," Teko jumped and landed on the two-step riser at the front of the stage. It slid away, sent him crashing onto his spine. His left hand clutched the mike, into which he continued to scream; his right hand, flailing to its beat even faster, had begun to bleed at the palm. Then he jolted off the floor, bit the mike, and launched into another song: "I get the feelin' you're gonna need a feedin'! Let's eat! Let's eat! Let's eat!"

A few minutes later, Clear Channel's man jammed himself into the edge of the crowd, grinning and rocking his head as the singer leaped from the stage and drove into the audience, swinging his bloody hand like a wrecking ball. Clear Channel's man loved it. Bryan Dilworth was a big man with small eyes and a head of thinning red hair that brought to mind Curly of the Three Stooges. He was in what he called "that moment." He grinned and rocked his head; he stopped scanning the room and actually watched the band. He elbowed me, nodding toward the Riverboat Gamblers, as if to say, "See? See?"

When the song ended, Dilworth stepped back from the crowd, returned to the bar in the next room, and ordered another Jameson's.

"Dude," he said. "*That* is what I'm fucking talking about."

Meaning the scene, the variables, "the combustibles": everything he claimed Clear Channel could never buy. That included himself. At various times, Dilworth told me he worked for Clear Channel, or didn't work for Clear Channel, or Clear Channel simply didn't matter. Sometimes he called Clear Channel "the evil empire"; sometimes he said it was the best thing that ever happened to his town. It was hard to know which Dilworth to believe: the one who took me up to the cluttered office of his private company, Curt Flood, two stories above the Khyber Pass, to play me tracks from one of his bands on a cheap boom box; or the one who took me on a tour of a Clear Channel hall and conceded that the paychecks that mattered came from Clear Channel, that he had a Clear Channel email address and a Clear Channel phone number, that he was in truth a Clear Channel "talent buyer" responsible for filling the calendars of a dozen Clear Channel venues around the city. At times Dilworth spoke of Clear Channel Philadelphia in the first person. "I am living proof," he told me more than once, "that Clear Channel Philadelphia is going to rock."

This flexibility was what made Dilworth such a valuable asset. Unlike Starbucks or Borders, Clear Channel does not build its empire from new franchises but rather goes from town to town and buys local operations. Clear Channel has Dilworths in every city with a scene, and what makes them so effective is precisely that their affiliation with the company is subject to doubt, even in their own minds. Dilworth develops "baby bands" in clubs like the Khyber on his own time and filters the most marketable of them to the more lucrative venues he books as his alter ego, a Clear Channel talent buyer. Such a double role appears to be part of the Clear Channel business plan, in which the independents who should be an alternative to Clear Channel instead become the company's farm team. As a result, live music is following the route taken by radio. Songs that sound the same are performed in venues that look the same and even have the same name: identically branded venues, all controlled by Clear Channel, brick-and-mortar embodiments of KISS, the FOX, and the ZONE.

"Everything is so fucked," said Dilworth, another shot of Jameson's at his lips. "Music business my ass. Take the 'music' off and that's what it is." He drank the shot, and then he was talking about the Riverboat Gamblers again: those dudes got it, they're going places, and Dilworth would take them there, Clear Channel all the way. That's not monopoly, said Dilworth, it's business in America. "Deregulation set this table a long time ago. I'm not taking a 'can't beat 'em then join 'em' attitude, but . . ." He trailed off, because, of course, he was.

Dilworth's contradictory relationship with Clear Channel extended even into his home life. His wife, Kristin Thomson, worked for the Future of Music Coalition, the leading activist group against consolidation. FMC's head, Jenny Toomey, had been a prominent witness against raising ownership caps during last winter's Senate hearings, at which she laid out a specific and compelling case for how Clear Channel has become a near monopoly. Thomson and Toomey had once been minor rock stars together, as the indie group Tsunami, and Dilworth thought his marriage to Thomson was a simple instance of "rocker dude meets rocker chick." He said they didn't talk about politics. Dilworth himself had given lectures for FMC on the music business. ("Fuck the art," he had advised a conference of musicians. "Put the hit first.") Thomson, for her part, felt that her husband wasn't like the rest of Clear Channel.

One night, when Dilworth and I were in his office, he showed me his first gold record, awarded for a small role he had played in the success of the band Good Charlotte. A very small role, he said; gold records get passed around freely when a record company sees a future in a relationship.

"A down payment?" I said.

"Yeah, man, it's like, a favor for a favor."

"What's the difference between that and payola?"

Dilworth guffawed and looked at me like I was the dumbest kid in school. "It's *all* payola, dude."

Then his shoulders slumped and he stopped laughing.

What determines the course of music today is not a zeitgeist or a paradigm or anything that can be dismissed simply as fashion. It's not even greed. What matters now is the process. "Cross-selling." "Clustering." A confluence of ear radios and concert halls, the drinks at the bar, the ticket that gets you in the door, the beat you dance to. "Anything you can do to be associated with the music, you try to do," a Clear Channel executive with forty years in radio told me. This is not entirely sinister, nor is it especially new. The music business, in its varied forms, has always depended on symbiosis. Clear Channel wants you to identify with the brand so fully that you don't recognize it as a brand at all but rather as yourself. The executive gave me an example. "Suppose you like Dave Matthews," he said. "We like Dave Matthews. We have Dave Matthews together."

To achieve this mind-meld, Clear Channel has designed itself as a self-contained, nationwide feedback loop, calibrating the tastes of its listeners and segmenting them into market-proven "formats." Today, Clear Channel operates in thirteen major music formats, and although some of these formats are nearly indistinguishable, they are nevertheless finely tuned: for example, listeners can choose between "AC" (Adult Contemporary) and "Hot AC," or among "CHR" (Contemporary Hits Radio), "CHR Pop," and "CHR Rhythmic." John Hogan, the radio division's CEO, boasted that in 2003 the company would make more than 2 million phone calls to survey its listeners, a process that would produce "around 10,000 local-audience research reports." As these reports are generated, the company can respond rapidly. "If we have a CHR PD"—program director—"in, you know, Dayton, Ohio, who figures out a great way to package up a bit, or a great promotion, or comes up with something clever and innovative, we can almost *instantaneously* make it available to CHR radio stations across the country." (At the time of our interview, Clear Channel owned eighty-nine CHRs.) Then, for a given advertiser, the company can align all its CHRs to hit one "formatic target"—a demographic. Hogan suggested teenage girls.

"A great advertiser would be the Crest Whitestrips. In the past, if Crest had wanted to use radio, they would have had to call a different owner in every market. There would have been no way to link together those stations with, you know, a common theme, or a common execution."

Such harmony extends to the company's concert business as well. "There's a lot of conference calling between cities," a booking agent named Tim Borror told me, "these former independents talking to one another, letting each other know what's going on." Another independent booking agent and a Clear Channel talent buyer, neither of whom would allow themselves to be named, confirmed this practice, adding that such calls take place almost on a weekly basis. The calls can launch a band or flatten it. "At a certain point, there's only one place to go—Clear Channel—and it doesn't matter whether or not they make you a fair offer," Borror said. "And pretty soon, they don't have to make you a fair offer. And they can decide what band is playing and what band isn't."

I asked John Hogan why I should believe that Clear Channel would never use its combined dominance of radio and live events to punish an artist—or a politician—who did not cooperate with the company. "I can't imagine a scenario where it would make any business sense at all," he replied. To use the power, he said, "would be to damage it." David T. "Boche" Viecelli, another booking agent, told me: "The thing people fear—legitimately fear—is that they're going to implement the threats they've intimated with radio airplay. It's not explicit. More often it's insinuation and innuendo." Clear Channel doesn't have to actively be "the evil empire," because everyone knows that it could be. With so much of music and entertainment determined by, produced by, broadcast by, measured by, and defined by Clear Channel, the company need not exercise its control in order to wield it. Clear Channel is a system so pervasive that it relieves its participants—consumers, bands, employees, even executives—of the responsibility to object, and the ability to imagine why they would ever do so.

In Denver, Clear Channel owns half the rock stations on the dial, as well as the region's number-one station, the news/talk KOA. It owns the Fillmore, co-owns the Universal Lending Pavilion, controls the rights to the Pepsi Center, and in 2001 pried a sweetheart deal out of the city for booking shows at the legendary Red Rocks Amphitheatre, carved out of the stone of the Rocky Mountain foothills—as much of a temple as pop music can claim.

I went to Denver to meet Jesse Morreale, an independent promoter who is suing Clear Channel. Morreale is one of the biggest independents in the country, but he is also one of the last. He persuaded one of the so-called Big Four law firms in Denver to represent him, but even if they can prove that Clear Channel Radio and Clear Channel Entertainment work together to shut out other promoters and threaten artists who work with them, there's a good chance his company, Nobody in Particular Presents, will be out of business by the time the case reaches any kind of conclusion. For now, Morreale has been silenced; Clear Channel won a protective order from the court, and although Morreale was happy to complain, he could not give me particulars.

Nor would the minor rock stars who came through town while I was there. The leather-clad lead singer of Cradle of Filth, a death-metal band from England, assured me that he would "never" say anything against Clear Channel. A punk-pop threesome called the Raveonettes at first said they hadn't heard of Clear Channel, then admitted that they had, then offered me a beer and asked if we couldn't please instead talk about rock-and-roll music. A record-company agent clinked shots with me and said, "Rock 'n roll!" but when Morreale told him I was writing about Clear Channel, he asked for my notes. "I'm going to need those," he said, trying to sound official. I would have said no, but since all I had written down was "Fred Durst," and the guy looked like he might cry, I tore the page out and gave it to him.

The next morning, I was driving around Denver listening to the radio when I heard a prerecorded spoof ad for "Butt Pirates of the Caribbean." It consisted mainly of the DJ reading, in a sneering lisp, a list of actors he considered "homo." Which is to say, it was nothing unusual. I had been listening to Clear Channel radio all over the country and had found that gay jokes ran second only to "camel jockey" or "towel head" humor. Such slurs, I began to think, were simply the comedic equivalent of the mannered rock "rebellion" in the musical rotation. Like the knee-jerk distortion of a Limp Bizkit song, the fag gags of the local morning crew are there to assure listeners that someone, somewhere, is being offended by what they are pretending to enjoy.

Back at my hotel, I called the local Clear Channel headquarters and asked for the man in charge. I was surprised to get a call back from Clear Channel's regional vice president, Lee Larsen, who invited me out to see him that very morning.

Larsen, who looked to be in his mid-fifties, was not a formal man. He put his loafers up on the coffee table between us and his arms behind his head and told me to fire away: he loved to talk about radio. Larsen wore his sandy hair in a modest pompadour, and although he had some girth on him, his tall frame and thick shoulders made him look like a linebacker. He started on the air forty years ago but made his career as a manager. On a pedestal near the center of his office sat an antique wooden radio, flanked by Broncos helmets facing inward. When I asked him what he listened to, he replied with a long and diverse list of stations—none of them Clear Channel—that marked him as a man of broad but refined tastes. Nevertheless, he was a staunch believer in Giving the People What They Want. "This whole society," he said, "is based on majority rules." There is no such thing, he said, as "lowest common denominator"; there is only democracy, and in the music world Clear Channel is its biggest purveyor. The best thing about democracy, which he likened to a pizza, is that there is so much of it. "If I take one slice of the audience, and it's the biggest slice, and it's the 'lowest common denominator' slice, whatever you want to call it, guess what? There's lots of slices for the other guy." As evidence of this bounty, he gestured over his shoulder. At first I thought he wanted me to look at the view of the Rockies behind him, but it turned out he was thinking of the franchise-lined highways I'd driven to get there. "Who'd have thought there could be so many different fast-food restaurants as there are?"

There were those among us, he said, who would complain nonetheless. People "at odds with the masses." People who believe that "the mass in our country are *stupid*." People who would tell you that you "should read *Atlantic Monthly*, not *Time*." But that was all right. "You can have anything you want," he said. "You just can't have what you want everywhere." He smiled. "Some people don't

like that." He leaned forward and patted the coffee table, a little gesture to let me know that he knew that I knew what he was talking
about, that I was, with him, part of "the mass."

I asked him about "Butt Pirates of the Caribbean." He reared
back and looked at me like I was Tipper Gore. In a gentle, rumbling
tone, he asked, "What are you saying? That it should not have been
on?"

"Well . . . ," I said, "switch 'Butt Pirates of the Caribbean' for
something like, say, 'Jigaboos of Jamaica,' and I think you can see
what I mean."

Larsen frowned. "I know clearly that you couldn't do a bit like
that that's *ethnic*. I know that, okay? Maybe, in the area you're talking about, that might still be open. Society's still trying to figure out
the line there. If you took that bit and put it on a classical-music
radio station and played it, well the people would be outraged. It's
out of context." But there was a time and place for such things. "If
every radio station was doing 'Butt Pirates,' then you would be saying, 'Well, what is this?' But they are not." At the station I had heard
it on, he explained, "the talent must have felt that was within the
bounds they could work within, *and* was something that the audience that was listening to *their* radio station could relate to."

I must have looked unconvinced, because Larsen seemed worried. "On the radio," he said, "the red light's on and you're talking.
And you say something. Just like you do in real life. And you go"—
he shaped his lips into an O and let his eyes bulge as he covered his
mouth—"I. Wish. I. Hadn't. Said. That." He shrugged his shoulders, held up his palms in a "what can you do?" gesture. "But it's too
late."

From Denver, I went to Oklahoma City to meet with former congressman Julius Caesar "J. C." Watts, who had recently been named
to Clear Channel's board of directors. During the hour and a half
we spent driving around and listening to the radio in his shiny new
black Cadillac Escalade, the congressman referred to Americans as
"dogs" five times. Not in the slang sense—Watts loathes what he
calls that "hip-hop be-bop rap" stuff—but in the idiom of business.
He was trying to get at what business is all about. He wasn't concerned about Clear Channel's overwhelming control of live music,

he said, because "the dogs are eating the dog food." He said that the reason talk radio is so conservative is that "the dogs ain't eating the dog food" offered by liberals: "You can't force bad dog food on people!"

A former football star for the Sooners and a Southern Baptist preacher at a church called Sunnylane, Watts has an easy manner that can nevertheless be disconcerting, as when he took both hands off the wheel at 75 miles an hour, turned, and gripped my arm, saying, "I'm ready to go to the American people with my dog food." Then he found a song he seemed to like, "Get Busy," by Sean Paul, and turned it up. It was hip-hop, but it did have a spiritual message: "From the day we born Jah ignite me flame/Gal a call me name and it is me fame/It's all good girl turn me on/Till the early morn'/Let's get it on."

The former fourth-ranking Republican in the House, Watts may be out of office at the moment (he chose not to run last year), but at age forty-five he still wields considerable power as chair of GOPAC, an organization designed to develop Republican candidates at the state level, and as the G.O.P.'s great black hope. When President Bush made his recent tour of Africa, he tapped Watts as a traveling companion. When Democratic fixer Vernon Jordan retired from Clear Channel's board, he pushed Watts, a man who considers LBJ to have been a "wild-eyed radical," as his replacement.

But I don't think Watts's connections—or his politics—are why he "aligns nicely," as Clear Channel CEO Lowry Mays put it, with the company. Rather, I suspect it has something to do with his mix of aggressive amiability and angry defensiveness. Watts often gets called an "Uncle Tom"; Clear Channel's radio and concert guys are sick of being called "sellouts." Watts thinks it's unfair that as a black man he should have to defend himself for also being a Republican; Clear Channel can't understand why people seem shocked when it competes as fiercely as it does. Both Watts and Clear Channel look at what they're doing as revolutionary, unsentimental, *necessary*. Watts thinks Clear Channel simply needs to do a better job of telling the American people—the dogs—what the company is.

We pulled into the parking lot of a motel next to a Denny's. Watts said, "In politics or in business, you're either on the offense or you're on the defense. If you're on the defense, you're losing."

Clear Channel, he explained, had to hit back, and hard. "Jeff, I think today that people are concerned with"—he reached out and banged the dashboard speakers of his Escalade— "this. They don't care where it's coming from!" Then he turned the radio on again and tuned it to his daughter's favorite station and cranked it up. "Get Busy," by Sean Paul.

"Same song!" Watts shouted. "Thirty minutes ago! I couldn't have planned that in a thousand years!" To Watts, this was a good thing.

He said Clear Channel needed a great slogan, like Fox's "Fair and Balanced."

"You mean," I said, "something like 'Clear Channel: We Give You What You Want.'"

"Yeah!" Watts slapped my shoulder. "Yeah! Or maybe . . ." He paused to think, then held up his hands to frame his idea. "Clear Channel, Your Community, you know, Involvement, you know, Network, or, or Station, or Whatever. . . .

"An enemy says, 'Jeff, I don't want you to have what you have. You know, I'm gonna be a self-righteous income distributor. And I'm gonna balance this thing out.'" (Watts believes in balance, so long as it isn't, as he put it, "Communist," which, presumably, pre-1996 radio in America was.) "'And I'm gonna take from all those who're producing and give to those that aren't producing.'" He shook his head. "Uh-uh. When we get to the point where people are envious and we say, 'We're not gonna allow [consolidation] to happen'" Watts clapped a hand over mine and shuddered— "that is a *fiendish* business."

Regulation of radio ownership—Watts's fiendish business—is rooted in the idea that the spectrum is a national resource, but as a reality the "public airwaves" are close to extinct. Even proponents of regulation now fight for it, perversely, in the language of business, touting ownership caps as a means to preserve the "marketplace of ideas." This phrase, or even the "free market of ideas," has become a rhetorical fixture of anticonsolidation activists, for whom it connotes a free and fair system by which ideas compete for the minds of the citizenry. Implicit in the phrase is that ideas compete in roughly the same manner as do brands of soap; that, given equal price and placement, the most effective ideas will win the day. By owning so many stations, the argument goes, Clear Channel reduces the number of songs, sounds, formats, and opinions from which American listeners can choose.

But to so frame the argument is already to have lost. Media corporations want nothing more than to create new, popular formats with which to segment their audiences on advertisers' behalf. As advocates of deregulation never tire of pointing out, the "diversity" of U.S. radio content—in terms of average number of different formats available in each market—has increased with consolidation since 1996, not decreased. In fact, nothing resembles a "free market of ideas" so much as Clear Channel itself, where infinitesimal changes in ratings are tracked, mapped, and responded to; where Boston's successful new format can appear in San Diego overnight. This is what Lee Larsen means when he speaks of giving the people what they want. It is what J. C. Watts was trying to express when he jabbed the tuner on his radio and shouted, *"This* is democracy!" Clear Channel is a *super*market of ideas, which sells scores of different products all made in the same factory.

Activists fret that Clear Channel is foisting a right-wing agenda onto its listeners. To the contrary, the company seems to advance no ideology whatsoever; nor does it seem to advance any aesthetic that could be called good, bad, ugly, or beautiful. Perhaps the most instructive example here is the controversy over what has come to be called The List: the roster of songs that, immediately after September 11, were not supposed to be played on Clear Channel stations. The List's recommendations ranged from the obvious (AC/DC's "Shot Down in Flames") to the saccharine (Billy Joel's "Only the Good Die Young") to the grotesque (Van Halen's "Jump") to the unexpectedly poetic (Phil Collins's otherwise unremarkable "In the Air Tonight"). Antiwar activists pointed out that The List "banned" Cat Stevens's "Peace Train" and John Lennon's "Imagine," but ignored the fact that The List also proscribed Judas Priest's "Some Heads Are Gonna Roll" and the Clash's "Rock the Casbah," said to have been popular with U.S. pilots on bombing runs over Iraq during the first Gulf War.

Everyone seemed to see The List as the ultimate case of censorship by a corporate head office, but in fact The List came together just as might a great promotion by John Hogan's hypothetical program director in Dayton, Ohio. On his or her own initiative (nobody knows for certain where, or with whom, The List started), a Clear Channel PD drew up a list of songs; this PD emailed The List to a PD at another station, and he or she added more songs, and so on. When, eventually, The List was leaked to the press, Clear Channel pointed out that it was the work of independent program directors who were free to play—or not to play—whatever songs they liked.

Confusing The List for ideological censorship reflects a fundamental misunderstanding of the meaning of Clear Channel. It reflects the misguided notion that the company means anything at all. All the Clear Channel talent buyers, "on-air personalities," news directors, and executives I spoke with shared a basic disregard for both the content of the product and its quality. The market would take care of those. Clear Channel's functionaries seemed to view the company as some marvelous but unfathomable machine with whose upkeep they had been charged. They knew only that it accomplished a miraculous task—satisfying the musical tastes of most of the people—and did not care to trouble themselves with how.

Bryan Dilworth swore to me he had nothing to do with Sean Agnew's show at the Church getting shut down. He said that any suggestion to the contrary was "Davy and Goliath bullshit." He claimed he walked into his boss's office and asked them if they had been involved. He told them he needed to know, because he would quit if they had. They swore innocence. I tried to confirm his story, but his bosses never returned my calls.

One Sunday I met Dilworth at his home in South Philly. His wife needed a nap, so we took his ten-month-old for a ride in his stroller. We walked through the Italian market, dead quiet at six on a Sunday evening, empty wooden stalls fronting pork shops and bakeries. We stopped to watch a group of boys on skateboards work a ramp they had set up in the street, performing for a video camera one of the kids was holding. Dilworth laughed. "The dudes who own those stores knew these kids were out here, skating on their stalls like that? They'd break their legs." This delighted him, all of it: the men who owned the stores who wouldn't give a damn for the law, the

kids who took over the street who didn't give a damn for the owners. "This place is totally . . . this place," he said.

I asked him how that squared with his working for Clear Channel, which seemed dedicated to making every place the same. Dilworth didn't look at me but he smiled. His grin pushed his baby-fat
cheeks up and made his eyes small.

"All of a sudden I'm supposed to be superevil?" he said. "FUCK
THAT."

"No, that's not what I meant," I said.

"FUCK THAT. I just wanted to make money doing something I
liked. There are different opinions about how far down the road
America is businesswise, but dude, whatever, it's too far gone for
anything to change."

He bumped the stroller up over a curb, and the baby began to
cry. We walked without talking for a few blocks, the clackety-clack
of skateboard wheels fading behind us. But closer to home, both he
and the baby mellowed. Dilworth stopped smiling, and his eyes
stopped squinting.

"Then," he said, "there's that feeling in your spine, and it's all
right." His voice went up in pitch and grew soft, as if he were
embarrassed. He was talking about rock. "When the arc is just starting to arc? And you're saying this could be Van Halen, this could be
Neil Young. It's like you're bearing witness. It's not, 'Ching-ching,
here we go.' It's 'I saw it. It does exist.' There's something really
there. It's not just a need for chaos. It's—yeah. That's what I want."
His voice deepened again, and his pace evened out. The baby had
nodded off. We stopped in front of Dilworth's stoop. "Clear Channel?" he said. "That's money. I need it to buy liquor and baby
clothes."

ROD SMITH

The Party at Pou Corner

"I don't get it," Pou croaked, handing the bright blue bong to Christophe Robin. "From the cover, it appears that the Animal Collective are an all-human band. But they don't *sound* the least bit human to me." Christophe Robin turned, resting the shiny implement on a wide, flat, light-gray rock festooned with wine bottles arrayed symmetrically around the center of attention: an enormous boom box that glittered in the light of the full moon like a miniature Oz. The young adventurer had liberated all of it just that afternoon, from the Big Box Canyon on the other side of the freeway from the Forty-Acre-and-a-Mule Wood. He'd also nabbed *Here Comes the Indian* (Paw Tracks), the Animal Collective's first proper release as a *ménage à quatre*. It happened entirely by accident, though. Christophe Robin had never even considered the possibility that the Flawmart staff might be capable of misfiling the disc in the "nature recordings" section. After all, the front of the digipack was all forest streaked with bright acid colors, not a human in sight. He'd figured it was just some real-gone termites or something.

Christophe Robin sparked the bowl and filled his lungs slowly, maintaining eye contact with Pou for the duration of his hit. "I wish there were girls in the Wood," Christophe Robin rasped, smoke spiraling from his nostrils. Suddenly, Tigre bolted to a sitting position. "I'll have one of those," he purred, reaching for the bong. "This

321

band sounds pretty human to me. Although I do have to say that the singer sounds a bit like a giant *anime* raccoon." The cat twisted around and handed the bong to Piglette, who raised it to a jaunty angle like a saxophonist taking a solo.

Christophe Robin merrily hoisted a bottle of vintage Châteauneuf-du-Pape and fully drained an eighth of its contents in one mighty draught. Then he wiped his mouth on his pirate shirt. "I think it sounds like the Residents," he chuckled, rolling in the grass like a tabby cat on heroin.

"*The Residents?*" Tigre roared. "That's the best one you've come up with since you lumped Joy Division with Black Oak Arkansas!"

"I dunno," Pou said gravely. "Only a few months ago, he insisted that Goldfrapp sounded like Marianne Faithfull." Pou, who always liked to have a little something or two at 11 in the evening, doubled Christophe Robin's wine intake in a few gurgles. "Get while the getting is good," he said. "At the rate we're going, it'll be back to the brothers Gallo by tomorrow afternoon." He wiped his muzzle on the hem of Christophe Robin's shirt.

Rabbit's voice leapt from a spot in the tall yellow grass near the big rock. "I suppose I can see the similarity in a crass, one-dimensional sort of way. But it's sort of like comparing John Coltrane and Jonathan Richman. The Animal Collective are far more sophisticated than the Residents—*and* more primal."

"Have you been able to pull up any kind of bio yet?" Pou asked the bespectacled leuciphore, who, having poised his laptop on an ice-cream carton that was discarded earlier in the evening, stood on his hind legs and worked the instrument's keys with his forepaws.

"We'll get to that," Rabbit countered. "First, I plead my case. Back it up to track two, 'Hey Light.'" Tigre tapped the button with a claw. "Good," Rabbit hissed, passing the bong to Pou. "Note, in order, the updated Throbbing Gristle vocal processing in the intro; then, the seamless consolidation of traditional rock instruments and electronics; then, the charmingly pastoral marriage of punk rock, psychedelia, and thoroughly post-Crash Worship tribalism in the body of the song; and finally, a reprise that is every bit as enchanting as it is unexpected. It pauses and then returns, as though a group of sailors were crooning wistfully at the end of the night. And that melody line is lovely enough to have sprung from the mind of Schubert, Mendelssohn, or even Brahms."

Rabbit bounded back to his makeshift workstation. Tigre peered over the tall grass to catch a glimpse of the laptop screen reflected in Rabbit's horn rims. How he loved that sight! "Check out these lyrics," Rabbit commanded. "'Hey light/Cut the curtain kids at noon/Dressed up in their bedtime suits/They should be out walking/Hey light/I've forgotten work today/Cause a kid can't work all day/You within me walking.' Nothing too Residential there," Rabbit asserted, taking a quick pull from the nearest wine bottle. "They're not nearly nerdy enough. If anything, they sound like they could have been written by one of us."

Pou loaded another bowl. "Actually," he mumbled, "I had a very similar illumination-related thought earlier today when I was out for my morning constitutional."

Suddenly, a wild braying sound startled the party. They looked up to see E. Hors, who had appeared in their midst as if by magic, doing a slow Pee-Wee Herman around the big rock. "Is this the new Residents?" the donkey queried, he ears twisting obscenely toward the boom box.

"Fuck the Residents!" Piglette squealed. "Animal Collective!"

"I know," the droopy-eared, sharp-hoofed ninja answered. "I've been spying from behind that tree over there. I don't think they sound like the Residents, either. I do have to say I like the more abstract material better than the pop stuff, though."

"Pop stuff?" Rabbit asked, passing the smoking bong to E. Hors. "I definitely hear a pop component, in a '60s psychedelic might-have-been sort of way. To me, the song I was just talking about sounds like something Brian Wilson might have done after *Pet Sounds* if he had gone native instead of nuts. And "Slippi" sounds like Brian Jones might have conjured up circa *Their Satanic Majesties Request* if he'd been collaborating with angels instead of fools. But there's not a straight pop song on the album. Even the most normal ones dissolve and morph in ways that lead me to peg them as experimentalists. We didn't even think they were human at first, for chrissakes."

"I can understand that," E. said coolly. "I guess I'm talking more about the tracks with no audible basis in pop music—the ones in the middle of the album."

"You mean the ones that sound like ritual music made by animals for animals? Or at least by humans and animals for same?" Tigre enthused. "I like those best, too!"

Pou had mixed feelings about the matter. True enough, he liked all the rich drones, with their combination of processed human voices, animal sounds, and electronics—the likes of which he'd never heard before. He especially liked "Panic," which sounded like the Animal Collective had enlisted the aid of mountain goats, musk oxen, and something that sound likes a cross between Piglette and Tigre back when Tigre was smaller and didn't eat nearly as much. "Would that be a Tiglette or a Pigre?" he wondered. But "Two Sails on a Sound" he could have sworn emanated from a sixth-dimensional Heffalump. And, goodness knows, the ordinary sorts of Heffalumps frightened him quite enough.

"I suppose I could fully embrace track six if I were in the right sort of ritual," he announced bravely, "and I was wearing a big sword. And a long purple robe, too."

"Silly bear," Christophe Robin giggled. "Although, I must say, this music does make me want to put on a loincloth."

Tigre laughed. "It'd beat those Zubaz you're wearing now!"

"Seriously, Chris," Pou cackled as he fell backward in the grass, "you should at least stop tucking them into your boots."

PHILIP STEPHENS

Fate and a Jukebox

If it weren't for Buck Owens and Brenda Lee, I would not exist. The Baron of Bakersfield and Little Miss Dynamite played no direct role in my birth, but two of their songs spoke for my parents, Carl Dean Stephens, "Poker," as he was known in high school, and the former Judy Lee Cunningham, or, as she was known, "Goose." The songs appeared on the charts when my parents were too young, or too scared, to speak their own minds. But Owens and Lee might just as easily have not recorded, and I might just as easily not exist. Listen. Music is as complicated as life. And vice versa.

My father was raised in West Aurora Springs, Missouri, a crossroads farming community on the Ozark Plateau. My mother grew up in Eldon, a railroad town a few miles north. In the ninth grade, West Aurora kids transferred from a one-room schoolhouse to Eldon High, where my mother and father met. In 1954 they started dating—my father a junior, my mother a freshman. They had a few things in common. They grew up in houses without indoor plumbing or electricity. They had hard-drinking fathers and long-suffering mothers. They smoked Pall Malls.

But they had their differences. My mother pitched on the softball team. My father did not make the cut in basketball—he lived too far from town to get to practice. My mother earned her nickname after she scolded a friend for goosing her. My father inherited his from his father, John Willard, who, as a boy, played cards in caves with Osage River toughs. My mother was a bright teenager who enjoyed talking more than studying. My father earned good-enough grades to make National Honor Society. For dates, they swam in the Lake of the Ozarks, ate foot-long chilidogs at the Cree Mee, and watched movies at the Corral Drive-In, where my mother scratched my father's head until, she says, he fell asleep. An innocent courtship. Somehow they fell in love.

In 1956, though, my father went away to college in Kansas City, earning an aeronautical engineering degree in two years. He took jobs in Texas, New York, and California, and my mother went on with her life. She dated Reed Bailey, a good dancer. She worked as a comptometer operator for Sears & Roebuck in Kansas City, going in the evenings to clubs and dancing to jazz, until one night from California my father called and said he wanted to marry her. "I think he'd been drinking," my mother says. After she moved back to Eldon to make wedding plans, my father sent her a Dear John letter.

A song is the culmination of experience, of celebration, suffering, or stoicism. It should be sung as such. A song can be the distillation of every note a singer has heard, every person whose eyes he's looked into but never known. Spirits of singers past and gone may dwell in a song. Who knows? At the time my father mailed his letter, country music had changed and was changing. The pedal steel and electric guitar had usurped the banjo and fiddle. If fiddles played, they were syrupy. Drums, pianos, and amps increased the volume. Radios were out, records were in, and these played on jukeboxes in bars. Celebrations of mother, home, and girls left behind were replaced with songs about drinking, carousing, and love lost.

Into that scene stepped Buck Owens and Brenda Lee.

Brenda Mae Tarpley was born in 1944 in a charity ward and raised in the Georgia backwoods—no plumbing, and no electricity. Most of the music she heard was gospel in church and Hank Williams tunes her mother Grayce sang. Still, she performed as a child on radio programs for free. They could have used the money. When she was eight, her father, an alcoholic and illiterate construction worker, died after a hammer fell on his head. Her mother remarried a man who worked for the Jimmy Skinner Music Center in Cincinnati. Brenda performed there on Saturdays. When they moved back to Georgia, she sang on the *Peach Blossom Special*, where the producer dubbed her the less-cumbersome Brenda Lee, and by age eleven she was on Red Foley's *Ozark Jubilee*, performing for television before her family even had one. She became the breadwinner, but couldn't get a recording contract because of her age. Finally, Decca in Nashville signed her; they didn't know what to make of her. She cut Hank Williams tunes, holiday novelties, rockabilly. At age twelve, she was marketed as a nine-year-old. At fifteen, though, she got her first number one hit—on the pop chart.

Alvis Edgar Owens, Jr., was born in 1929 in Texas in a house with dirt floors and no electricity. As a child he nicknamed himself Buck, after the family mule. When his family fled the Dust Bowl, they got as far as Mesa, Arizona, before the trailer hitch broke. They lived the migrant life, picking cotton, tomatoes, and peaches up into California. His mother played piano in churches along the way. Owens quit school at thirteen and taught himself whatever instrument a band might need. He hauled produce between Mesa and Bakersfield, California, an oil town with a burgeoning honky-tonk scene, then settled there. He married at eighteen, had kids, played sessions, divorced, and got a recording contract with Capitol, but his records sold poorly. He cut rockabilly tracks for the Pep label as Corky Jones, so as not to offend the country audience. He remarried, had more kids, and, figuring his career was shot, took a job as a DJ outside Tacoma in 1958. He got a country hit by 1960, when he was thirty, twice the age of Brenda Lee.

They were an unlikely pair to bring my parents back together. Lee used the best studio musicians in Nashville. Owens wouldn't record with anyone except his band, the Buckaroos, and he stayed out of Nashville as much as possible. Owens penned his biggest hits. Lee made other material her own. She was on the pop chart before changes in the industry forced her to the country chart, and she picked up vocal phrasings from Edith Piaf, Frank Sinatra, and Billie

Holiday. Owens was fed on Bob Wills, the Maddox Brothers and Rose, and Jimmie Rodgers, but he brought out the drums, bass, and Telecaster, making a raw-edged music that rocked against the string-heavy stuff, such as Lee's, that came from Nashville.

In July 1960, my father stopped in Missouri on his way to a job in New York City. About six months had passed since he'd penned his letter. Owens had finished his stint at No. 4 on the country chart, Lee had her No. 1 song on the pop chart, and both were on the jukebox at Frank Brown's, a chertstone roadhouse off Highway 54 between Eldon and West Aurora.

A young man named Audley Morris had been taking my mother out. One afternoon, he picked her up from her job as a switchboard operator and suggested Frank's. "Poker's back in town, though," Audley said. "He might be there." My mother said she didn't mind.

Frank's stood on an oak-covered rise in front of Shady Lawn, motel cabins for folks on their way to the lake. Nothing but a foundation is there now, but Frank's was a joint with a few booths and tables, and a jukebox by the door. It was a place where kids could drink and dance, but also the sort of place where, if soldiers came up from Fort Leonard Wood, Frank asked them to leave so they wouldn't bother the girls.

When my mother and Audley walked in, my father was seated on a stool in the far corner, drinking a beer. The only patron, he'd been there all afternoon. "Hi, Poker," my mother said, and he nodded. She and Audley took a booth along the far wall, where they ordered beers. Finally, my father went to the jukebox and fed it a dime and an "ooo, oooo," started up. Strings slid in, then Brenda Lee belted out in that smoky, almost-angry, alto of hers, "I'm sorry, so sorry/That I was such a fool." My father went back to his corner. "I think he winked," my mother says.

For two minutes and thirty-nine seconds, my mother tried to listen to Audley. When the song ended, she asked if he would play something on the jukebox. He punched up what she'd requested, and as he sat back down a pedal steel tore into the quiet and a bass thumped and a woody-sounding drum popped, and Buck Owens in that swooping voice of his sang, "You've got me under your spell again/Saying those things again/making me believe that you're just mine."

Of course, my father was not saying those things again. He is not a talkative man, and no romantic, and at age twenty-one, he probably didn't know what to say. "You tell me mistakes are part of being young," the song says, "but that don't right the wrong that's been done."

"I'm Sorry" has just eight bars of music. Producer Owen Bradley thought it monotonous until Lee recited a verse, a la the Inkspots. Lee fills those bars with a bewilderment and crackling undercurrent of self-loathing that only a girl who lived with poverty, loss, and a longing for success could have given it.

A similar emotional force churns through "Under Your Spell Again." Owens knew the helplessness love causes. He knew loss, poverty, and anger as well. "Under Your Spell Again" is a song in which the singer works to forget what he knows: "I swore the last time that you let me down/That I wouldn't see you if you came around/But I can't tell my heart what's right or wrong/And I've been so lonely since you've been gone." A nineteen-year-old girl on a date with another boy couldn't have made such an admission. Owens made it for her.

To my mother and father, though, it didn't matter who spoke for them. The next week they married in Miami, Oklahoma, where couples could get a blood test in a day. Just more than nine months later, my brother was born in New York. I came along five years after that.

To write a song, to perform one, requires faith—faith that words will come and true emotion will rise from the subconscious. There's faith in something else, too—that someone will hear the song, and it will matter.

To this day, if "I'm Sorry" plays on the radio, my father tenses. Sometimes he leaves the room. If "Under Your Spell Again" plays while my mother is working in the kitchen, she wants to dance. Reed Bailey was the good dancer, though, and my father does not like to recall how he caused my mother grief.

These days, I can't name a popular country song that could bring two estranged lovers together. At a bar I used to frequent, the jukebox held country tunes by a woman who wears skin-tight synthetics and cites the Backstreet Boys and Elton John as influences. For all their differences, Buck Owens and Brenda Lee, among many others, altered country music—maybe for the best, maybe not. What do I care? Their music ushered in my existence and commenced my parents' more-than-forty-year marriage. God knows, sometimes their relationship has been discordant, but sometimes it sings. And sometimes if they're in the kitchen and the right song plays, they dance.

COREY TAKAHASHI

Musical Masala

The DJ nodding attentively behind the turntables wears baggy pants, oversized earphones, and a tightly wrapped Sikh turban. His repertoire at this show in the South Bronx jumps from underground (Jurassic 5's "What's Golden") to ghetto fab (Clipse's "Grindin'") to rap-radio pop (Eminem's "Lose Yourself"). There's cutting, scratching, and smoothed-out blends. In between spins, there's also a surprise.

For about 200 uptown heads and downtown bohos, Indian-American alchemist Navdeep Nijher introduces a percussion instrument usually associated with Sikh devotional prayer. The tablas—classical Indian drums struck with bare hands like a bongo—make a sound more evocative of serene *gurudwaras*, Sikh temples, than rowdy hip hop parties. "It's not meant to dance to," confides Navdeep, as he is known on the DJ circuit.

Quite the opposite is true tonight, and that's because the musician recently jury-rigged his basketball-sized instruments with electronic microphones meant for Western snare and bass drums. Just as DJs in this section of New York City did with turntables nearly three decades ago. Navdeep has harnessed technology to flip a musical form. "Now all of a sudden, you have this whole new instrument in a digital context," says the bearded 25-year-old, a traditionally trained tabla player and acolyte of DJ Premier.

By 10:30 p.m., Navdeep's got the crowd rocking steady. He lets
the vinyl spin, passing the baton to fellow DJ Rekha Malhotra. "Oh,
no!" exclaims Nate Dogg on the hook. "Look at who they let in the
back door. . . . "

In an era when hip hop has moved beyond its early soul, funk,
and disco breaks, Navdeep is just one example of how a global perspective is steadily reshaping the genre. These stars of the South
Asian underground, like the black, Puerto Rican, and Filipino DJs
who came before them, raid their parents' record collections for the
finest source material. Their crates just happen to be filled with
Punjabi folk, soundtracks from Bollywood (as India's gigantic,
multibillion-dollar film industry is called), and remixes from their
Indian peers in England—in addition to Jay-Z and James Brown.

At the other end of the spectrum are a slew of non-Indian artists
who've gotten down *desi*-style, overtly riding Indian aesthetics—
from the sitar to the tablas to vocal samples—up the charts. Consider Missy Elliott ("Get Ur Freak On"); Lil' Kim ("Get in Touch");
Erick Sermon and Redman ("React"); Sean Paul (with his "tabla *rid-
dim*" version of "Street Respect"); or even Dan "the Automator"
Nakamura, who produced a critically acclaimed album called *Bombay the Hard Way: Guns, Cars & Sitars* back in '99.

Take a whiff of the simmering new melting pot in this era of
global hip hop. It can be detected whenever Navdeep sets off rounds
of "tabla hip hop," spinning back vinyl samples with one hand and
rolling his fingers over his drum set with the other. "The thing
that's really cool about it is that the motions on the tabla are very
similar to the motions that I do when I scratch," he says.

In the midst of one set last fall, Navdeep footnoted the East-
West symbiosis. "I cut in 'Nothin' by N.O.R.E.," he says. "But then
I started cutting in the Lata thing," he adds, referring to a vocal
sample of one of India's greatest singers. "People didn't even know
what it was at first 'cause it's the original!"

No doubt you know the Lata thing. The legendary singer Lata
Mangeshkar is to India what Aretha Franklin is to Detroit, what
Muddy Waters is to the Delta, what Biggie is to Brooklyn and
Tupac is to Cali. The mention of Lata's name inspires awe and rev-
erence among teens and grandparents, Hindus, Muslims, and Sikhs

alike—even at her ripe age of 73. She has worked in genres ranging from classical to pop, but her most famous stints have been in movies as a playback singer—the predubbed voice behind the lip-synching leading ladies of Bollywood, where movies play like three-hour musicals.

For most of her career, Mangeshkar, or Lataji as she's respectfully called, has been little more than a face on dusty LP covers in the West. But last spring, on the strength of the DJ Quik–produced track "Addictive," by Truth Hurts, a Mangeshkar-sung hook suddenly slipped into heavy rotation on MTV and urban and pop radio around the world.

"Addictive" had a run as the top-played video on BET, hit No. 2 on the *Billboard* R&B chart, and was a club banger from thugged-out nightspots in New York City and bhangra bars in London to upscale lounges in Bombay (officially renamed Mumbai). Along with a rollicking drum track, vocals by Truth Hurts, and a cameo by Rakim, the song was blessed by Lataji's show-stealing Hindi soprano.

Shari "Truth Hurts" Watson, 31, didn't have a clue who Mangeshkar was before she heard Quik's track. She was simply looking for a way to cut through the clutter of a stagnant urban-music scene. "We decided we wanted to keep it street but really get into Indian culture," says Watson, who wears *mehndi* decorations on her hands and back and flaunts Indian arm movements in the "Addictive" video. "We tried not to offend."

The inspiration for "Addictive" came to L.A. rapper/producer DJ Quik while he was watching the Indian cable network Zee TV. "It's a fly channel, man. I mean, even though you can't really understand the language, you can still feel the vibe. And the music is nothing less than incredible," says Quik, né David Blake, 33, who stumbled upon the "Addictive" sample while checking out *Jyoti*, a 1981 Bollywood flick. "Musically, they got the funkiest shit right now."

But in September, the Calcutta-based entertainment company Saregama India Limited, which claims ownership of the sampled song, filed a lawsuit against Truth Hurts's label, Aftermath Records, Dr. Dre, Interscope Records, and the Universal Music Group.

Truth Hurts and DJ Quik, among others, were added to the suit in November. It alleged copyright infringement for not clearing the sample, sought at least $500 million in punitive damages, and took exception to what the suit called "profanity and vulgar insinuations," on the song, which has Truth Hurts claiming to "like it rough" and Rakim boasting of "kilos to C-notes."

Mangeshkar's original tune, "Thoda Resham Lagta Hai" ("It Looks Silky"), is featured in a *Jyoti* scene, where a playboy chases around a hip-shaking, neck-swiveling temptress. Not exactly chaste by comparison, but the suit states the defendants showed a "lack of respect for Plaintiff's religious beliefs, culture, and legal rights." Howard King, Aftermath's attorney, says they've tried to negotiate a settlement with Saregama. A December pretrial date had been set at press time.

Ironically, after "Addictive" crossed over in India, the original Mangeshkar song was resung by the Indian artist Shashwati and remixed. The result? Another slick, new dance tune called "Kaliyon Ka Chaman," released by Universal Music India on the album *UMI–10, Vol. 3*. It quickly became a top seller, too.

The legal dispute hasn't dampened Quik's love for subcontinental sounds. "To me, it was a gesture of respect," says the daily Zee TV viewer, adding that there's an even deeper layer to it. In the wake of 9/11, the racial profiling of Indian- or Arab-American air passengers has become a new take on "driving while black." These tensions weren't lost on the rap artist from Compton, who says the timing of "Addictive" was partially political. "It's simple," says Quik. "It's like, Y'all, let's make some music, so motherfuckers don't have to think about this shit. And, no, Habib at 7-Eleven is not your enemy."

Truth Hurts says simply, "People are just happy that the cultures are mixing."

A noble conceit, to be sure, though DJ Navdeep refuses to play "Addictive" in his club sets. While he stops short of begrudging non-Indians who borrow from the culture, he has clear guidelines for doing so himself. "I want it to be Asian stuff, but it's slick. It's just not beating you over the head like, Ohhhh, Indian. Ohhhh, exotic," says the U.S.-born New Yorker, who grew up listening to hip hop and traditional Indian music in a Punjabi Sikh household. "We make stuff that sounds different, but that's like our soul, you know what I mean? It's not a gimmick."

"Addictive" wasn't the first time Mangeshkar was sampled. Indian DJs in the U.S., U.K., and South Asia have been cutting her warble with Western rhythms for decades. But thanks to African-Americans, the "Nightingale of India" crossed over to international pop.

The globalized gumbo of "Addictive" was reheated last June, when Truth Hurts and her dancers were invited to perform the hit song at the Bollywood Awards, an annual Academy Awards–like gala held at Nassau Coliseum in Long Island. The event draws glitterati from the Bombay film industry and from every corner of the Indian diaspora. When Truth Hurts announced near the end of her set, "This is how we do it in the West," she was representing for L.A., literally, and Western civilization by extension. After the performance, teenage girls shrieked with glee; sari-wearing grandmothers gasped.

In India, Truth Hurts is taken as yet another sign of Western Indophilia, already evidenced by Madonna rocking *mehndi*, Gwen Stefani and her *bindi*, and the crowds at London's hit musical *Bombay Dreams*, produced by Andrew Lloyd Webber with a score by Bollywood composer AR Rahman. "It's the other way around now," says MTV India VJ Nafisa Joseph, 24, whose Benetton sunglasses are tucked in the fashionably ripped collar of her white, midriff-baring baby T. "We're influencing the West."

In the daily program *MTV House Full*, Joseph, a Bangalore-to-Bombay transplant and former Miss India, offers the latest Bollywood dish, speaking an English-Hindi hybrid called Hinglish. Her persona reflects the *masala* motif: a bit of Ashanti's aura, Shakira's sex-appeal (the low-riding, candy-pink pants, at least), and Serena Altschul's polished TV presence. But for all the foreign culture absorbed by tastemakers like Joseph, they still like their grooves cut with something down-home. Hence, her preference for "Kaliyon Ka Chaman," the local remake inspired by "Addictive," over "Addictive" itself. "We saw the song, and we were like, 'Wow, that's nice.' But then what happened is that they [Indian singer Shashwati and producer Harry Anand] came out very quickly with a version of the song with a little bit of remix," says Joseph, "and that's caught on

like crazy. You go to any of the discos in India and you hear that
playing most of the time."

Curiously, the video for "Kaliyon Ka Chaman" features a crew of
young Indian dancers imitating the choreography of "Addictive"
right down to the belly gyrations and dress. The lyrics are sung in
Hindi, but seems less like an expression of Bombay pride than a cultural boomerang that started with Lata Mangeshkar, crossed over to
the West with Truth Hurts, then came whirling back with Shashwati's response.

Contemporary bhangra music bears a similar relationship: a Punjabi folk export gets laced up by Indian DJs in the West, then reim-
ported into India in newfangled fusions. A young crop of Indian
DJs, like the New Delhi–based MIDIval PunditZ, are now creating
that fusion at home. Featured on Mira Nair's *Monsoon Wedding*
soundtrack and a self-titled CD, the PunditZ are a local and global
operation, creating Indian-inflected club tracks for San Francisco's
Six Degrees Records and touring the world.

Ram Sampath, 27, is a member of the same tech-savvy generation as the PunditZ—the first in India to grow up with widespread
access to satellite cable, the Internet, hip hop, and disposable
income. Born and bred in Bombay, he's hoping to define the modern sound of India in the same way Navdeep has in New York. "We
can pioneer something. We can actually change the way the country
and the world listen to us," says Sampath, a musician and composer,
who supports his independent music projects by scoring jingles,
broadcast in India, for corporations like Coca-Cola and Levi's. "We
can also change the way people perceive India."

Sampath's hip hop tastes run from A Tribe Called Quest to Nelly.
His plan for his next solo project is to "translate what I learned from
Chuck D," during repeated listenings of *Fear of a Black Planet.* For a
country colonized by England for more than two centuries, and that
still embraces many British rituals and institutions (cricket is huge
in India), there's no mistaking the significance of American rap's
influence on a growing number of young Indians: "Black is the new
white," says Sampath, a Hindu with ancestral roots in the southern
Indian state of Tamil Nadu. "Kids around the world love hip hop."

Producers like DJ Quik may be fascinated with Bollywood as a
novelty, but Sampath, who previously worked in the film industry,

finds Bollywood music as clichéd and formula-driven as some American critics do commercial rap. So when Sampath wants authenticity, he takes his recorder to the streets to sample young beggars doing their renditions of Hindi film songs on Bombay's packed commuter trains, or folk musicians in the villages, or even the cacophony of the annual Ganesh Festival in Bombay, where giant elephant idols are hauled to the Arabian Sea.

Sampath wants to capture this "smattered culture" on wax the way early rappers once struggled to give the American ghetto its voice. "You have to understand," Sampath says of Bombay, "we're the New York City of the Third World."

The sun is setting on Bombay as Sampath's personal driver wheels a maroon 2000 Maruti Zen sedan past a south Indian–style Hindu temple adorned with gargoyles and gods, through the oddly harmonic honking of cabs, commuter cars, and motorbikes, on the way to Dharavi, the largest slum in Asia. "Sonically, translating the sound of the street and giving it a cultural filter, that's tough," says Sampath. "Because Bombay is chaos. And it takes a while to find structure in chaos, right?"

Later that evening, none of the young, chic Indians at the upscale lounge Athena, in south Bombay, seem to be looking for structure in chaos. But they're clearly seeking a link with urban American music. It is monsoon season in the financial capital, so when Nelly's voice over the speakers proclaims, "It's gettin' hot in herre," it's ridiculous understatement. And when Warren G's "Regulate" comes pulsating through, with the DJ shouting in Hindi-accented English, "This one's a classic!" that may be going too far in the other direction.

The repertory does, however, highlight an irony: this is an Indian club and an Indian crowd. The only thing missing is Indian music. The equal helpings of American hip hop and R&B that rule this floor could have easily come off the playlist at, say, Detroit's WJLB. There's no Bally Sagoo, no Malkit Singh, not even Talvin Singh.

But just after 2 a.m., the DJ throws on a track that casts a warm glow over Athena's cool, minimalist interior. Whole crews empty their seats, women rise onto platform heels and shuffle their way to the dance floor, drinks in one hand, the other raised and waving to the roof. The crowd in Athena is infused with a new energy. Some club-hoppers transition into traditional Indian dance styles, some mimic moves they've seen on "Addictive."

"He hits the spot," sings Truth Hurts. "He makes me hot."

It is undeniably an American import. But the dancing, the expressions . . . all the body language seem to say "Addictive" is also theirs. Truth Hurts and Lata Mangeshkar are in the house, rousing the crowd like no song before it.

Stepping out of the lounge, past the throngs of *nouveau riche* in dark club attire, one faces anew the very India from which Athena offered reprieve. There is row upon row of homeless bodies, splayed out on the Bombay streets. To the east is Elephanta Island, with its sixth-century cave temples and sculptures of the god Shiva; to the north, the gothic arches of the Gateway of India. History and tradition are everywhere, yet they are in tremendous flux. But the sights don't travel like the sounds, which follow you some distance from the club, echoing in your ears. This is the cross-continental call-and-response, ringing from the South Bronx all the way to south Bombay.

The Mystery of Lauryn Hill

In 1998, when Lauryn Hill was recording her debut solo album, she was on a mission. "She was aiming for big hits so she could outshine the Fugees and outshine Wyclef," says someone familiar with the sessions. Her 1996 album with the Fugees, *The Score*, had sold more than 17 million copies and made her rich and famous, but something was missing. After *The Score*, many perceived Wyclef Jean as the group's musical genius. Hill began plotting an album of her own that would change that. "Her solo career wasn't based on 'I wanna do an album,'" says Roots drummer Ahmir Thompson. "It was based on not being Wyclef's side girl."

Twelve million people bought *The Miseducation of Lauryn Hill*, and Hill was established as one of the great female MCs, a quadruple threat: a rapper as well as a world-class singer, songwriter and producer. She was critically acclaimed and extremely rich. In 1998 and '99, sources say, Hill grossed $40 million from royalties, advances, touring, merchandising and other revenues, and pocketed about $25 million of that. When Hill was thirteen years old, she already knew she would grow up to become an entertainer. In '98, Hill became an international superstar.

Hollywood beckoned her onto the A list. Sources say she was offered a role in *Charlie's Angels*, but she turned the part down, and

Lucy Liu took the job. Hill met with Matt Damon about being in *The Bourne Identity*, with Brad Pitt about a part in *The Mexican* and with the Wachowski brothers about a role in the last two films in the *Matrix* trilogy. She turned down lots of work. "Lauryn wasn't trying to do anything," says Pras Michel of the Fugees, almost lamenting. But she did begin developing a biography of Bob Marley in which she was to play his wife, Rita; started producing a romantic-comedy film set in the world of soul food called *Sauce*, in which she was to star; and accepted a prize part in the adaptation of Toni Morrison's *Beloved* but had to drop out because she got pregnant. The doors were open for Hill to create a multimedia entertainment empire of the sort that J. Lo, Janet and Madonna have built. Hill could have been J. Lo with political substance. Someone who once worked with Hill says with regret, "She woulda been bigger than J. Lo." Instead, she disappeared.

"I think Lauryn grew to despise who Lauryn Hill was," a friend says. "Not that she despised herself as a human being, but she despised the manufactured international-superstar magazine cover girl who wasn't able to go out of the house looking a little tattered on a given day. Because Lauryn is such a perfectionist, she always sought to give the fans what they wanted, so a simple run to the grocery store had to have the right heels and jeans. Artists are a lot more calculating than the public sometimes knows. It don't happen by accident that the jeans fall the right way, the hat is cocked to the side just so. All of that stuff is thought about, and Lauryn put a lot of pressure on herself after all that success. And then one day she said, 'Fuck it.' "

In 2000, Hill became close with Brother Anthony, a shadowy spiritual adviser, then abruptly fired her management team and the people around her. In 2001, she recorded her *MTV Unplugged 2.0*. Few bought the album, but many talked about how she could be heard on the record breaking down in tears and saying, "I'm crazy and deranged. . . . I'm emotionally unstable," and repeatedly rejecting celebrity and the illusions that make it possible. "I used to get dressed for y'all; I don't do that anymore," she said on the album. "I used to be a performer, and I really don't consider myself a performer anymore. . . . I had created this public persona, this public illusion, and it held me hostage. I couldn't be a real person, because you're too afraid of what your public will say. At that point, I had to do some dying."

Her honesty was both touching and confusing. She was rejecting so much of what she'd spent years being. The only thing that was clear was that she was suffering. "Artists do fall apart," a record executive says. "The most commonly held falsity in the game is that they have it all together. They fall apart. Look at Mariah, Whitney, Michael, all the great ones. They all have a moment where you go, 'Are they really all there?' And I think Lauryn chose to expose that to the world."

Until recently, the twenty-eight-year-old Hill lived in a high-end hotel in Miami with Rohan Marley, the man she called her husband, and her four children. Her fourth child was born this past summer. Sources say that not long ago, Hill moved out of the hotel and that her relationship with Marley may be over.

She now insists on being called Ms. Hill, not Lauryn, and is working on a new album, albeit very slowly. "I heard from a friend that she don't really wanna do music right now," Pras says. "I heard from another friend that she wants to do a Fugees album."

So what caused the Lauryn Hill of *Miseducation*, viewed as regal and brilliant, to morph into the Lauryn Hill of *Unplugged*, seen as possibly unstable, and then into someone willfully absent from the public? Confidential conversations with more than twenty friends and industry figures and a lengthy interview with Pras have clarified much of what has happened during the five years since her zenith. "I don't think she's crazy," Pras says. "People tend to say that when they don't understand what someone's going through. Walk in her shoes, and see what would you do."

Hill was born in 1975 and raised in middle-class South Orange, New Jersey. By her teens, she was determined to have a career in entertainment. At thirteen, she sang on *Showtime at the Apollo*. The audience was rough on her, and after the show she cried. In 1998, her mother, Valerie Hill, told *Rolling Stone* about her post-Apollo talk with her young daughter. "I said . . . now, if every time they don't scream and holler you're gonna cry, then perhaps this isn't for you," Valerie recalled. "And she looked at me like I had taken leave of my senses. To her, the mere suggestion that this wasn't for her was crazy." At seventeen, Lauryn had a role on the daytime soap *As the World Turns*; two years later she appeared in *Sister Act 2: Back in the Habit* and had a small role in Steven Soderbergh's *King of the Hill*. Meanwhile, she was also spending nights working on music with friends Wyclef Jean and Pras Michel. She was eighteen when the band's 1994 debut, *Blunted on Reality*, flopped, but, two years later, with *The Score*, the Fugees' cover of "Killing Me Softly" made her a star. She was sex-symbol beautiful, and her music and public persona seemed politically savvy and spiritually aware.

After the explosion of *The Score*, Jean began recording a solo album. Hill and Pras supported him emotionally and creatively. But when Hill started writing her own songs, Jean showed no interest. Pras says, "I remember when Pepsi wanted her for a commercial, and they were like, 'All we want is you. We don't need the other two cats.' She said, 'Without them I'm not doing it.' There's a lot of things she didn't do because of the group. Then when she goes to work on her [music] and she doesn't have the support, that can have an effect mentally. She felt—this is based on conversations we had— she felt there was no support on that angle. When you feel the ones you stuck your neck out for ain't doin' the same for you, it brings a certain animosity and bitterness."

Once, the three Fugees were close friends, but now Pras has little good to say about Jean. "He's the cancer of the [Fugees]," Pras says. "He's the cancer. You can quote me. He's the reason why it got wrecked to begin with, he's the reason why it's not fixed." Is he the reason for Hill's troubles? "Maybe, indirectly, she's where she's at because of him," Pras says. "Maybe. But not directly." Jean politely declined to be interviewed. "I'm somewhere else in my head," he says on the phone from his studio. "Certain things I don't talk about. I'm in another zone." He pauses. "I wish it didn't go down the way it went."

Hill responded to an e-mail request for an interview. "I am not available for free interviews at this time," she wrote. "The only interviews I will consider are those that amply compensate me for my time, energy and story." It was signed "Ms. Hill." She asks for money, friends say, because she feels she's been exploited by the media and the record industry. When *Oneworld* magazine contacted her about a cover story, she demanded $10,000.

People close to the Fugees say there has always been competition between Jean and Hill. "Not competing for something in particular," says one. "It's more competing just who's better, who's greater." Hill's solo music was intended to settle the matter. When Jean finally came around and offered his production assistance on the record, she no longer wanted it. "She said [to Jean], 'I'm thinking about working with this producer and that producer,'" a friend says. "He said, 'Oh, no—I'm producing your whole album.' She chewed on that for a minute and then said, 'Nah, I got my own vision.' That's when who Lauryn really is started to take form."

At the same time, Hill's love life began to get really complicated. For years she'd been clandestinely dating Jean. Their relationship started long before he married his current wife and continued afterward. But Pras says, "I think he was kinda, like, playing with her emotions."

But in the summer of '96, when the Fugees were on the Smoking Grooves Tour, she met Rohan Marley, who was on the tour with his brother Ziggy, both sons of Bob Marley. At first Hill was uninterested in Rohan—a former University of Miami football player—because she was still seeing Jean. "Honestly, she didn't even want the relationship," says a friend. "Everyone was pushing her towards [Marley] to get her out of the other thing. They pushed her towards him, like, 'Why don't you give him a chance, come on, go out on a date. Just do it,' not knowing that this man had all this other baggage and drama in his life."

Pras singled out Hill's first pregnancy as a turning point for the group. "When she got pregnant, definitely things started goin' on," he says. "Things got crazy." While Hill's stomach grew, the Fugees camp wondered whether the baby was Marley's or Jean's. Says a friend, "The conversation between everyone on the low was no one knew until that baby came out." The day Hill went into labor, Jean told a source he was flying to her side to see his new child. "People don't know how calculating she can be," a friend says. "Lauryn used Ro to pull herself out of the relationship with Clef, and she happened to get pregnant. She hoped that baby was Wyclef's, because it would've forced his hand. But it wasn't." Hill named her first child Zion Marley.

For years, Hill claimed that she was married to Rohan Marley, but at some point after Zion was born, Hill got another surprise: Someone told her Marley already had a wife. On March 18th, 1993, when he was a sophomore at the University of Miami, Marley married an eighteen-year-old woman from New Jersey in a ceremony in Miami. "The reason [Hill and Marley] aren't married is because Ro is already married," says a friend. Sources say Marley has two children from the marriage.

Hill decided to ignore it. "I think she was kinda like, 'Put it in the closet and don't even pay attention to it,'" says a friend. *Rolling Stone* could find no record of the dissolution of Marley's marriage, and even now it's unclear whether Hill and Marley were ever married in a conventional sense. "She has her own rules about life," another friend says. "According to her, she's married. Marriage to her is not a piece of paper, and it's not part of some civilization—civil-lies-ation. If you say to her, 'You're not married,' she'll say, 'What, do I have to get a government official to tell me I'm married?'"

It was critical that on *Miseducation*, Hill was credited as the sole auteur. "That was why she had to be seen as doing it all herself," says someone familiar with the sessions. "To show, 'I'm better than [Wyclef]. He's getting credit as the genius in the group. I'm the genius in the group.'"

But when musicians collaborate in the studio, it's often difficult to establish exactly who has written what. "It gets real gray in the studio," one artist says. At the time, people close to her suggested Hill needed documentation that would define everyone's role, but she was against the idea. "Lauryn said, 'We all love each other,'" a friend says. "'This ain't about documents. This is blessed.'"

The album was released crediting Hill with having produced, written and arranged all the music except one track, and Hill was established as a self-contained musical genius. Then she was sued by four men who had worked on the record who alleged that she had claimed full credit for music that they'd been at least partly responsible for. Her label, Columbia, urged her to settle, but she wanted to fight. "She felt settling would've been an admission of guilt," says a friend. "She was very concerned about credit. It's what eluded her from the past success [with the Fugees]. She didn't wanna be just a pretty face and a pretty voice. She wanted people to know she knows what she's doing." But she had to go into depositions and discuss making her art with lawyers. "That fucked with her," another friend says.

Eventually, Hill settled the suit. A source says the four producers were paid $5 million. It wasn't nearly as painful financially as it was emotionally. A friend says, "That was the beginning of a chain effect that would turn everything a little crazy." She was far from the first recording artist to have a crisis of faith and career, but few have had such a crisis so publicly.

She was a working mother of two, who, according to many, was unhappy in her relationship. She felt pressure to look like a model every time she left the house. She had several members of her family working for her or being supported by her. "To have your whole family depend on you for their well-being, that can be a lot of pressure," says Ahmir Thompson. "I said, 'If I was in that situation, I would snap.'" And she felt betrayed by the musicians she'd thought of as family and thus was increasingly mistrustful of people in general. Friends say she wanted to get out but didn't know how. "It was tough for her to admit all that to someone," a friend says. "So I think she spoke to God, and maybe it wasn't God, but somebody showed up." Another friend says, "A person came in, and they divided and conquered. They destroyed this whole thing." Around this time, Hill met a religious figure named Brother Anthony, a tall black man in his forties. Within three months she was going to Bible study with him two or three times a week. A friend says Brother Anthony taught Hill that "she should be whoever she wants to be, because she doesn't owe her fans anything. God didn't create us to be beholden unto people and entertain them. God holds us to be the people that we want to be."

The two became inseparable, and Hill began starting many of her sentences with the words, "Brother Anthony says. . . ." Shortly after recording *Unplugged*, Hill told MTV Online, "I met someone who has an understanding of the Bible like no one else I ever met in my life. I just sat at [his] feet and ingested pure Scripture for about a year." But Hill's friends found Brother Anthony bizarre. "His whole demeanor was real possessive, aggressive and crooked to me," a friend says. "You know how people are slick? He's a quick talker."

No one was certain what church he was from or what religion he belonged to. "I don't think he had a religion," a friend says. "I think he was more like, 'My interpretation of the Bible is the only interpretation of the Bible. I'm the only one on earth that knows the truth.'"

"Brother Anthony was definitely on some other shit," Pras says. "I had a tape of [his teachings]. That shit is ill. Fucked me up. I can't really explain it. It was some weird shit, man. It was some real cult shit. When I heard the tape, I couldn't believe that this dude was really serious. He was sayin', 'Give up all your money.' I don't know if that meant 'Give it to me' or whatever, but on the tape he said, 'Money doesn't mean anything.'"

Many believe Brother Anthony drove a wedge between Hill and the rest of the world. "It was like she was being brainwashed by this man," a friend says, "believing everything he was saying and tellin' her what to do." Another friend says, "I think he's just looking at a cash cow."

She recorded her *MTV Unplugged 2.0* in July 2001 while she was pregnant with her third child, Joshua. In a rehearsal the day before, Hill ripped up her throat but refused to reschedule, and on the record her voice is raspy and ragged. She accompanied herself on guitar, the lone instrument on the album, which was courageous given that she hadn't been studying very long. But a veteran industry executive says, "Anyone with ears can hear there are only three chords being played on every song. I saw it with a roomful of professionals, and someone said, 'I feel like jumpin' out a window.'"

"A lesser artist, it would've never been released," an industry insider says. "A lesser artist would've been shot and thrown out the window." *Unplugged* sold just 470,000 records, a failure. Another industry insider says, "I'm sure Columbia lost money on it." In the past few years, Hill has been in Miami, where she's working on a new album. She's determined to get full credit this time. "A lot of different people have been called down there and had strange experiences," says an industry figure. Sources say the musicians are required to sign a waiver giving Hill sole writing credit for the tracks they work on. The sessions have gone slowly. A few people spoke of her flying in a gang of top-flight musicians, putting them up in a nice hotel and paying for their time. But for more than a week they sat around each day, expecting to play, then getting a call saying, "We'll start tomorrow." Eventually they all left without ever getting into the studio. While no one is clear what stage of completion the tracks are in, those who've heard the music describe it as thrilling. "What she's doing and where she's going with it, ain't nobody even touching her," says an industry insider. "Nobody's even thinking that way. In the sad state of music we're in, I feel deprived knowing that she's got some real flavor that she's holding back."

"She gonna sit down and record until she feels happy," a friend says. "Whoever can't wait, she don't care." Some sources say she's spent more than $2.5 million, and Columbia has cut off her recording budget. The label denies this and maintains that Hill's new album will be out next year.

"Plenty of artists spend $2 million," says an industry insider, "but she had to fly all these people around and she had to build a studio in her Miami apartment, because she couldn't drive half a mile to the studio. Columbia bent over backwards for her, in pure self-interest, and I think they still believe in her, but you can't abuse the system like that. You can't do that."

Several of Hill's friends and associates are clearly worried about her. "She's Dr. Jekyll and Mr. Hyde," one says. "But not, like, two faces but, like, eight faces of that. You don't know who you're gonna get from one hour to the next. Not just one day to the next but one hour." Others recall Hill talking entirely in Bible-speak, "quoting Scripture, fanatically religious," one friend says. She sometimes answers business questions by saying things like, "We'll see what God has in store." A few tell a story in which Hill asked people to work with her on the new album, but when they asked how much they would be paid, she said, "Do it for God," meaning, do it for free, and God will reward you.

"I feel like she's lost," a friend says. "Something's not right. I just feel like she's sad and lonely and alone. I think she wants to cry out for help, but she has too much pride."

Others disagree. "Really, it's about restructuring her life and her lifestyle," an associate says. "I think maybe for a long time she thought she knew what she wanted. But, in reality, she didn't. She's gonna come through it, but she doesn't think anything's wrong with her. She used [Brother Anthony] to get rid of stuff in her life that she didn't wanna struggle with. She used him to her advantage, then she went too far, and she doesn't know how to come back. It'll be a process. It'll be a couple of years."

"She wants to do another album," a friend says. "Deep down, Lauryn is still Lauryn. She always wanted to be famous, she always wanted to sing, she always wanted to hear the applause. That's what she grew up to do. So to now not want it, that's not believable. She wants it the way Brother Anthony thinks it should be. His opinion is the only opinion that matters to her."

Many still have faith in her. "Sometimes people gotta find themselves, man," Pras says. "I don't believe that's crazy. People go through certain things, they gotta fight certain demons, and she's entitled to do that. Because her life isn't to please people. At the end of the day, Lauryn is not happy with herself. She's not gonna do some disc because she gotta make money for Sony. It just so happens that she's done something that captured a moment in people's lives. They want more of that, but she's not ready to give that."

OTHER NOTABLE ESSAYS OF 2003

Eric K. Arnold, "Hip-Hop Verite" (*East Bay Express*, June 25, 2003)

Andrew Beaujon, "Out of Step with the World" (*Spin*, May 2003)

Roy Blount, Jr., "Her Own Blues" (*Oxford American*, April 2003)

Will Blythe, "Authenticity Be Damned!" (*Oxford American*, April 2003)

Eric Boehlert, "The Greatest Week in Rock" (*Salon*, December 19, 2003)

David Cantwell, "Of Missing Persons" (*No Depression*, March–April, 2003)

Jeff Chang, "Missy E for President" (*Village Voice*, December 12, 2003)

Robert Christgau, "Black Elvis" (*Village Voice*, August 1, 2003)

Jon Dolan, "Resistance is Futile" (*City Pages*, October 29, 2003)

Baz Dreisinger, "Top Dogg" (*Salon*, August 22, 2003)

Chuck Eddy, "Mr. and Mrs. Used to Be" (*Village Voice*, April 11, 2003)

Sasha Frere-Jones, "Our Band Is Your Life" (*Village Voice*, June 20, 2003)

Bill Friskics-Warren, "Swamp Dogg: Up from the Dirty South" (*Oxford American #45*, Summer 2003)

Holly George-Warren, "She's About a Mover" (*No Depression*, November–December 2003)

Gary Giddins, "The Academy's Pulitzer" (*Village Voice*, April 30, 2003)

David Giffels, "My Brand-New Oakland Scarf" (*M–80*, Spring 2003)

David Hajdu, "Who's Got the Blues?" (*Mother Jones*, September–October 2003)

Howard Hampton, "Fairy Tails from Strangers" (*The Believer*, August 2003)

William Hogeland, "Imitating Nobody" (*Oxford American*, April 2003)

Todd Inoue, "Get Real" (*Metro*, July 10–16, 2003)

Lynne d Johnson, "Blurred Lines" (*Soul Patrol Digest*, Vol. 2, Issue 6, 2003)

Tom Junod, "Have You Met the Lips?" (*Esquire*, March 2003)

Monica Kendrick, "Expect the Unexpected" (*Chicago Reader*, October 10, 2003)

Rob Kenner, "On Fire" (*Vibe*, December 2003)

Kirk Kicklighter, "Georgia's Rockin' Fab Faux" (*DoubleTake*, Spring 2003)

Alan Light, "Sounds of the Spirit" (*Oxford American*, April 2003)

Melissa Maerz, "Atari Teenage Riot" (*City Pages*, July 23, 2003)

Greil Marcus, "Elvis Again" (*The Threepenny Review*, Winter 2003)

Peter Margasak, "Brass in the Blood" (*Chicago Reader*, July 25, 2003)

Katie Millbauer, "Mass Appeal" (*Seattle Weekly*, October 29–November 4, 2003)

Elias Muhanna, "Folk the Kasbah" (*Transition*, Issue 94, V12 N4, 2003)

Eric Nuzum, "Police on My Back" (*M–80*, 2003)

The Onion, "'90s Punk Decries Punks of Today" (Vol. 39, Issue 19, May 2Ⅰ, 2003)

Joe Nick Patoski, "The Cult of Ray" (*Austin Chronicle*, July 18, 2003)

Michael Perry, "Messenger of Jazz" (*Oxford American*, April 2003)

Dave Queen, "One Chord Wonders" (*Seattle Weekly*, November 26–December 2, 2003)

Stephen Rodrick, "Lost in the Music" (*The New York Times Magazine*, August 1, 2003)

Alex Ross, "Grand Illusions" (*The New Yorker*, May 19, 2003)

Carlo Rotella, "Linwood Taylor's Blues" (*The Washington Post Magazine*, August 24, 2003)

Roni Sarig, "Cat's Meow" (*Creative Loafing*, March 12–19, 2003)

John Jeremiah Sullivan, "That Don't Get Him Back Again" (*Oxford American*, April 2003)

Dave Tompkins, "For as Long as that Tick is Followed by that Boom" (*Waxpoetics*, Spring 2003)

Elijah Wald, "Respecting the Blues Makers" (*Living Blues*, June/July/August 2003)

Jim Walsh, "Into the Maw" (*City Pages*, September 10, 2003)

Lauren Wilcox, "Tough Mother for You" (*Oxford American*, April 2003)

Calvin Wilson, "Popularity Can Get an Artist Bounced from the Jazz Club" (*St. Louis Today*, July 13, 2003)

LIST OF CONTRIBUTORS

Grant Alden is coeditor and art director of *No Depression* magazine.

Dan Baum is the author of *Smoke and Mirrors: The War on Drugs and the Politics of Failure* (Little, Brown, 1996) and *Citizen Coors: An American Dynasty* (Morrow, 2000).

Elizabeth Méndez Berry is from Toronto, Canada, where she developed a taste for hockey and socialized health care. She now lives in Brooklyn, New York. She has had a paper route, worked as a lifeguard, and campaigned for a Colombian presidential candidate. She has also written about music and politics (and the Calgary Flames!) for the *Village Voice*, *Vibe*, the *Washington Post*, and *Blu*, among others, but dancing is still her favorite occupation.

Andrew Bonazelli has been a contributing writer at *Seattle Weekly* since 2000. He has also written for *Complex*, *CMJ New Music Monthly*, *City Pages*, and *Cleveland Scene*.

Geoff Boucher covers pop music for the *Los Angeles Times*, where during the past decade he has written about crime, politics, business, film, and other topics. He coauthored the 1997 book *Two Badges: The Lives of Mona Ruiz*.

William Bowers is a South Carolinian living in Florida whose work and reviews of books, film, and music have appeared in *The Oxford American*, *No Depression*, *Magnet*, *Esquire*, *People*, and Pitchforkmedia.com, as well as the anthologies *White Noise: The Eminem*

Collection and *Thesaurus Musicarum: The Pitchfork Year in Music*. A book, *All We Read Is Freaks*, is forthcoming from Harcourt.

Ta-Nehisi Coates is a staff writer for the *Village Voice*. His work has appeared in the *Washington Monthly*, *Vibe*, the *Washington Post*, and *Mother Jones*.

Michael Corcoran, a music critic for the *Austin American-Statesman* since 1995, has written a book, *All Over the Map: True Heroes of Texas Music*, to be published by the University of Texas Press in 2005.

Michael Eldridge teaches literature and culture at Humboldt State University in Arcata, California. He is working on a book about race and calypso in American culture.

Bill Friskics-Warren is music editor of the *Nashville Scene* and coauthor (with David Cantwell) of *Heartaches by the Number: Country Music's 500 Greatest Singles*. His work has also appeared in the *New York Times*, the *Village Voice*, the *Washington Post*, and *Da Capo Best Music Writing 2000*. He currently is working on a book about pop music and spirituality.

Robbie Fulks is a musician living in Chicago. He has released six records; his seventh, *Reality Country*, is due out in mid 2005.

Howard Hampton published his first rock criticism in the *Boston Phoenix* in 1982. He has written about music, movies, and culture for the *Village Voice*, the *LA Weekly*, *Artpaper*, *Artforum*, *Film Comment*, and the *Boston Globe*. He is currently writing *Badlands: A Psychogeography of the Reagan Era* for the Harvard University Press and is also preparing a collection of his essays and reviews.

Jessica Hopper is a Chicago-based writer. Her work has appeared in *SPIN*, *City Page*, *Urb*, *Grand Royal*, and she is a regular columnist for *Punk Planet*. Her forthcoming collection of essays on music and feminism will be published by Akashic Books in 2005.

T. R. Hummer's seventh book of poetry, *Useless Virtues*, was published in 2001 by Louisiana State University Press. He lives in Athens, Georgia, where he edits *The Georgia Review*.

David W. Johnson has been writing about music since the 1960s. During the 1990s, he was a regular contributor on folk music to the *Boston Globe* and other publications. Since moving to Virginia in 2001, he has written on traditional American music for the *Mars Hill Review*. He is researching biographies of A. P. Carter of the Original Carter Family and blues musician Bukka White.

Lynne d Johnson, a Bronx native, first started writing about hip-hop back in 1992. Since then she's moved to Brooklyn and expanded her writing coverage to include technology; literature; the arts; and youth, pop, and urban culture. Among the various media outlets she's written for over the years, the most recent include *Vibe*, *Urb*, *Colorlines*, *XLR8R*, *PopMatters*, and Africana.com.

Roy Kasten lives and writes in St. Louis, Missouri. He is a contributing editor at *No Depression* magazine and a frequent contributor to *The Riverfront Times*.

Chuck Klosterman writes for *SPIN*, *Esquire*, and the *New York Times Magazine*. He is the author of *Fargo Rock City: A Heavy Metal Odyssey in Rural North Dakota* and *Sex, Drugs, and Cocoa Puffs: A Low Culture Manifesto*. An expanded, book-length version of "6,557 Miles to Nowhere" will be published by Scribner in 2005 under the title *Killing Yourself to Live*.

Adam Mansbach is the author of the novels *Laugh/Riot* and *Shackling Water*, and the poetry collection *genius b-boy cynics getting weeded in the garden of delights*. The founding editor of the award-winning hip-hop journal *Elementary*, he serves as an artistic consultant to Columbia University's Center for Jazz Studies and a contributor to publications including the *Boston Globe*, the *San Francisco Chronicle*, and *JazzTimes*.

Michaelangelo Matos is the music editor of *Seattle Weekly* and the author of *Sign 'O' the Times* (Continuum). He contributes regularly to *SPIN*, the *Village Voice*, *City Page*, *Stereo-Type*, and *Tracks*.

Barry Mazor lives in Nashville and writes about music and media for *No Depression* (as a senior editor). He also contributes regularly to the *Wall Street Journal*, the *Village Voice*, the *Nashville Scene*, *Country Music Today*, and *American Thunder*. The Little Miss Cornshucks story, in expanded form, will appear as a chapter in his forthcoming book on key American musical performers who've been forgotten or underestimated for falling outside of historians' favored musical categories. The book will be published by the University of Massachusetts Press.

Andy McLenon is a Nashville-based freelance writer, pop culture observer, avid record collector, and archivist. He was also a principle in Prazis International, the record label/management company which launched Jason & the Scorchers and the Georgia Satellites, and at various times their roster also included Billy Joe Shaver, Steve Forbert, and John Hiatt.

Mark Anthony Neal is the author of four books, including the recent *Songs in the Key of Black Life: A Rhythm and Blues Nation* and the forthcoming *NewBlackman*. He is coeditor with Murray Forman of *That's the Joint!: The Hip-Hop Studies Reader*. Neal is a columnist for Africana.com and a regular contributor to PopMatters.com and SeeingBlack.com.

Alex Ross has been music critic of the *New Yorker* since 1996. His writing has also appeared in the *New York Times*, *The New Republic*, *SPIN*, *Slate*, and the *London Review of Books*. His first book, *The Rest Is Noise*, a cultural history of twentieth-century music, is forthcoming from Farrar, Straus & Giroux.

Carl Hancock Rux is the author of the *Village Voice* literary award-winning collection of poetry, *Pagan Operetta* (Fly By Night/Autonomedia), the novel *Asphalt* (Atria/Simon & Schuster), and the Obie award-winning play, *Talk* (TCG Press). He has also recorded two

CDs, *Rux Revue* (Sony 550) and *Apothecary Rx* (Giant Step Records). Rux is the recipient of the NYFA Gregory Millard Fellowship, NYFA prize, NEA/TCG Playwright in Residence Award, Rockefeller Map Grand, and a Herb Alpert CalArts award. He is working on a collection of personal essays.

Gene Santoro, *The Nation*'s music critic, also covers film and jazz for the *New York Daily News*. Santoro has authored two essay collections, *Dancing In Your Head* (1994) and *Stir It Up* (1997), as well as *Myself When I Am Real: The Life and Music of Charles Mingus* (2000).

Roni Sarig is the author of *The Secret History of Rock: The Most Influential Bands You've Never Heard*, and a contributor to *The Rolling Stone Album Guide*. From 1998 until 2004, he served as music editor of Atlanta's alternative weekly, *Creative Loafing*. He currently lives in New York with his wife and two kids and writes for *Rolling Stone*, *Vibe*, *Maxim*, and other magazines.

Joel Selvin has been covering pop music for the *San Francisco Chronicle* since 1970. He has written several books on the subject, including a biography of Ricky Nelson and *Summer of Love*, his best-selling account of the '60s San Francisco rock scene.

Jeff Sharlet is one of the founding editors of the online literary magazine KillingTheBuddha.com, winner of the Utne Independent Press Award, as well as a former editor of *Pakn Treger*, an award-winning magazine of Jewish culture published by the National Yiddish Book Center. Jeff has written about religion and culture for numerous publications, including *Harper's Magazine*, the *Washington Post*, *The Baffler*, and *Salon*. Jeff's most recent work is *Killing the Buddha: A Heretic's Bible*, coauthored with Peter Manseau. He lives in Brooklyn.

Rod Smith resides beneath the streets of Minneapolis, where he divides his time between writing and psychically engineering the controlled collapse of Western civilization as we know it. His work has appeared in the *Seattle Weekly*, *City Page*, and *Rain Taxi*, as well as sundry other publications. He is not now, nor has he ever been, a member of any political organization. His favorite food is weed.

Philip Stephens is the author of a collection of poems, *The Determined Days* (Overlook Press, 2000), which was a finalist for the PEN Center USA West award, and he has recently completed a novel. The creative writing administrator of the Sewanee Writer's Conference, he teaches at the University of the South in Sewanee, Tennessee.

Corey Takahashi is a freelance journalist, contributing to magazines, newspapers, and print documentary projects. He has worked as a reporter and editor in Manhattan and was most recently on staff at *Newsday*, where he wrote about the local and international cultures of New York City. Takahashi has reported on music, art, and contemporary culture in the United States and abroad.

Touré is the author of *Soul City*, a novel, and *The Portable Promised Land*, a collection of short stories. He's also a contributing editor at *Rolling Stone*, a contributor to CNN, and the host of MTV2's *Spoke N' Heard*. His writing has appeared in *The Best American Essays of 1999*, *The Best American Sports Writing of 2001*, and *The Best American Erotica of 2004*. He lives in Fort Greene, Brooklyn. (www.Toure.com)

CREDITS